THE EVICTION BOOK FOR CALIFORNIA

A HANDYMANUAL FOR SCRUPULOUS LANDLORDS AND LANDLADIES WHO DO THEIR OWN EVICTIONS!

EIGHTH EDITION

written by
LEIGH ROBINSON

illustrated by
DAVID PATTON

published by

express

P.O. BOX 1639
EL CERRITO, CA 94530-4639
http://www.landlording.com

FIRST EDITION	August, 1980
Revised	January, 1981
SECOND EDITION	October, 1982
Revised	September, 1983
THIRD EDITION	November, 1984
Reprinted	July, 1985
FOURTH EDITION	August, 1986
Revised	July, 1987
FIFTH EDITION	July, 1988
Revised	June, 1989
Revised	August, 1990
SIXTH EDITION	November, 1991
Revised	March, 1993
Revised	May, 1994
SEVENTH EDITION	March, 1995
Revised	February, 1996
EIGHTH EDITION	February, 1998

COVER AND BOOK DESIGN by David Patton

COMPOSED ON A MACINTOSH® USING ADOBE PAGEMAKER®

INTERNATIONAL STANDARD BOOK NUMBER: 0-932956-22-X

PRINTED IN THE U.S.A. BY FOLGER GRAPHICS, HAYWARD, CA

ExPress Publishing has a Web site (http://www.landlording.com) where, among other items of interest to landlords, you will find "what's news" about evictions.

The LANDLORDING SERIES™, of which this is Book Two, and the "Landlording Character," who first appears here on the preface page, are trademarks of ExPress and Leigh Robinson.

Preface

Originally, the nucleus of *The Eviction Book for California* was but a single chapter in *Landlording*, a book which I wrote in 1975 for scrupulous landlords and landladies doing business in California. Eventually that book began selling so well outside the Golden State that I felt obligated to prepare a completely new edition which might be useful to landlords and landladies no matter where they happened to be in the United States. So, early in 1980, I completed the third edition of *Landlording*, which was intended for distribution nationwide.

In preparing that third edition, I had to eliminate all the information in the earlier editions which was specific to California; consequently, all the legal information about evicting tenants in California courts had to go. After all, why should a landlady in Kansas care how her counterpart in California evicts a tenant through the courts for nonpayment of rent when the laws in her state dictate that she must use a very different procedure?

Because the eviction information in the earlier editions of *Landlording* had proven to be useful to many landlords and landladies in California over the years, however, I decided to expand it and publish it separately rather than toss it into my circular file.

You hold in your hands this descendant of *Landlording*. It is a rather specialized manual, a kind of companion volume to the national version of *Landlording*. I hope that you find it useful when you need it, but I also hope that you won't need it very often, for evictions are unpalatable and costly medicine.

Because they are so unpalatable and costly, I hope that you will take the time to learn how to prevent them. To help you learn how, I have included one short chapter here on the rudiments of preventing evictions, chapter 1, some of which

also appears in *Landlording*. This is material which always bears repeating. Although it may not be pertinent to the legal eviction that you want to pursue right now, it certainly will be pertinent to your situation when you regain possession of your rental dwelling once more and begin dealing with another tenant. Heed this advice, and you won't have to bother reading anything more about evictions ever again.

Chapter 2 also includes some material which appears in *Landlording*. These suggestions for getting problem tenants out without going to court will work as well in California as they will in Kansas or in the Land of Oz, and I should hope that you would consider trying the legal alternatives mentioned in this chapter before you ever go rushing headlong into the very uncertain and very imperfect world of the courts.

Courts are the provinces of attorneys and of judges, most of whom have been attorneys, and you may have wondered when you first picked up this book, why the letters "LL.B." or "J.D." did not appear after my name as an indication that I had paid my dues at law school and was fully qualified to write a manual explaining the intricacies of the legal procedure used in California to evict tenants. I don't use those letters after my name because I am not an attorney. In truth, I have never attended a single day of classes at even a store-front law school. I am a former high school English teacher who has toiled at landlording for years, and in doing so I have acquired certain knowledge about evictions which I have always believed would be useful to any other landlord or landlady struggling to survive, knowledge which attorneys may know but which they do not generally stress in a way most helpful to the distraught landlord or landlady who needs to get a tenant out today, right now, or go stark mad.

I became aware that my own approach to evictions was indeed different from those of attorneys when I appeared as a panelist at a public gathering hosted by the Berkeley Community Affairs Committee. The panel was comprised of four attorneys, all of whom had some unique perspective on housing problems, plus myself. One of the authors of the *California Tenants' Handbook* was there, along with two other attorneys sympathetic to tenants, and there was one attorney who specialized in representing property management companies. He and I were supposed to balance the panel. At one point in the discussion, the question arose concerning the shortest possible time an eviction for nonpayment of rent might possibly take, and there was only one person on the panel who knew the answer. You're right. I was the one. I knew the answer because it was in my interest to know. I'd already done the calculations. Besides, I had actually performed evictions myself in the shortest period of time allowed by law. They hadn't.

Attorneys don't particularly care how long evictions take, so long as the period of time is reasonable enough to keep their clients paying their bills. Only the landlord and landlady care enough about such things to find out, and then to turn that knowledge to their advantage.

My perspective on the subject of evictions, then, is not that of the attorney. It is the perspective of the landlord who has to deal on a daily basis, perhaps even on an emergency basis, with a tenant who is either a robber, a cheat, a devastator, or a nuisance. I want that tenant out as quickly as possible. For the sake of my business and my sanity, I have to get that tenant out. So my perspective is one similar to yours.

Because I have this perspective, I made it my business to develop certain eviction techniques which were as swift and as sure as possible, whether or not they involved going to court. I found out, for example, how best to offer bribes to tenants for moving and which days of the week are best for serving a 3-Day Notice to Pay Rent or Quit. The chances are good that you won't find an attorney who can give you such information because he won't have learned it in law school and he won't have taken the time to figure it out. It isn't in an attorney's best interest to know.

I do not mean to put down attorneys. Some of my closest relatives, some of my best friends, ahem, are attorneys. I am merely concerned that you understand my perspective as you read this book. I have walked in your moccasins, and I have trembled in them.

Table of Contents

Introduction

You, dear reader, are most likely involved in very painful circumstances, or else you wouldn't be reading this book. Somehow or other, you have become stuck with tenants who are constantly on your mind, tenants who are making your life miserable. You are plagued with self-doubts, and you are wondering whether you ought to be in this business at all, whether it's worth the trouble.

You have a substantial investment in your property, so naturally you have a lot to lose. Your tenants, on the other hand, very likely have nothing to lose by attempting to thwart your every effort to evict them, and they are doing just that.

You are wondering now what your options are, whether you can possibly get rid of the tenants without having to use an attorney, without having to wait very long, and without having to spend very much. You are wondering whether there is any good way for you to minimize your losses under the circumstances, whether there is any way you might handle the situation with a minimum of aggravation for all concerned so you might please almost everyone involved.

I can sympathize with you, for I have been in just such a mess more times than I care to remember. I have lost many hours of sleep while being involved with tenants who absolutely had to be evicted, and I have the gray hairs to show for the experiences, but I have survived, too, in spite of the threats on my life and the unmentionable damage which some tenants have done to my rental dwellings. Somehow I survived eviction after eviction with my life and my self-respect intact, and in the process I learned a few things about dealing with people under trying circumstances.

Rough as these experiences are to live through, you can, and you will, live through them just as I have. At least, I trust that you will. And even though you will undoubtedly ask yourself at times just why such revolting developments should happen to you of all people, don't expect any solid answers to questions like that, certainly not here. Do expect to find solid answers here to those nitty-gritty questions you have about evictions, answers which will enable you to get an eviction over with quickly and inexpensively so you can get on with more important business.

You will profit most from this book if you skim it quickly first, reading only the section headings in each chapter and the key points worth remembering which appear at the end of each chapter. They will give you a clue about what to expect so you can go directly to the section which answers the questions plaguing you now. If you are preparing to evict a tenant for breach of contract or failure to vacate, be sure you become familiar with chapter 5 first because it explains thoroughly the entire legal eviction procedure for nonpayment of rent, and parts of that procedure will apply to the other two. If you wonder what "breach of contract" or any of the other terms used in this book mean, look them up in the glossary before you plunge on. And if you happen to be unlucky enough to own property in a rent-controlled area, read chapter 4, by all means.

Incidentally, I believe that the laws governing evictions in California are outmoded. They are crying for reform. There are fairer, faster, less complicated ways to handle evictions (landlord-tenant courts modeled after small-claims courts are one possibility), and we should be clamoring for them to be adopted. You have only to be initiated into the eviction procedure yourself to realize how elusive, and hence frustrating, the pursuit of justice through legal channels can be. When merely the presence or absence of a single mark on a single piece of paper will give your tenant an extra fifteen days of free rent, you begin to wonder about our legal machinery for handling what should be a relatively simple matter. When your tenants are handed an opportunity at the eleventh hour to delay their impending eviction if only they will claim that one of their number wasn't named in the court papers and therefore they all should get to stay longer free of charge, you begin to wonder about fairness. Afterwards, you won't wonder any more why some landlords get so exasperated over the legal technicalities which prevent them from evicting a nonpayer promptly that they take matters into their own hands.

In theory, the eviction procedure is supposed to keep us and our tenants from taking advantage of one another. In practice, it has become a convoluted legal exercise which has undone more than one landlord I know and has given savvy tenants the opportunity to live rent free legally for many a month.

Little by little, some improvements are occurring (the streamlined complaint form approved by the Judicial Council of California is one; the law enabling court clerks to enter default judgments is another), but the whole machinery really needs to be overhauled, not patched piecemeal.

I hope that once you become familiar with the eviction procedure we have now, you will make some effort to change it. Write a letter or two to your state legislators. Tell them you think that the current procedure probably worked satisfactorily back in the good old days when people felt moral obligations to pay their bills on time and care for other people's property, when tenants would move out voluntarily if they were ever served with a notice to vacate, and when the attorneys who had to handle the few evictions which did actually reach the courthouse were charging a flat $25 per case and enjoying the challenge. Those days are long gone. Times have changed; eviction proceedings haven't. They need to be changed. Scream loudly enough. Your tenants are out there screaming, and look at what they have accomplished.

You should know that the information given here has been thoroughly researched and is believed to be accurate at the time of publication, but because certain practices vary from place to place and because the laws and the interpretation of those laws change all the time, whereas the words in this book are fixed on paper, you would be wise to consider double-checking what you read here.

To help you avoid the most common pitfalls in doing an eviction yourself, I have tried wherever possible to be conservative about the various decisions involved. There's always the chance that I might have been too conservative or not conservative enough or that I might have overlooked something. Should you encounter any errors in this book or any problems with your eviction which you think might fall within the scope of this book, please write me. I will share this knowledge with other landlords so they might avoid having to suffer as you did.

1
Preventing Evictions

Those people who are concerned enough about their health to exercise regularly and eat their apple a day, practicing preventive medicine all their lives, seldom wind up on an operating table undergoing the big fix, and they seldom suffer the many ailments common to those who ignore their health.

Preventive landlording is somewhat similar. Practice it religiously, and you should be able to avoid the numerous lighter ailments common to the landlord-tenant relationship. You should also be able to avoid landlording's big fix, an eviction. Preventive landlording is well worth the effort. It will keep your blood pressure and your pulse rate as near normal as possible, and it will contribute significantly to your overall success in this business.

So, how does one go about practicing preventive landlording as it relates to evictions? Are the methods some kind of magic or voodoo? Hardly! They are nothing more than well-developed, workable procedures for selecting tenants, insuring compliance, enforcing agreements, and collecting rents, all applied with as much diligence and consistency as possible.

Each of these methods in itself is a fascinating subject of particular importance to one's success in landlording. My intention here is not to expand on these subjects to any great degree. It is simply to underscore the relationship of these procedures to evictions and to suggest a few ideas worth remembering and using. Read the *Landlording* book for a detailed treatment of the subjects.

Selecting Tenants

To understand how evictions relate to tenant selection, think of each landlord-tenant relationship as a continuum with a short beginning, a lengthy middle, and a short end. Each relationship begins normally when you choose someone to be your tenant and that someone chooses you to be his landlord. It continues in a somewhat balanced fashion until the tenant chooses to leave and move on. You normally do not choose for the tenant to leave. You exercise only the one choice in the matter, at the very beginning of the relationship. If you fail to exercise that choice wisely or at all, you run the risk of having to end the relationship abruptly and abnormally, that is, with an eviction.

Since you surely don't want to evict tenants any more than you absolutely have to, you must choose your tenants wisely.

Even in this age of tenants' rights and landlords' responsibilities, you still do have some leeway in choosing your tenants. You don't have to rent to the first person who comes along and waves all the move-in money in your face. You only have to rent to the first person who comes along and meets all of your legal and consistently applied standards, standards which you yourself determine to a great degree.

When you set your tenant standards, you should set them according to what's legal and nondiscriminatory for the dwelling you want to rent out. These standards should include such things as amount of income, stability of income, credit rating, amount of assets, rental history, pets, number of vehicles, number of people in the household, smoking habits, drinking habits, permanence, and cleanliness. They should not include such things as whether there are any children in the household, whether the applicants are married, whether the applicants are Mexican-American, African-American, Chinese-American, or Italian-American, whether the applicants are 21 or 65 years of age, whether the applicants are atheists or holy rollers, or whether they are HIV-positive.

Once you have set your reasonable standards and put them in writing, you need to gather all the relevant information you can on the applicants. Give a rental application to everyone who is interested in renting from you. Then check the applications thoroughly to see whether the information is truthful.

Next, you must satisfy yourself as to whether the applicants measure up to your standards. All in all, you're mainly interested in determining whether they have the ability and the inclination to pay the rent, whether they will take care of your property, and whether they will likely get along with the other tenants.

Making these determinations requires some science and some sorcery. It's a judgment call, albeit an informed judgment call.

Just remember when you're making one of these judgment calls that a wayward suitor makes a wayward spouse, and a poor applicant makes a poor tenant. If you doubt whether an applicant will make a good tenant, don't rent to him. You're not going to change him. Remember, also, that a vacant rental is better than one rented to someone who is going to have to be evicted later. A vacant rental isn't going to drive your good tenants away, nor is it going to develop holes in the walls, burns in the carpets, clogs in the toilet, tears in the linoleum, cracks in the windows, and chips in the tile. It isn't going to generate any rent, that's true, but, on the other hand, neither will a dwelling which you've rented to a deadbeat tenant.

Refuse to rent to someone you believe would become one of your eviction statistics if you did rent to him. That is the cheapest, least agonizing "eviction" you can possibly perform.

Insuring Compliance

We Americans buy more insurance to cover ourselves for more calamities than any other people on this earth. We are insurance junkies. We can't seem to get enough of the stuff. Yet, we landlords seldom consider insuring ourselves in case an untested tenant turns sour. Believe it or not, nobody sells this kind of insurance. Nobody sells it because it's absolutely free. Because it's free, there's nobody promoting it, and we, therefore, tend to forget that it's available to us at all.

This insurance which I am referring to is *cosigner involvement*. When you're selecting ten-ants and you're somewhat dubious about whether a particular applicant would make a good tenant, request that he secure a cosigner, someone of means to insure that he will comply with the terms of the rental agreement. Get the cosigner to sign a cosigner agreement as an addendum to the rental agreement. Then, if the tenant does turn sour, you may proceed to collect on your free insurance policy from the cosigner.

Enforcing Agreements

When you and your tenant began your relationship, you should have agreed on any number of terms besides just the rent and how long the agreement was to last. Your terms might have covered the tenant's obligations regarding noise, cleanliness, pets, redecorating, damage, number of occupants, subletting, and the like.

If either of you manages to violate these terms you have agreed upon, the other naturally has grounds for a lawsuit.

Many times you may have grounds for a lawsuit, all right, and you may wish to hustle into court. Don't! Don't be hasty about going to court when you see a St. Bernard puppy sitting on the tenant's doorstep, when your new tenant begins practicing his trombone at 6 a.m., when an extra roommate appears, when the tenant paints all his walls flat black, or when the tenant drains his motor oil onto the driveway and into the gutter. But don't neglect those matters either. Instead of being hasty about settling them in court, be hasty about dealing with them on a person-to-person, face-to-face basis.

No problem you will ever encounter in this business will become any easier to deal with if you neglect it for a while. It will not disappear. It will only become tougher to deal with because it will have assumed greater proportions over time. Left alone long enough, the problem will result in neighbors' complaints, the departure of your best tenants (if the building is a multiple-family dwelling), the transgressing tenant's eviction, your property's deterioration, your impoverishment, your capitulation, or all six of these mournful eventualities.

Consider the St. Bernard puppy which has appeared mysteriously on the doorstep. It's a cute, cuddly animal when it's young, but it grows—fast. Confront the tenant when you first see the puppy, and the tenant will likely get rid of it or move. Wait some time before confronting the tenant, and you will likely have a battle on your hands that will lead you straight into court. Why? The tenant has become attached to his growing pet and has assumed that since you haven't approached him on the matter, you are permitting him to keep it in spite of what the agreement says. You are doing precisely that, too, if you don't enforce the agreement as soon as you recognize that it has been broken.

To its chagrin, the San Francisco Housing Authority, which operates San Francisco's public housing projects, had to learn the hard way about the problems of failing to enforce its own rental agreement some time ago. The agreement specifically prohibited "cats, dogs, snakes, etc.," but many tenants traditionally had ignored this ban, and the housing authority itself had overlooked the matter completely until certain tenants who were without pets began to grow weary of having to play hopscotch on the sidewalks and having to wear plugs in their ears in order to adapt to the habits of their fellow tenants' pets. These inconvenienced tenants finally complained so loudly that they couldn't be ignored. The problem had festered so long, and the controversy had escalated so dramatically that only the intervention of the mayor could quell it.

Actually, the tenants' landlord, the housing authority, had wronged them all, pets included, for when any landlord fails to enforce an agreement which has been broken by a single tenant, he is failing all the tenants, especially the ones who are conscientious about observing the agreement's terms in the first place.

Rental agreement terms are for the benefit of all concerned, yours as landlord, your tenants in general, and your tenants individually. You, in the role of agreement maker and enforcer, must try to be fair to all, and that means setting understandable, enforceable rules for your relationship in advance (if you can't understand a rule, don't include it in your agreement; if you can't envision yourself enforcing a rule, don't include it in your agreement). Make sure your tenants know what to expect of you from the very first (if you can, avoid changing the rules in the middle of your relationship), and then deliver. Rules and regulations serve no useful purpose otherwise. They become only a source of endless friction.

Notwithstanding the rental agreement, your tenants will test you constantly to determine what your limits are, (kids test their parents; students test their teachers; workers test their bosses; and spouses test each other). Testing for limits is human nature. Show your tenants at the outset, in your role as agreement enforcer, that you mean business, that you simply will not allow them to break the agreement you have made with them. Be tough in the beginning, and you won't have to resort to the courts to settle your disputes later. Going to court is a big waste of money and an even bigger waste of time, and you can never know for sure just how you'll be treated there. Stay out of court if you possibly can.

Collecting Rents

The last eviction prevention method is none other than a reasonable, lucid, and strict rent collection policy.

Remember that everyone hates to pay rent. Few would pay at all if they didn't believe they would be thrown out otherwise. Establish yourself, therefore, as a landlord who expects the rent to be paid promptly. When it isn't, you should become menacing, a force to contend with.

Make it more troublesome for your tenants not to pay you than not to pay anyone else they owe money to. Explain precisely what your policy is regarding rent collection. Tell them before you ever rent to them just when their rent is due, when it is late, and what's going to happen to them if they don't pay on time. I tell mine that their rent is due on the first, it is late on the fifth, and if it's not paid by the fifth, I'll give them only three days to pack up and leave. Talk tough. Be tough when you collect rents. You won't be understood any other way.

In practice, this four-day grace period works well. You no longer have to listen to those hackneyed excuses tenants make for not having paid you on or before the first. You know and, what's more, they know that if the rent hasn't been paid by the fourth, either they do have a serious excuse or they're making a conscious attempt to avoid paying altogether. You save innumerable calls and trips on the second or third or fourth of the month to inquire after the rent, and you can feel entirely justified in collecting a late fee from a tenant who has missed the due date by at least four days.

If your tenant hasn't paid you the rent or bothered to advise you that it'll be delayed for some good reason or another, visit him yourself on the fifth to learn what's the matter. Listen to his ex-

PAYMENT PLEDGE

Dear Landlord/Landlady:

On or before ___July 28, XXXX___ , I promise to pay you
$ ___750.00___ for rent and other charges now owing on the dwelling
which I rent from you located at the following address:

___45 Wellington Way, Apt. 367___
(Street Address)
___Bonkers___   ___California___   ___95556___
(City)   (State)   (Zip)

I expect to be receiving sufficient funds to pay you from the
following sources:

Name	Address	Phone	Amount Expected
Ellen Dore	Route 4, Box 221, Littletown, CA	123-0707	$250
One Arm Credit Union, 111 Main St., Littletown, CA		123-5000	$500

Should you wish to, you have my authorization to verify
these sources.

If I fail to honor this pledge, I understand that I will be
evicted and that this pledge will be used against me as evidence
of my bad faith in paying what I owe.

___ET___ I acknowledge receipt of a 3-Day Notice to Pay Rent or
Quit as required by law to begin eviction proceedings. I
understand that the 3-Day Notice may show a balance owed which is
different from that given above because a 3-Day Notice by law can
demand only delinquent rent. I also understand that the
three-day period mentioned in this Notice is being extended to
the date given above, at which time I promise to pay you what I
owe. If I fail to pay on or before that date, you have the right
to continue the legal eviction (unlawful detainer) procedure
against me without having to serve me another 3-Day Notice to Pay
Rent or Quit. I have already been served. I am being given the
extra time to pay only as a courtesy and only this once.

Signed ___Extra Terrestrial___
            Extra Terrestrial

Dated ___July 10, XXXX___

planation sympathetically, and then decide whether you ought to give him a little bit of leniency or none at all.

Whether he is to get leniency or not, he ought to get a 3-Day Notice to Pay Rent or Quit then and there (see chapter 5). Have the notice already filled out so you can hand it to him before you leave. Tell him, "We give everybody one of these notices if the rent isn't paid by the fifth, regardless of who he is. We treat everybody the same way."

If he doesn't deserve any leniency, tell him that

ber the details of the agreement, it helps both of you understand the situation more fully.

"Whoa, now," you might say, "there could be a problem here! If you're giving the tenant a 3-day notice at the same time you're getting him to sign a payment pledge stating that you'll still take the rent at some time after the 3-day notice expires, the tenant could argue in court that you're sending him confusing signals. On the one hand, you're saying, 'Pay up in three days,' and on the other, you're saying, 'It's okay to take more than three days to pay up.' Which is it?"

unless he comes up with the rent money in the next three days, he'd better get a move on and move out.

If you're inclined to show him some leniency, have him make a definite commitment to pay on or before a certain date, not over two weeks hence for the best of tenants and within just a few days for those doubtful ones. Put that commitment in writing using a payment pledge form like the one shown on the next page. It specifies exactly when the delinquent rent and other charges will be paid, how much will be paid at that time, what sources will provide the funds, and what will happen if the rent isn't paid by then. It formalizes whatever verbal agreement you make with the tenant. Not only does it help each of you remem-

So as not to be accused of giving the tenant confusing signals about when the rent really has to be paid in order to avoid court action, get the tenant to acknowledge that the 3-Day Notice to Pay Rent or Quit is being served at this time for legal reasons and that the tenant has until the date agreed upon in the payment pledge to pay. After that date, having already served him with the legal notice which initiates eviction proceedings, you may go right ahead and file the summons and complaint. Have him initial the acknowledgement to that effect on the pledge form.

Because you want to circumvent problems with 3-Day Notice to Pay Rent or Quit provisions which require that the final day for payment be a normal banking day, make the pledge's final day be a banking day as well. In other words, don't make the final day a Saturday, Sunday, or holiday; it should be any other day. And because you want to circumvent problems involving dollar amounts, make sure that your 3-day notice demands only rent, no late fees, no bad check charges, or the like. The payment pledge, however, may include whatever sums the tenant owes you, including late fees.

Incidentally, besides those already mentioned, there is another significant advantage in serving a payment pledge along with a 3-day notice. You get the tenant to acknowledge in writing that he has received the notice. You cannot understand how important this advantage is until you have to stand toe-to-toe with a tenant in court sometime and listen to him lie through his incisors, denying under oath that he ever received your notice. How are you going to prove otherwise? With a pledge form in hand, you have his initials and signature to prove that he received it. He can hardly deny that.

Also, going to the trouble of giving your tenant more time than the law requires will make you look good if you have to go to court later. You would not appear hasty. You would appear entirely reasonable. Giving the tenant the 3-day notice at the same time you come to terms using the pledge form is prudent, too. It's your fallback position in case he doesn't come through. You absolutely have to give your tenant some form of proper notice before you can proceed with his eviction. You might as well do it now.

If you fail to give the tenant notice along with the pledge, and he doesn't pay on the appointed day, you'll have to deliver it later anyway, and then you'll have to wait the required number of days following service of the notice before you can file your court papers. That wastes precious days. Whereas, if you deliver the notice on the fifth day after the rent due date, and the tenant doesn't pay up on the date agreed upon in the pledge, you may go right ahead, if you wish, and file your court papers the very next day because you have already served the notice and you should already have waited the required number of days specified in the notice. That's prudent indeed!

Taking the Consequences

Collecting your rents swiftly and doggedly on a scheduled basis will prevent evictions for non-

payment of rent more than anything else you might do. Your tenants will know full well what to expect of you. They may test you once, but they won't test you a second time. It's too costly. If they have to, they will borrow the money from someone else to pay you their rent rather than risk your wrath and risk being evicted.

Not collecting your rents systematically can only result in losses and frequent trips to the courthouse. I know. How I know! I estimate that I lost at least $6,000 in rents, which were owed to me but never paid, before I finally decided that collections were sufficiently important to warrant more careful treatment. How do you think I learned how to evict? That's right; I wore a path to the courthouse door.

If you stick with reasonable policies for selecting tenants, securing co-signers, enforcing agreements, and collecting rents, you will forestall at least 90% of all your potential evictions. You will be running a healthy business, and your own health will flourish as well.

- Select your tenants with care. While you still can, "evict" those applicants whom you'd likely have to evict later if they were to become your tenants.
- Get a cosigner to insure the compliance of an untested tenant.
- Be an "enforcer" of your rental agreement. Do not delay; enforce promptly. There's no time like this very minute!
- Be a "heavy" whenever you're collecting rent. Collecting rent is what landlording is all about. That rent money is your paycheck. There's nothing more important in this business than your paycheck, absolutely nothing!
- When you're inclined toward leniency, use the winning combination of a 3-Day Notice to Pay Rent or Quit and a written payment pledge.

2
Getting Problem Tenants Out Without Going To Court

There are legal and there are illegal self-help eviction methods which landlords and landladies may use to get obstreperous, obnoxious, deadbeat tenants to move. I recommend that you try whatever legal methods seem appropriate in your situation before you ever resort to the courts.

We Americans have become positively obsessed with litigation, running to court optimistically expecting to resolve every kind of problem imaginable, from determining what constitutes reasonable language for high school student assemblies to challenging our deceased Aunt Agatha's last will and testament, in which she left all her money to Rufus, her pet cockatoo. We have come to believe that we will be treated fairly only if we have our day in court, so we blithely file suit after suit after suit at a rate of more than 18,000,000 civil suits a year, and we pay our attorney's fees unquestioningly. We have been clogging our courts with patently frivolous suits; we have been spending more and more unproductive time on jury duty; we have been awarding damage claims so astronomical that they force old and established companies into bankruptcy; we have developed a fascination for watching law-related programs on television; we have been devouring convoluted legal thrillers written by attorneys; we have even elevated certain attorneys to celebrity status; and we have been educating far too many attorneys.

Japan has only one attorney for every 10,000 people; Germany has one for every 2,000; California has one for every 400; and San Francisco has one for every 50. Which geographical area is going to be the first to have one attorney for every single inhabitant? Which area will have nobody but attorneys? You can be sure that it will be someplace here in the United States, which houses a whopping 70% of the world's supply.

Will it be Boston, Chicago, Los Angeles, Miami, New York City, San Francisco, or Washington, D.C.? Stay tuned.

If you can stay out of the bailiwick of attorneys, that is, out of court, and still accomplish your primary objectives, do so. When faced with an eviction situation, whatever the reason, you obviously don't have to go to court to evict your tenant if you can come to some resolution of your differences between yourselves. At the very least, you should try something or other before suing your tenant in a court of law and subjecting yourself to a host of arcane procedures, new frustrations, and constant worries.

What might landlords try? Let's examine some of the legal alternatives available first. Then we'll take a look at some of the illegal alternatives. You ought to know the difference.

Legal Alternatives

• TALKING—How do you convince tenants to vacate simply by talking with them? Go to their dwelling. Do not summon them to yours and do not talk with them by telephone. Show them how important this matter is to you by making a personal appearance yourself on their turf. Make sure when you arrive that the decision-maker of the group is there. If not, arrange another meeting at a definite time later that day.

When you meet with them, ask them to explain, first of all, what unusual circumstances have occurred which might have forced them to break their agreement with you. Tell them you have had confidence in them in the past, and you have always felt that it was well placed. Then outline the situation matter-of-factly as you understand it, and suggest alternatives. After that, ask them what they would do if they were in your shoes. If they offer up some unacceptable solution, tell them quite frankly why it wouldn't work and pose your own.

Can you get someone to do something he absolutely doesn't want to do? No, you can't. Yet you can get people to do things which they never thought they would do. You convince them with diplomacy.

One of the many stories told about the redoubtable Winston Churchill occurred at the estate of a friend who was giving a lavish dinner party. The hostess became upset and frustrated when she happened to notice one of her wealthiest guests pocketing a sterling silver salt shaker. She didn't know how to go about retrieving her expensive heirloom without creating a scene and embarrassing the fellow, so she asked her good friend Winston for help. He told her to leave it up to him. Nonchalantly, Winston sidled up to the man later in the evening and engaged him in conversation, at the end of which he pulled a salt shaker from his own pocket and said to the fellow, "I think we've been seen. We'd better put them back." And so they both did.

What kind of a stir would Churchill have created had he approached the man like a policeman and told him he had been seen stealing a salt shaker and that if he didn't return it, he'd be arrested? It would have caused great embarrassment and lasting damage. The salt shaker would have been retrieved all right, but the man would have become a social pariah, and no one would have been pleased with the outcome. There is an immense difference between approaching someone as a companion in crime and approaching him as a strong arm of the law. The diplomat knows those two approaches and others and knows when to use each. He knows that one approach won't work in every situation with everyone. Had the salt-shaker thief been a streetwise Cockney beggar, the strong-arm approach would have worked well enough. The companion-in-crime approach, as a matter of fact, might have backfired, generating a very different response. The beggar would probably have told his supposed companion in crime that he was a fool for returning his shaker. "I am going to keep mine," he might have said.

Using diplomacy, you as landlord approaching a tenant who has failed to pay his rent when due could play the role of the strong-arm or the companion-in-crime. You know the strong-arm approach. That involves looking the tenant straight in the eye and telling him, "I want my money or else." Someone trying the companion-in-crime approach would say, "I have to pay my rent, too. I pay it to the bank. It's "rent" on the money I borrowed in order to buy this place, and I need your rent money to keep them from repossessing it."

Talk with your tenants using just the diplomatic approach which is right for the situation. Try to be understanding and try to reach an agreement that allows them to save face. You might want to put your agreement in written form, something like the payment pledge introduced in chapter 1. Then again, you might not. Be flexible up to a point. Give a little, take a little. Be reasonable. Be businesslike.

If you simply cannot reach an agreement you consider fair, tell them you are left with no alternative but to evict them in court. Tell them you are loathe to go to that extreme because they will be identified to the local property owners' association as having been evicted, and it will be more difficult thenceforth for them to rent in the area. Their credit rating will suffer because you report all such matters to the credit bureau, and the bill collection agency will begin hounding them. In addition, they will never again be able to answer honestly on rental applications that they have not been evicted (to some this may sound hilarious because they seldom tell the truth anyway; to others, unaccustomed to lying in matters such as this, it may be a serious prospect; you will have to decide whether to mention it at all). After stating these consequences candidly, see if the tenants still persist in being unreasonable. If so, depart and say, "I'm disappointed that you have left me no choice. I had very much hoped we could work something out." Don't get into an argument. Don't leave in a huff. Just go.

Your success or failure in using this maneuver will depend upon the kind of relationship you have already developed with your tenants, as well as upon your skills of persuasion and diplomacy. Tailor the appeal to the people you are dealing with. Above all, be firm and polite. Don't antagonize them. Don't call them names or impugn their ancestry. You may believe very strongly that they are doing you wrong, but keep your head. Swallow your pride. Keep the dialogue open-ended. If you cut off the dialogue, your impending eviction suit will be all the more difficult to pursue. You want the tenants to be available to be served with court papers as the case progresses.

You don't want to alienate them so much that they will avoid service and thereby delay your case ten days here and ten days there. That can be expensive.

For some good ideas on the subject of negotiating, read *Getting to Yes*, which appears among the listings in the References section of this book.

Perhaps you have already tried talking your tenants into leaving, or you feel that talk just wouldn't work. Well, how about bribery?

• BRIBERY—Bribery has several real advantages. It is quick and, comparatively speaking, it is inexpensive. If you required enough in depos-

handling the case) before making your offer, and you'll likely find that a bribe will cost you far less. Even if you do have to sweeten the offer somewhat out of your own pocket because you have delayed so long that there's only a paltry deposit balance remaining of, say, less than $100 (few tenants would move for less), you will come out ahead by bribing them to leave, and so will they.

There are some good variations on the bribery gambit, too. You might offer to store the tenant's goods in one of your garages or pay the rent at a self-storage facility for a few months. You might offer to arrange and pay for a U-Haul

its from your tenants before they moved in, you should, if you act fast, have enough money available from their deposits to pay them for leaving. This was one of the reasons for requiring a deposit in the first place, wasn't it?

Obviously, should you succeed in suing to evict them, the money judgment, including court costs, would be subtracted from their deposits, and they could expect to receive little or no money back. In fact, they'd probably owe you something. An offer to return what's left of their deposits after you deduct for the rent they owe you might be enough to get them moving. It's worth a try.

Calculate about how much an eviction and lost rent would cost you (especially if an attorney is

van and a small crew to move the tenant's possessions. You might cut a $100 bill in half right before the tenant's eyes, give him half, and keep half yourself until he has moved out completely. Or you might offer to buy his TV, stereo, appliances, furniture, aquarium, or pet parakeet.

Unless the tenant is unable to comprehend what an eviction will mean to him, you will likely be successful with one of these bribes. Don't be ashamed to try. Money, especially when offered in the right way, will get people to do things they wouldn't begin to consider doing without it. You have probably seen full-grown people making fools of themselves on those old television game shows, dressing up like half-grown ventriloquist dummies courting extraterrestrials, acting like escaped loonies, and chattering like blithering simpletons. Sure, they're exhibitionists, but they're also greedy when the price is right. Tenants, too, suddenly feel a great urge to make their move when the price is right.

• "OFFICIAL" INTIMIDATION—Another maneuver which is perfectly legal and ofttimes prompts tenants to vacate without your ever having to resort to the courts is "official" intimidation. I don't mean hiring goons or gorillas to intimidate. They're anything but official. I mean hiring a peace officer to scare your tenants out.

duty don't serve notices. Some are terribly slow. They may take more than a week to get around to yours. Before you hire one of them to serve your notice, ask them to estimate how long they'll take to serve it, and then weigh the intimidation factor of their serving the notice versus the time factor of your or someone else's serving it more quickly.

A variation of this method involves the direct hiring of an off-duty law-enforcement officer or a security patrolman to serve your notices. In most areas, they may wear their uniforms while off duty and may hire themselves out as process servers.

How? Have one of them serve your notices. Sure, you can serve the notices yourself, but you're too familiar a face to your tenants. You're simply not intimidating enough. You cannot possibly impress upon them the gravity of the matter as much as can an armed and uniformed peace officer who's handing out a notice signed by you and stipulating that the tenants have a fixed number of days to clear out. That is quite intimidating to most people. They simply do not want to get mixed up with the law if they can help it, and they frequently will mistake your notice for one which actually announces their impending eviction. It all looks so official and imperative.

CAUTION: Some peace officers on official

They look quite intimidating when they appear on a doorstep in full-dress attire complete with a firearm strapped to their waist and they hand your tenant his notice. They seem to carry *clout*, and they frequently get the desired response.

Illegal Alternatives

In some respects it's fortunate that there are laws to keep us landlords from acting rashly when we're trying to force problem tenants to move out. After being frustrated repeatedly, some of us might be driven to near distraction and feel compelled to take the law into our own hands, only to wind up doing something we regret later.

Unscrupulous, bull-headed, devil-may-care

landlords use illegal self-help eviction methods anyway, laws or no laws. These methods generally work as effectively as a gangster chieftain's dictum, but sometimes they don't. Sometimes the results are disastrous, and you read about them on the front page of your daily newspaper. No matter what the risks are, some people are willing to take them. So be it.

Just in case you don't know what these illegal self-help eviction methods are, I'll identify a few. Perhaps you weren't aware that they are illegal.

• CONSTRUCTIVE EVICTION—Unscru-

mises.

They might change the locks on the doors, rummage through the tenant's belongings, keep the good stuff, and throw the rest out on the sidewalk.

They might hire a burly bear of a man to scare the tenant out.

This monster man stops by at dinnertime and bangs threateningly on the tenant's door, perhaps loosening a hinge or two. When the tenant opens the door, he is staring directly into a hairy navel, and he hears a husky voice from on high echoing down to him, "Your landlord wants you

pulous landlords and landladies might disturb what the law calls "the tenant's right to quiet enjoyment of his domicile" by arranging for 130-decibel punk rock to play at all hours in an adjoining apartment or encouraging the elephants living upstairs to keep up their tap dancing. Like some of the other methods given here, this is what is known as a "constructive eviction," and the tenant's responsibility to pay rent ceases whenever a constructive eviction occurs.

They might cut off the water and lights, unhinge the outside doors, chop down the stairway to a second floor apartment, or collect the neighborhood population of rodents and keep them around by feeding them daily on the pre-

out of here by 6 o'clock tonight or we'll come by to move you out." Now that's an appeal that's mighty hard to resist. Few tenants do. They're cowed into submission. But it's as illegal as drug peddling, and the consequences can be just as disastrous.

Don't use any of these methods unless you're willing to risk a very angry tenant and legal action in which you are the defendant not the plaintiff, an action that may actually delay the tenant's departure and then cost you big bucks in a settlement.

You might wonder why laws keep us from using these methods. They seem so perfectly reasonable to use in certain cases. After all, it's our property, and we don't want the tenants to stay there anymore. If we want to remove the front door or chop down the stairway, that's our business. We own the place, including the door and the stairway. Why can't we do with it what we want to do with it? Why should such an act be against the law? The reason simply is that these eviction methods disturb the peace. They enrage tenants and endanger the lives and limbs of everyone concerned, yours too, to say nothing of the possible property damage they might cause. People get hurt when they're being tossed out. They break bones when they go to descend a

a neutral atmosphere.

Avoid illegal self-help eviction methods if you want to keep your property, your fortune, your health, and your life pretty much intact. Use them only if you don't mind taking the risk of losing plenty.

Still, I must admit that I know some landlords and landladies who resort to such methods when they believe the circumstances are right for these methods to work, that is, when they anticipate no complications. The secret to using self-help methods successfully, they say, is to keep a low profile, be unobtrusive and very canny.

flight of stairs and discover belatedly that the stairs have disappeared. People become infuriated when their belongings are peremptorily confiscated. People become incensed when someone "locks" them inside their home by removing the front door so they can't leave or when someone locks them out of their home by changing the locks. They strike back. Tempers flare. Problems grow out of all proportion, and the police have to be called in to quell the disturbances. Sometimes the coroner even has to be called in to cart off the dead. The object of these laws is to keep people from resorting to street remedies and to bring their potentially destructive disputes into court instead, where they can be judged impartially in

• LOCKOUT—One landlady told me how she locked out a tenant some time ago, seemingly a dangerous act, certainly an illegal one. Maybe it would have been dangerous in other circumstances, but she thought otherwise. You be the judge.

It so happened that one of her tenants was two weeks in arrears, and at great inconvenience to herself, she had been trying several times a day for the previous ten days to find him. Upon making inquiries, she learned that none of the neighbors had seen him during that period, and she was unable to reach any of the contacts listed on his rental application. To determine whether he had indeed flown the coop or whether he was just being evasive, she peered through the windows, and seeing what appeared to be little but trash inside, she decided to enter with her passkey. When she did so, she committed her first illegal act, forcible entry, believe it or not, but she rationalized her action by saying to herself that she thought the tenant might be dead and she'd better find out for sure. Strange to say, from what she saw in this house which she had rented out unfurnished, she couldn't tell whether he was still living there or not. There was a mattress on the floor in the bedroom and a table and chair in the kitchen. That's all there was for furniture.

ing to have trouble opening the lock herself. She gave him another key. They talked cordially. He apologized for not contacting her earlier about the rent. He said that all kinds of things had happened to him lately and he had just forgotten, but he promised to move out within two days, and so he did. In fact, the very next day he moved out everything.

She believed he had been eluding her all that time, coming in late and leaving early, and that he would have continued playing cat and mouse, occupying the premises rent-free much longer, if she had not forced him to meet with her. Her

On the back porch was a fair-sized heap of trash, and the usual junk one finds in a recently vacated rental was scattered throughout the rooms. The place looked abandoned.

Under these circumstances, she should really have used the abandonment procedure outlined in chapter 14 to regain possession, but she decided instead to change the locks, using old replacements exactly like the originals so that her locking out the tenant would not appear obvious to him if he did return. His key would fit into the keyway, but it wouldn't turn. That night at 2 a.m. the tenant called to let her know that he couldn't get his key to work. Apologizing for the "defective" lock, she let him in after pretend-

stratagem had worked. She had outsmarted her tenant. She had recovered possession of her house, and she had done it quickly, much more quickly than if she had followed the legal means available to her. Of course, her action might have resulted in her tenant's breaking a door or a window to get in. It might also have resulted in a lawsuit, but fortunately for her it resulted only in the tenant's departure, and that was her prime objective.

Do the ends justify the means? It's an age-old question. This landlady believed that they did in her case. Otherwise she would never have gambled and she never would have won.

The point of this narrative and the next is that

there are certain pragmatic methods which might accomplish one's objectives in a given situation quickly, cheaply, and painlessly should one choose to use them. I do not advocate their use because they must be carefully chosen and carefully executed, they require extra-careful judgment, they don't always work, they may actually backfire, and they are, after all, illegal, but I think you should be familiar with them and their drawbacks nonetheless, just as you should be familiar with the applicable legal eviction procedures.

• PHONY EVICTION—The next illegal method is rather an inventive one, staging a phony

To stage an eviction, the landlord follows all the steps of an ordinary legal eviction through the courts, but he forges the papers. Using originals of all the appropriate forms which he obtained from authentic cases against former tenants, he prepares forms for the phony eviction just as carefully as if he were going through court. He covers the original names, dates, and other particulars with correction fluid, photocopies the papers, types in the tenant's name and the other information relevant to this case, photocopies the doctored copies, and then serves those copies himself by posting them on the door. Each time

eviction. It capitalizes on the tenant's ignorance of the legal eviction process and his unwillingness to become a respondent in the case. When you examine the eviction procedures outlined in chapters 5-9, you will notice that none of them actually forces the stalwart but submissive tenant to appear in court. If he chooses not to answer the summons, he never goes near the courthouse. The legal machinery just keeps grinding away behind his back. He knows it is because he keeps getting papers from the court. The only thing he can hope to do is delay matters by making himself unavailable, and that insures the phony eviction's success. He never sees the landlord who's posting the notices on his door.

another form is "due," it too is forged and served. The tenant doesn't know the difference but believes that when the final date is set, he'd better clear out. The success of this method, to be sure, depends on the tenant's lack of sophistication in legal matters.

The landlord I know who uses this method claims that it saves him inconvenience and money and that it works especially well in cases where he has already delayed matters too long and the tenant regards eviction as inevitable anyway.

These illegal, self-help eviction methods are quite different one from the other, but they have one thing in common. They create some pretty apprehensive landlords and landladies.

- Avoid litigation if you possibly can.
- Try some friendly persuasion first.
- Consider how much litigation is going to cost you and then try offering your tenant some cash money as an enticement to leave.
- Eschew methods used by the unscrupulous.

3
Preparing for Your Court Case

When you have tried and failed to rid yourself of problem tenants by hook or by crook, you have no alternative but to try an eviction by the book. You need legal clout to get them out.

Before you begin, however, you should know a thing or two about legal terminology, eviction statistics, courts, attorneys, eviction services, local practices, court clerks, time demands, fictitious name statements, equipment and supplies, and costs, and if your property is located in an area under rent control, you should definitely know something about how rent control will affect your eviction. You'll find information about rent control in the next chapter. First, let's take a look at the various things which might have some bearing upon your eviction, no matter where in California you happen to be.

Legal Terminology

In almost every pursuit there's a jargon understood only by its initiates. Perhaps because those who practice law, work so much with words and try so hard to be precise, they have developed more special terminology than have people in most other pursuits. To help you understand certain special meanings of the terms you are likely to encounter when you handle an eviction through the courts, there is a glossary at the back of this book.

One term you will see so frequently that it should be introduced here is "unlawful detainer." Generally speaking, it means wrongfully possessing real property which belongs to someone else, but in the strict legal sense it refers to the legal proceeding which culminates in the sheriff or marshal's removing tenants from the landlord's property. Most frequently, it is used interchangeably with the term "eviction," but it will almost always be the term used in legal proceedings to refer to an eviction action.

Actually, the term "eviction" has a broader definition. You may say that you evicted a tenant when you merely asked him to leave and he went, when you served him with a notice and he left, when you made his dwelling uninhabitable and he moved, or when you filed a complaint against him in court and had the sheriff preside over his departure. Those are all evictions, but only the last one is an unlawful detainer.

Eviction Statistics

The news media love horror stories. They thrive on horror stories, so much so that you'd think Stephen King were every reporter's patron saint. If you pay any attention to the news media, you have encountered horror stories about evictions which took some poor landlord months to consummate and practically sent him to the poor house, and you may be wondering whether you might be embarking upon a horror story of your own as you prepare to evict some tenants. Well, just in case you're becoming apprehensive about your chances of successfully evicting your tenants in court, consider some statistics gathered by the California Apartment Law Information Foundation (CALIF) on unlawful detainers filed during 1990 in municipal courts.

In that year, there were 236,817 unlawful detainers filed throughout the state of California, and the plaintiff/landlord prevailed in 99.4% of them. Imagine that! Landlords won 99.4 out of every 100 unlawful detainers they filed! The Procter & Gamble people claim that Ivory soap is 99.99% pure, and we tend to think of that as being pretty pure. It is. Prevailing in 99.4% of all unlawful detainer cases is almost as sure as Ivory is pure. Think about that as you begin your own unlawful detainer action. You are going to prevail. You are not going to lose. The statistics are with you. They are with you overwhelmingly!

Don't let that 99.4% figure go to your head,

though. Whereas your eventual triumph is about as close to a sure thing as you'll ever find in this world, you still must jump through all the hoops which our antiquated legal system insists you jump through. Some of the hoops are flaming and may singe you slightly. Some are small and may be a tight squeeze. Some are moving and may require special concentration. Jump through them anyway. Jump through every one of them, or the bureaucrats, the badge wearers, and the black-robed potentates operating the system will not let you prevail.

Then there's the matter of time. Time is not on your side in an unlawful detainer action. Time is your enemy. The longer your unlawful detainer takes, the more your tenants gain. Time is on their side. It's their ally, not yours.

Let's look at some more eviction statistics gathered by CALIF, and we'll see just how tenants use time to their advantage in unlawful detainers. Statewide, the average unlawful detainer takes 48 days, that is, from the date when the landlord files his first document with the court until he gets his judgment. Mind you, this is not the elapsed time for the entire eviction cycle because it does not include the notice period before the first court papers are filed, nor does it include the lag time between the filing of the Writ of Execution and the actual departure of the tenants. The shortest amount of time the notice period might take is three days, and the final lag time is going to be at least five days, so we have to add at least eight days to the 48 days. The average unlawful detainer in California, then, takes at least 56 days. That's close to two months! That's a long time. That's a very long time when every one of those days is costing you money.

Hold on, it gets worse. On average, landlords in Los Angeles take a week longer than the statewide average to evict their tenants. Landlords in Berkeley take over two weeks longer than the statewide average. And landlords in Compton, of all places, require more than twice as much time to evict their tenants as landlords elsewhere. Sounds pretty bad, eh? Read on.

There are two primary eviction delaying tactics used by unscrupulous tenants. You'll be learning more about them later in this book. The one is a tenant claim that an adult actually living in the rental dwelling failed to receive proper notice of the landlord's unlawful detainer action. This is called an "Arrieta claim" because it's the result of a California Supreme Court decision in the Arrieta case [*Arrieta v. Mahon* (1982) 31 CA3d 381]. The other delaying tactic is bankruptcy, generally filed at the eleventh hour, right before the sheriff comes to turn the tenants out. If tenants make an Arrieta claim, statistics show that they require an extra month to be evicted. If they file bankruptcy, they require an extra five weeks to be evicted. And if they go for broke, making both an Arrieta claim *and* filing bankruptcy, they require an extra six weeks more than the average to be evicted, or three-and-a-half months in all!

Clearly, here is the tenants' ally–time. Initially, the statistics about unlawful detainers look good for the landlord. The landlord is going to win. It's a sure thing. Press the statistics further for information, however, and things change. Sure, the landlord is going to win in the end, but the tenant is going to be dragging his feet all the way out the door.

"Time" is the watchword in unlawful detainers. You have to be concerned as much about time in an unlawful detainer as anything else. It's important to you, very important. Ignoring time is not going to result in your losing your case completely, but it is going to result in your losing money, lots of it, and that after all is what most civil lawsuits are all about.

You *can* beat the time averages when doing an eviction yourself. I always do. I have never once needed as much time as the statewide average to consummate an eviction. My average is about half the statewide average. You should be able to beat the averages, too, even if you have never evicted a tenant through the courts before. All you have to do is pay close attention to the ticking clock while you're pursuing your unlawful detainer, and you will beat the averages.

Don't worry much about whether you will win or lose. Worry only about how long your winning will take. Stay tuned to your case. Follow it closely. Check out the various timetables in this book, and play "Beat the Clock."

Courts

Small claims courts can no longer hear eviction cases in California. Nowadays you must use either municipal or superior courts to evict your tenants.

In some ways, being denied access to small claims courts for evictions is no great loss for landlords because small claims courts were always notoriously slow in carrying an eviction through to its conclusion, no matter how justified it was. Landlords who chose to evict their tenants through small claims courts could wind up winning their judgments but losing their bank balances because the entire procedure was so slow and so weighted in favor of tenants. Any tenant bent on delaying his ouster as long as legally possible could stay on for months by taking advantage of the perfectly legal stratagems available to him and following a timetable far more unhurried than the one which applies to evictions pursued in the other courts.

for other money disputes involving tenants. Let's say that a tenant won't reimburse you for a window his son broke, or he drove his uninsured Ford into the side of your storage shed and refuses to pay for the damage, or he won't pay you the balance of the security deposit he promised to pay during the second month of his tenancy. Go after him in small claims court.

Just make sure that the compensation you seek falls within the monetary limits of the court.

Those monetary limits have been increased quite substantially over the years. You may have heard that you can now sue somebody for $5,000 in a California small claims court. You heard right.

Nonetheless, small claims courts did have certain advantages as eviction battlegrounds—neither landlord nor tenant could be represented by counsel; the landlord as plaintiff could expect special help with the paperwork from small claims court clerks skilled in advising neophytes about their cases; the landlord could expect to pay a cheaper filing fee; and the whole procedure was simpler. We can only hope that these advantages will return one of these days if the legislature ever gets around to establishing landlord-tenant courts using simple, straight-forward procedures and forms.

You may, of course, still use small claims court

It is $5,000. But there is one important condition. You may sue for a maximum of $5,000 *no more than twice in any given year*, whereas you may sue for anything up to $2,500 as often as you like.

The $5,000 limit applies to all small claims courts throughout the state, not to each of them separately. You can't sue twice for the maximum in San Diego, for example, and then twice in Los Angeles in the same year. You can sue once for the maximum in San Diego and then once in Los Angeles or any other place in the state in a single year, and that's all. After that, you have to limit your suits to $2,500 each until the following year.

Whenever you want to pursue a tenant who owes you money and you're not also trying to evict him, take him to small claims court. Before you go, though, locate a copy of the *Small Claims Court Handbook*, which is mentioned in the References section in the back of this book, and read it. Then proceed. You must know something about preparing your case for small claims court if you expect to convince a judge that you're telling the truth and deserve a favorable judgment.

Now that you no longer have the option of taking evictions to small claims court, which is the one court most people know something about from having seen "People's Court" on television, you should know a little about the courts you can use for evictions—municipal and superior.

First of all, you should know that these courts are under county jurisdiction, not city, not state, and not federal. Counties are responsible for administering them and maintaining their operations. Hence, you must know the county where your rental property is located, for you must use the courts in that county to evict. You cannot use the court which is nearest to your rental property unless it happens to be in the same county as the property.

Secondly, you should know that the names of these courts are misleading. Whereas juvenile courts and probate courts have names which indicate what kinds of cases they handle, municipal and superior courts have "poker-face" names. Their names offer no clues as to what happens there. Municipal courts are not "city" courts, and superior courts are not inherently "superior" to other courts. Forget what you might imagine is happening in these courts if you know no more about them than their names. Their names are not descriptive.

Still, these courts do have their differences.

The difference between municipal and superior courts is money limits, nothing more. Municipal courts may hear residential- and commercial-property cases where the total judgment requested does not exceed $25,000 (there is no longer any limit on the amount of the monthly rent or on the type of the property). If your case exceeds these limits, you'll have to file it in superior court or waive the excess. Use municipal court if you can. It's every bit as fast as superior court, and it has a lower filing fee.

No matter which court you find yourself in,

you may use the information given here to do your eviction. Although the forms in this book mention "municipal court" specifically where appropriate, they may be changed relatively easily with x's or correction fluid for use in superior courts.

Attorneys

Regardless of whether you do your own evictions or have an attorney do them for you, you should know an attorney to consult when there are legal entanglements. You'll feel more confident about handling your whole landlording business if you do. Besides, attorneys are absolutely indispensable in our society, regardless of how we feel about them and the whole business of litigation in America today.

They are not absolutely indispensable for doing evictions, however. In most eviction cases, ones which might be called routine, you can do the same thing yourself more quickly and more inexpensively. Attorneys, after all, delegate the paperwork to a legal secretary and become involved only when a court appearance is necessary.

Unless they have an "eviction mill" set up, most attorneys don't even want to do evictions for landlords (ah, but from reading the *California Eviction Defense Manual*, methinks there are those attorneys who get a perverse thrill out of championing the rights of "downtrodden" tenants) because they're penny-ante stuff compared to other types of legal cases. Many attorneys handle them for the same reason that some real estate agents handle rental property management operations, to promote themselves so you'll think of them first when you need their other more lucrative services.

Now you might think that an attorney, a professional in the field of law, would take less time to evict a tenant than you, a rank amateur, would. You might think that, but you'd be wrong.

Here are three reasons why an eviction handled by an attorney will take longer than one you do yourself. First, because you know that an attorney will charge you $200 to $500 in fees (depending on whether court appearances are necessary) plus attendant costs amounting to upwards of $190, you will tend to delay longer than you should before turning to him to begin eviction proceedings, accepting the tenant's excuses more credulously and hoping he will move out without your having to spend all that money. Second, an attorney will handle from 50 to 150 cases at one time, and yours may be delayed because another case needs attention at the same time yours does. Third, an attorney has no incentive to push your eviction through to completion as rapidly as is legally possible. You do. Every extra day the tenant stays without paying rent is money out of your pocket. On the other hand, the attorney is going to be compensated for his time regardless of how long the eviction takes.

You can do an eviction yourself in municipal court for between $190 and $220 in out-of-pocket costs and a total of two to five hours of your own time. If your time is more important than your money, hire an attorney to handle your evictions. It's an attorney's business. Otherwise, do it yourself.

Some have said that acting as your own attorney is akin to doing your own brain surgery. That may be true if you're trying to defend yourself on murder charges. Evictions are not murder charges. They're more like the common cold.

Do be shrewd enough to recognize when you need to engage the services of an attorney, however. Generally you need one when your tenants have hired an attorney themselves, when your tenants in an apartment house have organized against you (hell hath no fury like all the tenants in a building who are being evicted at one time), or when there are any complications you don't understand. That's when you should hire yourself an attorney, and remember that even though you have begun an action on your own, you may always hire an attorney to assist you whenever you feel you need one as your case progresses.

I should mention here that there are several special advantages in using an attorney for evictions if you're so inclined. Both relate to bungling. First, because attorneys are independent contractors, you can't be sued by your tenant if your attorney makes an error which gives the tenant a cause of action. Second, if the attorney bungles the paperwork so badly that you lose your suit to your tenant, you may sue your attorney for malpractice.

If you, on the other hand, bungle an eviction, you'll have to go back to square one and start all over again. You'll have nobody to blame for the bungling but yourself. Considering the advantages in handling routine evictions on your own, though, I'd say that the advantages in using an attorney really aren't substantial enough to warrant using one for every garden-variety eviction you have.

Eviction Services

The Yellow Pages in most metropolitan areas contain listings of eviction services, companies which specialize in doing evictions for the landlord or in assisting the landlord to do them himself. Because these companies vary all the way from secretarial service businesses to legitimate attorney's offices, you would be wise to choose carefully if you are ever inclined to turn to one for help. Some of them merely fill out forms for their clients; some actually engage in unauthorized legal practice; some privately offer unethical advice; and some honestly give good counsel. From an ad in the phone book you can't tell the difference between them, but you can tell from an ad whether the service is being run by an attorney or not, and only one which is run by an attorney can legally represent you in court. The others can only prepare you for court.

If you cannot make sense out of this book, if you feel too timid to handle an eviction yourself, if you live too far away from the court of jurisdiction, if you encounter difficulties doing an eviction yourself, or if you cannot call an apartment and property owners' association for recommendations, turn to the Yellow Pages and select an eviction service which mentions "attorney at law" in its ad. Only that eviction service can legally give you full eviction services. If you live in an area which has no eviction services listed in the Yellow Pages, check under "attorneys" (I guarantee you'll find some of them listed) and call several who advertise that they are a general practice law firm specializing in, among other things, landlord-tenant law.

To find the attorney in your area who ought to know more about evictions than any other, ask the court clerk for the name of the attorney who files the most evictions in her court. The clerk will know right away who that attorney is and will probably even have his telephone number memorized. In my local court, one attorney files more than half of all the evictions filed there. You can bet that he knows what he's doing.

Local Practices

Within California there are some variations in forms, practices, costs, and schedules. Some courts, for example, hear unlawful detainers on only one day a week; some allow a declaration in lieu of actual appearance in court to get a default judgment; some require that two-sided forms be copied always on one sheet of paper, never on two; and some have special forms all their own (forms approved by the Judicial Council of California are used throughout the state). Acquaint yourself with the forms and procedures given here first and then ask your court clerk certain questions about local practices when you first call her or when you actually file the summons and complaint. Then you won't be surprised later.

You will find in chapter 5 several cautions which relate to local practices discovered the hard way by readers of this book. Read them carefully. Don't let unusual local practices trip you up.

Court Clerks

Your primary contact with your court will be the court clerk. She can make your job easier and speedier in many ways, by giving you helpful hints when you need them, by supplying you with the correct forms for her court, by squeezing you onto an already full calendar, and by holding your hand as you traverse strange legal territory. She knows it all. Be patient around her (she's often harried), trust her (she's experienced), be nice to her even if she does sometimes appear gruff and uncivil (it's a stressful job), and she will be of great help to you. It wouldn't hurt for you to bring her a flower or two to cheer her up when appropriate. Courthouses aren't the most cheerful places in which to work, you know.

Lest you think that your court clerk is being especially aloof to you because you don't belong to the "attorney guild," consider this. One eviction expert, an attorney who has handled over 3,000 evictions himself, told me that three years elapsed before any of the court clerks in one of the courts he uses frequently, ever treated him civilly. Don't despair if your court clerk is unfriendly to you at first; she's not discriminating against you because you're an outsider; she very likely treats attorneys that way as well.

Time Demands

The eviction process will take some of your personal time. You will have to type up the papers, visit the clerk's and sheriff or marshal's offices, make telephone calls, possibly appear in court, and finally, supervise the actual eviction if necessary. Be certain you have the time necessary for the whole process. Either you or your spouse may do the work, but, for the sake of convenience, the one not tied to a daytime job should be the one to do it. Court offices are generally open from 8-12 a.m. and from 1-5 p.m., and your court hearing is usually set for 9 a.m. Be certain you can make your hearing.

As an added precaution, you should list both yourself and your spouse or partner as plaintiffs in the complaint, and then any one of you could appear in court. Some courts will allow your manager to appear in court as well, even though he is not mentioned in the complaint. If you live at a distance from your property or you would be greatly inconvenienced by appearing in court yourself, include your manager's name on the complaint as a plaintiff as well, and then he could appear, but he must be considered one of the owners if he appears in court on an unlawful detainer since the only one who may legally represent an owner in court is an attorney licensed to practice before the bar.

Fictitious Name Statements

If you have adopted a fictitious name for your landlording business or for a particular building you own *and* if your rental agreements are written in that name rather than your own (if rent checks are made out in the name of the building or in your business name, that doesn't matter; this requirement refers only to the name used on the agreement), you will have to file a fictitious name statement before you may evict a tenant through the courts. It's a simple procedure really, costing around $50 all told, but since it involves publishing a legal notice, it cannot be done overnight; it takes about four weeks. If you are using a fictitious name on your agreements, you must include a statement in your complaint verifying that you have filed the fictitious name statement. If you haven't filed one yet and you have been using a fictitious name, file immediately and then proceed with the first steps of your unlawful detainer. Only the court action itself need wait upon final publication of the name.

Where you file your fictitious name is important, for a devious attorney may attack your eviction action by claiming that you filed in the wrong county, and this claim may delay the eviction considerably. Remember to file it in the county where you conduct most of your business under a particular name. If you live in one county, own buildings in several other counties, and operate all of them under one fictitious name, then the location where you have your central office would be the county to file in. If you live in one county and have several properties in other counties, operating them under various fictitious names, file separate fictitious name statements, and file them in the counties where the properties are located.

Equipment and Supplies

To handle an eviction yourself, you won't have to invest in a three-piece suit, monogrammed

FORMS section of this book). With all that, this book, and, of course, your checkbook, you're ready to do battle with your tenant through the courts.

Eviction Forms Creator™

If you have a computer, you might want to consider something new to help you fill out the eviction forms. It's a program I wrote called Eviction Forms Creator. It runs on Windows machines and Macintoshes, and it's designed strictly to save you the drudgery of having to re-enter information. You enter information once, and then the program uses that same information wherever it applies.

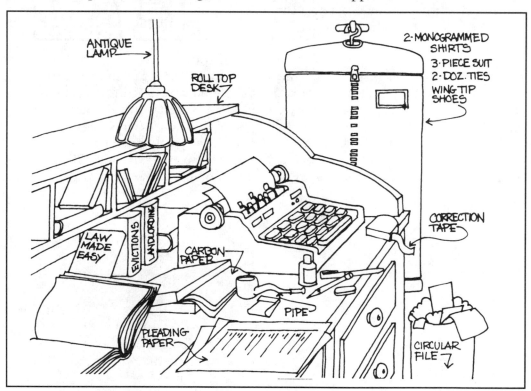

shirts, and wingtip shoes, trappings of the newly initiated attorney, but you will have to gather together some equipment and a few supplies, most of which you probably already have around the house. Get a ballpoint pen with black ink, a typewriter (preferably one with a correction key), typewriter correction tape (necessary only if your typewriter lacks a correction key), correction fluid (Liquid Paper® or White-Out® will do), carbon paper, copies of appropriate preprinted forms, and pleading paper (paper with numbers down the left margin; necessary only if you don't or can't use preprinted forms; you'll find a blank in the

You'll find some information about it in the References section. On the very last page of this book you will find more information and you will see what the main menu looks like.

Many of the sample forms shown in this book were created using Eviction Forms Creator. In all, it can create over fifty forms, including the mandated Judicial Council forms.

Costs

Your out-of-pocket expenses for doing an eviction yourself will vary according to the court you select (filing fees in superior court are greater than those in municipal court, which in turn are greater than those in small claims); the court of jurisdiction for your area (filing fees in municipal courts average around $80); the process server's fees (if you can con a friend into serving the papers for you, you may not have to pay anything; otherwise you'll pay $25-35 per service), and the number of tenants you serve (each one will cost extra because each one must be served a separate set of papers). There are other fees which you will have to pay for certain services as well, but they will hardly break you—issuing the writ by the court ($7) and evicting the tenant by the sheriff or marshal ($75). All together, your out-of-pocket expenses will be somewhere between $190 and $220 if you elect to use municipal court and do an unlawful detainer yourself.

Next

The particular reason you have for evicting your tenant will dictate the kind of notice you serve, as well as how you complete the complaint. In chapters 5-9, we will cover the steps used for evicting tenants legally for any of these reasons: 1) nonpayment of rent; 2) breach of contract; 3) waste, nuisance, or unlawful acts; 4) failure to vacate after receiving proper notice; and 5) failure to vacate after losing or relinquishing ownership. But before we do that, let's consider how rent control affects evictions. That's the subject of the next chapter.

- Start your eviction case expecting to win; stay with it in order to win promptly.
- Use municipal court for most evictions.
- Use an attorney only if you must.
- Be nice to court clerks.
- Learn the legal lingo and use it.
- Keep between $190 and $220 handy to pay your eviction costs.

4
Considering Rent Control's Effects on Evictions

Although many states, Massachusetts included, now prohibit their local governments from enacting any form of rent control, California is not among those enlightened states. Some form of rent control extends to approximately one-quarter of all the rental dwellings in the Golden State. In addition, many communities and counties have adopted rent control specifically for mobilehome parks.

Whereas the rent control bandwagon was rolling merrily along from the late '70s through the early '80s here in California, it hasn't been going anywhere lately. Having been lulled into a dream world with sweet songs about rent control's benefits, many people have come to their senses, for rent control's drawbacks are plain to see. We can only hope that something will happen soon at the ballot box or in a courtroom to eliminate this scourge from our state forever.

Fortunately, good things are happening because good people, such as the Pacific Legal Foundation, are challenging rent control's actual effectiveness in real life. We know that communism doesn't work in real life, and we know that rent control doesn't work in real life either. The world has rejected communism because it doesn't work, and California courts may soon reject rent control because it doesn't work.

Along these lines, the best thing to happen in many a year has been the appelate court decision in *152 Valparaiso Associates v. City of Cotati*. In that decision, the court held that "it is the result produced, not merely the result intended, which must be examined in determining whether a rent control ordinance has unconstitutionally taken private property without just compensation." The court challenged the city of Cotati to come up with evidence proving that its rent control law is benefitting the poor as intended. It is supposed to produce evidence that "poor people have in fact more recently flocked to Cotati to live in an increasing inventory of rental apartments [and] that respondents' rent control laws are applied so as to lure private investors and builders." If the city cannot come up with such evidence, then its rent control law must go. Imagine that, a court decision which makes perfect sense! The court is telling Cotati to prove that the good intentions in its rent control ordinances are actually coming true, or else the city must eliminate those ordinances.

The city of Berkeley saw the handwriting on the wall in this decision and tried to get it delisted, so that it could not be used elsewhere in supporting other decisions, but that naked attempt to thwart justice for all was denied.

While we are waiting for further developments to occur to restore the free market to all of California's rental properties, owners of rentals in rent-control areas must cope with the laws as they are, not as they will be in the future, and unfortunately those laws affect both rents and evictions.

Double Trouble

What many people do not realize is that the high-minded Robin Hoods who enacted rent control in certain California cities not only gave themselves a license to steal from landlords' pockets every month, they gave themselves a license to meddle with evictions. That's right! Where there are rent controls, expect to find eviction controls as well. Berkeley proudly and euphemistically calls its rent control ordinance the "Rent Stabilization and Eviction for Good Cause Ordinance." Controls on rents are only half the sad story of the "landlord bashing" going on there and elsewhere. Controls on evictions are the other half.

Why do the two occur together? You might say that once the rent control crusaders tasted power, they lusted after more, and you'd be at least partly right. They included eviction controls in their rent control ordinances for four primary reasons. Let's look at them one by one.

The first reason why rent control crusaders decided to meddle with evictions was to make vacancy decontrol provisions work. The vacancy decontrol provisions in some rent control ordinances permit landlords to increase their rents to market levels whenever there's a vacancy. So long as a tenant occupies a dwelling, the landlord must keep the rent as artificially low as rent control laws dictate, but as soon as the tenant vacates, the landlord is no longer bound by rent controls. He may charge whatever he likes, or so the rent control crusaders think.

(Actually, no landlord may ever charge whatever he likes; he may charge only whatever he can get, whatever someone will pay. The market sets rents. Landlords don't. You know that, and so does anyone else who's ever been in any kind of business.)

Okay now, if a vacancy were to release a landlord from rent control, even for a time, he'd be stupid not to create a vacancy periodically to take advantage of vacancy decontrol and increase his rents to market levels. Wouldn't he? Absolutely!

The rent control crusaders in their finite wisdom knew that such would be the case, so they added extra conditions to the steps normally required for landlord-initiated vacancies. They set up eviction controls. They felt they had to, to protect good tenants from being arbitrarily evicted by greedy landlords bent on getting rid of old tenants expressly so they could raise the rent on new ones.

They were right. Vacancy decontrol, to work at all, does require eviction controls. But not all rent control laws include vacancy decontrol provisions. Some control rents so strictly that if you decide to evict a tenant in order to move into your own building, what you are allowed to charge for rent whenever you finally move out must be based on whatever the rent was before you first moved in. Wow! In that case, there are no vacancy decontrol problems to worry about, are there?

The second reason why rent control crusaders decided to meddle with evictions was to protect tenants from landlord retaliation.

You can imagine how pleased you would be if a tenant of yours informed the rent control board that you were not complying with the rent con-

trol laws. You'd be eternally grateful, I'm sure. You want to be told when you're breaking the law, both good laws and bad, don't you? Other landlords wouldn't be so pleased. They would try to evict the informer at the first opportunity. That's why local eviction control laws prohibit evictions in retaliation against tenants who exercise their rent control rights.

The third reason why rent control crusaders decided to meddle with evictions was to "discipline" those landlords who refuse to register their rental property.

In most rent control areas, the rent control board raises revenue to pay for offices, paper shufflers, paper, and paper clips by charging landlords annual registration fees. Landlords who refuse to register are denying the board the revenue it needs to survive. That makes the board most unhappy, but there's not much it can do to collect because it doesn't have enough staff to force every landlord in town to pay his dues. So it requires that every landlord be registered in order to use the court system for an eviction. Evictions through the system have thus become the means for the board to exact its tribute, to demand its pounds of flesh. You must comply with the rent control ordinances in order to avail yourself of a court's authority to evict your tenant, and you must state in your complaint, even when the eviction is for a simple nonpayment of rent matter, that you have complied with all the applicable requirements of the ordinances. Presumably, if you are required to register your rental dwelling with the rent control board, and you neglect or refuse to do so, you would not be able to evict your tenants through the courts no matter what. You'd have to try some other way to get them out. What they're saying in effect is this, "Either you play our game or we won't allow you to play yours."

The fourth reason why rent control crusaders decided to meddle with evictions was to eliminate what they perceived to be "one of the great disasters of California law." What's that? You've never heard of a greater law disaster in California than rent control? You're right, of course. But rent controls are not a disaster from the crusaders' point of view. They're your disaster, not theirs. As far as they are concerned, rent-gouging landlords need controlling, so rent controls are fair and just.

The so-called "disaster" they're concerned

about is the state law which permits landlords to terminate a tenancy for no reason at all by giving a tenant a 30-Day Notice to Terminate. Rent control crusaders do not like this law one bit. They're certain that landlords abuse it.

Now, as any landlord knows, nobody is going to evict a tenant for no reason at all, just as no tenant is going to vacate voluntarily for no reason at all. There's always some reason, stated or not. Getting good tenants is too expensive a proposition for a landlord to evict a tenant for no reason, and moving is too expensive and traumatic for tenants to vacate for no reason.

Rent control crusaders don't know the economics or the agonies of the landlording business, so they don't know why it's utterly foolish for any landlord to evict a tenant unless there really is a good reason. They also don't seem to know why it's wise for a landlord to evict an uncooperative tenant without giving a reason (see chapter 8). Yet, when they as tenants can't get along with a fellow tenant, they want their landlord to "do something right away." Try getting rid of a tenant who's creating friction among other tenants or who's letting his dog loose to wander the neighborhood when you have to show a "just cause" for doing so. It's difficult, if not impossible. Judges won't let you evict a tenant from his home merely because he's being nasty to his neighbors or his landlord or because his dog is indiscriminate about elimination, not when there's a just-cause restriction on the books.

Believe it or not, there are some unscrupulous tenants in our world who make life miserable for all of us, scrupulous tenants and landlords alike, and those tenants are mighty hard to get rid of without 30-day notices. Rent control crusaders don't believe that. They believe that landlords would throw good tenants out on the streets if there were no just-cause eviction controls. It happens all the time in that three-quarters of California without eviction controls, doesn't it? You have to wonder how they would react if landlords tried to pass a law requiring that tenants must have a just cause to vacate. Then they would howl about a law disaster!

So much for why rent controls and eviction controls appear together. You might be wondering whether there are any local areas which have adopted eviction controls alone? No, there aren't. Crusaders can't get the people in a community quite so stirred up about controlling evictions as they can about controlling rents. Controlling rents appeals to people's greed; controlling evictions appeals to their principles. You know which one motivates them more. Once the rent control crusaders have organized and forced local authorities to adopt rent control measures, they say sweetly, "By the way, we can't just have rent controls unless we have eviction controls as well." You already know their reasons. After the struggle for rent control is won, there's no struggle for eviction controls. It's no contest, no contest at all. And so the landlord bashing goes on.

Local Eviction Controls

You should know that although courts have ruled that rent and eviction controls imposed by local ordinance are a legitimate use of "police power" (does that sound Orwellian or doesn't it?), local ordinances cannot ban evictions altogether, nor can they interfere with the summary nature of the proceedings as spelled out in state law. You see, evictions are entitled to summary treatment; it's the fastest treatment allowed in any civil case. It may not seem fast to you sometimes, but it's faster than anything else available. Local ordinances may not require longer time periods for the various steps in an eviction than are required by state law. They cannot, for example, require you to serve a 10-day notice to pay rent or quit since state law allows a 3-day notice, nor can they extend the time period provided for answering an unlawful-detainer summons beyond the five days state law allows.

Local eviction controls can, however, impose additional conditions on the eviction process, conditions which serve to make evictions more difficult and more expensive to conduct. Every attorney who handles evictions in both rent control and non-rent control jurisdictions knows this and charges extra for handling evictions in rent control jurisdictions. He knows they will take more of his time. He has to do more research to get everything right because there are more laws and legal precedents to review. He also knows that each eviction will be scrutinized all the more by the opposition.

The additional conditions in local eviction controls go beyond state laws. Here are the most common ones.

As a general rule, you cannot evict anyone from a rent controlled dwelling unless you have registered your rental property with the rent control board. That's pretty much a given wherever registration is required. Refuse to register and you can bet that your tenant will beat your eviction action, no matter how merited. All he has to do is reveal to the court that you haven't registered, and you'll lose.

You cannot evict a tenant from a rent controlled dwelling unless you are charging a legal rent. Should you and your tenant have mutually agreed in happier times on a higher-than-legal rent, you will not be able to evict him now that he's stopped paying you his rent altogether, at least not without complications.

You cannot evict a tenant from a rent controlled dwelling unless you follow whatever special notice requirements there are. You may have to submit to the rent board within ten days of service a copy of your 3-Day Notice to Pay Rent or Quit or any other notice you serve. You may have to state on the notice that there are tenant counseling services available from the rent control board at a certain address. Fail to do so, and you invalidate the notice.

Then there are the "just cause" requirements. You cannot evict a tenant from a rent controlled dwelling unless you have a just cause. They affect evictions more than anything else in rent control areas.

Just causes fall into two categories—those which are tenant-initiated and those which are landlord-initiated. Always the question is the same, "Is this matter substantial enough as a reason for the court to order an eviction?"

Here are the usual tenant-initiated just causes: failure to pay rent (state law applies in all areas), breaking the rental agreement, using the premises for unlawful acts, refusing to allow the landlord access, refusing to execute a new lease, creating a nuisance, and subletting.

Here are the usual landlord-initiated just causes: rehabilitating the unit, demolishing or converting the unit, going out of business, and moving himself or a relative into the unit.

Naturally, there are varying conditions and restrictions on these just causes, lots of them. San Francisco's ordinance, for example, specifically permits evictions when the tenant "habitually pays the rent late" or "gives checks which are frequently returned because there are insufficient funds in the checking account." Berkeley's ordinance, on the other hand, would not consider those as "just causes" for eviction. Tenants have

MAJOR RENT CONTROL BOARDS

BERKELEY
Berkeley Rent Stabilization Program
2125 Milvia St.
Berkeley, CA 94704
(510) 644-6128
http://www.ci.berkeley.ca.us/

LOS ANGELES
Rent Adjustment Commission
400 S. Main St.
Los Angeles, CA 90014
(213) 847-8360

OAKLAND
Residential Rent Arbitration Board
300 Lakeside Dr., 15th Fl.
Oakland, CA 94612
(510) 238-3721

SAN FRANCISCO
Residential Rent Stabilization & Arbitration Board
25 Van Ness Ave., Rm. 320
San Francisco, CA 94102-6033
(415) 554-9550

SAN JOSE
Rental Dispute Program
4 N. 2d St., Suite 600
San Jose, CA 95113
(408) 277-5431

SANTA MONICA
Santa Monica Rent Control Board
1685 Main St., Rm. 202
Santa Monica, CA 90401
(310) 458-8751
http://www.ci.santa-monica.ca.us/

WEST HOLLYWOOD
Rent Stabilization Dept.
8704 Santa Monica Blvd., 2d Fl.
West Hollywood, CA 90069
(213) 854-7450

If you have trouble locating your rent control board's Web site through a browser search, try http://tenant.net and you may find a link to the site you're looking for.

to be more than check kiters to get evicted in Berkeley.

The just-cause requirement for evictions sounds good. It sounds as if it's righting a wrong, but it doesn't work that way in real life. It's a nuisance, as are all eviction controls imposed on a local level.

What to Do, What to Do?

Local eviction controls make your job as a scrupulous landlord all the more burdensome, all the more exacting, all the more trying, all the more impossible. Of that there's no doubt. Landlording under local eviction controls is like playing tackle football without pads or helmet against a team suited up for gridiron combat. You get hurt a lot in such a contest. The other team doesn't feel a thing. You feel badly beaten sometimes when you try so hard to play fair and do the right thing and an unscrupulous tenant without hardly trying makes you suffer by taking advantage of the laws and legal interpretations so favorable to tenants today.

Short of throwing up your hands, mortgaging your property to the hilt, and surrendering it entirely to the rent control board or to your tenants (may not be such a bad idea; it would be a "just" reward, don't you think?), you are stuck with few alternatives when you want to evict a tenant. Until things change, heed these suggestions.

• GO TO THE SOURCE AND GET THE LATEST AUTHORITY—For specific information about local rent and eviction control ordinances, secure a copy of the full text of the latest ordinances from the same source your tenants use, the rent control board's office. Go there and ask for a copy, or look for the rent control board's Web site, and you'll likely find a copy of the ordinances there.

Do not expect the ordinances to speak for themselves. They won't, at least not at first. They're written in legalese. The rent control board knows that tenants don't understand legalese any more than you do, so they'll have a fifth-grade-vocabulary version available, too. Ask for one. At the same time, ask whether any recent ordinance has changed the information in either publication.

Remember, only the ordinances are the authority. A judge won't refer to the simplified version when he's deciding your case. Use the sim-

plified version to help you understand the ordinances, and refer to the ordinances themselves for clarification of fine points.

• FIND OUT WHETHER YOUR RENTAL PROPERTY FALLS UNDER EVICTION CONTROLS AT ALL—Read through the rent and eviction control ordinances carefully to learn whether they apply to your kind of rental dwelling. Whereas the rent control ordinances may exempt houses, condos, smaller owner-occupied buildings, new construction, and higher-priced units, the eviction controls may not exempt any kind of rental housing at all. You may be surprised to learn that although local rent controls do not apply to your little duplex because you occupy half of it yourself, local eviction controls do apply to it when you're trying to evict that tenant from the other half. Find out what the law says.

If you don't want to read through the ordinances or can't understand them, ask someone at the rent control board whether your kind of rental property must comply with local eviction controls. Or if you'd rather not push the rent control board's buttons, call your rental property owners association. Someone there will know.

• BECOME FAMILIAR WITH THE REQUIREMENTS—Learn the specific requirements you must meet in order to pursue the particular type of eviction you intend to conduct.

You already know that local eviction controls may impose special requirements about notices, legal rent, your registration status, and just causes.

Get the details. Find out what are the special requirements for conducting an eviction in your rent controlled area.

• COMPLY, COMPLY, COMPLY—You might as well save the money and time required to seek a legal eviction in any eviction-control area unless you intend to comply with the ordinances. Distasteful and difficult as it may be, you have to be prepared to jump through the rent control board's hoops, or you simply will not get the tenant evicted. It's their show. You're just a bit player to them, a bit player who must play his part perfectly or else. The court doesn't care whether you have a legitimate reason to evict a tenant for something so easy to prove as nonpayment of rent. You must comply with the local ordinances, or you will lose your case. Count on it.

What choice do you have?

- Expect rent control areas to have some kind of eviction controls.
- Familiarize yourself with the very latest rent and eviction control ordinances in your area.
- Comply with the ordinances or despair of ever evicting anyone legally.

5
Handling an Eviction for Nonpayment of Rent

You have tried everything possible short of going to court to get your deadbeat tenants either to pay you their delinquent rent or to leave the place, but they are as unyielding as they can be. Nothing moves them. You have despaired of ever getting them to pay you another cent, and quite frankly you have had enough of their excuses, their promises, their rubber checks, and their shenanigans. You want to get them out as soon as possible before you lose much more rent than what you have lost already.

Your best alternative now is to use the full strength of the laws written to protect you from deadbeats. Get the full force of the law behind you, and get them out.

To save yourself both time and money, you have decided to handle the eviction yourself, and you are now ready to proceed. Here are the steps you should follow, from preparing the proper notice to having them removed bodily, if necessary.

Step 1. Prepare a 3-Day Notice to Pay Rent or Quit.

If you have accepted any rent monies since you last served a notice or if you haven't already served a notice, you should now prepare a 3-Day Notice to Pay Rent or Quit. If you have already served a notice and it is still valid, proceed to Step 3.

Every unlawful detainer for nonpayment of rent must begin with a written notice served properly on the tenant. Because you hope that the very appearance of your notice will stimulate your tenant to react the way you want him to, use a form which is noticeable. The ones I use have large-letter headings which cannot be ignored. Anybody who sees one of them can tell at a glance from a distance of twenty paces what it is. They're eye-catching. They demand attention.

The notice itself ought to contain the following:
1) The name(s) of the tenant(s);
2) The address of the dwelling in question;
3) The amount of rent due;
4) The period for which this rent is due;
5) The date of the notice; and
6) Your signature.

Be careful that all of this information is complete and correct, and make it thoroughly consistent throughout your paperwork. Any deviation could give your tenant grounds for responding to your complaint on just this one technicality alone, and after you glance at chapter 10, you will understand a little better why you should avoid giving the tenants the slightest opportunity to respond.

• NAMES ON THE NOTICE—It's a sad reality of landlording these days that unless you specifically give notice to all the adults who claim to be living in a rental dwelling, regardless of whether they're mentioned in the rental agreement or are responsible for paying the rent, you may encounter difficulties in evicting anybody at all. So, make a special effort to discover whether any adults besides the original tenants are currently living in your rental, and mention them all by first and last names on the notice. Don't use "Mr. & Mrs. Richard Renter"; use "Richard Renter and Rose Renter" instead. And even though the cosigner, if there is one, is bound to be living elsewhere, include his name, too. He should know what's happening.

Don't bother to include on the notice the names of children who are eighteen years old or thereabouts unless they work and help pay the rent. Including the older children who don't work generally upsets the parents and needlessly complicates service of court papers later. Should their absence on the notice become an issue, you can always add their names if you have to. You are

3-DAY NOTICE TO PAY RENT OR QUIT

TO: <u>Richard Renter</u>

     <u>Rose Renter</u>

and all other tenants in possession of the premises described as:

<u>456 Sweet Street</u>
(Street Address)

<u>Littletown</u>   <u>California</u> <u>91111</u>
(City)   (State)   (Zip)

PLEASE TAKE NOTICE that the rent is now due and payable on the above-described premises which you currently hold and occupy.

Your rental account is delinquent in the amount itemized as follows:
Rental period <u>9/1/XX</u> through <u>9/30/XX</u>   RENT DUE $<u>780.00</u>

                                 less partial payment of $<u>50.00</u>

                          equals TOTAL RENT DUE of $<u>730.00</u>

YOU ARE HEREBY REQUIRED to pay said rent in full within three (3) days or to remove from and deliver up possession of the above-described premises, or legal proceedings will be instituted against you to recover possession of said premises, to declare the forfeiture of the Lease or Rental Agreement under which you occupy said premises and to recover rents and damages, together with court costs and attorney's fees, according to the terms of your Lease or Rental Agreement.

Dated: <u>September 12, XXXX</u>   *Lester Landlord*
                                         Owner/Manager

PROOF OF SERVICE

I, the undersigned, being at least 18 years of age, declare under penalty of perjury that I served the above notice, of which this is a true copy, on the following tenant(s) in possession in the manner(s) indicated below: <u>RICHARD RENTER</u>

[X] On <u>9/12/XX</u>, I handed the notice to the tenant(s) personally.

[ ] On _____, after attempting personal service, I handed the notice to a person of suitable age and discretion at the residence/business of the tenant(s), AND I deposited a true copy in the U.S. Mail, in a sealed envelope with postage fully prepaid, addressed to the tenant(s) at his/her/their place of residence (date mailed, if different _____).

[ ] On _____, after attempting service in both manners indicated above, I posted the notice in a conspicuous place at the residence of the tenant(s), AND I deposited a true copy in the U.S. Mail, in a sealed envelope with postage fully prepaid, addressed to the tenant(s) at his/her/their place of residence (date mailed, if different _____).

Executed on <u>9/12/XX</u>, at <u>LITTLETOWN</u>, California.

               Served by <u>*Lester Landlord*</u>

                                                            efc

You will find a blank copy of this form in the FORMS section of this book and in Eviction Forms Creator.

making provisions for such problems by having the notice read "and all other tenants in possession of the premises."

A single notice may have everyone's name on it.

• AMOUNT TO ASK FOR—In listing the amount of rent due, be sure you include only rent. You may not demand late charges or bad check charges or cleaning fees (if you use the discounted rent method described in *Landlording*, you may get away with asking for the entire non-discounted or gross rent, but don't count on it; to be safe, use the net rent when you calculate rent due). To recover whatever late charges or bad check charges or cleaning fees are owed to you, you may include them in the complaint filed later. Just don't include them here on the notice.

Rent is all you may ask for on the notice, and the rent stated there must be *delinquent* for the current rental period. For example, if you serve the notice on the seventh of June because the tenant hasn't paid any rent for May or June, and the rent is due on the first of the month, include June's rent, too, because his rent is also delinquent for June. Remember, though, that it must be delinquent, not merely due, to be included. If you serve the notice on the 29th or 30th of May, obviously it should include only May's rent and not June's because the tenant is not yet delinquent for the June rental period. But what do you do if you plan to serve the notice on the first of June and he hasn't paid for either May or June? Is June's rent delinquent on the first of June and should it be included in the notice? No, it isn't delinquent yet, and it should not be included in the notice. Don't hesitate to serve the notice on the first of June if he hasn't yet paid May's rent; just don't include June's rent on the notice.

Actually his rent may or may not even be delinquent on the second or third of the month either. Whether his rent is delinquent around the beginning of a rental period depends upon the availability of a banking day on which to pay and upon the grace period, if any, allowed by the rental agreement. If, for instance, his rent is due on the first, and the first falls on a Saturday, then legally he wouldn't have to pay his rent until Monday, which would be the first banking day after the due date, and if Monday were a holiday, then the first day he'd have to pay would be Tuesday. Unless otherwise stated in the rental agreement, you shouldn't count his rent delinquent until the day

after the first banking day following the rental due date, and if the rental agreement specifically allows, say, a four-day grace period, then the rent is delinquent the day after that grace period. Serving a 3-Day Notice to Pay Rent or Quit which includes any rent not yet delinquent could be regarded as premature and might precipitate a legal challenge.

Treat the second month involved in the same way you would treat the first month. Go ahead and serve the tenant with a notice whenever his rent is delinquent, but if you have already procrastinated a whole month, don't include the second month's rent on the notice unless it, too, is delinquent.

Whenever you're unsure exactly how much the tenant owes, estimate the amount with a figure which is certain to be below the actual amount. If you indicate on your three-day notice that the tenant owes you more than he actually does, you may lose your whole case on this one technicality alone and have to begin again from the beginning, all of which may affect you deleteriously by forcing you to drink too much, smoke too much, eat too much, worry too much, or become promiscuous. Don't let yourself go to ruin just because you lost an unlawful detainer on a technicality. Do the thing right the first time.

• "CORRECTING" THE NOTICE—After you have served your tenant a notice showing what you believe is the correct amount of rent owed and you discover that he owes you *more* because you just learned that his last check bounced or you somehow neglected to calculate properly, do not bother serving him another notice. You'll have the opportunity to prove he owed you more once you get into court. Ah, but should you discover that he owes you *less* than what you indicated as of the date on the notice, you will have to prepare a new notice with the correct figures and serve it. You cannot amend a notice once it has been served. An incorrect notice will cause you to lose your case if the tenant catches the error and answers you in court. It may even cause you to lose your case if the tenant doesn't answer you in court, but the judge happens to spot the error during the prove-up trial.

The notice doesn't mean much until you file your papers with the court. Then it must be absolutely correct, for it cannot be changed. Your case lives or dies on the correctness of that notice. Until filing, you can "correct" it all you want by serving new notices.

If you have to serve another notice, you will want to avoid any confusion regarding earlier incorrect notices. Indicate clearly on your "final" notice that this is the notice which counts, the "notice of notices." On the top of the notice, write or type something like this: "IGNORE PREVIOUS NOTICE. THIS IS THE CONTROLLING NOTICE." If you had served more than one incorrect notice, put this on top: "IGNORE PREVIOUS NOTICES SERVED ON [date] AND [date]. THIS IS THE CONTROLLING NOTICE."

• RENTAL PERIOD MENTIONED IN THE NOTICE—Although no law absolutely requires that you mention in the notice the rental period for which the rent is due, I recommend that you do mention it. Almost all preprinted notices to pay rent or quit, including the one given here and the one drafted by the California Apartment Association, contain space for the rental period. Judges, therefore, are accustomed to seeing the rental period on notices, and rightly or wrongly, they might question the legality, the completeness, or the clarity of your notice if you choose to omit it. You don't need the extra hassle of being called upon to cite a code or a precedent to prove your notice's legitimacy in court.

Mentioning the rental period in the notice also helps to clarify for your tenants just how you arrived at the total balance due.

If you use the 3-Day Notice to Pay Rent or Quit form which appears in this book, you should have no trouble indicating the period for which rent is owed and the amount of rent owed. That's in the notice's itemization section. Put down the rental period(s) for which there is any rent delinquent at all. Give the rent normally due for each of those periods. Add up those rents, subtract any partial payments which apply to the periods listed, and *voila*, there you have it, the TOTAL BALANCE DUE. You don't have to make any complex calculations.

If you are using a 3-Day Notice to Pay Rent or Quit form which calls only for the amount of rent due and the period for which it is due, you'll have no problem determining the period for which the rent is due or the amount, so long as the tenant owes rent for full months, but if the tenant owes you partial rent because you have accepted half a month's rent or some other sum less than usual, calculating the rental period for your notice can be confusing.

Do your calculating this way—divide the full month's rent by 30 (whether the month you're dealing with really has 28, 29, 30, or 31 days doesn't matter to the court; calculations based on a 30-day month are considered "fair"), and then divide that per-diem rental figure into the amount of partial rent already paid. Your answer will be in days paid, but it may include a fraction as well. The rental period for which rent is owed should start on the day after those days have been added to the previous full rental period for which rent was paid.

As an example, say that your tenant's rent is $585; the rental period is August 1 through 31; the amount paid by the tenant toward his August rent was $285; and you're serving the 3-Day Notice to Pay Rent or Quit on September 5th. We would divide $585 by 30 and get the rent per diem, $19.50; then we would divide the amount which the tenant paid toward his August rent, $285, by $19.50. Our answer would be 14.61. We would round this number off upwards to 15 and consider that 15 days' rent had been paid. The rental period which should be mentioned in the notice, then, would be August 16 through September 30, and the total amount of rent owed would be $885 (remember that we must now add September's rent because we are serving the notice after the delinquent date for September's rent.)

Whatever you do, be certain that the rent you are asking for covers *consecutive* periods and none of them over one year ago. Your case will be thrown out of court if you are asking for rent more than one year past due. As for consecutive periods, if your tenant failed to pay you any rent in January but did pay in February and again in March, you should give him a rent receipt for January when he pays in February and for February when he pays in March. Courts will not allow you to seek delinquent rents for periods with gaps in them, such as January and April. They assume that tenants who have a rent receipt to show for a recent period have paid rent for all prior months. If you somehow make the mistake of creating a gap in a tenant's receipts, forget about trying to collect for the gap. Go after rent for the most recent consecutive period only.

• THE ALTERNATIVE—Note that the 3-Day Notice to Pay Rent or Quit form shown here contains an either/or alternative. The alternative is this—either pay up or get out. If the tenant complies with the alternative, then the notice is of no further consequence. If you want the tenant to move even though he does comply with your notice and pays what he owes, serve him a 30-Day Notice to Terminate Tenancy, too.

Do not use the combination of these two notices indiscriminately. Any notice terminating a tenancy in thirty days has certain restrictions. You cannot use such a notice in certain California jurisdictions which have their own eviction controls except under special circumstances (see chapter 4), and you cannot, of course, use a 30-day notice if your tenant has an unexpired lease.

If a tenant moves out before the three days are up and still owes you rent money, don't go to municipal or superior court. It's a waste of money under the circumstances. Either proceed in small claims to get a money judgment and then set out to collect your judgment using the suggestions in chapter 13, or if you think there's little chance you might collect anything from him at all, be grateful the deadbeat's no longer your headache and chalk the whole affair up to experience, part of your schooling at Landlording's Hard Knocks School.

• THE DECLARATION—At the bottom of each notice is a declaration to prove to the court that the notice was, in fact, served on a qualifying date, in a prescribed manner, and by an eligible server. Some people use a separate sheet of paper for their declarations, but there's nothing wrong with saving paper and including it right on the notice itself. You do not have to fill out the declaration on the notice which is handed to the tenant but only on the copies which you keep for your own and for the court's use.

• COPIES—The first page of the FORMS section in the back of this book has suggestions you might want to follow in determining how many copies you need to make of the various forms.

Step 2. Serve the 3-Day Notice to Pay Rent or Quit.

• WHO MAY SERVE—You, your manager, a process server, or anyone else at least 18 years old may legally serve the notice. In some areas, you may even use the sheriff or marshal to serve the notice for you (see discussion in chapter 2 about using a uniformed officer or security patrolman to intimidate), but you don't have to. If you believe that your tenant is enough of a scoundrel to perjure himself and claim in court that your unlawful detainer against him should be thrown out because he never received a notice, you should consider any of the following so you'll be able to prove otherwise: serve a copy in person yourself and mail one, too, using the certificate-of-mailing method described shortly; serve it along with a payment pledge as outlined in chapter 1 and get the tenant himself to acknowledge service; serve it yourself in the presence of a witness; hire a professional to serve it; or get a friend or another tenant to do it. If your tenant swears that he did not receive notice and you swear that he did, the burden of proof rests upon you to show that he did. If you can't prove that he received it beyond your swearing that he did, you will lose in a standoff. Oddly enough, if you do elect to pay a professional to serve the notice, you may not count this as one of your reimbursable costs. Courts apparently consider this more a matter of convenience than of necessity.

• WHO SHOULD BE SERVED—You don't have to bother serving everyone named in the notice individually, for service of the notice on one of your tenants is considered to be service on all of them [*USC v. Weiss* (1962) 208 CA3d 759, 769, 25 CR 475]. Even so, some experts recommend that you make the effort to serve each tenant individually just to be on the safe side. I don't myself because I believe that serving notices should be a part of the rent collection process (see chapter 1), and I serve lots of them. If I had to serve each adult tenant individually every time I served a notice, I'd be wasting a lot of time trying to find everybody. Consequently, I serve one notice to a household, and I have yet to encounter a problem in an unlawful detainer which resulted from my serving tenants in this way.

If you feel convinced that your notice is going to be the first step in evicting certain tenants through the courts and that you are going to have to fight them every step of the way, consider serving them individually; otherwise, I don't think it's worth the trouble.

By all means, do prepare and serve a second copy of your notice if you are aware that the premises have been sublet, with or without your approval, for both the primary tenant and the subtenant should be notified of the nonpayment of rent and should have an opportunity to pay up.

See that any cosigner involved gets his own separate copy, too. Although you don't have to serve the cosigner in order to evict whoever's living on the premises, you should certainly make him aware of what's happening. Once he knows, he may pay you what the tenant owes or he may put pressure on the tenant in ways you cannot. After all, what's a cosigner for?

• THE SERVICE—To serve a 3-Day Notice to Pay Rent or Quit properly, you must serve it

that someone sixteen years old is "at an age of suitable discretion." Someone younger may or may not qualify. You'd be risking a challenge by serving the notice to a 13-year-old, a challenge which you might win, and then again you might not.

3) Do what attorneys call "nail and mail," that is, post the notice by the main entrance where it is unavoidable, *and* send a copy by first-class mail. Don't bother with registered or certified mail; just obtain proof that you mailed it.

You must try the first method first, personal

(keep the original to show the court or attach to the original complaint; serve a copy) in one of these three ways:

1) Hand it to the tenant personally;

2) Hand it to someone else on the property or at the tenant's place of business who is at an age of suitable discretion; make note somewhere of the person's name and/or of his description because you'll need this information later when you fill out the complaint; and also send a copy by first-class mail (to prove that you mailed it, take the stamped envelope to the post office; ask for a "Certificate of Mailing," USPS Form 3817; complete the form and hand it, the envelope, and 55¢ to the clerk; wait for the clerk to stamp the form and return it to you). Courts have held

service, and you probably ought to attempt to find the tenant both at his residence and at the place where he works. According to a recent appellate court decision [*Hozz v. Lewis* 215 CA3d 314, 263 CR 577], though, you do not have to try repeatedly to serve the tenant at home and at work. Once is enough. Having tried to serve the tenant in person, you may then resort straightaway to either of the other two methods, both of which are called "constructive-service" or "substituted-service" methods.

By the way, if the tenant refuses the notice when you hand it to him, that's his problem; you need only let him know he's being served and put the notice where he can get it. You may drop it at his feet, or if you're talking to him through a closed door, you may tell him that you're leaving it under the mat. You aren't expected to do the impossible. After all, it's for his benefit that you are serving him in the first place. You are taking the trouble to inform him that you are going to initiate some legal action which will affect him directly in some way or another.

If you can't find the tenant anywhere and you have good reason to suspect that he may actually have abandoned the premises, you may want to consider following the abandonment procedure as outlined in chapter 14. It has some very definite advantages over an unlawful detainer for nonpayment of rent, especially if you've already delayed serving a 3-Day Notice to Pay Rent or Quit for a couple of weeks. If fourteen or more days have passed since the rent became delinquent and you have seen neither skin nor hair of the tenant during that time, all you have to do then is send him a Notice of Belief of Abandonment and wait eighteen days for a response. If you get no response, you take possession. It's that simple.

Although you may use the abandonment procedure in conjunction with an eviction for nonpayment of rent and take advantage of whichever is successful sooner, you should not even think of using it as an underhanded legal maneuver just to profit from its advantages. That could get you into terrible trouble. Use it only as it was intended to be used, only if you honestly believe that the tenant has given up possession without notifying you. Don't use it if you think the tenant is merely trying to avoid being served. Use constructive service in that case.

• TIME TO SERVE—You may serve a 3-Day Notice to Pay Rent or Quit on the first day a tenant's rent becomes delinquent and not before. As mentioned already, a tenant's rent becomes delinquent the day after it is due unless the due date falls on a day when the banks are closed (Saturday, Sunday, or holiday), in which case it is delinquent the day after the first banking day following the due date, or it is delinquent the day after whatever grace period was specified in the rental agreement. Serving the notice before the rent is delinquent will cause your case to be thrown out of court as premature and will require you to begin the entire procedure again from the beginning.

• LEASES, LAST MONTH'S RENT, AND TIME TO SERVE—Some landlords puzzle over when they ought to serve a 3-Day Notice to Pay Rent or Quit to a tenant who's on a lease or to a tenant who's paid the last month's rent in advance. Should they delay serving the notice until the last month's rent is used up? No, no, no! Treat anyone on a lease and anyone who's paid the last month's rent in exactly the same way as you'd treat someone who's on a month-to-month agreement and hasn't paid any last month's rent. Serve them all a 3-Day Notice to Pay Rent or Quit as soon as their *current* rent is delinquent. Do not allow any tenant to apply his "last month's rent" to any month other than the "last month."

What happens to a tenant's last month's rent when he's evicted? Like his deposits, it's applied to the judgment.

• BEST TIME TO SERVE—You are more likely to serve a 3-Day Notice to Pay Rent or Quit belatedly rather than prematurely. Try to do neither. Keep on top of your rent collections and serve a 3-day notice to every tenant on a regular schedule the day after his rent becomes delinquent.

If you have procrastinated longer than that for some strange reason, you will be all the more anxious to evict your tenants as swiftly as possible, and you will want to take advantage of every opportunity to save time. One way to speed the process is to serve the notice when you may take advantage of every intervening day, including weekends. To get a decided advantage, serve the notice anytime Sunday or Monday (see calendars at the end of this chapter). Because of the way weekends affect the various time limits in an eviction, they're the two best days for serving a 3-day notice.

Even though the persistent landlord or landlady can hope to pursue an eviction within the shortest possible time by serving the notice on a Sunday or Monday, don't you wait for a Sunday or Monday to come along before serving your notice. The best time to serve it is *now, right now, today.*

• COUNTING THE DAYS—Begin your three-day countdown on the day *after* you serve your notice to everyone who's supposed to be getting a notice. If you serve the primary tenant on Friday and the subtenant on Sunday, start your counting with Monday. Count Monday, Tuesday, and Wednesday as the three days you are giving them to pay up. The earliest you may then file the summons and complaint is Thursday. You may wait longer if you want to, believing that they will either vacate or pay, but legally you don't have to.

Be aware that the third day after service must be a "business day." It may not be a weekend day or a holiday. If the third day falls on a Sunday and there's a Monday holiday the following day, you must give the tenant until Tuesday to pay, and you must not file your summons and complaint until Wednesday. If the third day falls on a Friday, though, you may file on the following Monday.

If you couldn't serve a tenant personally and had to resort to either method two or method three, you should consider waiting an extra five days before filing your summons and complaint. Then you will be safe from attack over your failure to allow the tenant sufficient time to act when the notice was entrusted to the mails.

You should be aware that according to an appellate court decision in Los Angeles [*Highland Plastics, Inc. v. Enders* (1980) 109 CA3d Supp 1, 167 CR 353], you do not have to wait the extra days. A 3-day notice means three days and no more, regardless of which legal method of service was used, and the same holds true for 30-day notices. The court held that the extra 5-day wait provisions of CCP (Code of Civil Procedure) §1013(a) do not apply to eviction cases which require notices to be served under CCP §1162. However, a more recent decision [*Davidson v. Quinn* (1982) 138 CA3d Supp. 9, 188 CR 421] held that *some* extra time has to be added in curable situations to allow for mail delivery (pay-rent-or-quit situations are curable; notice-to-terminate situations are not), but it didn't specify how much. If you are brave, wait only three days following constructive service. Otherwise, wait the extra days. Better still, go through hot coals or high water to serve the notice in person so you needn't risk involving yourself in this legal controversy.

• BEWARE ESTOPPEL—Did you know that by law your rents are not due in advance unless you stipulate in your rental contract that they are? It's true! Did you know also that if you continually accept a tenant's rent late, say fifteen days after it's due, and you decide one month to give him a 3-Day Notice to Pay Rent or Quit five days after the rent is due, that your case may be thrown out of court because you gave the notice prematurely? Well, it's true! In this latter situation, your tenant could argue the "estoppel defense." He could say that because you have shown by your past conduct that you have agreed to accept the rent late, you may not, therefore, give a 3-Day Notice to Pay Rent or Quit before the 16th day after the due date, or whenever in the month the tenant could establish was the day after which you have accepted his rent in the past without regarding it late. You set a precedent by accepting rent late on a regular basis, a precedent which becomes a danger to you when you're involved in an unlawful detainer.

To preclude the estoppel defense from being used against you in an unlawful detainer, set a definite grace period before you pass out pay-rent-or-quit notices every month, and then consistently give notices to everyone who hasn't paid you the rent by that day. In those cases where you have been accepting rent later than that in the past, give the tenants each a 30-Day Notice to Change Terms of Tenancy outlining your new rent collection policy. In any case where you have been accepting a certain tenant's rent late in the past and "late" is becoming "later" month by month, until it has finally reached the point where you are now pretty apprehensive about collecting any rent at all, give the tenant a notice one month and a day following the date when you last accepted rent and then proceed without fear that estoppel will be used as a defense against you.

• PARTIAL PAYMENT—You don't have to accept partial payment. No law requires you to accept part of the rent owed whenever a tenant claims to be unable to pay it all at once. You get to decide for yourself whether you ought to accept the fistful of dollars your tenant is waving in your face when you're there on his doorstep ready to serve him with a 3-Day Notice to Pay Rent or Quit. At this time, before you have served the notice, you have nothing to lose by accepting the money, no matter how much or how little it is. It's "found" money, money you're probably never going to see if you refuse it now. Take it, and tell the tenant that you will have to adjust the notice to reflect the amount of his partial payment. Make the adjustment then and there, and give him the revised notice. It's still a *three*-day notice, mind you. It still gives the tenant only three days to come up with the balance of the money or else. So what have you lost by accepting the money? You haven't lost any time because you aren't extending the notice by even one day. You may if you want to, but you don't have to. You haven't lost any money because you haven't paid out any court costs or attorney's fees just yet, and you have pocketed whatever money the tenant has paid you. You have also left the tenant with the impression that you are a reasonable person. That's a triple win for you.

Should the tenant offer you partial rent a few days after you serve the notice, accept it only if it's enough to warrant having to serve another notice and waste the time which has already elapsed since you first served a notice. Immediately after you accept it, serve another notice covering the balance, for your accepting even one dollar invalidates the old notice (actually the law is vague about this matter, but courts have held that landlords accepting partial payments after serving a notice are "interrupting their own proceedings" and must serve a new notice following acceptance of any rent monies).

• BAD CHECK—If you give your tenant a 3-Day Notice to Pay Rent or Quit and he gives you a bad check as payment, you needn't serve him another notice before you can file the summons and complaint. The original notice still applies because he never paid you what he owes you. He gave you a worthless piece of paper and nothing more. Just in case the tenant made an inadvertent accounting error, you might want to contact him and tell him that his check was worthless and that if he wants to keep from being evicted, he'd better pay you in full with a money order *today*. You aren't obligated to contact him, of course, just as you aren't obligated to serve him with another notice, but you should try.

• PAYMENT IN FULL—If the tenant offers you payment in full, take it; he has complied with your notice, and you have nothing to gain by refusing it. In fact, the law requires you to take it. If you have already waited the entire three days, and the tenant offers you the money on the fourth or fifth day, you may refuse it if you want to. I wouldn't, though, because I much prefer getting paid over evicting, and I know that I can always evict the tenant sometime later. If, however, you have already filed your summons and complaint, if the tenant offers to pay you the rent *in full*, and if you're inclined to take it, advise him that he owes you for your out-of-pocket expenses, too, but that they are much less than the court costs and attorney's fees which he probably agreed to pay in his lease or rental agreement. Sometimes I

split the expenses with the tenant if I want the tenant to stay and I believe that his reasons for paying so late are legitimate and unlikely to recur.

Decision Time

If your property is located in an area served by the Riverside Consolidated/Coordinated Courts, the Downey, El Cajon, North Santa Barbara County, or San Bernardino County Municipal Courts, or the Central Division of the Los Angeles Municipal Court (Los Angeles Judicial District), you may avail yourself of a somewhat different procedure from the one detailed here. It's a pilot project (CCP §1167.2) designed to reduce unlawful detainer delays and abuses.

What's good about it: 1) If requested by the court at a pretrial hearing, the tenant must put up a rent deposit of no more than 15 days' rent or $500, whichever is less. 2) The intentions behind this pilot project are good, and it may lead to some useful reforms of the unlawful detainer procedure in the future.

What's bad about it: 1) It requires you as landlord to use different forms and more of them. 2) It enables tenants to get into court merely by returning a reply form which you supplied them with their summons and complaint instead of having to go to the courthouse, get an answer form, complete it, and pay a filing fee or file another form pleading poverty in order to get their day in court. 3) It extends the unlawful detainer time frame. Using this option, you cannot apply for a default judgment five days after the summons and complaint were served because the tenant gets the opportunity to reply in person or *by certified or registered mail*. In an ordinary unlawful detainer, the answer must be filed in person only, so you may apply for the default judgment on the sixth day. You don't need to wait for mail to arrive at the courthouse. 4) The tenant gets two opportunities to appear in court, and you have to go to court twice if the tenant contests the unlawful detainer, once for the pretrial hearing and again for the trial. 5) The rent deposit covers none of the back rent the tenant owes. It covers only the delay caused by the use of this procedure.

If, in spite of this pilot project procedure's drawbacks, you wish to use it rather than the ordinary procedure outlined here, which may be used anywhere in California, go to the courthouse

SUMMONS
(CITACION JUDICIAL)

UNLAWFUL DETAINER—EVICTION
(PROCESO DE DESAHUCIO—EVICCION)

NOTICE TO DEFENDANT: *(Aviso a acusado)*
Richard Renter
Rose Renter
AND DOES 1 TO 10 INCLUSIVE

FOR COURT USE ONLY
(SOLO PARA USO DE LA CORTE)

YOU ARE BEING SUED BY PLAINTIFF:
(A Ud. le está demandando)
Lester Landlord
Leslie Landlord

You have **5 DAYS** after this summons is served on you to file a typewritten response at this court. (To calculate the five days, count Saturday and Sunday, but do not count other court holidays.)

A letter or phone call will not protect you. Your typewritten response must be in proper legal form if you want the court to hear your case.

If you do not file your response on time, you may lose the case, you may be evicted, and your wages, money and property may be taken without further warning from the court.

There are other legal requirements. You may want to call an attorney right away. If you do not know an attorney, you may call an attorney referral service or a legal aid office *(listed in the phone book)*.

Después de que le entreguen esta citación judicial usted tiene un plazo de 5 DIAS para presentar una respuesta escrita a máquina en esta corte. (Para calcular los cinco días, cuente el sábado y el domingo, pero no cuente ningún otro día feriado observado por la corte).

Una carta o una llamada telefónica no le ofrecerá protección; su respuesta escrita a máquina tiene que cumplir con las formalidades legales apropiadas si usted quiere que la corte escuche su caso.

Si usted no presenta su respuesta a tiempo, puede perder el caso, le pueden obligar a desalojar su casa, y le pueden quitar su salario, su dinero y otras cosas de su propiedad sin aviso adicional por parte de la corte.

Existen otros requisitos legales. Puede que usted quiera llamar a un abogado inmediatamente. Si no conoce a un abogado, puede llamar a un servicio de referencia de abogados o a una oficina de ayuda legal (vea el directorio telefónico).

The name and address of the court is: *(El nombre y dirección de la corte es)*
Saddleback Municipal Court
100 State Street
Littletown, California 91111

CASE NUMBER: *(Número del caso)*

The name, address, and telephone number of plaintiff's attorney, or plaintiff without an attorney, is:
(El nombre, la dirección y el número de teléfono del abogado del demandante, o del demandante que no tiene abogado, es)
Lester Landlord & Leslie Landlord   415-123-4567
123 Neat Street
Littletown, California 91111

(Must be answered in all cases) An **unlawful detainer assistant** (B&P 6400-6415) [X] did **not** [ ] did for compensation give advice or assistance with this form. *(If plaintiff has received **any** help or advice for pay from an unlawful detainer assistant, state)*:

a. Assistant's name: b. Telephone No.:

c. Street address, city, and ZIP:

d. County of registration: e. Registration No.:   f. Expires on *(date)*:

DATE:
(Fecha)

Clerk, by _____, Deputy
(Actuario)   *(Delegado)*

[SEAL]

NOTICE TO THE PERSON SERVED: You are served

1. [ ] as an individual defendant.
2. [ ] as the person sued under the fictitious name of *(specify)*:
3. [ ] on behalf of *(specify)*:

   under: [ ] CCP 416.10 (corporation)   [ ] CCP 416.60 (minor)
          [ ] CCP 416.20 (defunct corporation)   [ ] CCP 416.70 (conservatee)
          [ ] CCP 416.40 (association or partnership) [ ] CCP 416.90 (individual)
          [ ] other:
4. [ ] by personal delivery on *(date)*:
       (See reverse for Proof of Service)

Form Adopted by Rule 982
Judicial Council of California
982(a)(11) [Rev. January 1, 1997]

SUMMONS—UNLAWFUL DETAINER

Code Civil Procedure, §§ 412.20, 1167

You will find a blank copy of this form in the FORMS section of this book and in Eviction Forms Creator.

and get the special Judicial Council forms there, or download the forms from the Judicial Council's Web site (see References). If you study how to complete the ordinary forms here, you won't have any trouble filling out the pilot project procedure's counterpart forms.

Step 3. Prepare the Summons, Complaint, and Cover Sheet.

After you have served your notice and, as far as you are concerned, the tenant has made an inadequate response or no response at all in the time allowed, you should get ready to file a Summons (Unlawful Detainer) and Complaint (Unlawful Detainer), along with a Civil Case Cover Sheet, all of which are state-mandated Judicial Council forms.

• THE SUMMONS—The summons is a notice to the tenant that he is being sued and that he must respond to the complaint accompanying the summons within five days or risk certain eviction. Summons blanks are available at your court clerk's office, or you may copy the blank one found in the forms section of this book or use the one in Eviction Forms Creator.

Like many other Judicial Council of California forms, the summons form has two sides to it. The backside is upside down so that when the clerk mounts it in a two-hole top-grip binder, browsers won't have to keep turning the binder around every time they flip a page. The print will always be right side up. Any copies you make of the forms in the back of this book should preserve this page orientation, and they should also be two-sided if the originals are two-sided. Some courts will refuse to accept copies of a two-sided form made on two separate sheets of paper. In a pinch, you might get away with pasting two sheets of paper together so they resemble a double-sided copy. Whenever possible, though, copy a two-sided form on a single sheet of paper with the back side upside down.

If this is your first case as a lay attorney, at this point you should call the clerk of the court which has jurisdiction over the area where your property is located. You will find the telephone number under "Government Offices" in the Yellow Pages. (Connected to the Internet? Look for the court's Web site by going first to "http://www.courtinfo.ca.gov/otherwebsites/" and looking for a link to your court's Web site.) Tell the clerk that you are planning to file an unlawful detainer and that you need to know whether your particular rental property is within this court's judicial district. You also need to know what the filing fee is, whether the court will accept a personal check for the filing fee, what the names of the court and judicial district are, and where exactly the courthouse is located.

With this information, you should now be able to fill out the summons. Just below the words, "NOTICE TO DEFENDANT," put the names of all known adult tenants you want to evict. By the way, when you are filling out official court papers, you generally capitalize every letter in names and words of special importance. You don't have to follow this convention, however, if you prefer to follow standard capitalization usage. Either one is perfectly acceptable. By all means, do make sure that everything's legible. That's much more important than capitalization concerns.

In addition to naming the known tenants, put down a reference to all the *unknown* adult tenants you want to evict. Unknown tenants are known as "Does" in the legal world. They're fictitious people who may turn out to be real people later. Maybe they've been living on the premises all along or maybe they'll move in while your unlawful detainer is wending its way through legal channels. If a mother-in-law, her boyfriend, and his teenage son have all moved in with your tenant and his wife, and you don't know any of their names, you'll have to use "Does" for them here. This is a common legal maneuver to keep people who might be defendants in a lawsuit from being excluded. Mentioning "Does" will allow you to amend your complaint later if you make a "discovery" of people and names. Putting, say, "AND DOES 1-10 INCLUSIVE" on the summons can't hurt your case; it can only help. To learn what to do in case you do make a discovery, see Appendix A under the "Does" section.

Below the words, "YOU ARE BEING SUED BY PLAINTIFF," put your name and the name of anyone else who owns the property. You don't have to include the names of all the owners, just those who might be of some help in handling the case. When there are several people listed as plaintiffs, any one of them may handle the paperwork or appear in court. They don't all have to appear.

In the next space provided, put the name and

ATTORNEY OR PARTY WITHOUT ATTORNEY (Name and Address):	TELEPHONE NO.:	*FOR COURT USE ONLY*
Lester Landlord & Leslie Landlord 123 Neat Street Littletown, California 91111	415-123-4567	

ATTORNEY FOR (Name): Plaintiff in Propria Persona

NAME OF COURT: Saddleback Municipal Court
STREET ADDRESS: 100 State Street
MAILING ADDRESS:
CITY AND ZIP CODE: Littletown, California 91111
BRANCH NAME:

PLAINTIFF: Lester Landlord
       Leslie Landlord
DEFENDANT: Richard Renter, Rose Renter

[X] DOES 1 TO __10__ INCLUSIVE   DEMAND AMOUNT $730

CASE NUMBER:

COMPLAINT—Unlawful Detainer*

1. a. Plaintiff is (1) [X] an individual over the age of 18 years (4) [ ] a partnership
    (2) [ ] a public agency (5) [ ] a corporation
    (3) [ ] other (specify):
  b. [ ] Plaintiff has complied with the fictitious business name laws and is doing business under the fictitious name of
    (specify):

2. Defendants named above are in possession of the premises located at (street address, apt. No., city and county):
  458 Sweet Street, Littletown, Saddleback County

3. Plaintiff's interest in the premises is [X] as owner [ ] other (specify):
4. The true names and capacities of defendants sued as Does are unknown to plaintiff.
5. a. On or about (date): 12/14/XX defendants (names): Richard Renter
  Rose Renter
    (1) agreed to rent the premises for a [X] month-to-month tenancy [ ] other tenancy (specify):
    (2) agreed to pay rent of $ 700.00 payable [X] monthly [ ] other (specify frequency):
    The rent is due on the [X] first of the month [ ] other day (specify):
  b. This [X] written [ ] oral agreement was made with
    (1) [X] plaintiff (3) [ ] plaintiff's predecessor in interest
    (2) [ ] plaintiff's agent (4) [ ] other (specify):
  c. [ ] The defendants not named in item 5a are
    (1) [ ] subtenants (2) [ ] assignees (3) [ ] other (specify):
  d. [X] The agreement was later changed as follows (specify):
    Rent raised to $780 as of 7/1/XX
  e. [ ] A copy of the written agreement is attached and labeled Exhibit 1.

6. [X] a. Defendants (names): Richard Renter
    were served the following notice on the same date and in the same manner:
    (1) [X] 3-day notice to pay rent or quit (4) [ ] 3-day notice to quit.
    (2) [ ] 3-day notice to perform covenants or quit (5) [ ] 30-day notice to quit
    (3) [ ] other (specify):
  b. (1) On (date): 9/15/XX , the period stated in the notice expired at the end of the day.
    (2) Defendants failed to comply with the requirements of the notice by that date.
  c. All facts stated in the notice are true.
  d. [X] The notice included an election of forfeiture.
  e. [ ] A copy of the notice is attached and labeled Exhibit 2.
  f. [ ] One or more defendants was served (1) with a different notice, or (2) on a different date, or (3) in a different manner,
    as stated in attachment 6f. (Check item 7c and attach a statement providing the information required by items 6a-e
    and 7 for each defendant.)
*NOTE: Do not use this form for evictions after sale (Code Civ. Proc., § 1161a).
         (Continued on reverse)

Form Approved by the Judicial Council of California 982.1(90) [Rev. July 1, 1996]	**COMPLAINT—Unlawful Detainer**	Civil Code, § 1940 et seq.; Code of Civil Procedure § 425.12

You will find a blank copy of this form in the FORMS section of this book and in Eviction Forms Creator.

address of the court you are using, so the tenant will know which court he is being summoned to.

Put your name, address, and telephone number in the space for that purpose, and check one of the boxes to indicate whether you did or did not receive any assistance from an unlawful detainer assistant.

If you did receive assistance, provide information about the assistant where indicated.

Don't supply the date; leave that for the clerk. Do check the appropriate box under "NOTICE TO THE PERSON SERVED." In most circumstances, this would be box 1. Do not check box 4. Leave that for the process server and leave the back side for him to fill out as well to show proof of service.

Make an original and one copy of your prepared summons, and make one additional copy for each additional defendant whom you want to have served.

• THE COMPLAINT—The complaint which you must prepare for filing along with the summons form should do the following—review your arrangement with the tenant; declare that you have performed all the conditions according to your arrangement; state your case against him; indicate that you have complied with the laws about giving the tenant proper notice; ask the court to return the premises to you; and ask for a money judgment to cover the amount owed, your costs, and any damages.

To do all that in times past, you would have had to draft at least a three-page document following a certain legal format and using just enough legal jargon to sound impressive, or you might have used the three-page form which appeared in the first edition of this book (see the one in chapter 9 especially drafted for holdover owners). But in 1982 the Judicial Council of California came up with a straightforward two-page form which you may use to do the very same thing today. You don't have to use it if you don't want to. It isn't mandatory. It is a time-saver, though, and it will help you remember to include the essentials.

Ah, but don't be misled by the form's brevity. Because it has been condensed considerably, you will have to be all the more careful in filling it out. While getting used to your new trifocals, you might easily check a wrong box and find to your chagrin that your case was thrown out of court by a sharp-eyed judge. You will have to be hawk-eyed yourself to use this form correctly and stay out of trouble. Get accustomed to your trifocals while reading Ann Landers, not here. Use your most reliable reading glasses here.

I would suggest that when you have completed the form, you read it aloud to yourself or have someone else read it to you, reading only the portions you have checked. Think carefully about whether those statements reflect your own case accurately, and if they don't, change them so they do.

Here's an explanation of the entire form, line by line and box by box, and here's also a sample complaint form filled out as it should be if you were Lester and Leslie Landlord evicting Richard and Rose Renter for nonpayment of rent.

Complete the top portion of the complaint with the information called for. You'll notice that it has all the same elements as the summons except that they're in a different order. Immediately below your own particulars in the section "ATTORNEY OR PARTY WITHOUT ATTORNEY (Name and Address)," indicate that you are handling the case as "Plaintiff in Pro Per." "Plaintiff" is the legal term for the person who's doing the suing; "in pro per" is an abbreviation of the Latin expression, "in propria persona," all of which means simply that you are acting as your own attorney. Make certain that the names and the addresses are exactly the same on every document you prepare, right down to the middle initials if any. Again, do not use "Mr. & Mrs." Use first and last names. Do not use "Richard and Rose Renter" either. Use each tenant's full name like this: "Richard Renter" and "Rose Renter."

Beside "DOES 1 TO ___, " put the word "INCLUSIVE," and to the right of that put "DEMAND AMOUNT $XX." This demand amount should be the same figure you put in 16c of the complaint. It's the past-due rent.

1. Select the box after 1a which best describes who you as plaintiff are. If you are an individual, check the first box; if you are a church group, check the last box, "other," and then identify yourself as such. All that's easy, isn't it? Yes, but what if you are a husband and wife or two friends who have a "handshake" ownership arrangement? Are you a partnership? Not necessarily; you are a partnership only if you file a partnership tax return. If you are several individuals acting together as plaintiffs on some other basis, check the first

box.

Please note that if you are a corporation, you may not represent yourself in court as plaintiff in pro per. You must have an attorney represent you, but if you are an honest-to-goodness partnership, you may represent yourself as plaintiff in pro per, so long as you are one of the partners.

If you have adopted a fictitious business name such as Greenbrier Apartments or Overlook Terrace, and you have been using that name on your rental agreements and rent receipts (just having a sign out in front of the property doesn't count), then you must comply with the laws about filing that name with the county and advertising it in a publicly circulated newspaper before you may file an unlawful detainer. Use of a fictitious name which includes your surname, such as Lester Landlord's Sun Garden Apartments, won't require filing and won't require you to check this box unless you use Sun Garden Apartments in place of Lester Landlord on your rental agreement. If you are using a true fictitious name, as I do for certain of my property holdings, then be sure to check box 1b and give the name there (see the discussion of fictitious name statements in chapter 3).

2. Item 2 asks for the location of your property which your tenants, now the defendants in this case, are occupying—their street address, city, and county. In addition to that, be certain you include whatever apartment, suite, space, building, or room number further identifies the exact premises. This information should match what is shown on the notice and on the rental agreement.

3. Whether you own a minuscule percentage or one hundred percent of the property in question, check the owner box. If you are anything else, such as an original tenant trying to evict a subtenant, check the second box and state enough facts to show that you have the right to possession of the premises. Some courts will allow managers and agents to act as plaintiffs and handle unlawful detainers for absentee owners, and some won't. Check with your court about its requirements before you file. Even if your court does require the owner to be the plaintiff in an unlawful detainer, the physical presence of the owner would be required only for a court appearance, and even that may not be necessary. Everything else could be handled by someone else once the signatures have been obtained.

4. To take advantage of statement 4 in the complaint, put a number in the "DEFENDANT" section of the complaint up above, where you see "DOES 1 TO ____." This number should match the one you put on the summons.

5. In section 5, you have an opportunity to establish for the court the precise terms of the agreement made with the tenant. Indicate the date of the agreement and the names of those the agreement was made with. They should be the defendants named in the complaint. If the people you originally rented to have sublet to someone else, name here the original renters whose names appear on the agreement, even though they no longer live on the premises, and indicate in 5c whether there are any additional defendants and if so, what category they fit under. The term "other" in 5c might refer to guests, licensees, or trespassers. Include the names of the original tenants and the subtenants on your notice and in your complaint as defendants.

Next, indicate with a check whether the tenancy is month-to-month or another arrangement, in which case you should specify what kind of an arrangement it is, week-to-week, year-to-year, one-year lease, three-year lease, lease-option, or some such.

In the blank following "rent of $____," put down the net rent *as given in the rental agreement or as agreed upon verbally*. This may or may not be the current rent. Don't worry about that right now. Then indicate whether the rent is payable monthly or at some other interval and also when it is due, on the first or on some other day. Remember that these names, intervals, figures, and days should reflect what you agreed upon when you *first* rented the place to the tenant, and that they are not necessarily up-to-date. In item 5d, you have the opportunity to specify how the agreement has been changed.

Indicating whether the agreement is written or oral is extremely important, and that's what you do next. A crafty attorney taught me that lesson the hard way once by filing a demurrer (see Glossary) because my complaint failed to specify that the rental agreement was written. In the context of life, specifying whether an agreement is written or oral is about as important as the hair growing between your toes, but in the context of pursuing an unlawful detainer, it's as important as the hair on your head. Naturally this attorney's challenge was a frivolous one, made on a legal technicality, and designed only to delay the case, thereby winning the tenant a few more days of free rent. It was easily answered, but it was frustrating to be thwarted over something which appeared to be so insignificant to me.

If you were the one who made this agreement with your tenant, check the "plaintiff" box; if it was your manager or agent, check that box; if it was someone you bought the property from, a "predecessor in interest," check that; if someone else did it, check the "other" box and specify who it was.

Should there be any other defendants listed in your complaint whose names did not appear in 5a, check the box after "c" and indicate whether they are subtenants (renting from the original tenants and responsible to them), assignees (tenants who have assumed the original tenants' agreement and are responsible to you directly), or other (co-signers would fit into this category).

Unless the tenants being evicted are relatively new, you will probably have something to include in 5d. Check the box first and then list any relevant changes which have been made to the tenants' original rental agreement—rent increases, tenant additions or deletions, and the like.

You don't absolutely have to include a copy of your rental agreement as an exhibit attached to the complaint, and the virtuoso eviction attorney whom I consult for good ideas does not include one with his because he believes that omitting it "reduces the demurrability" of the complaint. In other words, he believes that including the rental agreement with the complaint increases the chances that the tenant or his attorney will find something to object to. If you follow this practice and omit the agreement from the complaint, you will have to make a copy available for the judge to see later, but not now. Bring it with you to court or else give it to the clerk with the Declaration for Default Judgment in Lieu of Personal Testimony referred to later. If you decide to include a copy of the agreement with your complaint anyway, type or print "Exhibit 1" on the top of the agreement and check box 5e.

6. This section refers to the type of notice you served and the people who received it. Check box 6 and list to the right the names of all those defendants who were served. Then check the box next to the type of notice you served. For non-

payment of rent, check the first one.

In 6b, give the date when the notice period ended. Be careful in making your calculations for this date. It should be exactly correct. Take the date given on the notice and add the number of days granted for compliance. If, for example, a 3-Day Notice to Pay Rent or Quit were given on July 12th, the notice expiration day would be July 15th. If it were given on July 31st, the notice expiration day would be August 3d. A 30-Day Notice to Terminate Tenancy given on July 3d would expire August 2d. "Thirty days" means thirty days; more would be all right, of course, but definitely not fewer. Electronic calculators aren't always helpful in your calendar calculations; fingers and toes are better.

Check box 6d if your notice included a statement requesting the tenant to forfeit his rental agreement. The 3-Day Notice to Pay Rent or Quit, 3-Day Notice to Quit, and 30-Day Notice to Terminate Tenancy given in this book all do include such a statement, but the 3-Day Notice to Perform Covenant does not. Look carefully at the particular notice you used. Whether the rental agreement is forfeited or not involves some legal complexities for underemployed attorneys to argue about. Suffice it to say here that when you do *not* elect to forfeit a rental agreement in a nonpayment-of-rent case, the court *may* allow the tenant to pay up and still continue to occupy the premises. When you serve any of the three notices above which request the tenant to forfeit his agreement, you want him to leave, not linger. When you serve him the 3-Day Notice to Perform Covenant, you may want him to leave, but you definitely want his tenancy responsibilities to continue, especially if there's a lease involved, so you do not request forfeiture.

So long as you disclose in your complaint all the pertinent facts about the notice you served on the tenant—type of notice, amount of rent delinquent and demanded, date of service, and type of service, all of which you reveal in various sections of the complaint form—you do not have to attach a copy of the notice itself to the complaint, and unless your court clerk tells you that you must, don't bother. It just increases your copying costs and gives the defendant another copy to replace the one he has probably lost already. You will have to take the original notice with you later when you either go to court or file your declaration because the judge will want to

PLAINTIFF *(Name)*: Lester Landlord	CASE NUMBER:
DEFENDANT *(Name)*: Richard Renter	

7. a. [X] The notice in item 6a was served on the defendants named in item 6a as follows:

(1) [X] by personally handing a copy to defendant on *(date)*:   9/12/XX

(2) [ ] by leaving a copy with *(name or description)*: _____ , a person
of suitable age or discretion, on *(date)*: _____ at defendant's [ ] residence [ ] business
AND mailing a copy to defendant at defendant's place of residence on *(date)*: _____
because defendant cannot be found at defendant's residence or usual place of business.

(3) [ ] by posting a copy on the premises on *(date)*: _____ ([ ] and giving a copy to a person found
residing at the premises) AND mailing a copy to defendant at the premises on *(date)*: _____

    (a) [ ] because defendant's residence and usual place of business cannot be ascertained OR

    (b) [ ] because no person of suitable age or discretion can be found there.

(4) [ ] *(not for 3-day notice; see Civil Code section 1946 before using)* by sending a copy by certified or registered
mail addressed to defendant on *(date)*: _____

(5) [ ] *(not for residential tenancies; see Civil Code section 1953 before using)* in a manner specified in a written
commercial lease between the parties.

b. [X] *(Name)*: Richard Renter   was served on behalf of all defendants who signed a joint written rental agreement.

c. [ ] Information about service of notice on the defendants named in item 6f is stated in attachment 7c.

8. [ ] Plaintiff demands possession from each defendant because of expiration of a fixed-term lease.

9. [X] At the time the 3-day notice to pay rent or quit was served, the amount of **rent due** was $ 730.00

10. [X] The fair rental value of the premises is $ 26.00   per day.

11. [ ] Defendants' continued possession is malicious, and plaintiff is entitled to statutory damages under Code of Civil Procedure
section 1174(b). *(State specific facts supporting a claim up to $600 in attachment 11.)*

12. [X] A written agreement between the parties provides for attorney fees.

13. [ ] Defendants' tenancy is subject to the local rent control or eviction control ordinance of *(city or county, title of ordinance,
and date of passage)*:

Plaintiff has met all applicable requirements of the ordinances.

14. [ ] Other allegations are stated in attachment 14.

15. Plaintiff remits to the jurisdictional limit, if any, of the court.

16. **PLAINTIFF REQUESTS**

a. possession of the premises.

b. costs incurred in this proceeding.

c. [X] past due rent of $ 730.00

d. [ ] reasonable attorney fees.

e. [X] forfeiture of the agreement.

f. [X] damages at the rate stated in item 10 from
(date):   10/1/XX   for each day
defendants remain in possession through entry of judgment.

g. [ ] statutory damages up to $600 for the conduct alleged in
item 11.

h. [ ] other *(specify)*:

17. [ ] Number of pages attached *(specify)*: _____

UNLAWFUL DETAINER ASSISTANT (Business and Professions Code sections 6400-6415)

18. *(must be answered in all cases)* An unlawful detainer assistant [X] did **not** [ ] did   for compensation give advice or assistance with this form. *(If plaintiff has received **any** help or advice for pay from an unlawful detainer assistant, state)*:

a. Assistant's name: b. Telephone No.:

c. Street address, city, and ZIP:

d. County of registration: e. Registration No.:   f. Expires on *(date)*:

Lester Landlord & Leslie Landlord	*Lester Landlord Leslie Landlord*
(TYPE OR PRINT NAME)	(SIGNATURE OF PLAINTIFF OR ATTORNEY)

VERIFICATION

(Use a different verification form if the verification is by an attorney or for a corporation or partnership.)

I am the plaintiff in this proceeding and have read this complaint. I declare under penalty of perjury under the laws of the State of
California that this complaint is true and correct.

Date: September 16, XXXX

Lester Landlord & Leslie Landlord	*Lester Landlord Leslie Landlord*
(TYPE OR PRINT NAME)	(SIGNATURE OF PLAINTIFF)

982.1(90) [Rev. July 1, 1996]   **COMPLAINT—Unlawful Detainer**   Page two

You will find a blank copy of this form in the FORMS section of this book and in Eviction Forms Creator.

take a look at it, but you don't have to attach it to the complaint. If you do elect to attach a copy anyway, identify it as "Exhibit 2" (if you did not include the rental agreement as an exhibit, identify the notice here as "Exhibit 1"; in that case, change the "Exhibit 2" in 6e on the complaint to "Exhibit 1") and check box 6e.

Check box 6f if you served other defendants with a different notice or you served them on a different date or in a different manner, and attach a statement to that effect as Attachment 6f.

In the box at the top of page two, put your surname as plaintiff and your tenant's surname as defendant, and leave the "CASE NUMBER" box blank for the court clerk to fill in.

7. Check the box directly after 7 and also check the appropriate one of the other boxes regarding service. If the defendant was served personally, the first method, check that box and give the date of service. If the notice was left with someone "of suitable age and discretion," check that box, give the name or description of the person whom the notice was left with, indicate whether it was served at the defendant's residence or place of business, and give the date when it was served this way. If the notice was posted and mailed, check that box, give the date when it was posted and when a copy was mailed, check whether a copy was also given to someone on the premises (it doesn't have to be), and then check one of the two boxes to indicate why you chose this method. If you used the fourth method, sending a copy by certified or registered mail, check that box and tell when it was sent (this method by itself may be used only for 30-day notices; it may be used for other notices only in conjunction with another method). Check box 7a(5) if you served a commercial tenant in some manner specified in your lease.

Check box 7b to indicate that you served one tenant on behalf of all those tenants who signed the rental agreement, and give the name of the person who was served.

Check box 7c if you checked box 6f and attach a statement explaining how you served the additional defendants referred to in 6f. Incidentally, you need not use a totally separate page for each attached statement. You may use one page for all the attachments. Use an additional page only if you need more room.

8. Check box 8 only if you are evicting the tenants because they failed to leave when their fixed lease term expired.

9. Check box 9 if you are evicting for nonpayment of rent and include the precise amount of rent due when you served the notice. This amount should be exactly what you put on the notice, regardless of whether more rent is now owed and delinquent.

10. Check box 10 no matter what kind of eviction you are pursuing and indicate the current rent per day. Regardless of how many days there are in the actual months involved, use a 30-day month for this calculation. Courts have held that a 30-day month is proper and consistent to use for rent calculations and that it represents a fair rental value. To calculate your rental's monthly value, merely divide the monthly rent by 30. If the rent were $850 per month, for example, the per-diem rent would be $28.33.

11. You are no longer entitled to treble damages awarded by the court for proving that the tenant was extra ornery in harassing or cheating you. Instead, you are entitled to a maximum of $600. I caution you against asking for this sum unless you believe you can prove beyond any doubt in an attachment that the tenant has been malicious. "Malicious" here would mean that he has threatened you, damaged the rental dwelling intentionally, or tried numerous and obvious delaying tactics. Calling you names wouldn't suffice. Brandishing a weapon at you would. These damages are seldom awarded, except in extreme cases, so I no longer include them in my complaints because they tend to complicate what I want to be kept simple. Some tenants' attorneys will file a motion to strike unless the request for such damages includes what might be considered an allegation of willfulness, in other words, behavior which is deliberate, intentional, or obstinate. If you are bent upon attempting to secure these damages from your tenant, include your allegations as attachment 11. As for myself, I wouldn't bother. Why ask for them and leave yourself open to an attorney's response when you have so little chance of being awarded them anyway and even less of a chance of collecting?

12. Check box 12 only if your rental agreement entitles you to ask for attorney's fees. Checking the box doesn't mean you are asking for attorney's fees; it means only that your agreement includes a clause which entitles you to ask for them.

Some agreements no longer ask that attorney's

ATTORNEY OR PARTY WITHOUT ATTORNEY *(Name and Address)* :	TELEPHONE NO.:	FOR COURT USE ONLY
Lester Landlord & Leslie Landlord 123 Neat Street Littletown, California 91111	415-123-4567	

ATTORNEY FOR *(Name)*: Plaintiff in Propria Persona

INSERT NAME OF COURT, JUDICIAL DISTRICT, AND BRANCH COURT, IF ANY:
Saddleback Municipal Court
100 State Street

Littletown, California 91111

CASE NAME:

LANDLORD VS. RENTER

CIVIL CASE COVER SHEET **(Case Cover Sheets)**	CASE NUMBER:

1. ☐ **32**   Case category *(Insert code from list below for the ONE case type that best describes the case)* :

01 Abuse of Process	18 Insurance Coverage/Subrogation
02 Administrative Agency Review	19 Intellectual Property
03 Antitrust/Unfair Business Practices	20 Enforcement of Judgment *(Sister State, Foreign,*
04 Asbestos	*Out-of-Country Abstracts)*
05 Asset Forfeiture	21 Partnership and Corporate Governance
06 Breach of Contract/Warranty	22 PI/PD/WD--Auto *(Personal Injury/Property Damage/*
07 Business Tort	*Wrongful Death)*
08 Civil Rights *(Discrimination, False Arrest)*	23 PI/PD/WD--Nonauto
09 Collections *(Money Owed, Open Book Accounts)*	24 Product Liability
10 Construction Defect	25 Professional Negligence *(Medical or Legal Malpractice, etc.)*
11 Contractual Arbitration	26 Real Property *(Quiet Title)*
12 Declaratory Relief	27 RICO
13 Defamation *(Slander, Libel)*	28 Securities Litigation
14 Eminent Domain/Inverse Condemnation	29 Tax Judgment
15 Employment *(Labor Commissioner Appeals,*	30 Toxic Tort/Environmental
EDD Actions, Wrongful Termination)	31 Unlawful Detainer--Commercial
16 Fraud	32 Unlawful Detainer--Residential
17 Injunctive Relief	33 Wrongful Eviction
	34 Other: _____

2. Type of remedies sought *(check all that apply)*: a. ☒ Monetary b. ☒ Nonmonetary c. ☐ Punitive
3. Number of causes of action: 1
4. Is this a class action suit? ☐ Yes ☒ No

Date: 3/16/XX

....   ▶ *Lester Landlord*
Lester Landlord
(TYPE OR PRINT NAME)   (SIGNATURE OF PARTY OR ATTORNEY FOR PARTY)

NOTE TO PLAINTIFF

• This cover sheet shall accompany each civil action or proceeding, except those filed in small claims court or filed under the Probate Code, Family Law Code, or Welfare and Institutions Code.
• File this cover sheet in addition to any cover sheet required by local court rule.
• Do not serve this cover sheet with the complaint.
• This cover sheet shall be used for statistical purposes only and shall have no effect on the assignment of the case.

Form Adopted by Rule 982.2 Judicial Council of California 982.2(b)(1) [New July 1, 1996]	**CIVIL CASE COVER SHEET** **(Case Cover Sheets)**	

You will find a blank copy of this form in the FORMS section of this book and in Eviction Forms Creator.

or legal services fees go to the prevailing party. Some landlords have been stung badly. After losing lengthy eviction suits, they have had to pay their own legal costs plus those of their tenants. Check your rental agreement to see what it says.

13. Check box 13 only if there is a rent or eviction control ordinance covering the premises. State whether it's a city or a county ordinance and give the title and date. If you don't know what to enter here, call your local rent control board and ask them for the information or look for it on the rent control board's Web site.

Note that item 13 also includes a statement saying that you as plaintiff have met all the applicable requirements of the ordinance. You have, haven't you?

14. Check box 14 only if you need to add some more allegations to your complaint, something which just hasn't been covered by any of the choices in the complaint form thus far. Add your allegations in an attachment.

15. In item 15, you agree to excuse the tenant for any monetary claims you may have against him which exceed the court's limits.

16. The eight requests under item 16 sum up the entire complaint. You have no choice about the first two. They're at the heart of every eviction. Request "a" states the first item of importance, that is, you want possession of the premises. Request "b" states the second item of importance, that is, you want your tenant to reimburse you for your out-of-pocket costs to pursue the eviction; these costs include filing fees, process serving fees, court reporter's fees for hearings and depositions if there are any, and witness fees. Request "c" echoes item 9 above; check box "c" if you checked box 9 above and put the same rental figure there, too. Request "d" asks for reasonable attorney fees. Don't check box "d" even if you did check box 12 above. Because you are acting "in pro per," you are not entitled to any attorney fees; if you decide to hire an attorney later, you may ask for them then. Request "e" asks for forfeiture of the agreement; check box "e" only if you checked box 6d and you want the agreement forfeited. Request "f" refers to damages, that is, what would otherwise be called "rent" from the end of the last rental period given in the notice to the actual eviction date; put in the blank here the fair rental value used in item 10. Request "g" echoes item 11 above; check box "g" if you checked box 11. Finally, check box

"h" if you have any further request which you want to specify, such as late fees, bad check charges, damages, legal services fees, etc.

Incidentally, if your rental agreement includes a clause which provides for "legal services fees" rather than or in addition to "attorney's fees," you may recover self-representation fees when filing "in pro per" [*Jacobson v. Simmons Real Estate* (1994) 23 CA4th 1285, 28 CR2d 699, 702-703].

17. Check box 17 only if you are attaching any pages to the complaint. Otherwise leave it blank. If you include your rental agreement and your 3-Day Notice to Pay Rent or Quit as exhibits, which I do not recommend, and each of them is on one page, then you would put a "2" after "specify."

18. As you do on the summons, you must indicate on the complaint whether you received any help from an unlawful detainer assistant. If you did, provide information about the assistant where indicated.

After completing item 18, type or print your name legibly on the two dotted lines below, sign your name on the two solid lines, and date the verification with today's date. Don't overlook the date. It's easy to overlook because it's in the same space where the plaintiff's typed or printed name goes in the verification, way down in the lower left corner.

Now that you have completed your complaint, go back to the first item and begin reading out loud, reading only those sections which you checked and the others which apply. See if it makes any sense to you and if it's consistent. When it does make sense and is consistent, you are ready to file your complaint with the court clerk and arrange to have it served.

• THE COVER SHEET—The cover sheet is a single-sided Judicial Council form which you must include with the summons and complaint when you first file your case. Your tenant won't be getting a copy when he's served because courts use cover sheets for statistical purposes only.

Completing a cover sheet is a simple matter. All you do is enter the same information in the upper-left-hand section of the form that you entered on the complaint. The case name is simply the plaintiff's (your) last name "vs." the defendant's (your tenant's) last name. In box #1, enter "32" for a residential eviction or "31" for a commercial eviction (look at the case category list to see where these numbers came from). After #2, put checks in boxes "a" and "b" because you are seeking both monetary and nonmonetary remedies in an eviction. After #3, put "1" because you have only one cause of action. After #4, check the "No" box because you are not bringing a class action suit. Then you date the form, type or print your name, and sign it.

Step 4. File the Summons, Complaint, and Cover Sheet.

• THE FILING—Now at last you're ready to file your initial paperwork with the court clerk. Take the correct number of copies of your paperwork to the court clerk's office which you located earlier. If possible, go in the morning so the process server will have a chance to serve the papers that same day.

Give the clerk the summons, complaint, and cover sheet originals, the copies, and the filing fee. She will assign your case a number and open a corresponding file, stamping your papers and hers with an array of rubber stamps so numerous and so varied that you'd swear she could write a book with them. Don't swear to that, though, not in this office. You don't want to perjure yourself.

After the necessary stamping and signing, she will hand you a receipt for the filing fee and return all the papers except the originals of your complaint and cover sheet. She keeps them for the court's records.

If she appears friendly, ask her for advice about serving the defendant, your tenant, with the papers. Practices and preferences regarding service vary, and you should listen carefully to the clerk's recommendations.

Since some courts hear unlawful detainers only on certain days of the week, ask also about specific scheduling so you can be prepared. There's no feeling worse than getting everything ready for court on the Friday before a three-day holiday, only to find out that unlawful detainers aren't heard on Fridays in your local court, and you'll have to wait until Tuesday before you can get in, thereby losing four days in the process. You might as well learn now what to expect in the way of court scheduling.

In addition, while you're still there, pick up at least three copies each of the Request for Entry of Default, the Writ of Execution, the Judgment by Default form used when the clerk enters the default judgment according to CCP §1169, and the Judgment by Default form used when the judge enters judgment. The first two may be copied from those given in the back of this book. Because the others are locally designed forms, you may or may not be able to use the ones in the FORMS section of this book. If not, ask the clerk to provide you with them now.

• DELAYED ACCESS—California municipal courts now delay public access to court papers in unlawful detainer actions for sixty days from the date of filing (see CCP §1161.2).

This delay is a real boon to landlords because it has virtually stopped the unscrupulous eviction defense services. They would send somebody down to the courthouse every day to sift through recently filed unlawful detainer complaints looking for potential business. They would identify who's being sued, and then they would contact the defendants directly with offers to obstruct the eviction as long as legally possible.

Believe me, almost any attorney can obstruct almost any eviction for some time if he wants to. Whether the case has merit or not doesn't matter in the least. The unscrupulous attorney knows all the gimmicks for exploiting the legal system. He can create a snowstorm of paperwork which will stop your eviction efforts cold, at least for a while. Any obstruction of the eviction is a "win" for your tenant, and when he's being evicted, he'd rather pay an attorney than pay you. These "eviction chasers" would also identify complaints which might have special value to them, complaints which might generate some damages assessed against you, you "rent-gouging, feelthy-reech landlord with them deep pockets and that bulging purse."

Now that public access to unlawful detainer filings is delayed, nobody can just go down to the courthouse and examine the paperwork. They have to wait sixty days, and by then, you should have evicted the tenants.

• SAVING TRIPS AND TIME—By knowing just what to do, which includes calling the court clerk at the right time of day, having certain papers already prepared, and taking advantage of weekends, you may save precious days in the eviction process, and you may also keep your trips to the courthouse to a minimum. I have had to make as many as three trips there in a single day because I wasn't completely prepared the first time. If you follow the advice given here and if your case is uncontested, you may be able to do everything in only two or three visits to the courthouse all told.

Step 5. Arrange Service of the Summons and Complaint.

Although you may legally serve the notice which initiates eviction proceedings yourself, you may not legally serve the summons and complaint yourself. That's absolutely *verboten*. You have to arrange for someone else to do it, someone who is impartial to the suit.

Any person in the following three categories may serve the summons and complaint for you:

1) A sheriff or marshal;

2) A professional process server; or

3) Someone else who is at least eighteen years old.

Personally, I prefer to have a uniformed law enforcement officer serve the papers if I think it will be intimidating to the tenant or if the tenant is potentially dangerous *and* if I know service will be fast. It appears legally sanctioned, as if you're "making a federal case out of the matter," one which has a foregone conclusion, and it stifles the tenant's will to respond. Since you want the tenant out as soon as possible, you don't want him wasting any of your time with a response to the complaint.

To have an on-duty law enforcement officer serve your papers, find out from the court clerk whether one can serve the papers (certain areas no longer have the manpower, so you may have to use somebody else) and where they have offices. Usually the office is close by. Ask them when they will make the first effort to serve your papers and when they might expect to complete the service. Some officers are extremely diligent. They'll attempt to serve the papers the very next morning between 5 and 7:30. That's 5 a.m. in the morning! In addition, they'll keep trying day after day until they succeed. Others act as if they have a monopoly on process serving in their bailiwick. They won't even try to serve the papers for two weeks.

You're going to be paying for the sheriff or marshal's service. You have a right to know how long they will take. Don't assume that your papers will be served quickly. Find out for sure. Time is extremely important here. Get the papers served as soon as possible so the eviction clock can continue ticking. Until they are served, nothing is happening to get the eviction moving. Its clock has stopped.

In most cases, a professional process server will do just as well as a sheriff or marshal, if not better, because he is bound to be more prompt and more diligent than a sheriff or marshal. For instance, if you file Friday afternoon, a sheriff or marshal probably won't make his first effort to serve until Monday morning because he doesn't work Friday nights or weekends, and that means you have just added two days to the eviction process. Professional process servers, on the other hand, will serve any time, any day, and speaking of diligence, process servers have been known to impersonate an Avon lady, climb up a ship's swaying mainmast, crash cocktail parties, and fend off killer pit bulls to get their papers served. That's free enterprise in action! You will find them listed in the Yellow Pages under "Process Serving." Check several of them out. Ordinarily they're quite competitive in price, but do compare their charges with the sheriff or marshal's before committing yourself, and also check to see that they are licensed by the state and registered with the county so their acknowledgment of service will be accepted readily by the court. Remember that professional process servers are dressed like ordinary people, and they don't look so imposing as does an officer of the law, but then this is sometimes an advantage, too, because tenants tend to be less wary about being served when someone ordinary-looking knocks on the door. You needn't worry whether ordinary-looking process servers will get the job done quickly and correctly. They will. After all, they're professionals.

If you want to save a few dollars, if you can't find a good professional process server, or if the tenant is successfully avoiding service, you can always have someone else serve the papers, and you can even accompany him to identify the defendant, but this is the least recommended method. It's just as legal a service, mind you, but it isn't quite so overwhelming as being served by a sheriff or marshal, and because an amateur's doing it rather than a professional, the service might get bungled. If you do elect to use a friend or acquaintance as your process server, make sure that he serves one copy of the summons and one copy of the complaint on each defendant and that he fills out the Proof of Service on the back side of the original summons.

Take a good look at the Proof of Service

PLAINTIFF: Lester Landlord

DEFENDANT: Richard Renter

CASE NUMBER:

PROOF OF SERVICE

1. At the time of service I was at least 18 years of age and not a party to this action, and I **served copies** of the (specify documents):

    Summons and Complaint

2. a. Party served (specify name of party as shown on the documents served):

    Richard Renter

    b. Person served: [X] party in item 2a   [ ] other (specify name and title or relationship to the party named in item 2a):

    c. Address: 456 Sweet Street, Littletown, CA 91111

3. I served the party named in item 2
    a. [X] **by personally delivering** the copies   (1) on (date): 9/16/XX   (2) at (time):   3:12 p.m.
    b. [ ] **by leaving** the copies with or in the presence of (name and title or relationship to person indicated in item 2b):

    (1) [ ] **(business)** a person at least 18 years of age apparently in charge at the office or usual place of business of the person served. I informed him or her of the general nature of the papers.
    (2) [ ] **(home)** a competent member of the household (at least 18 years of age) at the dwelling house or usual place of abode of the person served. I informed him or her of the general nature of the papers.
    (3) on (date):   (4) at (time):
    (5) [ ] A declaration of diligence is attached. (Substituted service on natural person, minor, conservatee, or candidate.)
    c. [ ] **by mailing** the copies to the person served, addressed as shown in item 2c, by first-class mail, postage prepaid,
    (1) on (date):   (2) from (city):
    (3) [ ] with two copies of the Notice and Acknowledgment of Receipt and a postage-paid return envelope addressed to me.
    (4) [ ] to an address outside California with return receipt requested. ← (Attach completed form.)
    d. [ ] **by causing** copies to be mailed. A declaration of mailing is attached.
    e. [ ] **other** (specify other manner of service and authorizing code section):

4. The "Notice to the Person Served" (on the summons) was completed as follows:
    a. [X] as an individual defendant.
    b. [ ] as the person sued under the fictitious name of (specify):
    c. [ ] on behalf of (specify):
        under: [ ] CCP 416.10 (corporation)   [ ] CCP 416.60 (minor)   [ ] other:
               [ ] CCP 416.20 (defunct corporation) [ ] CCP 416.70 (conservatee)
               [ ] CCP 416.40 (association or partnership) [ ] CCP 416.90 (individual)

5. **Person serving** (name, address, and telephone number):
    Bud Beans
    367 Hill Street
    Littletown, CA 91111
    555-1111

    a. **Fee** for service: $ 30.00
    b. [X] Not a registered California process server
    c. [X] Exempt from registration under B&P § 22350(b)
    d. [ ] Registered California process server
        (1) [ ] Employee or independent contractor
        (2) Registration No.:
        (3) County:
        (4) Expiration (date):

6. [X] **I declare** under penalty of perjury under the laws of the State of California that the foregoing is true and correct.

7. [ ] **I am a California sheriff, marshal, or constable and** I certify that the foregoing is true and correct.

Date: September 16, XXXX

▶ *Bud Beans*
(SIGNATURE)

982(a)(11) [Rev. January 1, 1997]

PROOF OF SERVICE
(Summons—Unlawful Detainer)

Page two
Code of Civil Procedure § 417.10(f)

You will find a blank copy of this form in the FORMS section of this book and in Eviction Forms Creator.

	SHERIFF or MARSHAL	PROFESSIONAL	OTHER (AMATEUR)
SPEED	varies, (check locally)	excellent	good
COST	good (check locally)	varies	excellent
INTIMIDATION POTENTIAL	excellent	poor	poor
SERVICE CORRECTNESS	good	good	poor

sample shown here to see how an unregistered amateur would fill out the form after having served Richard Renter personally on behalf of Lester Landlord. As you can see, it's reasonably straightforward. Sections 3 and 4, you might note, recount how the server completed the bottom of the front side of the summons; make sure that the server remembers to do so by checking boxes 1 and 4 there and dating it prior to service. Section 5 of the Proof of Service asks for information on the server, and there's a place (5a) where the server may put down a fee. $35, or whatever the law enforcement officers in your area charge, would be a reasonable figure. Your amateur server should check boxes 5b and 5c as well. You might like to know that "B&P §22350(b)," referred to in 5c, gives those who serve no more than ten summonses in any one calendar year an exemption from registering with the county.

Don't forget that there must be a separate Proof of Service form submitted for each person served, even if they were all served at once.

Which one of the three types of process servers you select to serve your summons and complaint will depend upon four factors: speed, cost, intimidation potential, and likelihood of completing the service correctly.

Check the chart on this page to see how the three possible process servers differ on the four factors.

Select the particular process server who's going to do the best job for you in a given situation.

Make the process server's job as easy as pos-

sible. Give whomever you select to serve the papers as much information as you can about the tenant, especially his appearance, his possible whereabouts at different times, and his occupation (process servers know that they're likely to catch a bartender at one time of the day and a carpenter at another). A picture would help if you have one (if you copied his driver's license when he moved in, show that photo to the process server). Make certain that the address correctly identifies the tenant's dwelling. If you tell the process server to look for the tenant at 140 Marina Way, and there are six apartments at that address, don't expect the process server to find which apartment this particular tenant lives in.

Step 6. Serve the Summons and Complaint.

• WHO SHOULD BE SERVED WITH THE SUMMONS AND COMPLAINT?—To evict all the adult tenants from a dwelling and make them all responsible for paying the judgment, you must mention each of them by name in the complaint and serve each of them separately with a summons and complaint. You could chance serving only the dominant adult or the breadwinner alone and hope that the eviction of that one person would precipitate a mass exodus, but you couldn't be absolutely certain of it, not nowadays anyway.

Some freeloaders know the legal loopholes in the eviction procedure well enough so that they can frustrate your best efforts to evict them, and the California Supreme Court (the old "Bird Court") gave them still another loophole to use in the Arrieta case. In it, the Court held that a sheriff or marshal can evict only those adults whose names appear on the complaint. He cannot remove an adult unnamed in the resulting writ who is physically present during the actual eviction, resists eviction, and claims a right of possession commencing before the unlawful detainer was filed. As you might imagine, this decision popped the lid off a bucket of worms, for it made evictions even costlier, more troublesome, and more time-consuming than they already were. If you want to get all the tenants out, you now have to prepare an additional set of papers for each defendant, pay added process servers' fees to serve each defendant, and wait until every one of them is served.

Consequently, you simply must name and serve all the adults who are currently living in your rental, regardless of whether they're mentioned in the rental agreement or are responsible for paying the rent. And if you want to forestall the possibility that some strangers might appear at the very last minute and claim that they, too, have tenants' rights and that nobody can be evicted as a consequence, you might want to take advantage of the "prejudgment claim" procedure, which I will explain shortly.

To get a judgment against a cosigner, you have to name and serve him as well, though most landlords prefer to ignore the cosigner during the unlawful detainer. They want to avoid any potential complications in getting the tenants out, and involving another person in the action tends to cause unforeseen delays. Once the tenants are out, the landlord proceeds against the cosigner in small claims court. Please note that some courts won't even allow you to proceed against both the tenant and the cosigner in an unlawful detainer. Ask.

As mentioned before regarding whose names should be on the notice, don't bother serving children who are upwards of eighteen years old unless they are mature enough to be helping support the family. Serving them antagonizes the parents. Serving them also tends to be difficult because they're hard to find at home.

• DECIDING WHETHER TO USE THE PREJUDGMENT CLAIM PROCEDURE— Eight years following the lamebrained Arrieta decision, after thousands upon thousands of fraudulent claims of right to possession had been filed against hapless landlords (only 3% of such claims were found to be legitimate), the state legislature finally came up with something to help the situation (CCP §415.46). It combines different methods of service and uses a special form called a Prejudgment Claim of Right to Possession (see FORMS section) to insure that nobody, known or unknown, with a claim could later plead ignorance about the unlawful detainer and put a halt to the eviction at the very last minute.

Here's how it works. You tell the court clerk that you intend to use the prejudgment claim procedure. You make up three additional copies of the summons and complaint. You attach a blank copy of the Prejudgment Claim of Right to Possession to each of these three sets of papers. One set is for whoever comes to the door; one is for posting on or near the primary entrance; and one is for mailing to the address of the premises. You tell the process server (must be a sheriff or marshal or a professional process server) that you want to serve any unknown occupants with a Prejudgment Claim of Right to Possession when you drop off all the papers you want served. You then wait ten days following service. If nobody responds with a claim during that period, you go right ahead and complete your normal unlawful detainer paperwork, except that you indicate on both the Request for Entry of Default and the Writ of Execution that you have complied with CCP §415.46 and that your judgment includes "all tenants, subtenants, named claimants and other occupants of the premises." That wording authorizes the sheriff or marshal to evict everybody he finds.

If one or more people do make a claim, they are added as defendants to the unlawful detainer, and they then have five days in which to respond to the summons and complaint. If they make no response within five days, you go ahead and file a Request for Entry of Default on them and proceed normally with your unlawful detainer. If they do make a response within five days, you treat the matter like any other contested case (see chapter 10).

Although some attorneys use this procedure as a matter of course now, you should be aware that it does have several disadvantages. It adds at least five extra days to the whole eviction process and it increases both the copying costs and the fees for service.

Should you use it anyway? Maybe yes and maybe no. If you believe that the tenants you want to evict are neither savvy nor devious enough to get somebody to file a post-judgment third-party claim, don't bother to use the procedure. If, on the other hand, you have reason to believe that they might file a claim because they know all the angles and aren't afraid to take advantage of them, or because they have proven to be devious people, or because they might really have somebody else living with them who is unbeknownst to you, or because you don't have a clue who is actually living there and you need to "smoke 'em all out," go ahead and use the procedure and save yourself any uncertainty about whether someone will show up out of nowhere to halt the eviction when the sheriff or marshal is there to put the tenants out on the street.

You may, and you should, of course, request entry of default on the named defendants five days after service upon them, so they cannot file a response later.

• SUBSTITUTED SERVICE—If, after three tries, your process server cannot find the tenant, then the process server must use "substituted service," a procedure which the officer or professional will resort to automatically. It will delay things a bit, but it will definitely advance them. The problems with substituted service, though, are that you need an additional copy of the complaint for each defendant served under substituted service, that somebody must be found on the premises to take the papers, and that the tenant has fifteen days to respond to the complaint rather than the usual five.

• POSTING—More and more, landlords are resorting to the posting procedure according to CCP §415.45 to serve those tenants who are difficult to find. Like substituted service, it gives the tenant fifteen days to respond and requires additional copies of the papers, but unlike substituted service, it does not require anyone to be found on the premises. You may use this procedure after the process server has made three attempts to serve the tenant on different days and at different times. Instruct the process server to return your papers with enough information so you can get an order for posting if you want to use this procedure. Then go to the courthouse and get your order signed by the judge. You'll find the forms and instructions for posting in Appendix A.

In exceptional circumstances, you may seek a Writ of Immediate Possession (see chapter 14), but you may find that proving what is necessary to get this writ is more difficult than the other alternatives.

• WAITING—When counting the five days, count every day including Saturdays and Sundays, but *do not count court holidays*, those twelve days a year when the courts are closed (currently, they are New Year's Day, M.L. King Jr. Day Observance, Lincoln's Birthday, Washington's Birthday Observance, Memorial Day, Independence Day, Labor Day, Columbus Day Observance, Veteran's Day, Thanksgiving Day, Day after Thanksgiving, and Christmas Day). The final day on which the tenant may respond to your complaint must be a business day, a day when court offices are open and he at least has the opportunity to file. If his final day falls on a Saturday, Sunday, or holiday, he has the following business day in which to respond. You cannot claim the tenant has defaulted until the day following the last day given him to respond to the complaint. If you have any doubts about waiting the prescribed number of days, consult Calendar 2 at the end of this chapter or ask your court clerk.

Whoever serves your summons and complaint will prepare the Proof of Service and return it to you. If you haven't received this evidence of successful service by the fourth day after you arranged service of the summons and complaint, by all means, take the initiative and call the server. Find out what's happening. Remember that you may begin counting the days allowed for the tenant's response only after service of the summons and complaint has been completed, so serving it promptly is extremely important.

Step 7. Inquire About a Response.

You are hoping that your tenant won't bother to file a response to your complaint because doing so will only delay and complicate matters for you.

If he does file a response with the court, you will receive a copy by mail, but you may have to wait a while for the U.S. Postal Service to deliver it, and you cannot afford to waste precious time doing so, especially if it wasn't filed until the last possible moment. So you should wait until the last day, and virtually the last hour, for the tenant to file before calling the court clerk's office to inquire whether he has filed a response. If the tenant has made a response to your summons and complaint, whether the response is substantial or frivolous in nature, go to chapter 9 to learn what to do next. If the tenant has not made a response, ask the clerk when is the earliest possible date she can schedule you on the court calendar, and then decide which of the alternatives in Step 8 to follow.

• LIKELIHOOD OF A RESPONSE BEING FILED—Fortunately the odds are in your favor that the tenant won't file a response (between 75 and 80% of all unlawful detainer complaints filed in my local court are never responded to). There are three reasons why responses are made infrequently to unlawful detainers for nonpayment of rent. Responses require 1) that the defendant either prepare a written paper himself or get an attorney to do it for him, 2) that he file the response with the court, and 3) that he either pay a filing fee or file a form stating that he's too poor to pay the fee. Most defendants are simply unwilling to take the time and spend the money to make a response when they know full well that they are most likely going to lose anyway. They'd rather spend their time and money finding new accommodations someplace else where they can begin the cycle of free living and troublemaking all over again.

Certain tenants may go so far as to contact a legal-aid attorney, and because you are representing yourself, you may get some phone calls about the matter, but if you have a good case and you explain it frankly and fully, the legal-aid attorney will seldom bother to file a response. He has plenty of other cases with real merit to work on. He doesn't have the time to defend a tenant who's up to no good.

Step 8. Consider Your Alternatives and Select One.

Let's say you happen to be lucky. Your tenant hasn't filed a response to your complaint, and now you face the pleasant prospect of evicting him legally within days. Don't start feeling too smug yet. There are still some pitfalls which could delay everything, and there are still more hoops you have to jump through before the sheriff or marshal puts him out.

Right now it's decision time. You have to select one of at least three, and in some cases four, alternative paths to follow, each with certain advantages. Consider the four carefully.

1) The first alternative used to be the only one available; not any more. It involves setting up a court date, doing the paperwork necessary to appear in court, actually appearing in court for what is sometimes called a "prove-up trial," and getting a judgment for the restitution of your rental dwelling and for the money owed to you. Consider using this option when you don't have to wait more than a day or two to get into court, and you have reason to believe that the tenant has attachable assets or garnishable wages.

2) The second alternative involves doing the paperwork necessary for the clerk to enter the tenant's default and to give you a default judgment for restitution. It's a timesaving procedure which is explained in CCP §1169. *You don't have to appear in court, but then neither do you get a money judgment.* As things are, only a judge can grant a money judgment. Consider using this alternative when you're in a hurry to get your tenant evicted and you despair of ever getting any money out of him. It definitely saves you time because you do not have to wait for a court date *or* appear in court.

3) The third alternative combines the best features of the first two alternatives. Just as in the second alternative, it involves doing the paperwork necessary for the clerk to enter the tenant's default and to give you a default judgment for restitution, so you do get the tenants evicted quickly. At the same time, however, you set up a court date to get a money judgment, too. You will have to take the time to appear in court before a judge, of course, but it's only routine. Consider using this alternative when you're in a hurry to have the tenant evicted and you think you might collect some money from him by attaching his assets or wages after he's long gone.

CAUTION: Some California courts are misinterpreting CCP §1169 altogether. They are not allowing this third alternative. They will give a landlord the clerk's default judgment. They can hardly deny him that, but then they require him to file a small claims action or another municipal court action to get a money judgment. Read the relevant text of CCP §1169 in Appendix B, and see for yourself what you're entitled to. You *are* entitled to get a money judgment as part of the same unlawful detainer action which yields you a default judgment for restitution. The language is quite clear.

Be realistic, however. Although you may be entitled to a money judgment, your court may not allow you to get one. Ask someone there whether this combination alternative is available to you *before* you decide which of the four alternatives you plan to follow. Then make up your mind. (You might want to show the clerk CCP §1169 and ask her why the court there doesn't follow it.)

4) The fourth alternative adds some paperwork and some time to the procedure, but it's convenient, for you don't have to appear in court, and you do get judgments for both restitution and money. It involves preparing and filing all the other paperwork, plus something called a Declaration for Default Judgment in Lieu of Personal Testimony. You should know, though, that this procedure is discretionary, that is, it depends entirely upon the practice decided upon by your local judicial district. Some courts allow a declaration, and some courts don't, and the only way you can find out whether yours does is to ask. Consider using this alternative when you don't want to, or can't, appear in court, but you still want a money judgment and you're willing to suffer some delay in the eviction.

Attorneys seem to favor the first alternative, the old-fashioned way, because they're used to it and it takes care of everything at once, restitution and money, but, as you know, attorneys aren't particularly interested in evicting their clients' tenants as quickly as possible. You have a different objective. You want the bums out sooner rather than later. I sure do. Consequently, I would recommend that you try the second or third alternative because either one of them should enable you to evict your tenants sooner. Getting into court generally means delays of one sort or another, and CCP §1169 recognizes this fact. Using it to expedite your tenants' eviction is, I believe, in your interest.

If you have any doubts about which alternative you ought to follow, read through Steps 9-14 for each alternative, and then decide. Note that the third alternative follows an "A" path first to get the judgment for restitution and then a "B" path to get the money judgment.

By the way, the fees for each alternative are identical.

Regardless of which alternative you select, plan to make a trip to the courthouse anyway on the sixth day following service of the summons and complaint. This is an extremely important trip, which is necessitated by your having to beat the tenant to the court clerk's office to file your re-

quest before the tenant gets around to filing his response. You see, after the tenant has had his five days to respond to your summons and complaint, he still has additional time to respond, up until you file the request. Once you file the Request for Entry of Default, you no longer need worry about whether your tenant will respond to the complaint. He can't. He has already had five days in which to respond and he has chosen not to. After you file the request, he gets no further opportunity to respond, even though you may not be able to get your default judgment immediately. You don't want to give him any more time than the law requires, so go ahead and beat him to the courthouse. Get there early, before the clerk has even had enough time to put on her lipstick.

CAUTION: In most California courts, the clerk takes the papers of the first person to get through the door on the sixth day following service of the summons and complaint. If you beat your tenant by one second, that's good enough. You'll get your default judgment. This practice follows the letter and the spirit of the law which gives the tenant five days to respond, not five and a quarter or six. But there are some courts which give the tenant more time to respond than they should. If you file your Request for Entry of Default at 8:15 a.m. in one of these courts, and the tenant files his answer at 4:46 p.m. on the same day, they give the tenant's answer precedence. As far as I am concerned, this is contrary to law, a practice obviously weighted in favor of tenants. Still other courts will refuse to enter your default request for several days, allowing the extra time for the tenant's paperwork to be forwarded from any court in the county. That, too, is just plain wrong. If you are treated in either of these ways, get mad about it. Scream "bloody murder" to all the powers that be, for you as a landlord are being taken advantage of!

Even if your court does give tenants extra time in which to answer and won't change its ways, you still should get to the court on the sixth day. That's the only way you can keep advancing your cause as quickly as possible.

Steps 9-14

These steps vary according to which of the four alternatives you selected in Step 8. To understand how they all work, you should note what they are once more:

1) Normal procedure requiring court appearance;

2) Clerk entering default judgment for restitution only;

3) Clerk entering default judgment for restitution, then judge awarding money judgment;

4) Default in lieu of personal testimony involving no court appearance, while providing judgment for both restitution and money.

VERY IMPORTANT!! VERY IMPORTANT!! VERY IMPORTANT!!

No matter which of the four alternatives you choose, you should be aware that your earlier decision to use or not to use the Prejudgment Claim of Right to Possession procedure outlined later *must be indicated* on the Request and the Writ. Both forms have check boxes for this purpose. On the Request, if you followed the prejudgment claim procedure, you should check the box [under 1e(1)] next to the words "Include in the judgment all tenants, subtenants, named claimants...." If you did not follow the procedure, do not check this box. On the Writ, if you followed the procedure, check box 9a(1). If you did not follow the procedure, check box 9a(2). Checking the boxes to show that you have followed the procedure alerts everyone that you are entitled to its benefits.

Please note—As shown here, the sample Request for Entry of Default and the sample Writ of Execution assume that Lester Landlord has *not* followed the prejudgment claim procedure.

Now follow the various steps for each alternative to its conclusion.

Step 9. (Alternative 1). Prepare Request, Judgment, and Writ.

Prepare the three forms: Request for Entry of Default, Judgment (Default), and the Writ of Execution as shown on the following pages (they must be typed).

Besides the usual information called for in the upper third of the Request for Entry of Default, check the "ENTRY OF DEFAULT" and "COURT JUDGMENT" boxes. Enter the date when you filed the complaint in item 1a. Enter your name in 1b. Check box 1c and enter the name(s) of the defendant(s) in item 1c; if you are proceeding against two tenants and neither tenant has answered, put both names here; if one tenant has answered and one hasn't, put here the name of the tenant who did *not* answer (use al-

ternative 2 to eliminate one of several tenants; you gain little by taking the time to follow alternative 1). Check box 1d. Under section 1e, check the box next to "Include in the judgment all tenants, subtenants..." if you served the Prejudgment Claim of Right to Possession.

In section 2a under "Amount," put the exact amount of your demand as given in the complaint.

Check box 3 because you are pursuing an unlawful detainer, and you are including unlawful detainer assistant information on the back side.

Now turn the form over. In section 3, indicate whether you did or did not use and pay an unlawful detainer assistant for help. If you did use and pay one, include the particulars.

Under "Memorandum of Costs," list what you paid for clerk's filing fees in 6a, process server's fees in 6b, and in 6d put "CCP 1039 sup. costs, $5" (these costs cover your various incidental expenses such as fuel, postage, stationery, etc.), and total them at 6e. Then bring forward this total from 6e and put it in the "Amount" column at 2d. Total these amounts at 2f.

At 2g, put down the figure given in the complaint as daily damages, and indicate in the space immediately following the words "per day beginning (date):" when these damages are supposed to begin. In nonpayment-of-rent cases, they begin the day following the rental period for which you have demanded rent in the complaint. Let's say, for example, that you demanded rent through September 30th in your complaint. Damages, being equal to rent not demanded in the complaint, would then begin on October 1st. In termination-of-tenancy cases, they begin the day following the expiration of the notice.

Below box 3, next to "Date:" put today's date, and type your name below that.

Turn the form over once more, and in the SHORT TITLE box type your surname "vs." your tenant's. Put the case number in the CASE NUMBER box. Check the second row of boxes under 4 to show that your action does not meet any of the criteria given. Check box 5b, put down today's date, and type the name(s) and address(es) of each defendant to whom you mailed the Request for Entry of Default. Follow the format shown. List each defendant separately. Then type today's date and your name under sections 5-7, and check box 7 to indicate that no defendant is in the military. Sign your name four times next

ATTORNEY OR PARTY WITHOUT ATTORNEY *(Name and Address)*:	TELEPHONE NO.:	FOR COURT USE ONLY

ATTORNEY OR PARTY WITHOUT ATTORNEY *(Name and Address)*:

Lester Landlord & Leslie Landlord   TELEPHONE NO.: 415-123-4567
123 Neat Street
Littletown, California 91111

ATTORNEY FOR *(Name)*:

Insert name of court and name of judicial district and branch court, if any:

Contra Costa Municipal Court
Littletown Judicial District, Bay Branch

PLAINTIFF: Lester Landlord
            Leslie Landlord

DEFENDANT: Richard Renter
            Rose Renter

REQUEST FOR (Application)	[X] ENTRY OF DEFAULT [ ] CLERK'S JUDGMENT [X] COURT JUDGMENT	CASE NUMBER: 1234567890

1. TO THE CLERK: On the complaint or cross-complaint filed
   a. On *(date)*: 9/16/XX
   b. By *(name)*: Lester Landlord, Leslie Landlord
   c. [X] Enter default of defendant *(names)*:
       Richard Renter, Rose Renter

   d. [X] I request a court judgment under CCP 585(b), (c), 989, etc. *(Testimony required. Apply to the clerk for a hearing date, unless the court will enter a judgment on an affidavit under CCP 585(d).)*
   e. [ ] Enter clerk's judgment
       (1) [ ] For restitution of the premises only and issue a writ of execution on the judgment. CCP 1174(c) does not apply. (CCP 1169) [ ] Include in the judgment all tenants, subtenants, named claimants, and other occupants of the premises. The Prejudgment Claim of Right to Possession was served in compliance with CCP 415.46.
       (2) [ ] Under CCP 585(a). *(Complete the declaration under CCP 585.5 on the reverse (item 4).)*
       (3) [ ] For default previously entered on *(date)*:

2. **Judgment to be entered**

	Amount	Credits Acknowledged	Balance
a. Demand of complaint	$ 730.00	$	$ 730.00
b. Statement of damages (CCP 425.11) *(superior court only)*†			
(1) Special	$	$	$
(2) General	$	$	$
c. Interest	$	$	$
d. Costs *(see reverse)*	$ 105.00	$	$ 105.00
e. Attorney fees	$	$	$
f. TOTALS	$ 835.00	$	$ 835.00

   g. **Daily damages** were demanded in complaint at the rate of: $ 26.00 per day beginning *(date)*: 10/1/XX

3. [X] *(check if filed in an unlawful detainer case)* UNLAWFUL DETAINER ASSISTANT information is on the reverse *(complete item 3).*

Date: 9/23/XX

....   ▶ *Lester Landlord*
Lester Landlord
(TYPE OR PRINT NAME)   (SIGNATURE OF PLAINTIFF OR ATTORNEY FOR PLAINTIFF)

† *Personal injury or wrongful death actions only.*

FOR COURT USE ONLY	(1) [ ] Default entered as requested on *(date)*:
	(2) [ ] Default NOT entered as requested *(state reason)*:
	Clerk, by: _____

(Continued on reverse)

Form Adopted by the Judicial Council of California 982(a)(6) [Rev. July 1, 1996*]	**REQUEST FOR ENTRY OF DEFAULT** (Application to Enter Default)	Code of Civil Procedure, §§ 585-587, 1169 *See note on reverse.

You will find a blank copy of this form in the FORMS section of this book and in Eviction Forms Creator.

SHORT TITLE:	CASE NUMBER:
LANDLORD VS. RENTER	1234567890

3. UNLAWFUL DETAINER ASSISTANT *(Business and Professions Code sections 6400-6415)* An unlawful detainer assistant
[X] did **not** [ ] did for compensation give advice or assistance with this form. *(If declarant has received **any** help or advice for pay from an unlawful detainer assistant, state):*
a. Assistant's name: b. Telephone No.:
c. Street address, city, and ZIP:

d. County of registration: e. Registration No.:   f. Expires on *(date)*

4. [ ] **DECLARATION UNDER CCP 585.5** *(Required for clerk's judgment under CCP 585(a))* This action
a. [ ] is [X] is not   on a contract or installment sale for goods or services subject to CC 1801, etc. (Unruh Act).
b. [ ] is [X] is not   on a conditional sales contract subject to CC 2981, etc. (Rees-Levering Motor Vehicle Sales and Finance Act).
c. [ ] is [X] is not   on an obligation for goods, services, loans, or extensions of credit subject to CCP 395(b).

5. DECLARATION OF MAILING (CCP 587) A copy of this Request for Entry of Default was
a. [ ] **not mailed** to the following defendants whose addresses are **unknown** to plaintiff or plaintiff's attorney *(names)* :

b. [X] **mailed** first-class, postage prepaid, in a sealed envelope addressed to each defendant's attorney of record or, if none, to each defendant's last known address as follows:
  (1) Mailed on *(date)*:   (2) To *(specify names and addresses shown on the envelopes)* :
       9/23/XX   Richard Renter
                                               458 Sweet Street
                                               Littletown, California 91111

I declare under penalty of perjury under the laws of the State of California that the foregoing items 3, 4, and 5 are true and correct.
Date: 9/23/XX

....   ▶ *Lester Landlord*
      Lester Landlord
      (TYPE OR PRINT NAME)   (SIGNATURE OF DECLARANT)

6. MEMORANDUM OF COSTS *(Required if judgment requested)* **Costs and Disbursements** are as follows (CCP 1033.5):
a. Clerk's filing fees .... $ 70.00
b. Process server's fees .... $ 35.00
c. Other *(specify)* : .... $
d. .... $
e. **TOTAL**............................. $ 105.00
f. [ ] Costs and disbursements are waived.

I am the attorney, agent, or party who claims these costs. To the best of my knowledge and belief this memorandum of costs is correct and these costs were necessarily incurred in this case.

I declare under penalty of perjury under the laws of the State of California that the foregoing is true and correct.
Date: 9/23/XX

....   ▶ *Lester Landlord*
      Lester Landlord
      (TYPE OR PRINT NAME)   (SIGNATURE OF DECLARANT)

7. [X] **DECLARATION OF NONMILITARY STATUS** *(Required for a judgment)* No defendant named in item 1c of the application is in the military service so as to be entitled to the benefits of the Soldiers' and Sailors' Civil Relief Act of 1940 (50 U.S.C. appen. § 501 et seq.).

I declare under penalty of perjury under the laws of the State of California that the foregoing is true and correct.
Date: 9/23/XX

....   ▶ *Lester Landlord*
      Lester Landlord
      (TYPE OR PRINT NAME)   (SIGNATURE OF DECLARANT)

* *NOTE:* Continued use of form 982(a)(6) (Rev. Sept. 30, 1991) is authorized until June 30, 1997, *except* in unlawful detainer proceedings.

982(a)(6) [Rev. July 1, 1996*]	**REQUEST FOR ENTRY OF DEFAULT** **(Application to Enter Default)**	Page two

You will find a blank copy of this form in the FORMS section of this book and in Eviction Forms Creator.

ATTORNEY OR PARTY WITHOUT ATTORNEY (Name and Address): TELEPHONE NO.: Lester Landlord & Leslie Landlord 415-123-4567 123 Neat Street Littletown, California 91111 ATTORNEY FOR (Name): Plaintiff in Propria Persona	FOR COURT USE ONLY
NAME OF COURT AND ADDRESS: Saddleback Municipal Court 100 State Street Littletown, California 91111	

PLAINTIFF: Lester Landlord
         Leslie Landlord
 	
DEFENDANT: Richard Renter
         Rose Renter
	CASE NUMBER:
	1234567890

UNLAWFUL DETAINER
DEFAULT JUDGMENT

The Defendant(s) hereinafter named, having been regularly served with summons and copy of complaint, having failed to appear and answer plaintiff's complaint within the time allowed by law, and the default of said defendant(s) having been duly entered, and after having heard the testimony and considered the evidence, or pursuant to affidavit on file herein, the Court ordered the following JUDGMENT:

IT IS ORDERED AND ADJUDGED that Plaintiff(s)

Lester Landlord, Leslie Landlord

have and recover from Defendant(s)

Richard Renter, Rose Renter

the restitution and possession of those certain premises situated, lying and being in the County of Saddleback, State of California, and more particularly described as follows, to-wit:

458 Sweet Street, Littletown, California, 91111

It is further Ordered, Adjudged, and Decreed that said plaintiff(s) have and recover from said defendant(s)

Rents and Damages	730.00	
Interest		
Costs	105.00	
Attorney Fees		
TOTAL	$835.00	

And that the lease or agreement under which said defendant(s) hold(s) said premises be, and the same is hereby declared, forfeited, void, and of no effect.

.... days stay of execution.

Dated: ....
                                        Judge of the Municipal Court
I hereby certify this to be a true copy of the Judgment in the above action.

Judgment entered on _____   _____, Clerk

Judgment Book_____ Page_____ By _____, Deputy Clerk

UNLAWFUL DETAINER DEFAULT JUDGMENT

efc

You will find a blank copy of this form in the FORMS section of this book and in Eviction Forms Creator.

ATTORNEY OR PARTY WITHOUT ATTORNEY *(Name and Address)* :	TELEPHONE NO.:	FOR RECORDER'S USE ONLY

[X] Recording requested by and return to:

TELEPHONE NO.: 415-123-4567

Lester Landlord & Leslie Landlord
123 Neat Street
Littletown, California 91111

[ ] ATTORNEY FOR   [X] JUDGMENT CREDITOR   [ ] ASSIGNEE OF RECORD

NAME OF COURT: Saddleback Municipal Court
STREET ADDRESS: 100 State Street
MAILING ADDRESS:
CITY AND ZIP CODE: Littletown, California 91111
BRANCH NAME:

PLAINTIFF: Lester Landlord
              Leslie Landlord
DEFENDANT: Richard Renter, Rose Renter

WRIT OF	[X] EXECUTION (Money Judgment) [X] POSSESSION OF [ ] Personal Property [X] Real Property [ ] SALE	CASE NUMBER: 1234567890 FOR COURT USE ONLY

1. **To the Sheriff or any Marshal or Constable of the County of:**
   Saddleback
   You are directed to enforce the judgment described below with daily interest and
   your costs as provided by law.

2. **To any registered process server:** You are authorized to serve this writ only in
   accord with CCP 699.080 or CCP 715.040.

3. *(Name)*: Lester Landlord & Leslie Landlord
   is the [X] judgment creditor [ ] assignee of record
   whose address is shown on this form above the court's name.

4. **Judgment debtor** *(name and last known address)* :

   Richard Renter
   458 Sweet Street
   Littletown, California 91111

   Rose Renter
   458 Sweet Street
   Littletown, California 91111

   [ ] additional judgment debtors on reverse

5. **Judgment entered** on *(date)* :   9/23/XX
6. [ ] **Judgment renewed** on *(dates)* :

7. **Notice of sale** under this writ
   a. [X] has not been requested.
   b. [ ] has been requested *(see reverse)*.
8. [ ] Joint debtor information on reverse.
   [SEAL]

9. [X] See reverse for information on real or personal property to be delivered under a writ of possession or sold under a writ of sale.
10. [ ] This writ is issued on a sister-state judgment.
11. Total judgment . . . . $ 835.00
12. Costs after judgment (per filed order or memo CCP 685.090) . . . . $
13. Subtotal *(add 11 and 12)* . . . . $ 835.00
14. Credits . . . . $
15. Subtotal *(subtract 14 from 13)* . . . . . . $ 835.00
16. Interest after judgment (per filed affidavit CCP 685.050) . . . . $
17. Fee for issuance of writ . . . . $ 7.00
18. **Total** *(add 15, 16, and 17)* . . . . $ 842.00
19. Levying officer:
    (a) Add daily interest from date of writ (at the legal rate on 15) of . . . . $ 0.23
    (b) Pay directly to court costs included in 11 and 17 (GC 6103.5, 68511.3, CCP 699.520(i)) . . . . $
20. [ ] The amounts called for in items 11-19 are different for each debtor. These amounts are stated for each debtor on Attachment 20.

Issued on *(date)*:   9/23/XX   Clerk, by _____ , Deputy

— NOTICE TO PERSON SERVED: SEE REVERSE FOR IMPORTANT INFORMATION. —

(Continued on reverse)

Form Approved by the
Judicial Council of California
EJ-130 [Rev. January 1, 1997*]

WRIT OF EXECUTION

Code of Civil Procedure, §§ 699.520, 712.010, 715.010
*See note on reverse.

You will find a blank copy of this form in the FORMS section of this book and in Eviction Forms Creator.

SHORT TITLE: LANDLORD VS. RENTER	CASE NUMBER: 1234567890

—Items continued from the first page—

4. ☐ **Additional judgment debtor** *(name and last known address)* :

7. ☐ **Notice of sale** has been requested by *(name and address)* :

8. ☐ **Joint debtor** was declared bound by the judgment (CCP 989-994)
   a. on *(date)* :   a. on *(date)* :
   b. name and address of joint debtor: b. name and address of joint debtor:

   c. ☐ additional costs against certain joint debtors *(itemize)* :

9. ☒ *(Writ of Possession or Writ of Sale)* **Judgment** was entered for the following:
   a. ☒ Possession of real property: The complaint was filed on *(date)* :   **(Check (1) or (2))**:
      (1) ☐ The Prejudgment Claim of Right to Possession was served in compliance with CCP 415.46.
             The judgment includes all tenants, subtenants, named claimants, and other occupants of the premises.
      (2) ☒ The Prejudgment Claim of Right to Possession was NOT served in compliance with CCP 415.46.
          (a) $26.00   was the daily rental value on the date the complaint was filed.
          (b) The court will hear objections to enforcement of the judgment under CCP 1174.3 on the following
             dates *(specify)* :
   b. ☐ Possession of personal property
      ☐ If delivery cannot be had, then for the value *(itemize in 9e)* specified in the judgment or supplemental order.
   c. ☐ Sale of personal property
   d. ☐ Sale of real property
   e. Description of property: 458 Sweet Street
                       Littletown, California 91111

— NOTICE TO PERSON SERVED —

WRIT OF EXECUTION OR SALE. Your rights and duties are indicated on the accompanying Notice of Levy.
WRIT OF POSSESSION OF PERSONAL PROPERTY. If the levying officer is not able to take custody of the property, the levying officer will make a demand upon you for the property. If custody is not obtained following demand, the judgment may be enforced as a money judgment for the value of the property specified in the judgment or in a supplemental order.
WRIT OF POSSESSION OF REAL PROPERTY. If the premises are not vacated within five days after the date of service on the occupant or, if service is by posting, within five days after service on you, the levying officer will remove the occupants from the real property and place the judgment creditor in possession of the property. Except for a mobilehome, personal property remaining on the premises will be sold or otherwise disposed of in accordance with CCP 1174 unless you or the owner of the property pays the judgment creditor the reasonable cost of storage and takes possession of the personal property not later than 15 days after the time the judgment creditor takes possession of the premises.
▶ *A Claim of Right to Possession form accompanies this writ (unless the Summons was served in compliance with CCP 415.46).*

---

* NOTE: Continued use of form EJ-130 (Rev. July 1, 1996) is authorized through December 31, 1997.

EJ-130 [Rev. January 1, 1997*]   **WRIT OF EXECUTION**   Page two

You will find a blank copy of this form in the FORMS section of this book and in Eviction Forms Creator.

to the triangular black pointers. Don't forget the one on the front side. Try to avoid getting writer's cramp when you're signing your name these four times. You won't qualify to receive worker's compensation if you do.

Sorry, you're not through yet. Look at the Judgment (Default-Unlawful Detainer) form shown here and try to identify similar elements in your own court's form. Fill yours out as best you can, but do not fill in any of the sums. The clerk will do that for you.

Next, you'll need to complete either an Application for Writ of Possession (see FORMS) or the Writ of Execution/Possession itself. Ask the clerk which form she wants you to complete. The two have such closely corresponding elements that we will assume that the clerk wants you to use the writ.

The writ should look pretty familiar to you by now. You already know how to fill in most of the upper third of the form. Go to it. In addition, check the box in the upper left-hand corner so you may record the writ. Check the "JUDG-MENT CREDITOR" box under your name, and check the "POSSESSION" and "REAL PROP-ERTY" boxes just above item 1 to indicate what specific type of writ this is. It's a "Writ of Possession of Real Property." Put your county's name in item 1. Put your name in item 3 and check the "Judgment creditor" box there. Put each judgment debtor's name and address separately under item 4, one per box (there's space for two more on the back). Skip item 5 for right now unless you know already when the judgment was entered. Skip item 6. Check 7a to show that you're not requesting any sale at this time. Skip item 8. Check item 9 to indicate that you have described your property on the back of the writ in item 9e. Skip item 10. That's all you can do on the front of the writ at this time. The rest has to wait until you get the actual judgment.

Now turn the writ over. The numbers on the back correspond to the numbers on the front. Complete the items on the back as appropriate. Be sure to check item 9 there, item 9a, and *either* 9a(1) *or* 9a(2), whichever one applies. Also, no matter which one you checked, 9a(1) or 9a(2), you must indicate in 9a(2)(a) the daily rental value, a figure you have probably committed to memory by now. Make sure you complete 9e, too; "description" here is merely the address of the property.

Step 9. (Alternative 2). Prepare Request, Judgment, and Writ.

If you're following alternative 2, make these *changes* in the request, judgment, and writ forms from the way they're shown here in the samples (see "very important" note on page 68): On the request, check the "CLERK'S JUDGMENT" box near the top rather than the "COURT JUDGMENT" box, check boxes 1e and 1e(1) rather than 1d, put nothing in section 2 and nothing in 6a through 6f; use a Judgment (Default) by Clerk form prepared by your judicial district; on the writ, omit the numbers on lines 11-18.

In addition, you may have to make up a simple application to use CCP §1169 or use a form prepared by your court for this purpose (ask the clerk); if you have to make one up, type the following on a piece of typing paper:

```
Court Clerk, [name & address of
the court]
    Due to continued occupancy of
resident defendant, I herewith
make application for you to enter
the default of [defendant's name]
and immediately enter judgment
for restitution of the premises
located at [address] and issue a
writ of execution.
    [Plaintiff's Signature]
```

Step 9. (Alternative 3). Prepare Request, Judgment, and Writ. (See caution on page 66.)

To follow the third alternative, prepare one set of these papers as outlined in step 9 (alternative 2) and prepare a second set to use for getting your money judgment *after* the tenants have been evicted (see note in Appendix B). When preparing the second set, make them exactly like the samples. You needn't change a thing.

Step 9. (Alternative 4). Prepare Request, Judgment, and Declaration.

Prepare the Request for Entry of Default and the judgment forms as shown in the samples (see "very important" note on page 68). Because you are proceeding under CCP §585.4, also known as §585(d), make sure that any relevant references

```
 1 | Lester Landlord & Leslie Landlord
   | 123 Neat Street
 2 | Littletown, California 91111
   | 415-123-4567
 3 | Plaintiff in Propria Persona

 4

 5

 6

 7

 8            IN THE MUNICIPAL COURT OF SADDLEBACK JUDICIAL DISTRICT,

 9               COUNTY OF SADDLEBACK, STATE OF CALIFORNIA

10 | LESTER LANDLORD
   | LESLIE LANDLORD
11 |                        Plaintiff,)      No. 1234567890
   |          vs.                     )
12 | RICHARD RENTER                   )      DECLARATION FOR
   | ROSE RENTER                      )      DEFAULT JUDGMENT IN
13 |                        Defendant.)      LIEU OF PERSONAL
   |_____  )      TESTIMONY (CCP 585.4)

14

15 |     I, _____Lester Landlord_____,

16 | declare that if sworn as a witness, I would testify competently

17 | within my personal knowledge to the following facts:

18 |     1.   That I am the plaintiff herein and the owner of the

19 | premises located at _____458 Sweet Street_____, in

20 | the City of _____Littletown_____, County of

21 | _____Saddleback_____, State of California.

22 |     2.   That on _____12/14/XX_____, prior to filing

23 | this action, the defendant rented said premises from me by

24 | _____written_____ agreement and agreed to pay the sum of

25 | $___700.00___ per month rental, payable in advance on the

26 | ___first___ day of each and every calendar month thereafter,

27 | current per month rental value being the sum of $_780.00_____ or

28
```

1

You will find a blank copy of this form in the FORMS section of this book and in Eviction Forms Creator.

1 $ ___26.00___ per day.

2   3. That by virtue of said agreement, defendant went into

3 possession of said premises and still continues to hold and

4 occupy same.

5   4. That on _____9/12/XX_____, I caused the

6 defendant to be served with a written notice stating the amount

7 of rent due and requiring payment thereof or possession of the

8 premises within three days after service of the notice.

9   5. That when at least three days had elapsed after service

10 of said notice on defendant and no part of said rent had been

11 paid, I caused the defendant to be served with a Summons and

12 Complaint on _____9/16/XX_____.

13   WHEREFORE, I pray that this Court render a judgment by

14 default against the defendants for restitution of said premises,

15 for costs of $___105.00___, for past due rent of $___730.00___, for

16 damages at the rate of $___26.00___ per day, and for forfeiture

17 of the agreement.

18   I declare under penalty of perjury that the foregoing is

19 true and correct.

20   Executed on ___9/23/XX___, at City of ___Littletown___,

21 County of _____Saddleback_____, State of California.

22

23

24

25   *Lester Landlord*
                        _____
                           (Signature)

26

27   Lester Landlord
                        _____
                            (Name)

28

efc

are checked. If you wonder whether you ought to check a particular box, especially on the judgment form your court uses, ask the court clerk. You must also prepare a Declaration for Default Judgment in Lieu of Personal Testimony. In the declaration, you restate your case much as you first stated it in the complaint, testifying in writing to what you would have testified in court had you made a personal appearance, and you sign your name to this statement under penalty of perjury. You may use the form given here by filling in the blanks as appropriate or you may make one up using this form as a guide. If you have to devise your own, remember to use pleading paper; that's the paper with numbers and a line down the left side. Put the heading for your declaration on the same lines which are used for that purpose on the sample.

Step 9B (Alternatives 1, 2, 3, & 4). If Asked to Do So by the Court Clerk, Prepare and Submit a Declaration of Plaintiff in Support of Writ of Possession.

If there is any discrepancy between the daily rental value as given on the complaint (at item 10) and again on the Writ of Execution (at item 9a.[2a]), you may be asked to complete a Declaration of Plaintiff in Support of Writ of Possession. This is nothing more than a statement of the daily rental value. There is no form for it as such, and I have not included one here because it is so simple and because you likely will never need one. On the off-chance that you might need one, however, here's what you do.

Make a copy of the blank pleading paper in the FORMS section, and type everything on the first fourteen lines to correspond to the declaration shown on page 75, except that instead of typing "DECLARATION FOR DEFAULT JUDGMENT IN LIEU OF PERSONAL TESTIMONY," type "DECLARATION OF PLAINTIFF IN SUPPORT OF WRIT OF POSSESSION."

Then, beginning on line 15, type the following (double-spaced, of course):

```
PLAINTIFF declares as follows:
    The daily rental value on the
date the complaint for unlawful
detainer was filed was $_____.
```

```
    I declare under penalty of per-
jury that the foregoing is true
and correct.
    Executed on _____ at
_____, California.
    [Plaintiff's Signature]
```

Step 10 (Alternatives 1, 2, 3, & 4). Mail Request to Tenant.

Mail one copy of the Request for Entry of Default to the tenant. It need only be mailed before the original is entered by the clerk; it need not be received by the tenant before you can proceed further.

Step 11 (Alternative 1). Prove Summons Service; File Request.

Whether or not you are able to get into court on the sixth day following service of the summons and complaint, bring the request, and Proof of Service of summons, with you to the courthouse. Show the clerk the back of the summons where the process server has indicated that your summons and complaint have been served. If it indicates that at least five days have passed since service on the defendants, your case will be listed on an upcoming docket calendar. The clerk will also ask you for the Request for Entry of Default. Having surrendered it, you are ready for your day in court, whenever it is.

Step 11 (Alternatives 2 & 3). Prove Service of 3-Day Notice and Summons; File Request, Judgment, and Writ.

Bring the request, judgment, writ, and written application (if required), as well as the Proof of Service of Summons and the 3-day notice, with you to the courthouse. Tell the clerk that you want a quickie eviction per CCP §1169; also tell her whether you want to go to court later for a money judgment. She'll scrutinize your papers with a well-trained eye and tell you whether everything's in order. She'll be looking for consistency primarily. Are all your dates and money amounts correct throughout the paperwork? Is everything legible? If it is, she may make the necessary entries in her books and give you the writ right then and there, or she may ask you to return later. Some clerks are so accommodating that they will let you leave with them a check for the sheriff or marshal and some simple instructions to him to evict your tenant (pick up the proper form from the sheriff or marshal's office or use the one in the FORMS section for this purpose); in that case, you won't have to return at all; the clerk will see that the papers are passed along.

Step 11 (Alternative 4). Prove Summons Service; File Request; Give Clerk Request, Judgment, and Declaration.

Gather up your papers and take them with you to the courthouse. Tell the clerk that you want to transfer the file to the judge, and show her that you have complied with the requirements regarding service of the summons and complaint, that you have waited five days, and that you have completed a Declaration for Default Judgment in Lieu of Personal Testimony. Give her the Request, the Judgment, and the declaration. Also, be sure you give her a copy of the rental agreement and the notice if you elected to omit them from the complaint as exhibits. The judge may want to see them to determine the merits of your case.

To get some idea how long the judge will take to examine your case and render judgment, ask when you might expect to hear from him and when you should call back if you fail to hear anything.

Step 12 (Alternatives 1 & 3B). Appear in Court.

Bring the proper judgment form and the writ with you to court, together with anything pertinent from your tenant files on this particular tenant, especially the rental agreement and the notice if you didn't attach them to the complaint. Arrive at least ten minutes before your court time. Generally, the courtroom clerk arrives early to see who is ready to appear, and you may approach her to indicate that you have the proper judgment form partially filled out and would like to have it completed as soon as the judge renders the verdict, so you can proceed with the eviction. The courtroom clerk will usually take the judgment form from you because she will otherwise have to do the whole thing herself, and you can then take a seat to wait for your case to come up.

Now you are in for a surprise, one of the few pleasant surprises that landlords and landladies can ever expect in this whole distasteful process. Unlawful detainers, praise some solon or other, are heard first, before all those other civil cases. You won't have to spend hours in court listening to Mabel and Clarence argue over custody of the family cow; you won't even have to hear the ribald details of how the housewife thought she was paying the plumber with her charms, that is, until she got his bill and learned that she was being charged not only for travel time and work time but for the entire time he was there as well. Evictions take precedence over other civil cases. They are entitled to what the legal world calls "summary proceedings."

When your case comes up, the judge will call you forward and you will have to repeat after the court clerk that you swear to tell no lies. During the oath, the judge will be reading your complaint. Then he will ask you whatever questions come to mind. He may ask to see the rental agreement and notice if they weren't attached to the complaint as exhibits; he may ask you why you're praying for such a big judgment; or he may ask what period of time is covered by the sum of money demanded in your complaint. Be prepared to provide him with this information if he should ask for it. Know exactly how much is owed as of the date you are in court and also as of the date when you can reasonably expect the eviction to be carried out, which is usually six days hence. Consult calendar 3 at the end of this chapter.

Step 12 (Alternatives 2 & 3A). Skip to Step 15.

Proceed directly to Step 15; lucky you, no appearing in court and no waiting!

Step 12 (Alternative 4). Wait.

By completing your declaration and transferring it to the judge, you have already done the equivalent of appearing in court. Now you'll just have to wait for the judge to reply with the judgment. If you don't like waiting, use another alternative and you'll undoubtedly complete everything a little more quickly.

Step 13 (Alternatives 1 & 3B). Get the Judgment.

The judge will consider for a moment and then

indicate the amount of judgment granted. Thank him and go to the court clerk's table in the courtroom to pick up your completed judgment form.

Step 13 (Alternative 4). Get the Judgment.

The court will send you the judgment by mail. If it doesn't arrive by the time the court clerk told you to expect it, call the clerk and ask about it. Tell her you haven't received it yet, and ask her whether you may come down to the courthouse and pick up a copy so you can proceed with your unlawful detainer.

Step 14 (Alternatives 1 & 3B). Fill in and File the Writ.

Your sweating's over, but don't go home yet. You still have a few things to do. Find a flat spot where you can do a little typing; get out the writs which you've already partially filled out, carbon paper (make two copies), and your portable Smith-Corona.

In item 5 of the writ, put the date when the judgment was entered. Put the dollar amount of the judgment which was awarded to you by the court in item 11. In item 12, put the sheriff or marshal's fee for posting the Writ of Possession and the Notice to Vacate, as well as for actually evicting the tenant. Add items 11 and 12 on line 13. In item 14, put any credits not already reflected in the judgment; and on line 15, subtract those credits from line 13. Skip line 16 unless you are filing a claim for interest by affidavit. In item 17, include the fee for issuing the writ. Total lines 15, 16, and 17 on line 18. The legal rate of interest for judgments is 10%. Multiply 10% times line 15, and divide by 365 to get the daily interest owed to you on your judgment. Put that in item 19a. Put nothing in item 19b; it's for the court to use to collect costs waived initially for public agencies and indigents. Check box 20 only if there's a difference in the amounts owed to you by each of your debtors and attach an explanation if there is. Date the writ in the "Issued on (date)" box. Now turn the writ over. If you haven't done so already, put your short title and case number at the top; check boxes 9 and 9a; give the date when the complaint was filed; check either box 9a(1) or 9a(2) as appropriate, and state the daily rental value in 9a(2)(a). In 9e, if you haven't done so already, put the street address,

unit number, city, state, and zip code. That's it! That's all!

Take the judgment and the writ to the clerk's office and pay the fee to file the writ. Ask the clerk to check your figures. If any of your figures are wrong, use the correction fluid in your lay lawyer's kit to mask the errors and then make the corrections.

Step 14 (Alternative 4). Fill in and File the Writ.

Once you have received the judgment, you'll have to fill out a Writ of Execution so the sheriff or marshal can act. Fill it out following the directions for alternative 1 above. Take it to the court and file it. Then proceed to follow the remaining steps the same as you would have had you appeared in court personally.

Step 15. Set the Eviction and Arrange Service of the Notice to Vacate.

You have now completed all the court-related work to regain possession of your rental property, but you must do one more thing to carry out the judgment. You must see the sheriff or marshal and give him the authority (that's just what the writ is) to take over your property, evict the inhabitants, and return the property to you. Naturally, you pay for this service, but it's well worth the fee, and it's chargeable to the tenants on the writ, for whatever that may be worth to you.

Visit the sheriff or marshal's office soon after you leave the clerk's office, and hand over the Writ of Execution original as well as your copies. Normally the deputy will hand you a simple form which lists your instructions to the sheriff or marshal, but you probably won't have to fill the whole thing out. A signature and some verbal instructions are usually sufficient to get the eviction set.

At last you're through! Hopefully, your court appointment was for 9 a.m., and you should now be at this point by 9:30. After what you've been through, since it's hardly martini time, you can decently celebrate at the corner watering hole with a midmorning screwdriver. Light up a big black cigar, too, an expensive one the likes of which you couldn't afford when your first child was born. You've earned it.

Step 16. Serve the Notice to Vacate.

The sheriff or marshal should be able to serve and/or post the Writ of Possession and the Notice to Vacate the very same day. At the same time he also leaves a copy of the form, Claim of Right to Possession and Notice of Hearing (more on it in a moment). He will set the eviction date and time, most likely six days later, and he will tell you that you'll have to appear at the designated time fully prepared to change the locks on the eviction. In some areas the sheriff or marshal appears automatically on the day set for the eviction, and in other areas he waits for some word from you. Ask what the practice is in your area and do what you must do to get him there.

Step 17. Evict the Tenant.

• THE RECKONING—If your tenants or their possessions are still there when you and the sheriff or marshal arrive, they will be put out bodily, if necessary, and the unit will be posted with an impressive-looking notice (see the front

the doors after the tenants have been evicted and the place has been posted. According to CCP §715.040, if the sheriff or marshal doesn't serve the Writ of Possession within three normal business days (excluding weekends and legal holidays) after it's turned over to him, you may retrieve it and have it served by a registered process server.

What tenants usually do once they have seen the handwriting on the door is simply move out. Some of the more contrary ones, however, will stay until the very last possible moment and even past it, always testing the limits.

Keep track of your tenant's movements if you can, so you can notify the sheriff or marshal if the tenant does move out before the time set for cover of this book) saying that it has been returned to your possession and that the tenants may not go inside without your permission. If they do, they will be subject to arrest.

While the sheriff or marshal is posting this notice, you should be changing the locks unless you have any reason to believe that the tenant might break into the place to recover his possessions after you change the locks. In that case, refrain from changing them now. Don't risk broken windows or a broken door just to keep the tenant's possessions. They can't be worth that much. Let him come and get them. Remember that the sheriff or marshal isn't going to remain there guarding your place simply because you have regained full rights to it, and remember that you can always call upon the police to remove the tenant if he tries any funny business after this.

Once the sheriff or marshal posts that notice and escorts the tenant off the premises, your civil action is at an end. His returning to the property after that becomes a criminal matter.

• CLAIM OF RIGHT TO POSSESSION— As mentioned previously, the California Supreme Court's poorly conceived decision in the Arrieta case prevents the sheriff or marshal from evicting any adult who isn't named in the writ and who claims a right to possession on the date you started your unlawful detainer action *unless* you elected to use the prejudgment claim procedure when you served the summons and complaint. Ordinarily, tenants first learn of their "Arrieta rights" when the sheriff or marshal gives them a blank copy of the Claim of Right to Possession and Notice of Hearing form (you don't provide this form; the sheriff or marshal does) at the same time he is serving them with the Writ of Possession and the Notice to Vacate (Step 16).

To some wily tenants this presents still another opportunity to take advantage of the system and remain right where they are at your expense, and there's nothing you can do about it legally. Neither arguing with the tenants nor hollering at the evicting officer will do any good.

If somebody claims to be a "nonparty occupant," that is, a person occupying the premises who was not a party to the unlawful detainer suit, he has every right to make a claim. He does have to make a formal written claim, however. He can't just sweet-talk the evicting officer and thumb his nose at you.

Here's how the claim procedure works (CCP §715.010 and §1174.3), and here's what you and the claimant do.

The claimant has to complete the claim form and bring it to the court or to the sheriff or marshal's office or, at the very least, present it to the evicting officer on the day set for the eviction. Within 48 hours, the claimant must then submit a filing fee to the court (just as you did when you first filed your complaint) or a *forma pauperis* (a sworn statement that he is too poor to pay the fee) *and* pay the court the equivalent of fifteen days rent. If the court receives all this, the clerk files the claim and sets a hearing not less than five days nor more than fifteen days later.

If the claimant submits nothing to the court within 48 hours of his having presented the claim, the court denies the claim automatically and orders the sheriff or marshal to evict all occupants within five days.

If the claimant submits the filing fee or the *forma pauperis* but not the equivalent of fifteen days rent, the hearing is set on the fifth day following the filing. In either case, the court will notify you of the hearing date. Because time is short, a clerk will usually send you a notice and phone you.

You must, of course, appear at the hearing prepared to prove that the claimant is a liar and not a nonparty occupant, and the claimant must be there to prove that he is telling the truth. If the court denies the claim (95% are denied), it orders the sheriff or marshal to evict all occupants within five days. If the court grants the claim, it then considers your summons and complaint to have been amended to include the claimant as a defendant, and it also considers the claimant to have been served with the notice which started the action, as well as with the summons and complaint. You don't have to do anything but wait. The claimant then has the usual five days in which to file an answer.

If the claimant fails to file an answer, you must prepare and file a Request for Entry of Default, a Judgment by Default, and a Writ of Execution (Steps 9-11), and then continue through Step 17. When preparing these papers, merely add the claimant's name to those of the other defendants even though the other defendants have already been eliminated. If the tenant does file an answer, you must request a trial and handle the matter as outlined in chapter 10.

By the way, the fifteen days of rent money which the claimant paid to the court goes back to the tenant if the claim is granted; if it is not granted, you will receive that portion of the money which covers the days during which the eviction was delayed, and the tenant gets the rest.

Whereas tenants have little to lose by pressing an Arrieta claim, you have a lot to lose. Just remember, though, that you don't have *every*thing to lose in this situation. It is aggravating. It is going to take more of your time and cost you more money in added fees and lost rent. That's for sure. But it's not the end of the world. Don't get discouraged. Don't even think of taking the law into your own hands. Be patient. Let the process run its course.

When it has run its course, write your state legislators about what you've been through. Explain the unfairness of Arrieta claims and suggest alternatives. What our legislators have come up with so far, the Prejudgment Claim of Right to Possession procedure, is a beginning, but it needs improving. For starters, the prejudgment procedure should allow five rather than ten days for a claimant to file, and it should require that the filing of the claim and the response to the summons and complaint be handled concurrently, not sequentially. Isn't that fair? Sure it's fair. It treats the non-named resident the same as a named resident, and it doesn't penalize those landlords who elect to use the prejudgment procedure by adding ten days to their unlawful detainer. Isn't an unlawful detainer supposed to be a summary action?

• LESSON—A final eviction notice on one door of an apartment building serves as a convincing lesson to other tenants that you know how to evict and that you will evict when necessary. Leave the notice on the door long enough for at least one other tenant to see it and then remove it yourself. The word will spread quickly. Don't leave the notice up longer than an afternoon, however, because you don't want other owners in the area to see it. They will wonder what's wrong with your building and will depreciate its value in their minds.

The final eviction notice on the door of a single-family dwelling should be removed as soon as the tenant's belongings are cleared out. It serves no useful purpose after that.

• COLLECTING YOUR MONEY JUDGMENT—See chapter 13.

• DISPOSING OF THE REMAINS—See chapter 14.

• FULFILLING ONE VERY IMPORTANT FINAL OBLIGATION—Whenever a tenant moves out, you have a legal obligation to return his entire deposit or provide a written accounting of what you did with it. If you fail to do so within twenty-one days, your tenant has every right to sue you for the deposit and for damages. Your having evicted the tenant does *not* relieve you of this obligation.

The tenant may have trashed your place when you evicted him, and the damages may have cost you a bundle to repair, much more than he ever gave you as a deposit, and you might think, quite naturally, that under these circumstances you shouldn't have to give him a written accounting at all. Wrong! Wrong! Wrong!

The law says that you must give an accounting of deposits to *every* tenant who vacates. "Every tenant" means every tenant, not just the ones you owe money to, not just the ones whose forwarding addresses you have available, not just the ones you hate to lose. Every tenant means the good ones, the bad ones, and the uglies.

Some landlords overlook this obligation because they can't understand why they should have to take the time to account for monies which they have no hope of recovering anyway. Such is the case most of the time, I'll grant you. But a law is a law, and you should comply with this law even when a tenant's departure is the result of an eviction.

Besides, when a tenant moves out and owes you money for damages, this accounting should serve as your itemized bill for what the tenant owes. You should be able to take this bill into small claims court and get a judgment against the tenant. If you haven't provided the tenant with an accounting as required by law, you cannot possibly win a small claims action to recover damages.

One landlord I know failed to give an accounting of deposits to an evicted tenant within twenty-one days because he couldn't assess all the damages within that period of time. When he finally did assess all the damages, he took the cosigner to small claims court. He produced evidence consisting of photos, documents, witnesses, and bills. His was an open-and-shut case, a sure thing, or so he thought. Then the cosigner told the judge that because the landlord had failed to provide a full accounting of the tenant's deposits as required by law within twenty-one days after the tenant vacated, the cosigner shouldn't have to pay a thing. The judge agreed with the cosigner. The landlord got nothing.

The twenty-one-day limitation is crucial in providing the accounting. Don't delay beyond the twenty-one days. If you can't complete the repairs within twenty-one days, make a reasonable estimate of what the costs should turn out to be and send the accounting off to the tenant. You can always quibble about the costs later if they become an issue.

Once you have prepared the accounting, send one copy to the tenant at his last known address, which may be the place you've evicted him from,

ATTORNEY OR PARTY WITHOUT ATTORNEY *(Name and Address):*	TELEPHONE NO.:	FOR COURT USE ONLY

Lester Landlord & Leslie Landlord   415-123-4567
123 Neat Street
Littletown, California 91111

ATTORNEY FOR *(Name):* Plaintiff in Propria Persona

Insert name of court and name of judicial district and branch court, if any:

Saddleback Municipal Court
Littletown Judicial District, Bay Branch

PLAINTIFF/PETITIONER: Lester Landlord
           Leslie Landlord

DEFENDANT/RESPONDENT: Richard Renter, Rose Renter

REQUEST FOR DISMISSAL

☐ **Personal Injury, Property Damage, or Wrongful Death**
     ☐ **Motor Vehicle** ☐ **Other**
☐ **Family Law**
☐ **Eminent Domain**
☒ **Other** *(specify):* Unlawful Detainer

CASE NUMBER:
1234567890

— A conformed copy will not be returned by the clerk unless a method of return is provided with the document. —

1. **TO THE CLERK: Please dismiss this action as follows:**

   a. (1) ☐ With prejudice   (2) ☒ Without prejudice

   b. (1) ☒ Complaint   (2) ☐ Petition
       (3) ☐ Cross-complaint filed by *(name):*   on *(date):*
       (4) ☐ Cross-complaint filed by *(name):*   on *(date):*
       (5) ☐ Entire action of all parties and all causes of action
       (6) ☐ Other *(specify)* :*

Date: 10/15/XX

Lester Landlord
....
(TYPE OR PRINT NAME OF ☐ ATTORNEY ☒ PARTY WITHOUT ATTORNEY)

* If dismissal requested is of specified parties only, of specified causes of action only, or of specified cross-complaints only, so state and identify the parties, causes of action, or cross-complaints to be dismissed.

▶ *Lester Landlord*
                (SIGNATURE)
Attorney or party without attorney for:
☒ Plaintiff/Petitioner   ☐ Defendant/Respondent
☐ Cross-complainant

2. **TO THE CLERK: Consent to the above dismissal is hereby given.****

Date: 10/15/XX

Lester Landlord
....
(TYPE OR PRINT NAME OF ☐ ATTORNEY ☒ PARTY WITHOUT ATTORNEY)

** If a cross-complaint—or Response (Family Law) seeking affirmative relief—is on file, the attorney for cross-complainant (respondent) must sign this consent if required by Code of Civil Procedure section 581(i) or (j).

▶ *Lester Landlord*
                (SIGNATURE)
Attorney or party without attorney for:
☒ Plaintiff/Petitioner   ☐ Defendant/Respondent
☐ Cross-complainant

(To be completed by clerk)

3. ☐ Dismissal entered as requested on *(date):*
4. ☐ Dismissal entered on *(date):*   as to only *(name):*
5. ☐ Dismissal **not entered** as requested for the following reasons *(specify):*

6. ☐ a. Attorney or party without attorney notified on *(date):*
       b. Attorney or party without attorney not notified. Filing party failed to provide
          ☐ a copy to conform   ☐ means to return conformed copy

Date: _____   Clerk, by _____, Deputy

Form Adopted by the
Judicial Council of California
982 (a)(5) [Rev. January 1, 1997]

REQUEST FOR DISMISSAL

Code of Civil Procedure, § 581 et seq.
Cal. Rules of Court, rules 383, 1233

You will find a blank copy of this form in the FORMS section of this book and in Eviction Forms Creator.

and keep one copy for your files.

Dismissal

Every so often tenants will vacate shortly after you file the summons and complaint, that is, before you've had a chance to request a default judgment. What you do next will depend upon whether they still owe you any money after you deduct what they owe you from their deposits.

If they owe you any money, you should forge ahead and get the default judgment so you'll have some legal entitlement to this money and can try to collect it in the future or at the very least ding their credit. If they wind up owing you nothing, you should file a Request for Dismissal form to advise the court that it can close its books on the case.

Fill out the request as shown. Note that you have the option of dismissing with or without prejudice. You should dismiss "without prejudice." If you dismiss "with prejudice," you cannot file another complaint based on the same facts as the dismissed complaint. If you dismiss "without prejudice," you are free to file another complaint later based upon the same facts. Don't limit yourself. You never can tell what might happen when you're dealing with wily tenants.

Settlement Before Judgment

See chapter 10 for a discussion of "Settlement Before Trial." That discussion concerns how you might settle with your tenant after he files an answer to your complaint and before you go to trial.

What should you do if your tenant hasn't filed an answer to your complaint and he approaches you with an offer to settle before you get the default judgment?

First, listen to everything the tenant has to say. In filing an unlawful detainer lawsuit against him, you might just have awakened him out of his complacency, and he might now be ready to agree to terms which meant little to him before.

Second, understand that you and your tenant might each have something to gain by settling now. You might get everything or almost everything you wanted in the first place, and your tenant might get to stay right where he is without having to deal with a money judgment on his credit record.

Third, agree to nothing unless it is in writing and signed by both of you.

The settlement you reach may be expressed as an ordinary written agreement in plain English or as a Stipulation for Entry of Judgment, which may or may not be filed with the court (see chapter 10). A filed stipulation is better for you. It's "official."

If your tenant fails to comply with your settlement and you have a stipulated agreement, you don't have to go back into court to get him evicted. You can get the judgment and writ immediately and have him evicted in short order.

If your tenant fails to comply with your settlement and you have a plain English agreement, you will have to go into court to get a judgment, and then you may find that you cannot get a judgment because you have accepted partial payments. You may have to start all over again.

Whereas you should consider initiating an effort to settle when a tenant answers your complaint, you should not initiate an effort to settle when a tenant has failed to answer. Let your tenant do it. In filing the summons and complaint, you have already fired a salvo at your tenant. Now it's his turn to respond. If you initiate an effort to settle, you may hurt yourself in two ways—1) by appearing too eager and thereby diminishing your bargaining position and 2) by calling his attention to the whole unlawful detainer matter and thereby increasing the likelihood that he will answer the complaint. Play your hand right.

If you do settle amicably with the tenant, file a Request for Dismissal.

- Study the entire eviction procedure carefully.
- Proceed with each step cautiously.
- Fill out each required form painstakingly.
- Observe the time restraints attentively.
- Pursue the eviction relentlessly.
- When the smoke clears, fulfill your obligations religiously.

AN UNCONTESTED UNLAWFUL DETAINER FOR
NONPAYMENT OF RENT
(Step-by-Step Procedure, Alternative 1)

Step	Person	Place	Time
1. Prepare 3-Day Notice	You	Home	Anytime
2. Serve 3-Day Notice	You or third party	Tenant's dwelling or place of business	Same day as step 1
3. Prepare Summons and Complaint	You	Home	Late on 3d day after step 2
4. File Summons and Complaint	You	Court clerk's office	Early on 4th day after step 2*
5. Arrange service of Summons and Complaint	You	Sheriff or marshal's office	Same as step 4
6. Serve Summons and Complaint	Process server	Tenant's dwelling or place of business	Same day as step 4
7. Inquire about a response	You	Home (by phone to court clerk's office)	Late on 5th day after step 6
8. Set court hearing time	You	Home (by phone to court clerk's office)	Same day as step 7
9. Prepare Request, Judgment, and Writ	You	Home	Same day as step 7
10. Mail Request to tenant	You	Mailbox	Same day as step 7
11. Prove Summons service; give clerk Request	You	Court clerk's office	Early on day after step 7
12. Appear in court	You	Courtroom	Same as step 11
13. Get Judgment	You	Courtroom	Same as step 11
14. Fill out and file Writ	You	Court clerk's office	Same as step 11
15. Set eviction date with sheriff or marshal; arrange service of Notice to Vacate	You	Sheriff or marshal's office	Same as step 11
16. Serve Notice to Vacate	Sheriff	Tenant's dwelling or marshal	Same as step 11
17. Evict tenant	Sheriff	Tenant's dwelling or marshal and you	6th day after step 16

*The third day following service of a 3-Day Notice to Pay Rent or Quit must be a "business day," that is, neither a weekend day nor a holiday. If it is not a business day, you must give the tenant a business day to pay before you file the Summons and Complaint.

Calendars for Determining the Important Days in an Uncontested Unlawful Detainer Which Begins with a 3-Day Notice to Pay Rent or Quit (Best Case)

Instructions

Find the day of the week when you served the 3-Day Notice to Pay Rent or Quit, and note the number which appears next to the "N." For Tuesday in calendar 1, it's a 3 (outlined and enlarged for easy identification). Then look for the next time a 3 appears. It's on Monday of the next week, and there's an "S" by it (it's outlined and enlarged, too). Being where it is, this "S3" means that if you serve a 3-Day Notice to Pay Rent or Quit on a Tuesday, you cannot file the Summons and Complaint until the following Monday. If you do file the Summons and Complaint on that Monday and have the tenant served the very same day, then the earliest you can get into court is on the following Tuesday, which is where the next 3 appears. It's by a "J" this time. If you go to court that day and you take care of all the paperwork afterward, including arranging with the sheriff or marshal for service of the Notice to Vacate, then the eviction will be set when the last 3 appears. It's by an "E," and it's on the following Monday. All together, then, the eviction will be completed on the twentieth day after the Tuesday when you served the 3-Day Notice to Pay Rent or Quit.

Now try following the 2's on calendar 1 to see what advantage there is in serving the notice on Monday. You save a few days, don't you?

This first calendar should help you visualize the relationship of all the important days in an unlawful detainer action so long as everything goes according to schedule and there are no delays. You won't often be able to evict a tenant in a total of sixteen days from service of the 3-Day Notice to Pay Rent or Quit to the actual eviction, but you *can*. I know. I've done it. It does take some cooperation from the court clerk and some good luck. That I'll admit. But it can be done.

Do remember when you're thinking about the timetable for a nonpayment-of-rent eviction that the third day after service of the notice must be a business day. It may not be a weekend day or a holiday. If the third day falls on a Saturday, for example, you must give the tenant through the following Monday to pay up. You must not file your Summons and Complaint until Tuesday. If the third day falls on a Friday, though, you may file your Summons and Complaint on the following Monday.

Refer to calendar 2 if, for some reason, there is a delay in the procedure. For example, if the process server tried to serve the tenant with the Summons and Complaint on Monday but couldn't do it until Thursday, switch from calendar 1 to calendar 2 and follow the 5's to see what the next important days are. The court day would be the following Wednesday, and the eviction day would be the Tuesday after that.

Refer to calendar 3 if there is a delay in getting the Writ of Execution to the sheriff or marshal after the court hearing. If the writ is issued on Wednesday (J3), but you can't get it to the sheriff or marshal until Thursday (J4), follow the 4's, and you'll see that the eviction will be set for the following Wednesday. Simple, eh?

1. Calendar for Determining Summons Days, Judgment Days, and Evictions According to Notice Days

Sun	Mon	Tues	Wed	Thurs	Fri	Sat
N1	N2	**N3**	N4	N5; S1	N6; S2	N7
N8	`N9; **S3**	S4-6	S7; J1	S8; J2	S9	○
○	○	**J3**-7; E1	J8; E2	J9	○	○
○	**E3**-7	E8	E9	○	○	○

Abbreviations:
N = *Day of service of 3-Day Notice to Pay Rent or Quit*
S = *Day of service of Summons and Complaint*
J = *Judgment day (Judgment [Default] entered; Writ of Execution issued)*
E = *Day set for the eviction*

Summons days on this calendar assume that the filing and service of the Summons and Complaint occur on the same day. You cannot, of course, file on either Saturday or Sunday although you may serve the Summons and Complaint on weekends. If service is completed on a weekend day, see Calendar 2 for the followup.

If you want to complete an unlawful detainer in the shortest possible time, you will find that Sunday (here represented by N1) and Monday (here represented by N2) are the best days for serving a 3-Day Notice to Pay Rent or Quit, and Tuesday (N3) and Wednesday (N4) are the worst days. Don't wait for a Sunday or a Monday to come around just because they're the best, though. Serve the notice any day you're ready to, because there may be some delays in the process somewhere, and the earlier you serve it, the better off you'll be. Even though Tuesday (N3) through Saturday (N7) are poor notice days when compared with the previous Sunday (N1) and Monday (N2), they still wind up with a one-day advantage in this whole stream-lined eviction process over the following Sunday (N8) and Monday (N9). Don't delay the eviction by even one single day!

2. Calendar for Determining Judgment Days and Evictions According to Summons Days

Sun	Mon	Tues	Wed	Thurs	Fri	Sat
S1	S2	S3	S4	**S5**	S6	S7
○	J1	J2-4	**J5**	J6	J7	○
○	E1-4	**E5**	E6	E7	○	○

Sheriffs and marshals do not serve Summons and Complaints on Saturday or Sunday, but private process servers do, so all seven days of the week are included here. Naturally, you may file the Summons and Complaint only on a business day when the courts are open.

3. Calendar for Determining Evictions According to Judgment Days

Sun	Mon	Tues	Wed	Thurs	Fri	Sat
○	J1	J2	J3	**J4**	J5	○
○	E1,2	E3	**E4**	E5	○	○

Please note that all evictions are set by the sheriff or marshal as soon as you bring him the Writ of Execution. If you do so early in the day, he may be able to post the writ and the Notice to Vacate that very same day, and the tenant will then be evicted within the timeframe indicated on all three calendars. Otherwise, the eviction will be delayed. A Monday court day, as the calendar above shows, is the one exception. Since evictions are set the same for both Monday and Tuesday judgment days, bringing the writ to the sheriff or marshal late Monday won't make any difference.

6
Handling an Eviction for Breach of Contract

Your tenant in Apartment 6 has had a noisy party every night for the last four nights, and all the neighbors are on the warpath, complaining to you every chance they get and urging you to get rid of him right away; you can't even watch the nightly news without some tenant's telephoning to complain and inform you of more pressing news on the local scene. Or your tenant in that little bungalow on Bissell has just acquired an Irish Setter from a friend who's dying of AIDS, and he has resisted your every reasonable request to get rid of the dog, which is specifically forbidden in the rental agreement. Or your tenant in that sunny studio now has three people living with her who aren't listed on the rental agreement, and she has as much as told you that they're all staying because she needs them to help her pay the rent.

What are you going to do about these problems, landlord? You have to do something. You can't expect them to cease if you overlook them. They will only get worse. If you don't get that noisy tenant out, all of your good tenants are going to be leaving. If you don't get rid of the one tenant who has the dog, you're going to find that a second and a third tenant will be acquiring pets of their own without ever consulting you. Let that mass of humanity stay in the one-room dwelling you rented to a single woman, and you will be paying considerably higher maintenance costs.

Before your building empties or deteriorates, you are going to have to do something about these problems, each of which is known in legal circles as a breach of contract and can be dealt with legally through the courts. "Breach of contract" means simply that the tenant is breaking the agreement outlining those terms which the two of you agreed would govern your relationship when it all began.

Other breach-of-contract evictions might be for installing a wood-burning stove, painting the walls without your permission, working on cars at all hours, cluttering the yard, denying you access to inspect or work on the premises, changing the locks, subletting to others, or anything else which was legitimately prohibited in the agreement.

As you might imagine, breaches of contract involve interpretations and misunderstandings, and they generally involve some personality conflicts and hard feelings, too. The landlord wants to maintain some semblance of order on the premises while the tenants naturally want to exercise their independence by testing the rules and doing as they please. These situations are different from those as clear-cut as nonpayment of rent, unlawful acts, or failure to vacate. Consequently, many landlords will forego the quicker dispatch of an unlawful detainer for breach of contract because it will sometimes cause protracted and costly complications in court, and they will seek to evict their breachers by using a 30-Day Notice to Terminate Tenancy instead. This tactic enables the tenant to save face. He doesn't feel obligated to marshal his forces to fight the eviction. He has more time to think things over, understand that he can't continue living where he is, and find another place. So, he usually just leaves.

Because evictions for failure to vacate, which are explained in chapter 8, have become subject to certain limitations in those localities with rent control (see chapter 4), you may no longer have the choice. You may have to evict for breach of contract, knowing full well that such an action may precipitate opposition every step of the way. Don't despair. Do it and get the breacher out. You'll have little peace from the other tenants until you do.

You should know that an unlawful detainer action for breach of contract will involve your having to prove that the tenant is, in fact, breaching the contract, and you would be wise to gather as much evidence as you can to support your case later on. It will likely be needed. This evidence may be a sound recording, a videotape recording, a photograph, or the testimony of witnesses. Gather the evidence openly if you can. If possible, try to be seen in the act of speaking into the microphone of your cassette recorder: "This recording is being made at 11:32 p.m. on the 12th of April outside the front door of 1128 Sutter Street, Apartment 6, residence of Tom

era and snap away when you think you might arouse the interest of the offending tenant. Tell him what you are doing and why. You might find that the tenant will be more cooperative after that, and then again he might not be. Even if your evidence-gathering activity does not serve to intimidate the tenant into mending his ways, you still have great evidence to introduce in court. Judges love to see things such as pictures and tapes entered into evidence and generally give great credence to them.

We're supposing here that you have already tried to handle the matter with either a direct approach or a well-calculated psychological ap-

Twit, to be kept as evidence of the noise level which his neighbors have been complaining about, noise disturbing to the general peace and quiet." Then hold up the microphone ostentatiously. Perhaps you might even knock on the door and mock-innocently inform the occupants that you are taping the noise as evidence for the court case you are preparing. They will respond much differently to that approach, I can assure you, than they would if you were there all by yourself without your electronic monitoring equipment.

If it's a messy yard or the presence of a pet which constitutes the breach, get out your cam-

proach or both. If you haven't tried these approaches fully yet, go back to chapter 2 and mine it for any ideas pertinent to your situation. Try them first.

Whatever you do, do not set up your own amplifier and blast the noisemakers with Beatles or Bach. Do not poison the dog. Do not go for your six-shooters. Use your head. Don't get angry yourself, and don't get your tenants angry. Keep cool. Understand what you want and what they want, and try to come to some compromise that suits all of you. Be diplomatic, tough as that can be at times. Finally, if you cannot come to a mutual understanding and if you believe you have given the tenant every opportunity to mend his ways, go about using the legal means available to you to get him out.

Before handling any eviction for breach of contract, familiarize yourself with the basic procedure of an eviction for nonpayment of rent in chapter 5, for there are many similarities between these two basic unlawful detainer procedures. Once you are familiar with how you go about evicting a tenant who doesn't pay, you will have a better understanding of how you go about evicting a tenant who doesn't comply with the rental agreement.

Now that you have been introduced to evic-

or a jury that your tenant is not living up to the agreement you made with him and that you are telling the truth about the situation. Fill out your notice like the sample shown here, quoting chapter and verse from the rental agreement's pertinent covenants and giving the tenant three days to "clean up his act" or leave.

Note that this notice states specifically that it does not terminate or forfeit the rental agreement. If the tenant has a long-term lease or certain obligations stated in the agreement which you do not want canceled just because he was evicted for breach of contract, then those terms can still be enforced. His obligation to pay rent

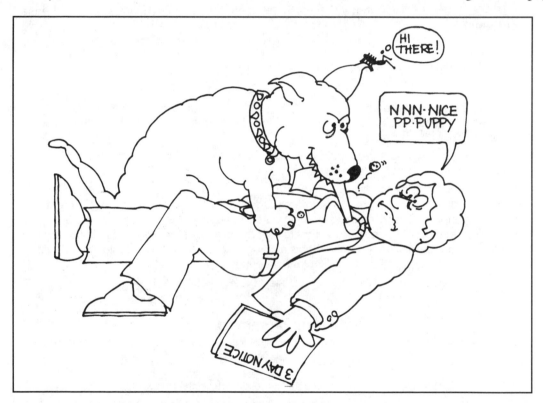

tions for breach of contract, and you know what they're all about, let's look at the steps involved in handling this particular kind of an eviction. (The step numbers correspond exactly to the ones used in chapter 5.)

Step 1. Prepare a Notice to Perform Covenant.

The first step in an eviction for breach of contract is the preparation of a notice stating precisely which covenants the tenant has broken in your rental agreement. State one or more, but make certain you can *prove* each one you mention with evidence sufficient to convince a judge

under an unexpired lease, for example, would continue. As the notice states, "If, after legal proceedings, said premises are recovered from you, the owners will try to rent said premises for the best possible rent, giving you credit for sums received and holding you liable for any deficiencies arising during the term of said Lease or Rental Agreement." You are not releasing the tenant from his obligations to you.

Like the notices used to initiate the other types of unlawful detainers described in this book, this form combines both the notice and the proof of service. You ought to fill out the proof of service after you hand a copy of the notice to the tenant,

NOTICE TO PERFORM COVENANT

TO: Richard Renter

Rose Renter

and all other tenants in possession of the premises described as:

456 Sweet Street
(Street Address)

Littletown   California   91111
(City)   (State)   (Zip)

PLEASE TAKE NOTICE that you have violated the following covenant(s) in your Lease or Rental Agreement:

Only the following persons and pets are to live on said premises: Richard and Rose Renter. No other persons or pets are to live there without plaintiff's prior written permission.

You are hereby required within ____three (3)____ days to perform the aforesaid covenant(s) or to deliver up possession of the above-described premises which you currently hold and occupy.

If you fail to do so, legal proceedings will be instituted against you to recover said premises and such damages as the law allows.

This notice is intended to be a ____three (3)____-day notice to perform the aforesaid covenant(s). It is not intended to terminate or forfeit the Lease or Rental Agreement under which you occupy said premises. If, after legal proceedings, said premises are recovered from you, the owners will try to rent the premises for the best possible rent, giving you credit for sums received and holding you liable for any deficiencies arising during the term of your Lease or Rental Agreement.

Dated: _August 15, XXXX_   _Lester Landlord_
                                 Owner/Manager

PROOF OF SERVICE

I, the undersigned, being at least 18 years of age, declare under penalty of perjury that I served the above notice, of which this is a true copy, on the following tenant(s) in possession in the manner(s) indicated below: _RICHARD RENTER_

☒ On _8/15/XX_____, I handed the notice to the tenant(s) personally.

☐ On _____, after attempting personal service, I handed the notice to a person of suitable age and discretion at the residence/business of the tenant(s), AND I deposited a true copy in the U.S. Mail, in a sealed envelope with postage fully prepaid, addressed to the tenant(s) at his/her/their place of residence (date mailed, if different _____).

☐ On _____, after attempting service in both manners indicated above, I posted the notice in a conspicuous place at the residence of the tenant(s), AND I deposited a true copy in the U.S. Mail, in a sealed envelope with postage fully prepaid, addressed to the tenant(s) at his/her/their place of residence (date mailed, if different _____).

Executed on _8/15/XX_____, at _LITTLETOWN_____, California.
                    Served by _Lester Landlord_

You will find a blank copy of this form in the FORMS section of this book and in Eviction Forms Creator.

not before. The tenant's copy needn't have the lower section filled in when it's served because that section tells how the notice was served (past tense). It should be completed following service.

Step 2. Serve the Notice.

In aggravating, but otherwise tranquil, situations which require a notice for breach, the best time to serve a 3-Day Notice to Perform Covenant, stating that the tenant is doing something he agreed he would not do or that he isn't doing something he agreed he would do, is shortly after the rent has been paid, for you must consider that the tenant won't be too eager to pay any rent after he receives the notice if he expects to be, and intends to be, evicted. If the case goes to court and all goes well, you might be rid of the tenant before the next rent payment falls due, thereby losing no rent whatsoever.

In those crisis situations which require immediate attention, the best time to serve the notice is *now*. Do not even consider whether you might lose a month's rent if you serve the notice at an inopportune time of the month. Rather, consider whether you might lose your property, your good tenants, your health, or your sanity by waiting. What are they worth to you? If they're worth more than a few days of rent, serve the notice right now.

Try repeatedly to serve the notice directly to the person you're evicting, and when you serve it, be friendly, even if you encounter a grumpy tenant.

If you can't find the tenant, you'll have to resort to one of the other methods for serving a 3-day notice. See the bottom of the notice itself for the choices.

Step 3. Prepare the Summons, Complaint, and Cover Sheet.

Use the same summons form for this kind of unlawful detainer as you would if you were evicting the tenant for nonpayment of rent, and fill it out the same way, too.

Your complaint form will be the same as the one used for nonpayment of rent, but you must fill it out differently. The differences begin with item 6. Check the box after 6; put the defendant's name after the word "names" which appears in parenthesis; and under 8a, check "3-day notice to perform covenants or quit."

Complete 6b by giving the date when the no-

tice expired, but do not check box 6d, whatever you do. You did not ask for forfeiture of the tenant's rental agreement in the notice, remember? Check 6e if you decide to attach a copy of the notice to the complaint (see discussion of this subject in chapter 5).

Fill in items 7, 10, 11, 12, and 13 as appropriate, and omit items 8 and 9 completely. Check item 14 for sure because you'll have to attach a description of the particular kind of breach the tenant is committing, and you'll be calling it Attachment 14.

Under item 16, sometimes referred to as "the prayer," check box "f." If the tenant owes you any rent following your service of the notice, that rent is now known as damages, and the judge or court clerk, at your direction, will determine what it is from the per-diem rate you put in item 10. If you have any other requests, such as charges other than rent which the tenant still owes you, check box "h" and specify what they are.

Check box 17 because you will be adding an attachment, and put the number of pages attached after "specify."

Finally, check the first box in item 18 to indicate that you did not use an unlawful detainer assistant.

Attachment 14 should follow the format of the sample shown here referring to a breach involving an unauthorized pet. Attachments for other kinds of breaches might be worded as follows in these samples:

For a breach regarding messiness or filth—"By the terms of said agreement, defendant covenanted and agreed to keep yards and garbage areas clean; defendant does now maintain the aforesaid premises in an unclean and unsanitary condition."

For a breach regarding subletting—"By the terms of said agreement, defendant covenanted and agreed that only Richard Renter and Rose Renter would live on said premises and that no other persons would live there without written permission; defendant has sublet the premises to a third party now occupying same; and plaintiff has never given permission to defendant to sublet the premises."

For a breach regarding alterations—"By the terms of said agreement, defendant covenanted and agreed not to alter the dwelling; defendant has constructed or caused to be constructed a metal storage shed in the front yard of the de-

1 SHORT TITLE-- LANDLORD VS. RENTER

2 ATTACHMENT(S) 14

3   By the terms of said agreement, defendant covenanted and

4 agreed to have only the following persons and pets live on said

5 premises: Richard and Rose Renter, and to have no other persons or

6 pets live there without plaintiff's prior written permission.

7   Defendant does now harbor a pet dog on said premises, and

8 plaintiff has never given permission to defendant to harbor a dog

9 on said premises.

10

11

12

13

14

15

16

17

18

19

20

21

22

23

24

25

26

27

28

efc

To create your own attachment, use the blank pleading paper in the FORMS section of this book or use a blank attachment in Eviction Forms Creator.

mised premises; plaintiff has never given permission to defendant for construction of said shed."

For a breach regarding noise—"By the terms of said agreement, defendant covenanted and agreed to keep from making loud noises and disturbances and to play music and broadcast programs at all times so as not to disturb other people's peace and quiet; defendant has deliberately disturbed other people's peace and quiet on various occasions so as to cause complaints from neighbors about said noise."

Surely from these examples you can devise your own attachment sufficient to describe your tenant's particular breach, whatever it is. Couch your description in typical legalese if you possibly can. Use at least one "aforesaid," "plaintiff," "defendant," or "covenanted" in the wording to make it all sound reasonably consistent with the gobbledygook an attorney might use.

Complete a cover sheet to accompany your summons and complaint. Follow the instructions for doing so in chapter 5.

Steps 4-17. (Follow those given in chapter 5.)

• • • • • • • • • •

Should you, in the course of your unlawful detainer for breach, encounter any response to your complaint, turn to chapter 9 for information about what to do next.

If you go to court for your default judgment, you won't have to bring any witnesses to testify, but you should consider bringing either audio or visual evidence of the breach. Although the judge will take your sworn testimony as sufficient evidence that your tenant has indeed breached the contract, he will be all the more convinced by a

tape recording or some pictures.

The one big difference between nonpayment and breach cases is that in a breach-of-contract case you would be approximately even with the tenant in terms of money, especially if you gave him his notice shortly after he paid the rent. He may owe you some money, or you may owe him some. Once he moves, rejoice and heave a sigh of relief that he has actually departed. Then treat him like any other tenant who has moved out of your rental property. Settle up with him according to the terms of his lease or rental agreement.

• Gather concrete evidence of the breach of contract if you can.
• Use a 30-Day Notice to Terminate Tenancy and the entire procedure explained in chapter 8, if that option is available in your area, if you believe the tenants might feel challenged by your proceeding against them and might be tempted to contest the case, and/or if the breach can wait that long.
• Serve the Notice to Perform Covenant shortly after the tenants pay their rent so you will have plenty of time to conduct your court case and incur the least loss of rent possible.

7
Handling an Eviction for Waste, Nuisance, or Unlawful Acts

In the course of everyday landlording, you may have the misfortune to happen upon some tenants who have more personality disorders than Dr. Jekyll, more faces than Eve, more sinister pals than the Godfather, more marijuana than a Mendocino pot grower, more cocaine customers than a Colombian cartel, more delusions than a Watergate burglar, more armaments than an American Nazi, more gentlemen callers than Sally Sanford, more corn whiskey than a Kentucky moonshiner, or more problems of some other sort than even a soap opera could dramatize or a Pollyanna could handle. For whatever reason, these people are not what they seem, and you unfortunately do not discover what they are truly like until after they have managed to gain possession of your rental dwelling. They may have convinced you to rent to them by appearing quite normal when they made an application to rent or by resorting to some form of deception, such as renting through the personal appearance of a comely friend. How they gained possession doesn't matter; the fact is that they have possession. They are living in one of your rentals, and you want them out; you have to get them out before they damage your property any more, hurt somebody, involve you in a lawsuit, alienate every neighbor within two stones' throws, or provoke a police raid. You can't really evict them using any of the other three types of evictions because they are current in their rent, they haven't specifically broken any provision in the rental agreement, and they must be dealt with before thirty days have elapsed. So how do you deal with them?

You evict them on the grounds that they are committing waste, committing a nuisance, or committing unlawful acts. The law is reasonably specific about what these grounds are: "waste" is abusing or destroying property; "nuisance" is "anything which is injurious to health, or is indecent or offensive to the senses, or an obstruction to the free use of property, so as to interfere with the comfortable enjoyment of life or property..."; and "unlawful acts" are any acts committed in violation of the law.

The problem you face in trying to evict a tenant on any of these grounds, of course, is that you have to prove that he is guilty. You have to be the first judge of whether the bothersome behavior is substantial enough and whether the evidence you have gathered to prove your allegations about this tenant's bothersome behavior is good enough to convince a real judge, and perhaps a jury, that the tenant should be evicted. In a way, you are like the wife who is afraid that her husband is going to kill her but she's unable to prove to the police or the courts just how great the danger is in order to get protection. No one quite believes her until she turns up dead.

You may be damned if you do try to evict a tenant who you feel is destructive, dangerous, troublesome, or law-breaking, and you may be damned if you don't. Yes, I said "damned if you don't." That Dr. Jekyll who has laid your property waste already by kicking holes in the doors and uprooting the wall heater will keep right on destroying the place if you ignore him, and he'll no doubt accelerate his demolition if you attempt to evict him. That naughty lady who's a nuisance to her neighbors because she parades about the hallways in her boa, mules, and birthday suit soliciting tricks is going to drive your good tenants to vacate if you don't force her to vacate first, and she'll undoubtedly rail at you and charge you with unmentionable sins if you try to force her out. That drug dealer who brazenly peddles cocaine out of his apartment at all hours will attract more criminal elements to your property if you look the other way when you discover what's

3-DAY NOTICE TO QUIT
FOR WASTE, NUISANCE, OR UNLAWFUL ACTS

TO: Boom Boom Suess

and all other tenants in possession of the premises described as:

456 Sweet Street
(Street Address)

Littletown _____ California ____ 91111
(City) _____ (State) ____ (Zip)

PLEASE TAKE NOTICE that you are hereby required within three (3) days to deliver up possession of the above-described premises which you currently hold and occupy because you have committed the following waste, nuisance, or unlawful act(s):

Committing acts of prostitution on the premises on at least two occasions, August 6th and August 15th, as evidenced by police reports.

As a consequence of your having committed the foregoing acts, your Lease or Rental Agreement is hereby declared canceled under California law (CCP §1161.4).

Should you fail to comply with this notice, legal proceedings will be instituted against you to recover said premises and such damages as the law allows.

Dated: August 16, XXXX _____ *Lester Landlord* _____
Owner/Manager

PROOF OF SERVICE

I, the undersigned, being at least 18 years of age, declare under penalty of perjury that I served the above notice, of which this is a true copy, on the following tenant(s) in possession in the manner(s) indicated below: BOOM BOOM SUESS

☒ On 8/16/XX , I handed the notice to the tenant(s) personally.

☐ On _____, after attempting personal service, I handed the notice to a person of suitable age and discretion at the residence/business of the tenant(s), AND I deposited a true copy in the U.S. Mail, in a sealed envelope with postage fully prepaid, addressed to the tenant(s) at his/her/their place of residence (date mailed, if different _____).

☐ On _____, after attempting service in both manners indicated above, I posted the notice in a conspicuous place at the residence of the tenant(s), AND I deposited a true copy in the U.S. Mail, in a sealed envelope with postage fully prepaid, addressed to the tenant(s) at his/her/their place of residence (date mailed, if different _____).

Executed on 8/16/XX , at LITTLETOWN , California.

Served by *Lester Landlord*

efc

going on, and he'll likely threaten you with foul play if you dare to begin eviction proceedings against him. You are trapped in a no-win situation. You probably won't turn up dead if you attempt to evict the tenant who discharges his arsenal in the backyard of your rental property, and you probably won't turn up dead if you actually evict him, but you might find yourself involved in a costly and protracted lawsuit if you do nothing.

Remember, landlord, that you have what attorneys call "deep pockets," and you are constantly being pickpocketed in suits which blame

of these people live in a netherworld where life is short and cheap. If you are particularly fearful, consider hiring an attorney to handle the whole thing for you, though even then you may face danger if the tenant knows where you can be found and wants his revenge. At the very least, keep someone else informed of your whereabouts all the while you are involved in this kind of an eviction, to increase the chances that the tenant will be caught if he tries to "waste" you.

Step 1. Prepare the Notice.

State law allows you to evict a tenant on

you whenever something actionable happens which is remotely connected with your property, regardless of whether you were directly responsible or not. You may have been nowhere near the backyard of your property when a tenant fired the bullet which paralyzed a neighbor, but if you were aware that your tenant might discharge a weapon in the yard, then you, along with the gunslinger would likely be held accountable for the injury. Why you? You got the bucks, dearie. You may not want to do anything, but you have to. There's no sensible alternative.

You cannot be idle in these situations.

You may be putting your own life in danger when you initiate this kind of an eviction, for some

grounds of waste, nuisance, or unlawful acts without offering him the opportunity to reform his behavior. In other words, the 3-Day Notice to Quit which is used in this situation does not have to include an alternative. It may have one, but it doesn't have to, and you will notice that the one provided here does not (in some rent-control areas, this kind of notice must include an alternative; check your local rent-control ordinances). This is very serious business. You are saying, by not providing an alternative, that the tenant cannot remain even if he does mend his ways. He has squeezed the toothpaste out of the tube, and he can't force it back in. The notice informs the tenant why he is being evicted, and it gives him three days to leave. That's all. No alternatives, no and's, no if's, no but's, no maybe's. You should take advantage of your opportunity to be tough here, for nobody, not even a psychic psychiatrist, could possibly determine whether a tenant has reformed enough within three days to be a suitable tenant again. Besides, you would still be held accountable if he lapses back into his errant ways in the future, and you would still have to answer to the other tenants for allowing him to stay. They tend to be unforgiving of people with a past. You have to get that bad-acting tenant out!

When you prepare the notice, be careful to list only those grounds which you feel confident you can prove in court. If you can't prove them to be utterly and undeniably true, use some other pretext to evict the tenant. Don't bother listing all the derogatory tidbits you can possibly remember about the tenant. List the most flagrant ones only, the ones you can photograph, tape-record, or get witnesses to verify.

On the notice itself, describe the grounds for the eviction something like this: Discharging a gun through the floor of Apartment 212 at 11:35 on the night of September 12; growing marijuana plants on the balcony of the tenant's domicile in violation of state and federal laws; dealing drugs on the premises, resulting in an arrest on October 11; committing acts of prostitution on the premises on at least two occasions, August 6th and August 15th; violating City Fire Ordinance 112.3 regarding the operation of a kerosene heater inside a living area; disturbing the neighbors with loud quarreling, loud music, obscene language, drunken disturbances, all of which required a police visit on January 6; fencing and storing stolen goods on the premises; harboring two illegal aliens in a storeroom on the premises; dismantling stolen automobiles in the garage on the premises; operating a bookmaking business on the premises.

Don't try to evict a tenant on these grounds unless the incident or activity which you are citing in the notice occurred recently or continues to occur. If a tenant used to commit acts of prostitution on the premises months ago but has obviously reformed since then, and you did nothing earlier to evict her, don't try to evict her now on those old grounds. Your case would be thrown out of court. She'd be given the benefit of the doubt if she claimed that she had reformed and was a new woman now.

Step 2. Serve the Notice.

If you consider the tenant to be dangerous, do not serve the notice yourself. Hire a sheriff, marshal, off-duty peace officer, security guard, or professional process server to serve it for you.

If the tenant has always been friendly to you and isn't somebody you'd consider dangerous, screw up your courage and approach him directly with notice in hand, when he might think you have come merely to reprimand him; only don't just hand him the notice and leave. Talk with him. Try to convince him that his moving would be in your mutual interest. Tell him he should begin looking immediately for some other accommodations where he'll be able to live more freely according to the lifestyle he has chosen for himself. If he wants to be destructive, tell him to rent a dilapidated place which the owner wants to tear down anyway. If she wants to peddle her favors, tell her to look for a place in the part of town where such assignations are commonplace. If he wants to discharge weapons any time of the day or night, tell him to look for a place with fewer neighbors. Be polite, yet firm. Tell him you have to get him out so all the neighbors will quit bugging you. Tell him you don't want to have to call the police about his marijuana, but you will if you have to. You are challenging the tenant directly, so expect to be yelled at, perhaps even threatened.

The best time to serve one of these notices is when the tenant is committing the waste, nuisance, or unlawful act. That establishes a one-to-one causal relationship between what he is doing and what you are doing; your approach becomes a kind of just retribution, prompt and exacting. If you can't serve it then, serve it anytime. Because the vandalous, nuisance, or lawbreaking tenant tends to keep irregular hours and may be difficult to catch, however, you may have to lie in wait until he appears or else ask a cooperative neighbor to alert you when he returns.

Step 3. Prepare the Summons, Complaint, and Cover Sheet.

Should your tenant refuse to heed the 3-day notice, you will have to proceed against him in court, and as in other kinds of evictions, that entails preparing a summons, complaint, and cover sheet. Fill out the summons and cover sheet forms not a whit differently from those in chapter 5. Unlawful detainer summonses and cover sheets are all the same.

Fill out the same complaint form you would use for nonpayment of rent as shown in chapter 5, and fill it out in the same way through item 5. Check the box after 6 on the form, and put the defendant's name after the word "name"; under 6a, check "3-day notice to quit," since that is the kind of notice you should have served to initiate this kind of eviction. Indicate when that notice expired in 6b, and check 6e if you want to attach a copy of the notice to your complaint.

Fill in items 7, 10, 11, 12, and 13 as appropriate, and omit items 8 and 9 completely. Check item 14 to indicate that you are attaching a statement about the tenant's wrongdoing.

Under item 16, check box "e" because you are canceling the agreement. Check box "f" to entitle yourself to any damages. If you have any other requests, such as charges other than rent which the tenant still owes you, check box "h" and specify what they are.

Check box 17 because you will be adding an attachment, and put the number of pages attached after "specify."

Finally, check the first box in item 18 to indicate that you did not use an unlawful detainer assistant.

In your Attachment 14, you needn't try to be creative. In fact, you shouldn't be. State the facts as you know them, simply and directly, following the description of the grounds for the eviction which you stated originally in the tenant's notice. Refer to the tenant in the attachment as the defendant rather than as your tenant, and refer to yourself as the plaintiff. This attachment is not supposed to prove that the tenant did what you say he did. It can't do that. You are merely stating in it what the tenant is doing or has done to commit waste, nuisance, or unlawful acts.

Steps 4-17. (Follow those given in chapter 5.)

• • • • • • • • • •

Once you have endured this kind of an eviction, you will have earned your landlord's hard nose, pitchfork, and pointed tail. You may appear autocratic and even satanic to the meek souls you know socially because you'll be all the more suspicious of people and especially of anyone who applies to rent from you. You'll have changed.

Churchill is credited with having said, "If you're not a liberal by the time you're twenty, you have no heart, and if you're not a conservative by the time you're forty, you have no brains." We landlords are on an accelerated schedule. We become conservative soon after assuming the name "Landlord," regardless of our age. This kind of an eviction makes us so.

• Recognize that this kind of eviction is the most trying of all.
• Understand that you may be damned if you don't evict and damned if you do.
• Document your case carefully.
• Keep your loved ones informed of your whereabouts at all times during one of these evictions.
• Keep good help in the wings, an attorney and a process server.

8
Handling an Eviction for Failure to Vacate

You are planning to renovate a rental dwelling; you are selling a rental house and the new owner wants to move in but insists that you get the current tenants out; your father-in-law and his ladylove want to move into one of your rentals; you are tired of having to chase after one tenant who's always at least fifteen days late with the rent; your tenant has already caused one small fire with his careless smoking, and you're afraid that next time he may burn down the whole building; your tenants have some destructive monsters masquerading as innocent babes; your tenant won't use the "pooper-scooper" you gave him last Christmas; or you've had it up to your eye sockets with two chronic complainers because you can't do enough for them, and still they complain, complain, complain.

In any of these situations involving tenants who are paying their rent and may or may not be breaching their rental agreement, the best way available for you to get rid of them is to give them a 30-Day Notice to Terminate Tenancy. Then you add crossed fingers to your already crossed eyes, and you hope that they move before the 30-day period is up so you don't have to spend the money and time necessary to evict them through the courts.

Before you begin passing out 30-day notices to all your tenants who are in situations like the ones above, however, you must consider three very important questions:

1) Are these tenants leasing from you rather than renting; that is, do they have an agreement which permits them to occupy your rental dwelling for a certain period of time, a period which has not yet expired?

If they have such an agreement, you may not serve them with a 30-Day Notice to Terminate Tenancy because you may not terminate the lease on your own initiative. The lease may be terminated prematurely only if you and the tenants together agree to terminate it or if you can show cause. If that lease has expired, though, and you have not signed a new one yet but have continued accepting rent from the tenants, then you may use a 30-Day Notice to Terminate Tenancy because the tenancy has automatically become a month-to-month tenancy.

So what do you do if you have a valid lease with the tenants which precludes your evicting them with a 30-day notice, yet you still want them out? You have a number of options: Try to buy them out of their lease; find a significant breach which they are committing and evict them on that ground; pounce on them with a 3-Day Notice to Pay Rent or Quit as soon as their rent first becomes delinquent and hope that they don't pay within the three days so you can evict them for nonpayment of rent; or wait until their lease expires and tell them beforehand that you will not renew it.

Incidentally, if they refuse to move at the expiration of a fixed-term lease which you have chosen not to renew and if you do not accept any rent from them beyond the lease's expiration date, you may have them served with a summons and complaint without first serving them a notice. In that case, fill out the complaint form as appropriate, and make sure to check box 8, which makes your demand for possession at the end of a fixed-term lease. Although giving them some kind of notice that you aren't going to renew their lease is not obligatory unless called for in the lease, you would be wise to do so; you want the tenants to know what your intentions are in plenty of time for them to move.

2) Is the rental dwelling located in any area which requires that you have a "just cause" for an eviction? (See chapter 4.)

In those areas, you may certainly evict for nonpayment of rent or for a legitimate breach of contract if you want to, but you may evict for failure

103

NOTICE TO TERMINATE TENANCY

TO: Herman Lockyear

Preston Lockyear

and all other tenants in possession of the premises described as:

458 Sweet Street
(Street Address)

Littletown   California   91111
(City)   (State)   (Zip)

PLEASE TAKE NOTICE that you are hereby required within ___thirty (30)___ days to remove from and deliver up possession of the above-described premises, which you currently hold and occupy.

This notice is intended for the purpose of terminating the Lease or Rental Agreement by which you now hold possession of the above-described premises, and should you fail to comply, legal proceedings will be instituted against you to recover possession, to declare said Lease or Rental Agreement forfeited, and to recover rents and damages for the period of the unlawful detention.

In compliance with local housing ordinances, this notice is being given for good cause as follows: Owner desires to move into this dwelling.

Dated: ___June 5, XXXX___   _Lester Landlord_
                                                          Owner/Manager

---

PROOF OF SERVICE

I, the undersigned, being at least 18 years of age, declare under penalty of perjury that I served the above notice, of which this is a true copy, on the following tenant(s) in possession in the manner(s) indicated below: __PRESTON LOCKYEAR__

☒ On __JUNE 5, XXXX__, I handed the notice to the tenant(s) personally.

☐ On _____, after attempting personal service, I handed the notice to a person of suitable age and discretion at the residence/business of the tenant(s), AND I deposited a true copy in the U.S. Mail, in a sealed envelope with postage fully prepaid, addressed to the tenant(s) at his/her/their place of residence (date mailed, if different _____).

☐ On _____, after attempting service in both manners indicated above, I posted the notice in a conspicuous place at the residence of the tenant(s), AND I deposited a true copy in the U.S. Mail, in a sealed envelope with postage fully prepaid, addressed to the tenant(s) at his/her/their place of residence (date mailed, if different _____).

☐ On _____, I sent by certified mail a true copy of the notice addressed to the tenant(s) at his/her/their place of residence.

Executed on __6/5/XX__, at __LITTLETOWN__, California.

Served by __Lester Landlord__

efc

You will find a blank copy of this form in the FORMS section of this book and in Eviction Forms Creator.

to vacate only if you have a so-called "just cause," and some of the situations given at the beginning of this chapter do not constitute such a cause. Check the local ordinances. You'll find that they vary quite a bit. Habitually paying late, for example, may be a just cause in one eviction-controlled area but not in another.

3) Does this particular rental dwelling fall under any special circumstances?

Owners who participate in the HUD Section 8 program must give their Section 8 tenants a just cause (also known as a "good cause") to terminate midterm. Owners who rent out single-family dwellings in some rent-controlled areas do not need to give a just cause because they're exempt from the ordinances. Check.

Once you have determined that you may legally use a 30-Day Notice to Terminate Tenancy, you may follow steps similar to those given in chapter 5 to evict your tenant.

Step 1. Prepare the Notice.

Fill out the notice form by following the sample given here. Put something in every blank as indicated. Note that there's one blank where you're supposed to insert the number of days allowed for the tenant to move. Normally the number you'd put there would be thirty because this is supposed to be a *30-Day* Notice to Terminate Tenancy. Right? Yep, but if, and only if, you've specified another number of days in your rental agreement, then you may use that number here, and that number may be less than thirty; it may be as little as seven. It'll automatically be seven for a week-to-week rental agreement unless a larger number is agreed upon; it'll automatically be thirty for a month-to-month agreement unless a smaller number is agreed upon.

In those situations where just-cause requirements apply, indicate on the notice itself your just cause(s) for giving the notice. What you consider a "just cause" must, of course, correspond to what HUD or your rent control ordinances consider a "just cause." Type or print the following on the notice in the space above the date: "In compliance with local housing ordinances [or HUD requirements], this notice is being given for good cause as follows: [describe your reason briefly]."

In other situations, you need give no reason at all for your notice, and you shouldn't give a reason because a reason will only serve to antagonize the tenant.

Step 2. Serve the Notice.

• THE SERVICE—There is some controversy surrounding service of the 30-Day Notice to Terminate Tenancy, and you would be wise to sidestep it if you can. The controversy involves whether such notices may be served by mail alone or whether service by mail must also be accompanied by the server's either leaving a copy with someone on the premises or posting a copy by the main entrance, too, as he must for 3-day notices. Some interpret the requirements for service one way, and some the other. Naturally, personal service is still the best type of service for this kind of notice as it is for all the others, and you should try to serve the notice personally to avoid getting entangled in this controversy. If you can't serve it personally, I would recommend that you take the more conservative position and serve it both by mailing it and leaving or posting a copy. And while you're being conservative, you might as well go all the way and send it by certified mail rather than regular mail. Whether or not you have your certified mail receipted, the post office keeps records on it for two years, and delivery can always be verified within that period of time if the need arises.

• CONFUSING TWO TYPES OF 30-DAY NOTICES—I have heard some landlords say that the only time to serve a 30-Day Notice to Terminate Tenancy is on the rent due date. That's piffle! They're probably confusing the Notice to Change Terms of Tenancy (used primarily for increasing rent), which is also a 30-day notice, with the 30-Day Notice to Terminate Tenancy. You may serve a 30-Day Notice to Terminate Tenancy any old time, and it becomes effective thirty days from when it was served (a Notice to Change Terms of Tenancy may be served anytime, too, but it is generally served on or before the rent due date, to give the tenant at least thirty days' notice before the rent is increased).

• BEST TIME TO SERVE—The best time to serve a 30-Day Notice to Terminate Tenancy is shortly after the rent has been paid. You should know that as soon as you serve the notice, the tenant's desire to pay rent diminishes drastically, even though he is legally liable for rent for every day he stays. You may lose some rent if the tenant does prove to be recalcitrant and remains for the entire thirty days and on into the eviction proceedings, but it will be the least amount you could possibly lose.

Incidentally, you should serve the tenant with a 3-Day Notice to Pay Rent or Quit if at any time during the 30-day waiting period he becomes delinquent in his rent. That way you can evict him all the more quickly, and you can sue for back rent in your complaint as well. A 30-Day Notice to Terminate Tenancy demands possession not rent, and should you fail to serve the 3-day notice, you might find yourself in an unfortunate position where you have evicted the tenant successfully without at the same time receiving a judgment for his unpaid rent [*Castle Park No. 5 v. Katherine* (1979) 91 CA3d Supp 6, 154 CR 498].

• COUNTING THE DAYS—If you serve the tenant a 30-Day Notice to Terminate Tenancy on June 16th, begin counting with the 17th as the first day and stop counting with July 16th as the thirtieth day. On the following day, July 17th, you could file the summons and complaint. If you serve it January 10th, February 9th is the thirtieth day.

Again, to be conservative, if you serve the notice by mail, add an extra five days.

• PITFALLS—The biggest pitfall you face after serving a 30-Day Notice to Terminate Tenancy is accepting rent beyond that 30-day period. Doing so would invalidate your notice, requiring you to start all over again, and you know what that would necessitate—serving another notice and biding your time for another thirty days. The tenant may offer you rent money beyond the 30-day period as many times as he wants to, but so long as you refuse it, you can safely follow up on your notice in court. If the 30-day period expires near the end of the month and the tenant offers you rent for the entire month, take his rent through the exact date when the notice expires, and write his receipt to reflect that his rent was paid through that date.

This same pitfall becomes all the more hazardous when you are holding the tenant's last month's rent (security and cleaning deposits have no bearing on the situation; as a consequence, I recommend that you eliminate the practice of charging last month's rent and charge higher deposits instead). That last month's rent is supposed to be used for, what else, the last month's rent. When you give notice to terminate tenancy in thirty days, you are, in effect, telling the tenant that this is his last month, so the last month's

rent you've been holding should be applied. Make sure that the expiration of your notice does not fall on a date before *all* the tenant's prepaid rent has been used up, whether that prepaid rent was paid to you recently or some time ago, when he moved in.

Another pitfall is not waiting a full thirty days following service of the notice before filing the summons and complaint. Remember that you must wait at least thirty days following actual service, not thirty days after the date when you thought you'd be able to serve the notice. Remember that thirty days do not necessarily equal one month. You are giving thirty days' notice, not one month's notice. Count off the thirty days on a calendar.

Step 3. Prepare the Summons, Complaint, and Cover Sheet.

Use the same summons, complaint, and cover sheet forms as those referred to in chapter 5, but prepare the complaint differently to reflect the special nature of this kind of unlawful detainer.

Fill in the top part of the complaint form and the first five items in the same way they're done in chapter 5. Indicate in 6a that the tenant was served with a 30-day notice to quit, which is the same as a 30-Day Notice to Terminate Tenancy, and check 6d because the notice included an election of forfeiture. Reveal how the notice was served in item 7, and complete items 10, 11, 12, and 13 as appropriate. You may omit items 8, 9, 14, and 17. There's no need to include any attachments with this kind of complaint either; it's really the simplest of them all.

Check 16e and f. You are entitled to "damages" equivalent to per-diem rent for all the days the tenant refuses to vacate following the expiration of the 30-day notice. Check 16h if the tenant owes you for anything other than rent.

Finally, check the first box in item 18 to indicate that you did not use an unlawful detainer assistant.

Steps 4-17. (Follow those given in chapter 5.)

Should you be following the fourth alternative under step 8 as it's described in chapter 5, you will have to submit a Declaration for Default Judgment in Lieu of Personal Testimony. The first page of the failure-to-vacate declaration is exactly the same as that of the nonpayment declaration, but the second page should be slightly different. Change paragraphs 4 and 5 and the "prayer" to read as follows:

```
    4. That on _____, I
caused the defendant to be served
with a written thirty-day notice
terminating tenancy and requiring
possession of the premises within
thirty days following service of
the notice.
    5. That when at least thirty
days had elapsed after service of
said notice on defendant and de-
fendant was still in possession
of the premises, I caused the de-
fendant to be served with a Sum-
mons and Complaint on _____.
    WHEREFORE, I pray that this
Court render a judgment by de-
fault against the defendant for
restitution of said premises, for
costs of $_____, for damages at
the rate of $_____ per day
(calculated from the 31st day
following service of said notice,
that 31st day being
_____, through the date
of the expected eviction), and
for forfeiture of the agreement.
```

• • • • • • • • •

The major advantage of this kind of unlawful detainer is that there are really only two substantial defenses a tenant might raise against it, and the burden of proof is on him. He might say, "My landlord is discriminating against me," or "My landlord is retaliating against me." Discrimination according to the Unruh Civil Rights Act is illegal when you are selecting tenants, as well as when you are arbitrarily evicting them. Don't do it!

The retaliation referred to here involves your evicting a tenant arbitrarily within 180 days after he has exercised, or attempted to exercise, some legal right which is considered by the court to be of substantial importance. This would include a complaint to a governmental agency about conditions of the dwelling which violate housing or safety code requirements. It would also include the tenant's good-faith use of his right to "repair and deduct."

If you're interested in examining the law regarding retaliatory evictions, look at Civil Code §1942.5.

• Know your local housing ordinances well enough to understand how they relate to a 30-Day Notice to Terminate Tenancy.
• Don't accept any rent money from your tenant for the period following the expiration of the notice.
• Wait a full 30 days after the notice was served before filing your summons and complaint.

9
Handling an Eviction of Holdover Owners

You have just acquired a property, and you would like to move into it yourself or rent it to somebody else, except that the former owners still occupy the place and don't appear to be in any hurry to vacate. In fact, they appear determined to stay there as long as they can without paying anybody anything and without lifting two fingers to take care of things. The place could fall down around them, and they wouldn't care.

Whether the sale occurred voluntarily (with the owners' cooperation) or involuntarily (without the owners' cooperation as the result of a foreclosure, an IRS sale, a writ of execution, a trust deed default sale, or a default sale under a conditional sales contract) doesn't matter. What does matter is that you hold title to the property and that you want to take possession now.

What should you do?

First, you should communicate with the former owners and try to entice them to vacate.

Enticing Holdover Owners to Vacate

Enticing holdover owners to vacate is no different from enticing tenants to vacate. You assess the situation, including how much you're hurting, how much they're hurting, how much you'll have to pay in costs to evict them, how much time an eviction will require, and how immediate your need is to gain possession. Then you approach them, discuss their options and yours, make them an offer, and come to an understanding.

You will get the best results if you take the time to learn why they haven't vacated and you consider how to address their most pressing needs. You may find, when you ask them why they haven't vacated, that they need guidance from you more than they need money. Perhaps they had plans to vacate prior to the sale, and those plans fell through, and now they need help in assessing their options and formulating new plans.

Try talking with them. Try reasoning with them. Try helping them.

Owners whose property you acquired without their cooperation may require lots of enticing. You may have to pull out all the stops. Go ahead and pull them out. Don't be cheap, either. Bribery does work, you know. A little money offered to people who have recently lost all legitimate claims to their home and could be both despondent and obstinate might work wonders. When you tally the overall costs of evicting the former owners—the legal fees, the loss of use, and the repair of all the damage they could do to the property—even if you do handle the eviction yourself, you'll find that the dollars mount up in a hurry. You might offer them $500 to leave within three days and be much better off than you'd ever be if you'd "gone all the way" and evicted them through the courts.

If your holdover owners won't vacate in spite of your best efforts to get them out, you'll just have to force them out legally, of course. There is a way (CCP §1161a), and you can do it yourself. It's a straightforward unlawful detainer procedure requiring, most importantly, some proof that you actually do have title to the property.

Keep in mind that you may use this particular procedure only when you're evicting an owner who is holding over, an owner who has not become a tenant. If the property you acquired is occupied by a tenant or if you turned the holdover owners into tenants by executing a rental agreement with them or by accepting rent from them, then you should be using the normal tenant eviction procedure outlined in earlier chapters, for you are bound by whatever contract the previous owner had with his tenants or whatever expressed or implied contract you now have with

NOTICE TO QUIT

TO: Allen Barnes
Marion Barnes

and all other tenants in possession of the premises described as:

456 Sun Valley Rd.
(Street Address)
Dallasville   California   95555
(City)   (State)   (Zip)

PLEASE TAKE NOTICE that your possession of the above-described premises is without the consent of the owner and is in violation of California law regarding
[ ] forceable entry (CCP §1159 & §1160).
[x] holdover after foreclosure or execution (CCP §1161a).

You are hereby required to remove from and deliver up possession of said premises within ___three (3)___ days, or legal proceedings will be instituted against you to recover said premises and such damages as the law allows.

Dated: ___March 4, XXXX___   *Bruce Buyer*
                                      _____
                                      Owner/Manager

PROOF OF SERVICE

I, the undersigned, being at least 18 years of age, declare under penalty of perjury that I served the above notice, of which this is a true copy, on the following person(s) in possession in the manner(s) indicated below: ALLEN BARNES

[x] On ___3/4/XX___, I handed the notice to the person(s) in possession personally.

[ ] On _____, after attempting personal service, I handed the notice to a person of suitable age and discretion at the residence/business of the person(s) in possession, AND I deposited a true copy in the U.S. Mail, in a sealed envelope with postage fully prepaid, addressed to him/her/them at his/her/their place of residence (date mailed, if different _____).

[ ] On _____, after attempting service in both manners indicated above, I posted the notice in a conspicuous place at the residence of the tenant(s), AND I deposited a true copy in the U.S. Mail, in a sealed envelope with postage fully prepaid, addressed to him/her/them at his/her/their place of residence (date mailed, if different _____).

Executed on ___3/4/XX___, at ___DALLASVILLE___, California.
                    Served by ___Bruce Buyer___

ef(

the owners-turned-tenants. Tenants who have a legitimate two-year lease on the property which still has six months to run, for example, cannot be evicted until the lease expires unless the tenants break the lease or the lease provides for cancellation upon notice that there has been a change of ownership.

Let's say that there's no doubt about your holdover owners. They definitely are the former owners of the property, they are still living there, you haven't turned them into tenants by accepting rent from them, and you want them out. You want possession yourself. You have tried reasoning with them and you have tried enticing them, all to no avail. They're standing their ground, protecting what they still think of as "their castle." What's next?

Study the eviction procedure you must follow. Then get busy and evict them as soon as possible.

Five Things You Should Know About Holdover Cases

The eviction procedure for holdover owners is little different from any other eviction, but there are a few things you should know.

First of all, you should know about and understand the difference between "holdover tenants" and "holdover owners." I cannot emphasize enough how important this difference is in holdover cases. The term "holdover tenants" refers to those tenants who have given notice that they plan to move as of a certain date, and then they "hold over" after that date. The term "holdover tenants" also refers to those tenants whose long-term leases have expired, and they are "holding over" following the expiration of their lease. The term "holdover owners" refers to occupants who used to be owners of a property but no longer are. They have neither property rights nor tenancy rights, but they continue in possession of the property. Evict holdover owners using the procedure explained in this chapter. Evict holdover tenants using the procedures explained in other chapters.

Second, you should know that you must serve a notice to begin the eviction of holdover owners. You should serve the notice as soon as possible because you cannot ask for any rent from holdover owners in your complaint. You cannot ask for rent because the holdover owners are not tenants, but you can ask for damages to begin

once the notice expires.

Third, you should know that you cannot use the Judicial Council's complaint form in holdover cases. You may have noticed that the current Judicial Council complaint form even has a note at the bottom which states specifically: "Do not use this form for evictions after sale."

Fourth, you should know that you must attach a verification to your holdover complaint. Look at the end of the Judicial Council complaint form for unlawful detainer, and you'll see that a plaintiff's verification is a part of the complaint. A similar verification must be included as part of a holdover complaint. The verification needs to be on a separate sheet of pleading paper and attached to the complaint. You may use the verification form included in the FORMS section of this book.

Fifth, in case there are any local eviction controls in your area (see chapter 4) which might prevent a new owner from filing an unlawful detainer against holdover owners following a sale, you may still file an action against them to get them out, but it'll have to be some other kind of action, such as an ejectment, and you won't get to take advantage of the summary nature of an unlawful detainer. (Should you have to file an ejectment, consult *California Practice Guide: Landlord-Tenant* for details.)

Step 1. Prepare the Notice.

Use the Notice to Quit form which refers specifically to holdover owners. Identify the holdover situation right on the notice, and give the holdovers three days to quit.

Step 2. Serve the Notice

Since the notice used to evict holdover owners is a three-day notice, you should serve it the same way you serve other three-day notices (see chapter 5). Be diligent in trying personal service first before you resort to one of the other two methods.

Don't be so naive as to expect the holdover owners to move out within the three days. Be realistic. Spend this interval preparing to file the required legal papers rather than preparing to move in.

Count the days correctly. If you gave the holdover owners their notice on Friday, the 9th, the date when the notice expired would be the 12th. The 9th doesn't count. The count begins with

```
 1   Bruce Buyer
     1223 Pinehurst Ct.
 2   Dallasville, California 95555
     555-555-5555
 3   Plaintiff in Propria Persona

 4

 5

 6

 7

 8         IN THE MUNICIPAL COURT OF ____DALLASVILLE____ JUDICIAL DISTRICT,

 9         COUNTY OF _____BACKBONE_____, STATE OF CALIFORNIA

10

11   BRUCE BUYER_____,)
                         Plaintiff,)
12            vs.             )        NO.
     ALLEN BARNES             )
13   MARION BARNES            )
     _____,)            COMPLAINT FOR
                      Defendant.)    UNLAWFUL DETAINER
14   _____)    (CCP §1161a)

15   Plaintiff alleges as follows:

16        1. At all times mentioned herein, plaintiff was and now is a

17   competent adult residing in the City of __Dallasville__, County of

18   Backbone_____, State of California.

19        2. Plaintiff is the owner of the premises located at

20   456 Sun Valley Road_____ in the City

21   of __Dallasville_____, County of _____Backbone_____, State of

22   California.

23        3. Plaintiff believes that defendants are competent adults

24   residing in the City of _____Dallasville_____, County of

25   Backbone_____, State of California.

26        4. The true names and capacities of defendants sued as Does are

27   unknown to plaintiff. Plaintiff will seek leave of court to amend this

28   complaint when said true names and capacities have been determined.

29        5. At all times mentioned herein, each of the defendants,
```

You will find a blank copy of this form in the FORMS section of this book

the 10th and ends with the 12th, which is the third day following the 9th and the last day for them to comply with your 3-day notice.

Step 3. Prepare the Summons and Complaint.

You already know that you cannot use the Judicial Council's complaint form in holdover cases. You must use a complaint especially drafted for your holdover case, and it must be printed on pleading paper. There's nothing magic about the verbiage except that it must include a certain few things, such as the exact relationship between plaintiff and defendants which entitles the plaintiff to possession, the method used by the plaintiff to obtain title, and an allegation that the title was perfected through compliance with all legal requirements.

The sample complaint form shown here might be used in any holdover-owner case. For example, let's suppose that you want to evict holdover owners who sold you their house and now won't vacate the place after you have paid them for it. You would need to fill in the blanks on the complaint and select the first of the choices in paragraph 7. That choice identifies you as the owner of record, holding legal entitlement to the premises as purchaser from the defendants through a voluntary sale.

Be sure that you indicate the proper date when damages begin. That date is four days following service of the Notice to Quit. In other words, the holdover owners have three days to vacate following service of the notice. If they don't vacate by then, one day later damages begin.

Per-diem "damages" amount to a rental equivalent for every day the owner holds over following expiration of the notice period. Since the property hasn't been rented, there is no established rent, and you must determine what the fair rental value would be if the property were available for rent. You can determine a fair rental value for the premises by checking the classified ads for similar properties and phoning the landlords of those properties. Discuss the size, condition, amenities, location, and rent of their property. Compare that information with everything you know about your property, and come up with a fair rental value. When you pick a figure, make sure it's reasonable and be prepared to justify it. You don't want to pick a figure which is so unreasonable that the holdover owners will want to answer the complaint strictly to dispute your damages figure.

Along with the complaint, you will need to prepare a verification. A self-explanatory verification form appears in the FORMS section.

Steps 4-17. (Follow those given in chapter 5.)

Because holdover owners are not tenants, they cannot raise the normal tenant defenses, such as warranty of habitability or retaliation. You prevail against them merely by proving to the court that you, not they, are now the undisputed owner of record and hence are entitled to possession.

- Find out why the holdover owners haven't vacated.
- Entice them to vacate as best you can.
- Once you realize the futility of enticements, follow the legal procedure to evict them.
- Serve the Notice to Quit promptly to start the "damages" clock.

10
Handling the Contested Case

Your tenant has chosen to file a response to your complaint, and you are absolutely livid that he would dare to use a legal means to oppose your efforts to evict him. He's a scumbag, an absolute scumbag. He lies and cheats and uses the system to further his own ends. You know that you are entirely in the right, that his claim against you is on a par with Iraq's claim against Kuwait before the Gulf War, but you are also uncertain about what to do next.

Calm down first. A response to one eviction complaint doesn't portend the end of the world. It doesn't even portend the end of your rental property business. It means only that the eviction will be delayed somewhat; that's all. Worse things could happen, and in this business, you can be sure that they will.

Once you have calmed down and your blood pressure has returned nearly to normal, read the response your tenant has made. Read it over and over until it makes good sense to you, eighty-three times if need be. Only then will you be in any position to decide what you should do next. Don't despair. You have plenty of options, and you are going to prevail. Take some time while you're reviewing your options to consider again what your primary objective is and how you might best achieve it now that you know your tenant is trying to use the law to stymie your efforts to get him out. That objective of yours should still be to evict your tenant as quickly and as cheaply as possible. The question is—How can you evict him quickly and cheaply under these changed circumstances?

Let an Attorney in Your Life?

Earlier I tried to dissuade you from paying an attorney to crank up his eviction mill and have his secretary fill out a few forms in order to perform a perfunctory eviction for you, especially when the chances are slim that you will encounter any opposition.

Once a response has been filed, however, the chances are good that you will encounter further legal complications which may require the expertise of an attorney. Understand that a wily attorney for the tenant can create a flurry of paperwork which can delay your case a month or more. Ask yourself whether you can afford these delays. Your securing the services of an attorney now will cost you some bucks, that's for sure, but it may save you many in the long run. Weigh your alternatives.

Naturally you don't have to hire an attorney to represent you at this point, but you may if you want to. You may hire him to take the case over completely or you may elect to buy half an hour of his time and ask him to review your case and offer you some advice about what you should do next. You should seriously consider hiring an attorney if your tenant has hired one, though, and you'll know whether he has when you see the words "Attorney at Law" somewhere on the written response.

Read further in this chapter to learn what's in store for you whether you hire an attorney or not, and if you think then that it all sounds too complicated for you to do by yourself, get help. Remember that you may secure legal counsel at any time you think you need it.

The Various Responses

Having read the tenant's response through carefully to know what it says, you should know whether it is a motion to quash service, a demurrer, a motion to strike, or a straightforward answer to your complaint. It could be any of them, and it could be totally groundless, filed for no other reason except to gain some additional free possession of your rental. So don't imagine that simply because your tenant has filed a response that there is any merit to it. There probably isn't, not in the least.

Let's examine the most likely responses in some detail so you will know what each one is all about.

A *motion to quash service* is used to seek dismissal of a case by alleging that there was some defect in the summons. The defect might be that you as a party to the suit served the summons, that the wrong person was served, that the summons failed to mention the five-day period available for responding, that the summons mentioned the wrong court or judicial district, that the wrong kind of summons was used, or even that the summons was never served. You can avoid this kind of a response by using the proper summons form and by seeing that it is filled out and served correctly. Remember, all the same, that even if you do everything properly, the tenant may still file a motion to quash just to be obstinate and gain time, knowing full well that he will lose the motion when you come forward to prove that you did handle the summons and service correctly.

A *demurrer* is used to delay or seek dismissal of a case by alleging that whereas the matters of fact may be true as stated, the plaintiff really has no case at all. It may allege that either the notice or the complaint was inadequate. The inadequacy might be that the notice wasn't in writing, that it wasn't signed by the right person, that it wasn't dated, that it didn't give the right address, that it was served before the tenant was delinquent, that it was improperly served, that it wasn't specific enough, that it wasn't in the alternative if it was supposed to be, that it requested rent which was higher than it should have been according to the complaint, or that it requested money other than rent. A demurrer filed concerning the complaint might mention that the complaint failed to indicate whether the rental agreement was oral or written, that the complaint was vague or inconsistent, that it failed to mention whether the required notice was served, that it failed to indicate whether the plaintiff was either the owner or the authorized agent, that it was filed before it should have been, or that it revealed a defect in another relevant notice such as one given for a rent increase. (You might want to know that there is some controversy in legal circles about what constitutes proper grounds for a demurrer in an unlawful detainer action [*Delta Imports, Inc. v. Municipal Court*, 146 CA3d 1033, 1036 194 CR 685, 687 (1983)]. Look at this case should someone file a demurrer against you.)

A *motion to strike* is used to seek a delay or dismissal of a case by alleging that the complaint contains irrelevancies, redundancies, or some other defect. These might say that the complaint includes much about the tenant which is irrelevant or repetitious, that it is not verified, that it asks for a reasonable rental value but fails to mention what a reasonable rental value is, that it asks for extra damages but fails to indicate maliciousness on the tenant's part, that it asks for attorney's fees but fails to say whether the rental agreement authorized them, that it asks for damages but fails to support the claim sufficiently, or that it asks for damages beyond the holdover period.

An *answer* to the complaint is used to defend the tenant on any of a variety of grounds, some of which are the same as those allowed under the other responses already mentioned. For example, an answer might allege that the tenant never received a notice, that the notice didn't give the correct rent owed, that the notice was unclear, that the notice failed to offer an alternative when it should have, that either the notice or the complaint was served prematurely, that the landlord refused to accept rent within the three days after serving the notice, that the rent demanded was different from what was agreed upon, that the complaint failed to specify which rental agreement provision was broken, that rent was accepted when it shouldn't have been, that the tenant was not guilty of bad faith in holding over and shouldn't be charged treble damages, that the eviction is retaliatory, that the eviction is racially motivated, that the landlord breached the warranty of habitability and isn't owed any rent, that the landlord violated local rent control or eviction ordinances, or that some other reason should be considered.

Take a look at the answer form shown here which the Judicial Council of California in its evenhandedness made available to tenants at the same time it made its complaint form available to landlords. You can see that it's much the same as the complaint form you're already familiar with, even to the point of referring to specific items in the complaint.

Now that you know what kinds of responses your tenant might make and the likely grounds for each, you should know something about handling them.

ATTORNEY OR PARTY WITHOUT ATTORNEY *(Name and Address)* (415) 123-4567 TELEPHONE NO.	FOR COURT USE ONLY
LESTER LANDLORD AND LESLIE LANDLORD 123 NEAT STREET LITTLETOWN, CA 91111	

ATTORNEY FOR *(Name)*:   Plaintiff in Pro Per

NAME OF COURT   SADDLEBACK MUNICIPAL COURT

STREET ADDRESS   110 STATE STREET

MAILING ADDRESS:

CITY AND ZIP CODE: LITTLETOWN, CA 91111

BRANCH NAME:

PLAINTIFF: LESTER LANDLORD AND LESLIE LANDLORD

DEFENDANT: DANA CHEEP AND MURETTA SHODDI

ANSWER—Unlawful Detainer	CASE NUMBER: 987654

1. Defendant *(names)*: DANA CHEEP AND MURETTA SHODDI

   answers the complaint as follows:

2. ***Check ONLY ONE of the next two boxes:***
   a. ☐ Defendant generally denies each statement of the complaint. *(Do not check this box if the complaint demands more than $1,000).*
   b. ☒ Defendant admits that all of the statements of the complaint are true EXCEPT
      (1) Defendant claims the following statements of the complaint are false *(use paragraph numbers from the complaint or explain)*:

      6a; We did not receive the 3-day notice.

      ☐ Continued on Attachment 2b(1).
      (2) Defendant has no information or belief that the following statements of the complaint are true, so defendant denies them *(use paragraph numbers from the complaint or explain)*:

      ☐ Continued on Attachment 2b(2).

3. AFFIRMATIVE DEFENSES   *(NOTE: For each box checked, you must state brief facts to support it in the space provided at the top of page two (item 3j).)*
   a. ☐ *(nonpayment of rent only)* Plaintiff has breached the warranty to provide habitable premises.
   b. ☐ *(nonpayment of rent only)* Defendant made needed repairs and properly deducted the cost from the rent, and plaintiff did not give proper credit.
   c. ☐ *(nonpayment of rent only)* On *(date)*:   , before the notice to pay or quit expired, defendant offered the rent due but plaintiff would not accept it.
   d. ☐ Plaintiff waived, changed, or canceled the notice to quit.
   e. ☐ Plaintiff served defendant with the notice to quit or filed the complaint to retaliate against defendant.
   f. ☐ By serving defendant with the notice to quit or filing the complaint, plaintiff is arbitrarily discriminating against the defendant in violation of the Constitution or laws of the United States or California.
   g. ☐ Plaintiff's demand for possession violates the local rent control or eviction control ordinance of *(city or county, title of ordinance, and date of passage)*:

      (Also, briefly state the facts showing violation of the ordinance in item 3j.)
   h. ☐ Plaintiff accepted rent from defendant to cover a period of time after the date the notice to quit expired.
   i. ☐ Other affirmative defenses are stated in item 3j.

(Continued on reverse)

Form Approved by the
Judicial Council of California
982.1(95) [Rev. January 1, 1997]   **ANSWER—Unlawful Detainer**   Civil Code, § 1940 et seq.
Code of Civil Procedure, § 425.12

For obvious reasons, you will not find a blank copy of this form in the FORMS section of this book or in Eviction Forms Creator.

PLAINTIFF *(Name)*: LESTER LANDLORD AND LESLIE LANDLORD	CASE NUMBER
DEFENDANT *(Name)*: DANA CHEEP AND MURETTA SHODDI	987654

3. AFFIRMATIVE DEFENSES *(cont'd)*

    j. Facts supporting affirmative defenses checked above *(identify each item separately by its letter from page one)*:

    (1) ☐ All the facts are stated in Attachment 3j.   (2) ☐ Facts are continued in Attachment 3j.

4. OTHER STATEMENTS

    a. ☐ Defendant vacated the premises on *(date)*:

    b. ☐ The fair rental value of the premises alleged in the complaint is excessive *(explain)*:

    c. ☐ Other *(specify)*:

5. DEFENDANT REQUESTS

    a. that plaintiff take nothing requested in the complaint.

    b. costs incurred in this proceeding.

    c. ☐ reasonable attorney fees.

    d. ☐ that plaintiff be ordered to (1) make repairs and correct the conditions that constitute a breach of the warranty to provide habitable premises and (2) reduce the monthly rent to a reasonable rental value until the conditions are corrected.

    e. ☐ other *(specify)*:

6. ☐ Number of pages attached *(specify)*:

      UNLAWFUL DETAINER ASSISTANT (Business and Professions Code sections 6400-6415)

7. *(Must be completed in all cases)* An **unlawful detainer assistant** ☒ did not ☐ did for compensation give advice or assistance with this form. *(If defendant has received any help or advice for pay from an unlawful detainer assistant, state)*:

    a. Assistant's name: b. Telephone No.:

    c. Street address, city, and ZIP:

    d. County of registration: e. Registration No.:   f. Expires on *(date)*:

    DANA CHEEP   ▶ *Dana Cheep*
    (TYPE OR PRINT NAME)   *(SIGNATURE OF DEFENDANT OR ATTORNEY)*

    MURETTA SHODDI   ▶ *Muretta Shoddi*
    (TYPE OR PRINT NAME)   *(SIGNATURE OF DEFENDANT OR ATTORNEY)*

(Each defendant for whom this answer is filed must be named in item 1 and must sign this answer unless his or her attorney signs.)

                              VERIFICATION

    (Use a different verification form if the verification is by an attorney or for a corporation or partnership.)

I am the defendant in this proceeding and have read this answer. I declare under penalty of perjury under the laws of the State of California that the foregoing is true and correct.

Date: August 10, XXXX

    DANA CHEEP   ▶ *Dana Cheep*
    (TYPE OR PRINT NAME)   *(SIGNATURE OF DEFENDANT)*

982 1(95) [Rev. January 1 1997]   **ANSWER—Unlawful Detainer**   **Page two**

For obvious reasons, you will not find a blank copy of this form in the FORMS section of this book or in Eviction Forms Creator.

Handling Responses

No matter what the response, you will have to participate in a hearing, but unless you opted to file a Declaration for Default Judgment in Lieu of Personal Testimony or to have the court clerk enter a default judgment for restitution, you would have had to appear in court anyway for the prove-up trial even if the tenant failed to respond, so it's nothing unusual, and it's certainly nothing to fear. The only difference here is that there will be an adversary facing you in court.

If the tenant files a motion to quash, a demurrer, or a motion to strike, the court hearing will be set automatically, and you should plan to be there well prepared to substantiate your position. You will get a notice in the mail, of course, but you may certainly ask the court clerk about the hearing date before the notice reaches your mailbox. If the tenant files an answer, you will have to take the initiative and request a trial date (see below).

If the response is a demurrer or a motion to strike and it alleges some deficiency which might be corrected, you would have an opportunity to correct the deficiency after the hearing. If the response is a motion to quash or an answer, and either were judged in the tenant's favor, you would lose your case and you would have to begin anew by serving the tenant with another notice in order to pursue the eviction.

Remember, the notice you serve to begin your unlawful detainer action is extremely important to your case. It must be correct. Once you file the complaint, anything found to be deficient in your notice cannot be corrected. That's why you must be absolutely certain that your notice is entirely correct *before* you file the complaint. Before you file, you may "correct" an incorrect notice by serving a new one (see chapter 5). After you file, forget it. The notice might as well have been cast in bronze. Your unlawful detainer is dependent upon that notice's correctness for its very life.

Two Defendants, One Response

Whenever you serve more than one tenant with a summons and complaint, each becomes a defendant, and each must respond to your complaint. Sometimes only one will make a response; the other doesn't bother. When that happens, be sure you get a default judgment against the one who did not respond (follow the steps in chapter 5), or you will not be able to evict that person even when you do get a judgment against the party who responded. Get the non-responding party out of the picture as soon as possible.

Settlement Before Trial

Even though your case appears to be working its way into court at this point, you may still want to work something out with your tenant before actually going to trial in order to resolve everything more quickly and to leave nothing to chance. After all, you're still looking at a delay of at least twenty-five days before the tenant is evicted if you do prevail in court, and you can't really know whether you will prevail in court until the judge gives judgment. No matter how good your case is, the judge may show your raggedy tenant some leniency or even rule against you entirely because your tenant cries bigger tears than you do.

A settlement now may be to your advantage and to your tenant's advantage as well, a true win-win arrangement.

Should your tenant or his attorney call you to suggest a settlement before trial, listen to the suggestion and give it some serious consideration as an alternative to going to trial. You may even want to contact the tenant or his attorney yourself with your own suggestions for settling your differences before trial.

In determining whether you ought to settle, you must understand what your primary objectives are. Do you want your rent money more than you want the tenant to vacate? Do you want the tenant to vacate more than you want the rent money? Do you want to minimize the hassle in continuing the eviction through the courts? In these cases and in any number of others, you may want to reach a settlement before trial because a settlement will likely save you money and time and hassles.

Remember that in most contested nonpayment cases, no matter how favorable the judgment is to you, you can't win. All you can do is try to control your losses. Forget fairness, forget ego, forget pride, but don't forget money. Don't forget that you are a business person. Don't forget that you are in the landlording business to make money. You must always keep your mind open to the many different ways there are in this business to make money and if not to make money, then to control losses.

Settlement before trial could be one of those ways.

Remember that there's now a certain amount of pressure to settle which didn't exist before you filed your unlawful detainer. You have put some pressure on the tenant by filing the unlawful detainer, and your tenant has put some pressure on you by filing an answer. As a result, both of you are likely to be more agreeable to coming up with a settlement you can live with. You may agree to terms that you wouldn't have agreed to before, and your tenant may do the same.

You both know what you're facing if you don't come to a settlement yourselves. You're facing uncertainty.

Face it, you have nothing to lose in trying to settle before trial, that is, if you believe that you are dealing with someone who can be dealt with, someone who is neither a professional deadbeat nor a genuine ignoramus nor a real loony.

Should you decide that you might be able to settle with your tenant, rehearse what you're going to say to him. Stress the advantages of settling over the disadvantages of not settling.

Start by asking something like this, "Do you know what's really going to happen to you as a result of your being evicted through the courts?" Most tenants don't have a clue.

"First of all, I'm going to get a judgment against you which will go down on your credit rating immediately and remain there for seven years. Second, the sheriff is going to come out here and humiliate you in front of your neighbors by throwing you out on the street and locking the door behind you. Third, I'm going to inventory your belongings and move them into storage. Fourth, I'm going to hire a bill collector to hound you for the money you owe me from now until kingdom come. Fifth, you're going to have trouble renting from any other landlord in the future. Sixth, I'm going to tell the IRS that you had income equal to the amount of the judgment against you, and you're going to have to pay taxes on it. Do you want all this to happen to you?"

Finish up by saying, "Consider what you stand to gain by fighting this eviction. There is only one thing. You stand to gain a few extra days of staying here. That's all. There's nothing more. Just remember, once you've been evicted from here, that eviction is going to haunt you long after you leave."

Next, try to figure out what the tenant's concerns really are. Does he need a little more time to find another place? Does he need a little more time to raise the money to pay you off? Would he be ready to move today if you were to agree not to seek a judgment against him? Does he need some help of one sort or another? What can the two of you do right now to settle the case?

If you can establish some terms agreeable to both of you, write them down and sign them. You could summarize them in a simple agreement, something like this:

```
Lester Landlord agrees to drop
his unlawful detainer action
against Richard Renter provided
that Richard Renter vacates the
premises known as 456 Sweet St.,
Littletown, CA, completely as of
tomorrow, March 12, xxxx.

Richard Renter agrees to leave
the premises clean and undamaged.

Richard Renter agrees to allow
his entire security deposit to be
applied to his past-due rent and
other charges.

Once Richard Renter has vacated,
Lester Landlord will ask the
court to dismiss the case without
prejudice and will send a copy of
the dismissal to Richard Renter.

Dated:      Signed: [both parties]
```

Use a simple agreement only if the tenant agrees to pay you in full or vacate immediately. Do not use a simple agreement to spell out a payment scheme, for if the tenant makes only one payment and refuses to make any more, you will have to start the eviction from scratch.

In order to keep your unlawful detainer alive while still giving your tenant a chance to perform whatever terms you agree upon, you should use a stipulated agreement. There's a big difference between an ordinary agreement and a stipulated agreement. Whereas you can create an ordinary agreement anytime (the payment pledge introduced in chapter 1 is one example of an ordinary agreement), you cannot even consider creating a

```
 1  Lester Landlord & Leslie Landlord
    123 Neat Street
 2  Littletown, California 91111
    415-123-4567
 3  Plaintiff in Propria Persona

 4

 5

 6

 7

 8      IN THE MUNICIPAL COURT OF ____LITTLETOWN____ JUDICIAL DISTRICT,

 9      COUNTY OF _____SADDLEBACK_____, STATE OF CALIFORNIA

10      LESTER LANDLORD
        LESLIE LANDLORD
11      _____,)
                            Plaintiff,)    NO. 1234567890
12              vs.                    )
        RICHARD RENTER                 )    STIPULATION FOR ENTRY
13      ROSE RENTER                    )    OF JUDGMENT
        _____,)
14                          Defendant.)
        _____)

15          Plaintiff(s) and Defendant(s) named above hereby agree to settle

16      the above-entitled action, which is for unlawful detainer of premises

17      located at 456 Sweet Street

18      in the city of Littletown

19      in the above-named county, state of California.

20          The settlement terms and conditions are as follows (applicable

21      paragraphs are checked):

22          [X] Plaintiff shall have immediate judgment for restitution of

23      premises. Execution on this judgment shall [cross out one] (not be

24      stayed)  (ｘｅ ｘｓ ｔａ ｙｅ ｄ ｘ ｘｘｘ ｘｘXXXXXXXXXXXXXXXXXXXXXXXXXXXXXXX).

25          [X] Defendant(s) agree to vacate the premises on or before
                September 30, XXXX
26

27          [X] Defendant(s) agree to pay Plaintiff(s) the sum of $ 730.00 ,

28      of which $  730.00    is payment in full of the rent owing for the

29      period from  September 1, XXXX  through September 30, XXXX          ,
```

You will find a blank copy of this form in the FORMS section of this book and in Eviction Forms Creator.

1 and of which $ XXXXX   is for the following:

2

3 Defendant(s) agree to pay this sum [cross out one] (immediately) ~~(on or~~

4 ~~before~~XXXXXXXXXXXXXXXXXXXXXXXXXXXXXXXX). If Defendant(s) fail to pay as

5 agreed, Plaintiff(s) shall make an ex parte application to the court

6 for a judgment or amended judgment for the portion of this sum owing

7 and for immediate restitution of the premises.

8   [X] The deposits of $ 500.00   being held for security on the

9 premises shall be applied as follows: $105.00 for accrued costs,

10 and the balance to be returned after Defendants have moved out.

11   [X] Plaintiff(s) and Defendant(s) agree to drop any and all other

12 claims they may have made against one another as landlord(s) and as

13 tenant(s).

14   [X] Plaintiff(s) and Defendant(s) agree that this stipulation

15 makes no conclusion as to which side has prevailed in this legal

16 action.

17

18 Dated: September 17, XXXX   *Lester Landlord*

19   *Leslie Landlord*
                                   _____
                                          Plaintiff(s)

20

21 Dated: September 17, XXXX   *Richard Renter*

22   *Rose Renter*
                                   _____
                                          Defendant(s)

23

24

25

26

27

28

29

You will find a blank copy of this form in the FORMS section of this book and in Eviction Forms Creator.

stipulated agreement without first having filed a lawsuit. It's part of a lawsuit. If a tenant does not abide by a stipulated agreement, you can have the tenant evicted legally in short order.

In order to create a stipulated agreement, you will need two legal documents. The one is called a Stipulation for Entry of Judgment, which outlines the terms of the stipulation and is signed by the parties involved. The other one is called a Judgment Pursuant to Stipulation, which is the judge's approval of the stipulation agreement and is signed by the judge.

You will find versions of both these legal documents in the FORMS section, but only the first one appears here in example form to show how it might be filled out. The second one does not appear here as an example because it simply summarizes the information in the first document.

You may submit the two stipulation documents to the court straightaway, or you may choose to wait. In the end, you may never submit them at all if the tenant performs as promised. What you do about submitting and filing these documents will depend upon how the tenant views his credit rating. Keep this possibility in mind when you're bargaining with him. He may want to keep the judgment from being filed badly enough to make certain concessions to you.

Preparing for Trial—The Judge

You may think that your case is so one-sided in your favor that you needn't even be concerned about which judge will hear your case. You may think that nobody could possibly side with your tenant once you have an opportunity to present your case. You may think, too, that judges are completely impartial, or else they wouldn't be sitting on the bench.

Think again.

Some judges are not impartial. They tend to side with tenants or with landlords most of the time. Well, you certainly don't want to appear before a judge who favors tenants, not if you have a choice in the matter. You may indeed have a choice in the matter, and you may want to do a little sleuthing down at the courthouse to learn whatever you can about the judges you could get.

To find out pretty quickly, ask the clerk which attorney handles more evictions than anybody else in the jurisdiction and then ask whose courtroom this attorney is appearing in today. That courtroom will likely have the judge who's most fa-

vorable to landlords.

Now, even though you may not request that your case be heard by a particular judge, you may be able to request that it be heard at a particular time, a time which is most convenient for you. Use this available option to request a time when the judge who is most likely favorable to landlords will be hearing unlawful detainers.

Of course, you may find that the judge you think would be favorable to landlords is not favorable to landlords who appear *in pro per*, and the whole effort to find the right judge may backfire. That's just a risk you take.

Preparing for Trial—The Paperwork

When a tenant files an answer to your complaint, you will have to request a trial date yourself using the form entitled Memorandum to Set Case for Trial (you'll need an original and two copies, plus a copy for each additional defendant who answered). Either you or the tenant may request a jury trial, but whoever requests it will have to pay more costs, and generally no one wants to pay unless the tenant is willing to gamble on still another delaying action.

Have someone other than yourself mail a completed copy of the memorandum form to the defendant, and then have that person sign it to declare that you have complied with the service requirements.

Take the original and the other copy of the memorandum to the court clerk's office, and ask that your trial be set for the earliest possible date. Fortunately, there's an important law, CCP §1170.5, which requires courts, except under unusual circumstances, to schedule unlawful detainer trials within 20 days following the filing of a memorandum. When you get your date, make sure it's within the legal limits.

Sometime before the trial, you should prepare a Judgment (Unlawful Detainer—After Trial) form and a Writ of Execution. You are an optimist, aren't you? This judgment form is similar enough to its counterpart in a defaulted case for you to use the default sample as a guide. The writ is the same in both situations.

Both you and the tenant have the right before trial to try to discover certain things about the other's case which might help your own, and for that the Judicial Council has prepared a form. It's called Form Interrogatories—Unlawful De-

Name, Address, and Telephone No. of Attorney(s)

Lester Landlord & Leslie Landlord
123 Neat Street
Littletown, California 91111
415-123-4567

Space Below for Use of Court Clerk Only

Attorney(s) for Plaintiff in Propria Persona

MUNICIPAL COURT OF CALIFORNIA, COUNTY OF SADDLEBACK
LITTLETOWN JUDICIAL DISTRICT

Lester Landlord
Leslie Landlord   Plaintiff(s)
      vs.

Richard Renter
Rose Renter
             Defendant(s)

Case Number 1234567890

MEMORANDUM TO SET CASE FOR TRIAL

I hereby represent to the court that this case is at issue, and request that it be set for trial.

Nature of the case: Unlawful Detainer

Jury trial ___is not___ demanded. Time necessary for trial: ___1/2 hour___
      (is or is not)   (Estimate carefully)

This case ___is___ entitled to legal preference in setting ___C.C.P. 1179a___
      (is or is not)   (If so, state reasons)

_____ . Reporter ___is not___ requested.
                                                       (is or is not)

The following dates are NOT acceptable to me: April 8, XXXX, April 10, XXXX

Names, addresses and telephone numbers of attorneys for other parties, or of parties appearing in person:

Lester Landlord & Leslie Landlord   Richard Renter & Rose Renter
123 Neat Street   456 Sweet Street
Littletown, California 91111   Littletown, California 91111
(510) 123-4567   (510) 123-9876

Dated: ___March 22, XXXX___   *Lester Landlord*
                                        (Note: Must be signed by attorney or party requesting setting)

PROOF OF SERVICE BY MAIL — CCP 1013a, 2015.5

I declare that: I am a (resident of / employee in) the county of _____Saddleback_____, California.
                                                           (County where mailing occurred)

I am over the age of eighteen years and not a party to the within entitled cause; my (business / residence) address is:
_____12 Chanslor Ct. Orangevale, CA_____

On ___March 22, XXXX___, I served the attached MEMORANDUM TO SET CASE FOR TRIAL on the
      (Date)

___defendant(s)___ in said cause, by placing a true copy thereof enclosed in a sealed envelope

with postage thereon fully prepaid, in the United States mail at ___Orangevale, CA___ addressed as follows:

Richard Renter & Rose Renter
456 Sweet Street
Littletown, California 91111

I declare under penalty of perjury that the foregoing is true and correct, and that this declaration was executed on
___March 22, XXXX___, at ___Orangevale, CA___, California.
   (Date)   (Place)

___George Bunn___   *George Bunn*
(Type or Print Name)   (Signature)   efc

This is a "local" form; ask the clerk for the one your court uses, or try one of several included in Eviction Forms Creator.

tainer. Because it's seven pages long and doesn't require any explanation to complete for someone who has come this far in handling his own unlawful detainer, you won't find it reproduced here, but you will find a blank copy of it in the FORMS section.

Both discoveries and the form itself would appear to benefit the tenant more than the landlord, for there are many more things a tenant might discover about your case against him than you might discover about his defense. Still, you might want to use the form for a few things under exceptional circumstances, such as for discovering the names and tenancy dates of un-

interrogatories no sooner than five days following service of the summons and complaint. Normally an opponent has thirty days to respond, but since an unlawful detainer trial must be set no more than twenty days following the filing of the Memorandum to Set, answers to unlawful detainer interrogatories must be returned within five days following service (CCP §2030[h]).

As your trial date nears, review your complaint and the tenant's answer before you go to trial, make notes about what you're going to say, and arrange to bring along whatever witnesses, documents, photographs, or tapes might be helpful to your case. Don't suppose that you will win

knowns who are living on your property, discovering the basis for a tenant's warranty of habitability defense, and discovering various facts involved in any affirmative defense the tenant might claim to be making. Don't use the form to harass the tenant, that is, don't check off every conceivable question. That kind of harassment could backfire on you if the tenant were to call it to the judge's attention. Use the form strictly to discover relevant information.

If you are going to use your discoveries at the trial, you must receive the answers to your interrogatories before the trial, so you'll need to serve them relatively soon. However, you may serve

simply because your cause is just or because you've kissed the Blarney Stone. You have to convince the judge that your cause is just, and you must have the proof on hand to do it. Otherwise it's your word against your tenant's, and he may have kissed the Blarney Stone more passionately than you did.

Remember, that judge you're appearing before doesn't know you or your tenant from Eve or Adam. If he did know either of you, he'd have to disqualify himself. For all he knows, your tenant might be a good Samaritan, and you might be an ogre of a landlord who is accustomed to exacting pints of blood from tenants just for late fees. If you are that predatory, don't look it in court at least; look honest, tolerant, long-suffering, and maybe even a little oppressed.

Every successful trial lawyer in the country spends a good deal of pre-trial time grooming his clients for court. A client may be as guilty as a hit man caught with a smoking gun in his hand, but in court he shouldn't look guilty.

You should pay attention to what you look like in court, too. Don't prejudice your case by looking like an unscrupulous, filthy-rich landlord. Leave your pinkie rings, your gold chains, your monogrammed shirts, your designer jeans, your Rolex watch, and your Gucci shoes at home. Put on your plain pockets jeans, your Penney's work

opportunity. Understand what you need to do in court, and then do it.

If your complaint is for nonpayment of rent, you will have to prove that your notice was served properly, that it accurately stated the amount of rent due, and that the rent was not paid. If your complaint is for breach of contract, you will have to prove both that the tenant has breached the contract and that he has been properly served. If your complaint is for waste, nuisance, or unlawful acts, you must prove that the tenant committed the acts you allege and that you served him proper notice. If your complaint is for termination of tenancy and you're not in a rent-control area, you need prove only that the notice was

shirt, your Timex wrist watch, and your well-worn jogging shoes. Look like the salt of the earth. Justice may be blind, but judges are not, and the judge is the law in that courtroom where you'll be appearing. Judges are only human, and they will be scrutinizing you and your tenant in court for clues which will sway their judgment one way or the other.

One thing which will sway a judge is organization. All told, you and your tenant get around twenty minutes in court. To make your portion of this time count, you must organize your evidence and your remarks well for this one brief

properly served. The burden is on the tenant to show that the eviction is discriminatory or retaliatory.

In the Courtroom

Should you feel especially apprehensive about appearing in court, find out when other contested unlawful detainer cases are scheduled to be heard. Attend one and observe what goes on. Imagine yourself appearing and speaking on your own behalf. You'll find that what goes on in your local court isn't so very different from the "People's Court" television programs you've seen. The only difference is that attorneys are allowed.

To free your stomach's butterflies on your big day, rehearse what you're going to say before you walk into the courtroom. When the judge calls upon you to present your case, speak up and tell the truth, the whole relevant truth. Don't waste the court's time with irrelevancies. Remember that you and your tenant together have twenty minutes. That gives you less than ten minutes to tell your side of the story. Don't try to tell the history of the world in that amount of time. You can't. Be brief in your remarks. Address yourself to the judge, and don't argue with the defendant.

Also, remember what every experienced courtroom lawyer says about questioning witnesses, "Don't ask any question unless you already know what the witness's answer is going to be." Unanticipated answers have a way of blindsiding you and demolishing your case.

Your courtroom dialogue might go something like this:

Judge: All right, Lester Landlord, what do you have to say for yourself?

Lester: Your honor, my name is Lester Landlord, and I am the plaintiff in this case. I am the owner of a little duplex at 456 Sweet Street right here in town and am entitled to possession of the premises. In order to save the court's time, I would like to call the defendant to the stand now and ask him to testify to certain facts in this case. May I do that, your honor?

Judge: You may. Call Richard Renter to the stand.

Bailiff: Richard Renter, do you swear to tell the truth, the whole truth, and nothing but the truth, so help you God?

Richard: I do.

Lester: Please state your name.

Richard: My name is Richard Renter.

Lester: Where are you currently living?

Richard: I live at 456 Sweet Street, Littletown.

Lester: Did you rent 456 Sweet Street from me for $360 on December 16th, XXXX, and did you sign this written agreement to that effect?

Richard: Yes, I did, but you raised my rent last month.

Lester: Is the rent there now $434 per month?

Richard: Sure is.

Lester: And did I serve you with a notice like this one on January 12th, more than a month and a half in advance, that your rent was going to go up on the first of March?

Richard: You did, but I told you then that I was going to be laid off and that I wouldn't have any money to pay you the rent for a while.

Lester: Did you pay me the rent on March first?

Richard: No, I didn't. I just told you I got laid off and didn't have the money to pay my rent.

Lester: Your honor, I would like to ask the court to disregard the defendant's reason for not paying his rent. That was not part of my question.

Judge: Sustained. Do you have any further questions?

Lester: Yes, your honor. Richard Renter, were you served on March 12th with a 3-Day Notice to Pay Rent or Quit like this one?

Richard: Yes, I was.

Lester: I have no further questions, your honor.

Judge: You may step down.

Lester: Would you like me to take the stand and testify to these same facts that Richard Renter has already testified to, your honor?

Judge: No, that won't be necessary. Richard Renter, would you like to testify now on your own behalf?

If Richard does testify, write down any points he makes which you feel should be dealt with in a cross-examination, especially if he is lying about something crucial to the case, like not receiving the notice. Don't worry if he tells his hard-luck story to the court, even if he embellishes it enough to move the entire courtroom to tears, yourself included. His being out of work is not relevant to the case, and while it may gain him the sympathy of the court, it's not enough to gain him the right to live rent-free in your rental. The court is concerned only about whether he rented the place from you at an agreed-upon rent, whether he paid the rent when it was due, whether you gave him notice that the rent was delinquent, whether you have taken any rent money from him since giving him the notice, and whether he still lives there. If he says anything to refute what you establish about those concerns, then you should make note of them and attempt to prove he is wrong.

The judge may or may not render his verdict

as soon as he has heard both sides. If he does render his verdict right then, and it's in your favor, submit your judgment form to the courtroom clerk for approval and signing. Then follow the same procedure for filing the writ, etc. as it's explained in chapter 5 for a default hearing. If the judge decides to take the matter "under submission," he will have the judgment form mailed to you, and you will have to wait before proceeding any further.

If the judge's verdict is not in your favor, figure out exactly what you need to change in order to be assured of success before you make another attempt to evict the tenant. Waste no time. Go right ahead and begin the process all over again. Do it right this time.

By the way, each time I have had to begin the process all over again with the same tenant, and I've had to do so only twice, I have won in short order. The tenants recognized that they wouldn't stand a chance using the same arguments twice, and they didn't even bother to answer the complants.

- Make every effort to understand any response your tenant files.
- Consider hiring an attorney more seriously if your tenant responds to your complaint and is himself represented by an attorney.
- Consider the advantages of settling before trial using a stipulated agreement.
- Be well prepared to prove your case in court.

11
Handling the Bankruptcy Case

For some time, declaring bankruptcy was a popular last-ditch measure which unscrupulous tenants would take to delay their inevitable eviction. Just by filing bankruptcy they'd get an automatic stay. The stay would put the brakes on the landlord's every effort to evict them until the bankruptcy court allowed the eviction to continue. In the meantime, the tenants stayed put.

Fortunately, one bankruptcy judge and a majority of California's law makers came to recognize that these tenants, prodded by unscrupulous eviction-delay services, were declaring bankruptcy for one reason and one reason only—to beat their landlords out of as much rent as they possibly could. The judge and the law makers have tried to put a stop to this practice.

Statistics now show that they have been largely successful. Back in 1991 the percentage of bankruptcy cases filed primarily to stop evictions was a whopping 16.9%. Today it's a minuscule 1%!

Nowadays there's little likelihood that you will find yourself stymied by a tenant who declares bankruptcy primarily to keep you from evicting him in a timely manner. Still, you ought to know what has happened to curtail this abuse and what you need to do to see an eviction through to completion if your tenant does declare bankruptcy during eviction proceedings.

The Judge and *In Re Smith*

After hearing hundreds of patently frivolous cases where tenants were trying to delay their eviction by filing bankruptcy, one judge decided that he'd heard enough, and he wrote an opinion so revealing that I have reproduced it in its entirety in the back of this book as Appendix D. The judge who wrote this opinion was Vincent Zurzolo, and his opinion is referred to as *In re Smith* 105 B.R. 50 (Bkrtcy.C.D.Cal. 1989).

Take a few minutes to read it. It's not too technical for us lay folks to understand. It reveals much about the practical side of life inside the bankruptcy court system, and it might put a smile on your face. It put such a big one on mine when I first read it that I sat right down and wrote the good judge a thank-you note.

Basically, Judge Zurzolo concludes that a month-to-month residential tenancy itself has inconsequential monetary value, and therefore, an unlawful detainer which terminates such a tenancy should not be stayed at all by the filing of a bankruptcy. Only the money judgment should merit the concern of a bankruptcy court, not the judgment for possession.

Holy toilet tanks! Here's a court opinion which makes perfect sense, doesn't it? Why in the world should a bankruptcy, of all things, allow a tenant to continue living in your rental dwelling rent free when you already have a judgment entitling you to reclaim possession?

That's a travesty of justice. A bankruptcy is supposed to insure that justice is done, not frustrated. It's supposed to help both debtors *and* creditors settle their affairs in an organized fashion. The bankruptcy court identifies all the debtor's assets, liabilities, and creditors and then determines who should get what. That's the way the system is supposed to work. Identify everything of value, identify everybody involved, distribute the assets in some equitable fashion, and get on with life. Well and good. So where does the tenancy fit in?

What Judge Zurzolo is saying in his opinion is that the *tenancy* which the debtor wants to prolong with a bankruptcy filing *is not an asset.* It has no monetary value whatsoever. It's more of a condition, like an ability or an achievement or an illness or a job at Burger King. What're they worth? Nothing, really. Can they be pawned or auctioned or sold? Nope. As a consequence, none of them warrants protection from a bankruptcy court. The bankrupt tenant's eviction shouldn't

129

be held up by the bankruptcy filing at all.

Wow! This is important stuff for any landlord confronted with tenants who think they're going to pull a fast one at the very last minute and enjoy still more rent-free living! The tenants might think they're entitled to an automatic stay by filing bankruptcy, but they are in for a big surprise when they discover that you are entitled to get automatic relief! At least you would be entitled to automatic relief if Judge Zurzolo had his way.

The trouble is that Judge Zurzolo's decision is not binding in other bankruptcy courts, and it may not get you anywhere if you try to use it to your benefit wherever in California you happen to be. Nonetheless, here's what he says in his conclusion:

"I further observe that this opinion will have absolutely no effect on this problem unless residential landlords, and the attorneys who represent them, call it to the attention of the state courts that issue unlawful detainer judgments and convince those state courts to order the proper state law enforcement officials to evict debtor/tenants without first requiring residential landlords to obtain relief from the Stay. If this chain of events results, there is a chance that this widespread and daily abuse of the Bankruptcy Court system and the shameless defrauding of thousands of tenant victims will cease."

Judge Zurzolo urges us to avoid taking our cases to bankruptcy court unless our municipal courts absolutely refuse to allow enforcement of the judgment. He goes on to state emphatically in the end of Section VI. The Scope of the Stay:

"I conclude that the Stay does not enjoin a landlord from regaining possession of residential premises from a wrongfully holding-over bankruptcy debtor/tenant, as long as the landlord seeks only to repossess the property and not to enforce any other portion of his unlawful detainer judgment against the debtor and the bankruptcy estate, such as collecting money damages."

Much as we would like to take advantage of Judge Zurzolo's common-sense decision, we may not be able to take advantage of it. We may be stymied because his decision holds no sway in bankruptcy courts outside the Central District, where he holds court, and it may not even hold sway outside of his own court. We have no way of knowing for sure.

As a consequence, I would suggest that you not even try to take advantage of Judge Zurzolo's decision when you encounter a tenant who declares bankruptcy at the very last minute in order to gain a few more days of rent-free living before being evicted. You'd be wasting your time.

CCP §1162.2 and §715.050

No doubt mindful of the thinking behind *In re Smith*, California's legislators have tried to help those unfortunate landlords whose tenants declare bankruptcy in order to delay an eviction. They passed two laws to help.

The first one, CCP §1162.2, already referred to in chapter 5, delays public access to unlawful detainer paperwork for sixty days. As a consequence, the unscrupulous eviction defense services which used to be able to access court documents to learn the names of tenants being evicted and could then solicit them as clients, can no longer find the tenants so easily. Since they can't find the tenants, they can't use their bag of tricks, including the filing of bankruptcy, to delay evictions.

The second law is CCP §715.050, and here's what it says:

"Except with respect to enforcement of a judgment for money, a writ of possession issued pursuant to a judgment for possession in an unlawful detainer action shall be enforced pursuant to this chapter without delay, notwithstanding receipt of notice of the filing by the defendant of a bankruptcy proceeding."

Major Conflict

Before you try using this second law to your advantage, however, you should know that it is a state law. Bankruptcy law is federal law. Wherever there is a conflict, federal law takes precedence. Even though CCP §715.050 is still on the books, it has been found to be in conflict with federal bankruptcy law (*In re DiGiorgio* (CD CA 196) 200 BR 664, 675). Much as you might like to use it, and much as bankruptcy court judges like Judge Zurzolo would like you to be able to use it, you simply cannot. It has been found to be "unconstitutional on its face."

Since you cannot proceed with the eviction without first getting the stay lifted, you have no real choice any longer. You cannot hope to proceed with your unlawful detainer in municipal court. You must go to federal bankruptcy court.

Proceeding in Bankruptcy Court

When you have to go into bankruptcy court to petition for early relief in order to evict a tenant, you are going to feel pretty hostile toward the no-good tenant who is costing you all this extra time and money. Grit your teeth and press on, knowing that the tenant is going to get his comeuppance eventually.

Bankruptcy courts look more favorably upon landlords' petitions to proceed with evictions nowadays. The bankruptcy ploy, which used to gain tenants a delay of at least sixty days, is now gaining them as little as seven days, and it's costing them far more than they realize when they resort to it. It scars their credit and haunts them for years.

To get into bankruptcy court, you'll first need to note the court's physical location and its telephone number.

There aren't nearly as many bankruptcy courts as there are other courts. In all, California has only twelve bankruptcy courts spread throughout the state.

Call the court and tell the clerk the situation. You'll find that bankruptcy clerks are generally quite helpful, and they know what they're doing because they handle stays all the time. In fact, most bankruptcy litigation consists of motions for relief from stay. She will tell you that in order to get relief, you will need to get a hearing date directly from the calendar clerk first. Go ahead and get the earliest possible date.

Next, you prepare and file a Relief from Stay Cover Sheet, a Notice of Motion for Relief from the Automatic Stay, a Motion for Relief from the Automatic Stay (Unlawful Detainer), and a Declaration in Support of Motion for Relief. Then you pay a filing fee and serve the papers as directed.

Tell the clerk that you live some distance from the court and that you would like to keep your trips there to a minimum. Ask her whether she has any suggestions. You might be able to minimize your trips by taking a portable typewriter with you on your very first visit, so that you can fill out all the paperwork right then and there and file it immediately.

Make sure that you have a copy of the tenant's paperwork with you when you prepare your own. You'll need it for reference, and you'll need your

BANKRUPTCY COURTS

NORTHERN DISTRICT
235 Pine St.
San Francisco, CA 94120
(415) 705-3200

1300 Clay St., Rm. 300
Oakland, CA 94604
(510) 273-7212

280 S. First St., Rm. 3035
San Jose, CA 95113
(408) 291-7286

99 S. "E" St.
Santa Rosa, CA 95404
(707) 525-8539

EASTERN DISTRICT
8308 U.S. Courthouse
650 Capitol Mall
Sacramento, CA 95814
(916) 551-2662

2656 U.S. Courthouse
1130 "O" St.
Fresno, CA 93721
(209) 487-5217

1130 12th St., Rm. C
Modesto, CA 95354
(209) 521-5160

CENTRAL DISTRICT
255 E. Temple St.
Los Angeles, CA 90012
(213) 894-3118

34 Civic Center Plaza
Santa Ana, CA 92701
(714) 836-2993

699 N. Arrowhead Ave., Rm. 105
San Bernardino, CA 92401
(909) 383-5717

222 E. Carrillo St., Rm. 107
Santa Barbara, CA 93101
(805) 897-3870

SOUTHERN DISTRICT
U.S. Courthouse
325 West "F" St.
San Diego, CA 92101
(619) 557-5620

checkbook for funds to pay the filing fee. As for the paperwork, the clerk will supply you with the Relief from Stay Cover Sheet, and she may have forms similar to Judicial Council forms for the Notice of Motion and the Motion itself. Use what forms she has available.

If you have to make up these documents from scratch yourself, ask the clerk whether you should use pleading paper (there's a blank in the FORMS section of this book) or ordinary typing paper. You can't go wrong using pleading paper, of course. No matter what kind of paper you use, you must follow a particular format in the upper section of the first page of each document. This particular format enables the court's paper shufflers to identify each case's paperwork readily. Below is what it looks like.

You should double-space the text, which appears next in the document, and number each page at the bottom.

Incidentally, in all of this paperwork, you refer to yourself as the "movant." You're akin to somebody who makes a motion at a meeting, saying, "I move that we adopt the resolution." This person in legalese would be a "movant." Because you are making a motion before the bankruptcy court in this case, you are the "movant."

The Notice of Motion for Relief from the Automatic Stay should read something like this:

NOTICE IS HEREBY GIVEN that on [date] at [time], the above-en-titled Court, located at [street address, including city], Movant in the above-captioned matter will present a motion to have the automatic stay terminated, conditioned, modified, and/or annulled. The particulars of said motion are described in the accompanying Motion, Declaration, and other such evidence as may be presented to the Court on the above date. Debtors and trustee, if any, are hereby informed that no written response is required to oppose this motion. Further, no oral testimony will normally be presented at the above-described hearing. However, the debtors and/or the debtors' attorney and the trustee must appear at said hearing, or the relief requested by the Movant will be granted. The applicable law is United States Bankruptcy Code 11 U.S.C. 362 and Bankruptcy Rules of Procedure 4001 and 9014.

Dated this [day] of [month and year].

Respectfully submitted,
[Movant's Name]
Movant

The Motion for Relief from the Automatic Stay

```
 1 ‖ Lester Landlord
     Leslie Landlord
 2 ‖ 123 Neat Street
     Littletown, CA 91111
 3 ‖ (510) 123-4567
     Movant in Propria Persona
 4 ‖

 5 ‖                 IN THE UNITED STATES BANKRUPTCY COURT
                    FOR THE XXXX DISTRICT OF CALIFORNIA
 6 ‖                          XXXX DIVISION
                    [use the appropriate court identification]
 7 ‖
     IN RE:                              )  CASE NO. XXXXX
 8 ‖                                     )  CHAPTER XX
     RONALD E. ROTTER and               )  RS NO. [number stamped by clerk]
 9 ‖ HAZEL C. ROTTER                     )  HEARING TO BE HELD
                                         )  DATE:  XXXX
10 ‖ DEBTORS                             )  TIME:  XXXX
                                         )  PLACE:  COURTROOM XX
11 ‖
             NOTICE OF/MOTION FOR RELIEF FROM THE AUTOMATIC STAY
12 ‖                  [use the appropriate title]
```

(Unlawful Detainer) should read something like this (remember that this motion is a separate document all its own and that its first page should include a properly formatted first-page heading):

MOTION FOR RELIEF FROM THE AUTO-
MATIC STAY (UNLAWFUL DETAINER)
[use the appropriate title]

1. Movant in the above-captioned matter moves this Court
for an Order granting relief from
the automatic stay on the grounds
set forth herein.

2. A Petition under Chapter
[Chapter number of Debtor's filing; either 7, 11, 12, or 13] was
filed on [date].

3. Movant alleges the following
in support of its motion:
a. Debtor occupies the premises
commonly known as [street address, including city].
b. Debtor occupies the premises
[select one of the following: on
a month-to-month tenancy; on a
holdover tenancy; pursuant to a
lease in default; on a tenancy at
will; after a foreclosure sale;
or pursuant to a terminated
lease].
c. Debtor last paid the monthly
rent of $[amount] on [date],
which paid for the period through
[date], and has paid no rent
since.
d. The procedural status of
Movant's case against debtor in
state Court is as follows [in-
clude only those which are appli-
cable]:
i. On [date], Movant served a Notice to Pay Rent or Quit on the
Debtors.
ii.
On [date], Movant filed a Complaint for Unlawful Detainer in
State Court.
iii.
On [date], a Judgment was entered
on said Complaint by the State
Court.

[THIS ENTIRE SECTION IS OP-
TIONAL] 4. Movant alleges that

Debtor filed this bankruptcy case
in bad faith based upon the following [include only whatever is
appropriate]:
a. The Debtor filed what is commonly referred to as a "face
sheet" filing of only a few pages
consisting of the Petition and a
few other documents. No Schedules or Statement of Affairs accompanied the Petition.
b. The landlord and/or the
landlord's attorney was the only
creditor listed on the master
mailing matrix.
c. Movant is informed and believes
that the Debtor filed the Petition herein for the sole purpose
of attempting to obstruct a State
Court unlawful detainer proceeding and without intending to seek
a fresh start as provided under
the Bankruptcy Code. Debtor's
use of the bankruptcy system for
such purpose is an abuse of such
system.

5. Movant attaches the following supporting evidence pursuant
to Local Bankruptcy Rule
112(3)(a) [include only whatever
is appropriate]:
a. Declarations under penalty of
perjury which include any material to which the declarant would
be allowed, under Federal Rules
of Evidence, to testify if called
as a witness at the hearing.
b. Copy of State Court Unlawful
Detainer judgment.
c. [Other evidence].

6. There are [number] attached
pages of supporting documenta-
tion.

WHEREFORE, Movant prays that
this Court issue an Order granting the following [include only
whatever is appropriate]:

Relief from the automatic stay,
or alternatively, for adequate
protection.

Prospective relief and findings
under Bankruptcy Code §109(g).

Attorney's fees and/or sanctions as requested in the supporting Declaration and Order.

Dated this [day] of [month and year].

Respectfully submitted,
[Movant's Name]
Movant

The Declaration in Support of Motion for Relief, which you have to make up to accompany the other paperwork, should read something like this (use an appropriate first-page heading):

I, [give your full name], am over eighteen (18) years of age, and declare as follows:

1. I am the Movant in this action and have personal knowledge of the facts stated herein and am competent to testify about them.

2. Judgment was entered for the Movant in [name and address of municipal court] on [date] for possession of the premises located at [address] and for $[amount of judgment].

3. Movant is owner of and entitled to possession of said premises.

4. Debtor remains in possession of said premises.

5. There is a need for this stay to be lifted because Movant is incurring additional costs on a daily basis as a result of Debtor's continuing possession.

6. To the best of my knowledge, information and belief, the Debtor has no equity in the property, and the property is not necessary to any effective reorganization by the Debtor.

I declare under penalty of perjury under the laws of the State of California that the foregoing is true and correct.

[Dated] [Signed]

You need an original plus two copies of all this paperwork.

You also need to provide a Proof of Service. Word it as follows (because it is really a part of other documents, the proof need not include a first-page heading):

PROOF OF SERVICE

I, the undersigned, do hereby certify that a true and correct copy of the Notice of Motion for Relief from the Automatic Stay and Motion for Relief from the Automatic Stay and the Declaration in Support of Motion for Relief was forwarded to all interested parties at their last known address in this action by placing a true and correct copy thereof in a sealed envelope with postage thereon fully prepaid in the United States Mail at [city], California, addressed as set forth below on this [date].
[Type your name below this statement and sign it.]
[Give the names and addresses of everyone to whom you sent these documents, and also indicate how you sent them.]

Send copies of the documents to the debtors, their attorney, and to the trustee, if any. Send them by certified mail, return receipt requested, and include the post office's certified mail number as well.

Ask the calendar clerk about the time frame for sending these documents, and make absolutely certain that you send them in plenty of time to comply.

Then prepare the Order for Lifting the Automatic Stay, the paper you need from the bankruptcy court to show the municipal court that you have had the stay lifted. Take the original and three copies of it with you into court. It should read something like this (use an appropriate first-page heading):

Upon reading the Movant's MOTION FOR RELIEF FROM THE AUTOMATIC STAY and the DECLARATION IN SUPPORT OF MOTION FOR RELIEF and hearing this matter, the Court appears satisfied therefrom that there exists no reason to stay the Movant's action for unlawful detainer against Debtor.

IT IS HEREBY ORDERED therefore that Movant is authorized, to the

```
extent that such authority is re-
quired, [either to continue the
unlawful detainer in state court
or to enforce the judgment] to
regain possession of the premises
from Debtor.
    [Dated] [Signed, Judge of the
Bankruptcy Court]
```

At your hearing, you ask the court to remove the automatic stay so you can get the tenant out. In order to receive approval, you'll have to establish that the lease rate is not substantially less than the fair rental value for the property, that your getting the property back will in no way harm either the tenant's other creditors or the reorganization plan itself, and what's more, that you will suffer irreparable damages if you don't get the property back doggone soon.

Come prepared with everything you need to support your position. Gather every scrap of paper you have on the tenant, including the rental application, rental agreement, and rent receipts. Come up with some evidence, perhaps current rental listings, that the property's rental value is at or near market level. And put together a listing of the expenses you normally pay out of your rental income, so you can show that you are suffering damages from the tenant's continuing to stay without paying any rent.

Chances are good that you won't have to say much in court because the tenants are unlikely even to show up.

As Judge Zurzolo remarked in *In Re Smith*,

"These relief from Stay motions are rarely contested and are never lost, as long as the moving party provides adequate notice of the motion and competent evidence to establish a *prima facie* case."

As soon as you have proof from the bankruptcy court that the automatic stay has been lifted, go back to municipal court and continue your unlawful detainer from where you left off.

You may be detoured, but you will prevail!

- Become familiar with *In re Smith*.
- Should your tenant declare bankruptcy while you're trying to evict him, try to take advantage of the state law written to help you evict without delay; recognize, however, that this law may not help you because bankruptcies are governed by federal law.
- Get thee to bankruptcy court without delay when you have no other choice.

12
Handling Non-payment & Non-compliance in a Mobilehome or RV Park

The laws governing residency in mobilehome (MH) and recreational vehicle (RV) parks, both of which used to be lumped together under the term "trailer parks," have expanded right along with the length and width of the coaches being manufactured (the term "coach" here refers to mobilehomes and recreational vehicles of all sizes).

As you might imagine, this proliferation of laws would tend to restrain park management and unshackle park residents. It has. Management used to be able to hitch the park's pickup truck up to a coach occupied by deadbeats, haul them out into the street while they were having dinner, and put a lien on the coach to boot.

Today that's no longer possible. First of all, a park's itty-bitty pickup truck couldn't begin to budge most residents' yacht-sized coaches from their moorings; second, management must meet all sorts of conditions before evicting anybody at all; and third, even when those conditions have been met, there are still further limitations to the remedies available.

So how do you proceed against a problem resident today? To begin with, you must determine who is the registered owner of the problem resident's coach, who is the legal owner, what type of space it occupies, whether the coach is classified as an RV or a mobilehome, and how long it's been where it is.

If you own the coach and you rent it out as a residence on a month-to-month tenancy, regardless of where it sits or who owns the real property beneath it or what type of coach it happens to be, so far as you and that resident are concerned, the laws governing conventional rental dwellings apply. The resident might as well be renting an apartment or a house from you. If this is the case and your resident should give you trouble, go ahead and use the appropriate procedures as outlined in previous chapters.

If the coach is situated on a space designated for RV's, and it is, in fact, an RV, how you proceed against the occupants will be determined by how long it's been parked where it is. If it's been there less than thirty days, its occupants are entitled to get a 72-hour notice before you can act to have it moved out; if it's been there for at least thirty days but less than nine months, they're entitled to get a 30-day notice before you can take action; and if it's been there longer, they're entitled to the same treatment as mobilehome occupants.

To be considered an RV (included are motor homes, truck-mounted campers, fifth wheelers, travel trailers, camping trailers, and the like), the coach must not require a special moving permit to be out on the highway. If it does require a permit, then it's a mobilehome.

This distinction between RV's and mobilehomes is an important one because each is governed by a separate set of laws. RV's can travel about the highway as readily as prairie schooners, so they're governed by laws more like innkeeper statutes and vehicle codes. Mobilehomes may be called "mobile," but once set up with awnings, skirting, landscaping, and fencing, they aren't much more mobile than tract houses, so they're governed by laws more like those for conventional housing, to be specific, §§798, et seq., of the Civil Code, commonly referred to as the "Mobilehome Residency Law" (MRL). Recreational vehicle parks, on the other hand, are governed specifically by the "Recreational Vehicle Park Occupancy Law," which is §§799.20, et seq., of the Civil Code.

The MRL has become a kind of accounting of the battles enjoined by the opposing mobilehome-related associations—in the one corner, the Golden State Mobilehome Owners League (GSMOL), representing park residents, and in the other, the Western Mobilehome As-

72-HOUR NOTICE TO VACATE

(Recreational Vehicles)

TO: Dennis Sampson

Vernagae Sampson

and all other occupants in possession of the premises described as:

2020 Cherry Hill Rd., Space 26
(Street Address)

Lemon   California   91222
(City)   (State)   (Zip)

PLEASE TAKE NOTICE that you have failed to pay for your occupancy or failed to comply with the reasonable written rules and regulations of the park provided to you upon registration. You are hereby required within seventy-two (72) hours to remove from and deliver up possession of the above-described premises which you currently **hold and occupy.**

Should you fail to comply with this notice, your recreational vehicle will be removed from the park pursuant to the procedure described in that part of the California Civil Code (CCC §799.20 et seq.) commonly known as the Recreational Vehicle Park **Occupancy Law.**

Dated: _____ 2/8/XX _____   *Dan Coffey* _____
                                   Owner/Manager

PROOF OF SERVICE

I, the undersigned, being at least 18 years of age, declare under penalty of perjury that I served the above notice, of which this is a true copy, on the person(s) indicated below and in the manner(s) indicated below:

DENNIS SAMPSON

☒ On __2/8/XX__, I handed the notice to the occupant(s) personally.

☐ On _____, after attempting personal service, I handed the notice to a person of suitable age and discretion at the address above or at the place of business of the occupant(s), AND I posted a true copy in a conspicuous place at the address above, AND I deposited a true copy in the U.S. Mail, in a sealed envelope with postage fully prepaid, addressed to the occupant(s) at the address above. I also deposited a true copy in the U.S. Mail, in a sealed envelope with postage fully prepaid, addressed to the occupant(s) at the following address given on their registration agreement:

_____.

☒ On __2/8/XX__, I [cross out one] (~~sent by certified mail~~) (hand-delivered) a true copy of the notice to the police or sheriff's department serving the area where the premises are located.

Executed on __2/8/XX__, at __LEMON__, California.

Served by __*Dan Coffey*__

efc

---

sociation (WMA) and California Mobilehome Parkowners Alliance (MPA), representing park owners and managers. Each of them has its lobbyists in Sacramento vying for legislators' ears.

Whereas mobilehomes are always governed by the MRL, RV's are not always governed by laws written for RV's. RV's are chameleon-like. They become mobilehomes when they act like mobilehomes, that is, when they occupy a space designated for mobilehomes or when they occupy a space designated for RV's for more than nine months. Then they, too, are governed by the MRL, unless, that is, they are motor homes, truck

more responsible about paying their bills than other renters and because moving a mobilehome is such an expensive proposition nowadays, park owners and managers tend to use what may seem to apartment owners and managers to be a lenient approach to collecting delinquent rents. They operate more on the premise that mobilehome residents will pay their rent if given proper notice and a reasonable period of time in which to pay it.

Here's the collection routine followed by one experienced mobilehome park manager, a manager who has never had to resort to the courts to

campers, or camping trailers, which are always RV's.

Before outlining the eviction procedure dictated by the MRL, I'd like to describe a pragmatic collection procedure which you might use yourself for handling those residents whose rent doesn't arrive when it's supposed to. Some sort of collection procedure should always precede an eviction for nonpayment.

Nonpayment

Because those who own their own coaches (called "homeowners" in the MRL but also referred to as "residents" if they occupy the coach) and rent space in a mobilehome park tend to be

evict a resident for nonpayment and has never failed to collect all the rent owed to his park in more than a dozen years as manager of a 113-space park. Throughout, it provides the resident with proper notice and allows him a reasonable period of time to pay.

Central to this collection routine are consistency, persistence, reasonableness, and four informal notices, written on imprinted, half-sheet, two-part park stationery and sent to the resident by first-class mail. At the bottom of each notice the manager puts the following:

```
Copy to:
File Space [number]
Attorney [name of actual attorney
```

3-DAY NOTICE TO PAY RENT OR QUIT

TO: Peter Romstead   Roseanne Romstead

_____ and all other residents or occupants in possession of the premises described as:

2020 Cherry Hill Rd., Space 14, Lemon, California 91222

PLEASE TAKE NOTICE that the rent is now due and payable on the above-described premises which you currently hold and occupy. Your rental account is delinquent in the amount itemized as follows:

Rental period ___3/1/XX___ through ___3/31/XX___

RENT DUE $	285.00
less partial payment of $	0.00
equals TOTAL RENT DUE of $	285.00

YOU ARE HEREBY REQUIRED to pay said rent in full within three (3) days or to deliver up possession of the above-described premises to the park manager, who is authorized to receive same, or legal proceedings will be instituted against you to recover possession of said premises, to declare the forfeiture of the Lease or Rental Agreement under which you occupy said premises and to recover rents and damages, together with court costs and attorney's fees, according to the terms of your Lease or Rental Agreement.

3-DAY NOTICE TO PERFORM COVENANT OR QUIT

PLEASE TAKE NOTICE that you have also failed to perform that covenant in your Lease or Rental Agreement requiring that certain other charges be paid along with your rent. These charges are itemized as follows:

Other charges Water _____ TOTAL other charges due $___12.29___

You are hereby required to perform this covenant within three (3) days or to deliver up possession of the above-described premises to the park manager. If you fail to do so, legal proceedings will be instituted against you to recover said charges and to recover said premises and such damages as the law allows.

PLEASE NOTE WELL: If you fail to pay the total amount of rent due and owing within three days, your tenancy is terminated. The additional time period allowed in the "60-Day Notice" below is strictly to give you time to locate a place to move your mobilehome. It does not extend the time you have to pay what you owe.

You may advertise your mobilehome for sale and sell or transfer it if you wish, but you may not represent that it may remain where it is when sold or transferred. In fact, it may not remain where it is. It must be moved.

60-DAY NOTICE TO TERMINATE TENANCY

PLEASE TAKE NOTICE that you are hereby required within sixty (60) days to deliver up possession of the above-described premises, which you currently hold and occupy. Compliance with this notice requires removal of your mobilehome so that the space can be re-let.

Rent being delinquent, this notice is being given for good cause, and it is intended, pursuant to California Civil Code §§798-9, commonly known as the "Mobilehome Residency Law," for the purpose of terminating the Lease or Rental Agreement by which you now hold possession of the above-described premises.

SHOULD YOU FAIL TO COMPLY WITH THIS (THESE) NOTICE(S), legal proceedings will be instituted against you to recover possession, to declare said Lease or Rental Agreement forfeited, and to recover rents and damages for the period of unlawful detention. Your mobilehome may be sold at a sheriff's sale to pay for any money judgment entered in favor of the park owner.

Please be advised that your rent, utility bills, and other charges on said premises are due and payable up to and including the date of termination of your tenancy under this notice.

Dated: ___4/15/XX___   ___Dan Coffey___
                                                    Owner/Manager   efc

---

PROOF OF SERVICE

I, the undersigned, being at least 18 years of age, declare under penalty of perjury that I served the above notice, of which this is a true copy, on the above-mentioned resident(s) in possession in the manner(s) indicated below:

☒ On ___4/17/XX___, I handed the notice to the resident(s) personally.

☐ On _____, after attempting personal service, I handed the notice to a person of suitable age and discretion at the residence/business of the resident(s), AND I deposited a true copy in the U.S. Mail, in a sealed envelope with postage fully prepaid, addressed to the resident(s) at his/her/their place of residence (date mailed, if different _____).

☐ On _____, after attempting service in both manners indicated above, I posted the notice in a conspicuous place at the residence of the resident(s), AND I deposited a true copy in the U.S. Mail, in a sealed envelope with postage fully prepaid, addressed to the resident(s) at his/her/their place of residence (date mailed, if different _____).

☒ On ___4/17/XX___, in addition to service on the resident(s) as described above, I deposited a true copy of the notice in the U.S. Mail, in a sealed envelope with postage fully prepaid, addressed to the legal and registered owner(s) (if other than resident(s)) as follows: [legal owner] _____ ;
[registered owner] _PACIFIC FINANCE, 32 ORANGE AVE., SUNSET CALIFORNIA_.

Executed on ___4/17/XX___, at ___LEMON___, California. Served by ___Dan Coffey___ given on final two notices]

The first notice acknowledges that the resident's rent, which is due on the first and delinquent on the seventh of the month at this particular family park, has not been paid. The manager sends the notice on the tenth. Here's the exact wording he uses for this first notice:

```
Dear [resident], Space [number]:
   Your space rent in the amount
of $xx was due on [date] and be-
came delinquent on [date]. Please
drop this by our office today,
and don't forget to add the late
fee of $xx, too. Your rent is now
late.
     Thank you.
```

The second notice, sent out five days later if the resident has made no effort to contact the manager with either rent payment or excuses, is more formal than the first one. It reads as follows:

```
Dear [resident], Space [number]:
   THIS IS A FIVE (5) DAY NOTICE
to pay space rent of $xx due on
[date].
   As stated in your Rental Agree-
ment, "When rent is paid after
the seventh (7th) day of the
month for which rent is due,
Homeowners must pay a late fee of
$xx." The amount now due of $xx
includes the late fee, as it is
now past the 7th day of the
month.
     Thank you.
```

The third notice, sent five days following the second notice, assumes that there has been some contact with the resident, that the resident has assured the manager his rent and late fee would be paid by a certain date, and that the resident has failed to perform. It's a little more insistent than the others. Here's what it says:

```
Dear [resident], Space [number]:
   On [date], you promised to pay
your delinquent space rent of $xx
and a late fee of $xx. This
promise has not been kept. We
shall expect payment within
twenty-four (24) hours!
     Thank you.
```

The final notice is the most insistent of all and threatens to involve an attorney and court action.

It says the following:

```
Dear [resident], Space [number]:
   We are sorry that you have
failed to pay the delinquent rent
due on Space [number]. Please be
advised that your account will be
turned over to our attorney for
collection processing and evic-
tion action if not paid at our
office by [date given is five
days hence].
     Thank you.
```

Should the resident fail to respond to this final informal notice from the park, the manager takes the first legal steps required to evict the resident. He completes a 3-Day Notice to Pay Rent or Quit, a 3-Day Notice to Perform Covenant or Quit (necessary to demand payment of the other charges commonly included in mobilehome parks' monthly statements), and a 60-Day Notice to Terminate Tenancy. A single page combining all three notices is shown here; the 60-Day Notice must include a bonafide good cause, such as "nonpayment of rent" in this case.

Then the manager makes an effort to jolt the resident. He hires any uniformed peace officer (sometimes just a security guard) he can find, someone intimidating and unfamiliar, to serve the notices (within ten days, as required by law, he also sends copies by certified or registered mail, return-receipt requested, to the coach's registered owner and legal owner, if they happen to be someone other than the resident, and to any junior lienholders). He never serves the notices himself, so he can keep the process on a businesslike plane and keep from injecting anything personal into what he now considers a serious matter. Although the resident may have scoffed at the earlier informal notices, he begins to get serious now. He seldom scoffs at these notices, served as they are by a stranger, and somehow he always seems to find the money needed to pay his rent. The manager then drops the matter, having accumulated plenty of paperwork to fatten that resident's file in case it's needed later to substantiate legal action.

Eviction Through Court

If you had to follow up on the notices and pursue your case still further in the courts, here's what you'd do.

You'd wait sixty to sixty-five days before doing anything. (Just like ordinary tenants, mobilehome owners get only three days to pay up. If they don't pay up within that three-day period, they should be looking around for some other place to move their mobilehome. Mind you, they aren't getting the extra time to pay what they owe. They're getting the extra time so they can find a place to move their mobilehome).

Then you'd file a summons, complaint, a cover sheet, and a Prejudgment Claim of Right to Possession, the same Judicial Council forms covered in chapter 5. You'd wait the appropriate number of days, depending upon the method of service used and whether you'd decided to use the prejudgment claim procedure (recommended because of the long wait following service of notices).

In non-contested cases, you'd file a Request for Entry of Default and a Writ of Possession, and you'd get a lockout date. In contested cases, you'd file a Memorandum to Set, argue your case in court, and if successful, get a judgment, a Writ of Possession, and a lockout date.

With the resident locked out, you'd follow a procedure dictated by whether there's a legal owner different from the registered owner.

If the legal owner and the registered owner were one and the same, you'd get the sheriff or marshal's office to return the Writ of Possession to the court. You'd get a Writ of Execution from the court, and you'd instruct the sheriff or marshal's office to sell the mobilehome to satisfy the judgment. If there were no bidders, you would get the title and could submit the necessary papers to Housing and Community Development (HCD) to clear the title.

If the legal owner were different from the registered owner, you'd give notice of a lien sale and wait ten to fifteen days for the legal owner to pay the lien. If the legal owner were to pay, he would get the mobilehome. If he didn't pay, you'd publish notice of the lien sale and hold the sale. If there were no bidders, you would get title and could clear it with HCD.

Unoccupied Coaches

The ordinary nonpayment problem isn't the only nonpayment problem encountered in mobilehome parks. There's another one which we should consider here, one which is unique to mobilehome parks. It involves unoccupied coaches.

Because fewer than 5% of the mobilehomes placed in parks ever take to the road again, there are always some for sale on their sites when homeowners move on and leave their mobilehomes behind. As far as the park is concerned, if a coach occupies a space, there's rent due on that space, whether anyone is living in the coach or not. Sometimes absentee homeowners continue paying their space rent while the coach is up for sale and sometimes they don't. When they don't, you as the park owner or manager could initiate an unlawful detainer against the owner of the coach as explained above, but you'll find that it's an exercise in futility. You really needn't bother. You might not want to bother, either, if you're already plagued with vacancies.

Since there's a large asset involved, the coach itself, you're better off being patient about getting paid, but there are a few things you might want to do to safeguard your position. Notify the mobilehome's legal owner about the situation right away (you should have a file of the registered and legal owners of every coach in the park; homeowners are required by law to furnish this information to the park, and you should prod them if they don't respond). The legal owner becomes a kind of bail bondsman trying to preserve the money he put up to finance the coach in the first place. He has an interest in keeping the coach right where it is because a well-situated coach is worth more than a coach which is out on the street, and the lender's depreciated collateral might not be enough to cover the loan balance if he were to foreclose. To protect that interest, he will sometimes promise to pay the space rent while the coach is vacant, although he may not pay it until the coach changes hands.

He may try to sell you his security interest in the mobilehome, but in most cases, you shouldn't buy it because you'd still have to foreclose on the resident to get the space back and the rent owed. Instead, you should refuse the lender's offer and remind him that he may foreclose himself and pay you or he may let you evict the resident and pay yourself out of any proceeds from the lien sale. In other words, you stand to get your money without paying the lender anything for his interest.

Whatever you do, keep the meter running all this time, and continue calculating the rent and late charges since the rent was last paid. Then, when you approve the new buyer, find out who's handling the escrow on the transaction, and present your claim for the unpaid charges to that escrow holder. If the registered owner's equity is large enough, you'll get the rent from him. If the legal owner has to foreclose on the coach, you'll get the rent from him. Just keep abreast of what's happening, be patient, and you stand a good chance of getting the rent in the end.

Abandonment

Every so often a homeowner will abandon his mobilehome or at least appear to abandon it. Perhaps he'll owe some rent on the space. Perhaps he won't. Perhaps he'll own the mobilehome outright. Perhaps a bank will. The situations vary.

One thing which doesn't vary is this. An abandoned mobilehome has nobody looking after it or its yard. It will soon become a blight on the neighborhood. Because no park can afford to have one abandoned coach or many abandoned coaches dragging it down, you as park management must make a serious effort to contact the registered owners first and the legal owners second to ask permission to take over the maintenance of the space. If you cannot locate anyone with an interest in the coach, you should post a notice about space maintenance, and then take over.

Keep work records just in case you are able to recover some or all of your costs later, but don't fret if you can't recover anything. The primary reason for your taking over the space maintenance of abandoned coaches is to preserve the park's reputation and value.

With the space maintenance resolved, you can work on sorting out the details of the abandonment in order to restart the income stream which the space should be generating. There are at least three ways to handle abandonments.

The first way is to pursue an ordinary unlawful detainer for nonpayment of rent. Because there's nobody available to accept personal service, you serve the notices by "nailing-and-mailing" and the summons and complaint by posting. Then, when nobody answers your complaint, you get a default judgment and a writ of execution. You go all the way to a lien sale, where the coach is sold, and you either get your money or the title to the coach.

The second way is spelled out in full in CC §798.61. It's a well-defined procedure specifically for handling abandonments. Do note, however, that this second procedure applies only to those mobilehomes (1) which are located in a park on a site for which the rent is at least sixty days in arrears, (2) which are unoccupied, and (3) which reasonably appear to be abandoned.

Should you decide to follow this second procedure, look it up and follow it carefully. It begins with the posting and mailing of a notice and ends with the public sale of the mobilehome and disposition of the proceeds. Because it's not particularly complicated and involves no adversary, you should be able to do it yourself.

The third way, which works only if there is a lienholder, is to conduct a lien sale for the unpaid charges.

Which of the procedures should you use? The answer depends upon whether there's a lienholder. If there is, use the uncomplicated third procedure. If there isn't, the answer depends upon how long you've already waited since the abandonment. If sixty or more days have elapsed since you last received any rent from the resident, you're better off using the second procedure. It assumes that you have been patient, and it gives you a head start as a consequence. If only a few days have passed since you last received rent, and you have reason to believe that the coach has been abandoned, use the first procedure.

Noncompliance

There are probably fewer uncooperative residents in mobilehome parks than in conventional rentals, but there are always some, no matter what. These uncooperative residents are the type who let their pets roam about freely, fertilizing the streets. They set up an auto repair business in their front yard. They party late and loudly. They whoop it up and discharge their firearms through the walls. They build unsightly spite fences and paint them gaudy colors, or they find some rule to break just to antagonize their neighbors or the park management. Litigation having become the national pastime that it is, you have to do something about these people or your other residents will haul you into court for failing to act. You're between Half Dome and a hard place.

When you encounter such a resident, follow the procedure outlined in chapter 2 of this book first, and while you're doing that, consider the role you should be playing. Act more like the park mayor than the park cop. Try to make the

60-DAY NOTICE TO TERMINATE TENANCY

TO: Virgil Lutz

Victoria C. Lutz

and all other residents or occupants in possession of the premises described as:

2020 Cherry Hill Rd., Space 19
(Street Address)

Lemon   California   91222
(City)   (State)   (Zip)

PLEASE TAKE NOTICE that you are hereby required within sixty (60) days to deliver up possession of the above-described premises, which you currently hold and occupy. Compliance with this notice requires removal of your mobilehome so that the space can be re-let.

This notice is intended, pursuant to California Civil Code §§798-9, commonly known as the "Mobilehome Residency Law," for the purpose of terminating the Lease or Rental Agreement by which you now hold possession of the above-described premises.

SHOULD YOU FAIL TO COMPLY WITH THIS NOTICE, legal proceedings will be instituted against you to recover possession, to declare said Lease or Rental Agreement forfeited, and to recover rents and damages for the period of unlawful detention. Your mobilehome may be sold at a sheriff's sale to pay for any money judgment entered in favor of the park owner.

This notice is being given for good cause as follows:

Homeowners have been given adequate notice to remove the three inoperable and unlicensed junk cars and debris on their space. Their space is unsightly, and they are in violation of park rules, paragraph 22, section 3.

Please be advised that your rent, utility bills, and other charges on said premises are due and payable up to and including the date of termination of your tenancy under this notice.

Dated: _____4/15/XX_____   ___Dan Coffey___
                                        Owner/Manager

PROOF OF SERVICE

I, the undersigned, being at least 18 years of age, declare under penalty of perjury that I served the above notice, of which this is a true copy, on the following resident(s) in possession in the manner(s) indicated below: VIRGIL LUTZ, VICTORIA LUTZ

☒ On ___4/16/XX___, I handed the notice to the resident(s) personally.

☐ On _____, after attempting personal service, I handed the notice to a person of suitable age and discretion at the residence/business of the resident(s), AND I deposited a true copy in the U.S. Mail, in a sealed envelope with postage fully prepaid, addressed to the resident(s) at his/her/their place of residence (date mailed, if different _____).

☐ On _____, after attempting service in both manners indicated above, I posted the notice in a conspicuous place at the residence of the resident(s), AND I deposited a true copy in the U.S. Mail, in a sealed envelope with postage fully prepaid, addressed to the resident(s) at his/her/their place of residence (date mailed, if different _____).

☒ On ___4/16/XX___, in addition to service on the resident(s) as described above, I deposited a true copy of the notice in the U.S. Mail, in a sealed envelope with postage fully prepaid, addressed to the legal and registered owner(s) (if other than resident(s)) as follows:

LEGAL OWNER _____

REGISTERED OWNER BANK OF LEMON, 1 MAIN ST., LEMON, CALIF.

Executed on ___4/16/XX___, at ___LEMON___, California.

Served by ___Dan Coffey___

efc

You will find a blank copy of this form in the FORMS section of this book and in Eviction Forms Creator.

resident understand why he should shape up. Take a written agreement with you when you talk with him, and if you can, get him to agree in writing that he will remedy the problem within a given period of time.

When you have exhausted the talking stage without results, you may want to hire an attorney to write the scoundrel a nasty letter outlining the steps you will be forced to take next. Most of the time that works. When it doesn't, consider hiring an attorney to seek an injunction. Unless the court requires the attorney to appear personally to get an Order to Show Cause, in which case an injunction can become rather expensive, an injunction will be cheaper and quicker than an eviction.

To get an injunction, the attorney goes to superior court and asks for a court order requiring the resident to stop certain behavior, such as threatening his neighbors, discharging his handgun on park property, entertaining a nightly procession of people of the opposite sex, or breaking those particular park rules he's being uncooperative about. After listening to your attorney and examining the declarations of the people affected (they don't have to appear in court), the judge alone makes the decision (juries are never involved).

An injunction is much more effective than your talking with the resident or an attorney's writing to him, for he can be hauled off to jail or fined for failing to observe an injunction. It does have some teeth.

When you're dealing with someone who's truly difficult, though, someone who's hardheaded or downright crazy, you ought to pursue the one solution with plenty of teeth for the situation, an eviction. Whereas the resident might be hauled off to jail or fined as the result of an injunction, he'll be back. You can count on that. After an eviction, he's out for good, although you could get the resident to stipulate to an injunction as a settlement of the eviction case. That can work well, too.

Sometimes, like it or not, the most expeditious and least costly way to "evict" a problem resident in a mobilehome park nowadays is for the park owner to buy that resident's coach and resell it to someone else. Such a solution may not seem fair to the park owner because it ties up his cash, frequently causes him to lose some space rent, and sometimes results in a loss on the sale,

but, given the time-consuming and expensive legal alternatives, it should certainly be considered.

If you've considered every other possibility and you still want to pursue a problem resident's legal eviction, serve him with a Notice to Perform Covenant (7 days), and then, if he persists in his noncompliance after the 7-day period, give him a 60-Day Notice to Terminate Tenancy just like the sample shown here. After that, I'd suggest you hire an attorney to handle the court work because the chances are good that the resident will hire an attorney to defend himself, and you might as well be well prepared for battle.

A Word About Experts

Few attorneys are experts in the laws governing mobilehome parks and recreational vehicle parks. It's a specialty which requires study and experience, and the chances are good that the family attorney who wrote your will, handled your first divorce, or defended your teenage son when he was arrested for drunk driving would not be able to do a good job representing you as a park owner or manager. Most attorneys don't even know that such a thing as the Mobilehome Residency Law exists, so much of what you'd be paying them to represent you would be spent on their schooling to become minimally proficient in this field of law.

To find experts who specialize in mobilehome parks and mobilehome park law, contact the Western Mobilehome Association, (916) 448-7002, or the California Mobilehome Parkowners Alliance, (916) 441-1882.

NOW REMEMBER THESE KEY POINTS!

- Distinguish between recreational vehicles and mobilehomes and treat them appropriately.
- Familiarize yourself with the laws governing mobilehomes and recreational vehicles.

- Adopt a reasonable rent collection routine designed to yield rents and keep you out of court.
- Maintain the spaces which have abandoned coaches on them, all the while using the legal means available to you to collect the rent.
- When dealing with park residents, act more like the park mayor than the park cop.

- To get rid of the uncooperative resident without wasting time and money going to court, consider buying his coach and reselling it to someone else.
- Keep an expert attorney in the wings for serious mobilehome and RV evictions.

13
Collecting the Money Judgment

With the actual vacating of your rental dwelling by a nonpaying tenant behind you, you have accomplished one of the two goals you set for yourself when you began your eviction action for nonpayment of rent. You have forced your tenant out. He's gone, gone, gone. Hooray and hallelujah, he had it comin' to 'im, oo ya!

Ah, but you still haven't received any of his back rent, and, in addition, you're now out of pocket more than a few dollars for the various fees and charges you've had to pay to get him out. Your judgment entitles you to all of this money, that's true. The trouble is that getting what you're entitled to requires still more effort on your part. Evicted tenants are certainly not going to pay you anything willingly (they tend to think like Abbott, who told Costello in one of their old comedies which you might catch during the wee hours when you're awake from worry about some landlording problem or other: "Paying back rent is like betting on a dead horse."), and nobody from the courthouse or the police department is going to come forward spontaneously to collect it for you. You are going to have to take some initiative yourself to get what you're entitled to.

Unfortunately, the laws today do not favor creditors as they once did. Gone are the days when you could just walk off with a debtor's belongings and the money that came in his mail, leaving him nothing but a barrel and suspenders. You can't send your deadbeat tenant to debtors' prison any more, and you can't garnish a judgment debtor's checks from sources other than wages (wage garnishments do have their limitations, you know). You can't even pull up in front of where he lives with a big sign on the side of your car saying "WE COLLECT DEBTS FROM DEAD-BEATS" to shame him in front of his neighbors. That's been tried, and it's been judged to be "harassment"! Bah, humbug!

So what can you do to collect? Go hat in hand to your tenant asking for spare change to apply to the judgment? Ha, ha! You could do that if you wanted to. I wouldn't. There's no force behind such a plea to pay. He'd laugh in your face. After all, you had to force the tenant to leave. You'll have to force him to pay.

Don't despair. There are still some very legal and very effective things you can do to get your money, and there are also a few little tricks you can use to exact some sweet revenge for all the misery your tenant has put you though.

Before you try any of them, however, you ought to determine whether there's somebody other than the tenant whom you might tap for the money and if not, then whether the tenant himself has the ability to pay you anything at all.

Tapping the Cosigner

When you originally rented to the tenant you evicted, did you happen to secure a cosigner to guarantee the tenant's financial compliance with the rental agreement? You did? Well, aren't you the smart one!

Your foresight should finally start to pay off now, for you probably have somebody of substance to tap for the judgment, somebody who cares about his credit rating and will do something to protect it. A cosigner is just as liable for paying what's owed to you as the tenant is. A cosigner on a rental agreement is like the cosigner on a bank loan. He's on the hook for the full amount.

Although you could have included him in your unlawful detainer from the very beginning if you'd wanted to, doing so tends to complicate service of the necessary papers. Most landlords, therefore, after being ignored by the cosigner when they've contacted him about the trouble with the tenant, concentrate on getting the tenant evicted first. Then they go after the cosigner in small claims court. Armed with the unlawful detainer judgment against the tenants and the cosigner agreement, the landlord has an open-and-shut case in small claims, and the cosigner has no choice but to pay up.

If the cosigner proves reluctant to pay as well, you may proceed against him using any of the ways mentioned here just as if he were the deadbeat tenant.

Determining Whether the Tenants Have the Wherewithal to Pay

In many cases there's not a chance in hades that you'll ever collect one clad dime on your judgment because tenants who have to be evicted tend to lack attachable assets and steady employment. They're what attorneys call "judgment proof." Their pockets are shallow; their purses, empty. Just as turnips lack blood, they lack money, and whatever they lack to begin with, you'll certainly never be able to squeeze out of them, no matter how hard you try.

The question is, then, how do you know whether they really do lack money and attachable assets? They might be fooling you. You look for clues. That's what. Did they pay you the rent with cash or money orders in times past? Then they probably don't use banks and don't have their savings where it can be attached. You can't attach money stored in a mattress. Did they stay around the house a lot? Did they party all night and sleep all day? Then they probably don't work, at least not steadily, and you won't be able to attach their wages. Do they drive an old car? It'd cost you more to impound and auction the heap than what you'd derive from the sale. Are they welfare, disability, social security, child care, unemployment insurance, or workers' compensation recipients? Their checks from these sources can't be touched. Are they underground economy types who handle their money transactions with rolls of cash? Maybe the IRS can get to their cash. You can't. Such assets are virtually unattachable.

If you strongly suspect that your evicted tenant has nothing you can get at now and has little hope of ever acquiring anything which you might be able to get at in the future, then you might as well drop the matter before you spend any more of your precious time or good money in trying to collect what is quite likely uncollectable. Put this loss behind you and get on with your land-lording business. Get busy and find a prompt-paying tenant to replace the deadbeat you've just evicted.

Exacting Your Revenge—Part 1

Before you drop the matter entirely, you can, and you should, at the very least smirch the bum's credit rating so that other people proposing to do business with this malefactor will know what to expect of him and be able to protect themselves if they merely take the precaution of checking him out through a credit bureau or an unlawful detainer registry.

Smirching his credit is easy. In fact, it's automatic when you've already gone to the trouble of securing a money judgment against an evicted tenant and had it recorded. Credit bureaus search out such information as a matter of course. They thrive on it. You needn't worry about whether it will get into the tenant's file. It will. Once there, it remains for years, and anyone who bothers to check the file will discover that there was a judgment against the tenant and that it remains unpaid. If it ever is paid, the file will reflect that as well.

When you don't secure a money judgment, however, because the tenant skipped out after receiving either your 3-day notice or your summons and you dropped your case, the tenant's credit file will not automatically reflect what he owes you. After all, how could the credit bureau know something like that? Whereas almost everything pertinent which is a matter of public record will appear in the tenant's file, things which aren't in the public records will appear only if they're reported. That's how a department store's late-payment information, for example, gets there. It's reported by creditors who themselves rely on such information when extending credit.

Although credit reporting agencies won't take nonpayment-of-rent information from every Tom, Dick, and Harriet landlord, they will take such information from their "members." That's right! As a member of a credit reporting agency, you may report negative credit information on your tenants so that it will appear on their credit report (if your apartment and property owners association does credit reports for you, ask whether you may report negative credit information through them). As a member, you are considered to be a small business owner, and you have the same rights and responsibilities a small business owner has in using the credit system. You may report a tenant who moves out and owes you money even when you haven't had to evict him through the courts. You may also report a tenant who habitually pays late.

By the way, unlawful detainer registries report both filings and judgments, so merely filing against your tenant will alert other landlords that he might be suspect.

If you want any chance of recouping monies owed to you by a tenant who moved out before you filed court papers against him and you want to smirch his credit rating through public records, go to small claims court and get a judgment against him. That will get the information into the public records and might get you the money, too. If he moved out after you filed court papers against him, go ahead and get the judgment, so you can have it recorded. You've already paid the bulk of the fees. Getting the judgment and having it recorded won't cost much more. Follow through.

Exacting Your Revenge—Part 2

There's yet another method you might use to exact your revenge against a former tenant who owes you money which you know you'll never collect. Give him an IRS Form 1099-MISC. The form notifies the IRS that the tenant has received income from you. This "income" is equal to the amount of money the tenant owes you. The tenant will then be liable for paying income tax on this amount.

The tenant may have been able to dodge your every effort to collect, but he won't be able to dodge the IRS. Underworld characters can't even dodge the IRS. Your deadbeat tenant doesn't stand a chance against this formidable adversary.

Please note that if you do elect to file a 1099-MISC, you will be relinquishing all claims to the money the tenant owes you. You are essentially forgiving the debt, and you must file an Acknowledgment of Satisfaction of Judgment form with the court (explained later in this chapter) as well.

Also note that the amount shown on the 1099-MISC should be $600 or more, and that it should be the exact amount owed. You will get yourself into trouble if you exaggerate the amount. Don't.

In order to complete a 1099-MISC, you will need to include the tenant's name, address, and Social Security number on the form (don't worry too much if haven't a clue as to the tenant's

whereabouts; the IRS will locate him in its files according to his Social Security number). You did get the tenant's Social Security number when he moved in, didn't you? If you didn't, don't despair. A credit reporting agency can secure it for you for a price.

For explicit instructions in preparing and filing a 1099-MISC, ask the IRS for its instruction booklet on the subject.

Filing an Abstract of Judgment— A Small Gamble

If you've already gone to the trouble of securing a money judgment and you don't want to give up on ever getting the money from the tenant, you might want to take a small gamble. The gamble necessitates your filing something called an Abstract of Judgment form with the county. It's easy, it costs only a few dollars, and it entitles you to payment with interest if the evicted tenant ever attempts to buy or sell any real property in that county during the next ten years (the odds of your getting a payoff on an abstract are a whole lot better than those in the lottery). You may file in other counties as well, and you may renew the judgment for a second decade if you wish.

Collecting It Yourself

Depending upon your past relationship with the evicted tenant, your time available, your intestinal fortitude, and your estimate of the ease of collection, you might wish to try collecting the judgment yourself. After all, you evicted the so-and-so yourself, didn't you? Well, there's no reason why you can't try collecting the judgment yourself, too. By that I don't mean that you should camp on his doorstep, follow him around demanding payment, walk off with his coveted black velvet paintings, drive away in his Corvette, take his large-screen Zenith, or petnap his pedigreed Doberman. What I mean by "collecting the judgment yourself" is that you should use the legal recourses available to you through the sheriff or marshal in the county where the tenant's job or his assets are located. The sheriff or marshal is duly authorized to collect the judgment on your behalf. You don't have to make personal contact with the tenant and risk bodily injury. All you have to do is point the sheriff or marshal in the right direction and pay some upfront costs.

To collect your judgment, you have to know where the tenant works, where he lives, and/or where he keeps his money. Then you can file the papers necessary to get the sheriff or marshal busy.

Involving the Co-Tenants

Keep in mind that you have the legal right to pursue everyone mentioned in the judgment when you're trying to collect. Each person mentioned is liable for the entire amount, not just a pro-rated share. You may go after any one of them for the entire amount, but once that entire amount has been paid, you may not try to collect any more money from any of them.

Suppose Richard and Rose Renter, the couple you evicted, have now decided to split up, and you are able to locate Rose working in a neighboring town. You can attach her wages for the entire amount of the judgment if you want to, and she will have to find Richard to collect his share from him. You don't have to collect half from her and then try to find him to get the other half. Once she realizes that she's going to have to pay the entire judgment herself, she may take pains to help you find something of Richard's to attach for at least part of the judgment so she doesn't have to pay it all herself.

Whether you go after one tenant or all of them doesn't really matter so far as you are concerned. What matters is finding somebody, anybody, who has the wherewithal to pay.

Finding Your Former Tenant

Uh, oh, there is one problem you may not have encountered before this. You used to know where to contact the tenant. He was living in your rental dwelling, wasn't he? Now that he doesn't live there anymore, you may not have a clue where to find him, and you have to be able to tell the process server where he is, or you won't be able to get your papers served.

Take heart. Remember that you can have the tenant served anywhere he happens to be. You don't have to know exactly where he's living right now if you know where he's working or what bar he frequents after work or where he bowls every Tuesday or which motorcycle gang he hangs out with on Saturday nights.

Don't be shy about asking your remaining tenants where this former tenant may be found. Sometimes they'll know and won't think twice about divulging the information to you. Sometimes they'll know and won't tell you, but they will tell somebody else. If you don't mind re-

sorting to a little deviousness, have somebody you know, preferably a woman with a smile in her voice, call and say something like this, "Hello, I'm Sally Smith from Smith's Dry Cleaners (Smith's Photo Shop). Your neighbor, Richard Renter, left some clothes (film) here to be cleaned (developed) quite some time ago, and he hasn't stopped by to pick them (it) up. We think he may have forgotten, and we haven't been able to reach him at the telephone number he gave us. Do you know how we might find him?" It usually works.

If every avenue you take turns into a blind alley, remember that the post office might be of some help. Your tenant wants his mail forwarded; that's pretty sure. He's still expecting his Auntie Nelly to die and leave him a large inheritance, and he certainly wants to get all of his Reader's Digest Sweepstakes mail. He knows that some day he'll be a winner and surprise everyone by paying back his many debts.

To locate him using the post office, ask the postal carrier who delivers mail to the tenant's old address whether there's a change of address on file for him and if so, what it is. If that doesn't work, try dispatching an envelope to the tenant at his old address. Stuff it with a copy of the judgment and your reckoning of his deposits. Include your return address, and write the words "PLEASE FORWARD AND MAIL ADDRESS CORRECTION TO SENDER" below the tenant's address. The post office will send you whatever forwarding address it has on file.

Don't give up. He hasn't vanished off the face of the earth. He's probably even closer than you think. Few people move any distance away from where they've been living unless they're in the armed forces or work for a nationwide company which rotates its employees periodically. They tend to stay within a certain geographical radius because that's where their friends and relatives are, that's where they're accustomed to living and playing, and that's where everything is familiar to them. Your former tenant is around somewhere, and he has left his tracks. Chase him down.

To locate him using the phone system, dial 411 and ask for the tenant's current phone number. He may already have a telephone installed at his new place.

To locate him using the Internet, consult the nationwide directories now available there. Go to "Yahoo.com" and do a "people search"; go to

"Excite.com" and use the "people finder"; or go to "Switchboard.com" and tap into its vast nationwide people database. I've been pleasantly surprised by how many people I've been able to find through these sites. The cost is right, too. It's absolutely free.

For specific, helpful hints in tracking down your tenant, consult a book like *How to Find Missing Persons or You Can Find Anyone*. People who earn their living looking for bail jumpers, child support shirkers, swindlers on the lam, teenage runaways, elusive heirs, and wayward waifs have their own ways of finding those who seem to have vanished as if from a magician's trunk.

Looking Around for Something to Collect

You may know already where the tenant works or has attachable assets. Good for you! You're smart to have kept track of such things. Now don't wait. Get going. Take this information to the sheriff or marshal and fill out the proper forms so collection can begin right away, before the tenant knows what's happening.

If you suspect that your evicted tenant may have attachable assets, but you don't know what they are or where they are, you may do one or both of two things—run a credit check or order an examination at the courthouse.

Running a credit check has enough advantages so that you ought to think about trying it before resorting to an examination. First, it preserves the element of surprise. You may catch the tenant unawares before he has had an opportunity to hide his attachable assets. Second, it saves you time because you don't have to arrange, prepare for, and conduct a face-to-face examination. Third, it takes no mental toll on you because you don't have to put yourself in the presence of the lousy scoundrel who's caused you all this trouble in the first place. That's no fun.

Of course, running a credit check does require authorization, doesn't it? But you got that when the tenant first filled out his rental application, didn't you? The rental application I use states specifically: "I authorize verification of my references and credit as they relate to my tenancy and to future rent collections."

The credit report may tell you enough about the tenant's assets to point you in the right direction to get at them, and then again it may not. The information in his credit report may be so dated that you may be able to tell the credit agency things about the tenant which they didn't know before. If so, you will have to go further and order an actual examination.

Ordering an Examination

An examination involves personal testimony before a court or before a court-appointed referee. The tenant has no choice but to come. He absolutely has to appear at an examination just as he has to appear in court when subpoenaed or he will be held in contempt of court and will face the humiliation of being arrested. He must tell the truth about his assets, too, or he will be guilty of perjury, which carries both a jail sentence and a fine.

To arrange this examination, use the Application and Order for Appearance and Examination (Attachment—Enforcement of Judgment) form. You're already familiar with the format of other similar Judicial Council of California forms. This one is simpler than most. Fill it out as shown here and take it to the court clerk's office to get an appointment for the examination. There is no additional cost for this hearing. All you pay for is the service of the papers. Once you have set the appointment, take the order to a process server. The form must be served in person at least ten days prior to the examination.

Generally the examination is held in impersonal surroundings at the courthouse in the presence of a clerk. You are the examiner.

The examination, you hope, will be revealing, but you must know what questions to ask, for your former tenant isn't going to volunteer any information. You can be quite sure of that.

Here are some questions you may want to ask:

1) What's your current address? What's your current phone number?
2) Who are your dependents, and how are they related to you?
3) How do you propose to pay me the money you owe me?
4) What's your occupation? Who's your employer? How long have you worked there?
5) What's your salary? How is it paid? When is it paid?
6) What's your spouse's occupation? Who's your spouse's employer? How long has your spouse worked there?
7) What's your spouse's salary? How is it

paid? When is it paid?

8) Do you have an interest in any business? How much of an interest do you have? What kind of business is it? How does the business get its money? Where does the business keep its money?

9) What other income do you have?

10) Do you own your own home now? What is the home's value? What mortgages are there on it? Who holds the mortgages? What are the payments? When was your home homesteaded?

11) Are you renting now? How much is the rent? When and how is it paid? What's your landlord's name and address?

12) Do you own any real estate either by yourself or with someone else? Where is it located? How do you hold title to it? Is it mortgaged? Who holds the mortgages? What are the payments?

13) Where do you have your checking account? What's its number? In whose name is it? What's the balance in the account? Do you have any checks with you?

14) Where do you have your savings account? What's its number? In whose name is it?

15) Do you have any more bank accounts? If so, what are the particulars?

16) Do you have any money in an individual retirement account (IRA)? Where is it? Do you have any money in some other retirement account? Where is that?

17) Do you have a safe deposit box? If so, where is it?

18) How much cash do you have on you? Where else is your cash kept?

19) Do you have any stocks, bonds, or other securities? What are the particulars about them?

20) How much life insurance do you have and with what company is it? Who's your insurance agent?

21) Where is your jewelry kept? What would you estimate its value to be?

22) Do you have a share in someone's will or estate? What are the particulars?

23) Who is the registered owner of the car you drive? Who and where is the legal owner you make payments to? What is the value of your car? How much are your car payments? What is the unpaid balance? You say you don't have a car?

Then how did you get here?

24) Do you own or have a share in any other vehicles? What are the particulars?

25) Have you ever filed for bankruptcy before? When? Where?

26) Do you have any property, such as furniture, tools, office equipment, or appliances, which you have pledged to pay a debt? What are the particulars?

27) Who are your parents? Where do they live? What's their telephone number?

28) Give the names of two other relatives or of friends who live in the vicinity.

29) Is there anything else relative to your financial situation which I may have overlooked?

Deciding What to Go After

Well, how do things look? You should have a lot of information by now. What are you going to do with it all? Look for things to seize and attach, that's what. Are there forthcoming wages. Is there something of value which your former tenant possesses that you might be able to get your hands on? Did he say during the examination that he had $200 in his wallet? Did he say that he had some checks?

First things first—if the tenant admits to having jewelry or cash on his person during the examination, ask him to turn them over to you voluntarily to help satisfy the judgment. Ask him to take out two of those checks he said he has with him and write them to you, one for a third of what he owes you, the other for two-thirds (you want two checks just in case the bank won't cash a check for the entire amount because of insufficient funds; it will cash one for a smaller amount if he has enough in his account). Then run directly to his bank to cash them. If he won't cooperate, get a court order immediately to force his cooperation. Whoever's acting as the impartial third party during the examination will know exactly what to do.

The next best sources of payment after his most readily available assets are wages, a till tap, bank accounts, and vehicles.

Wages are the best of the lot. They're paid on a regular basis, and there's little he can do to stop you from garnishing them. Once you know where he works and how much he earns, you have all the information you need to garnish his wages.

If he's self-employed and he doesn't receive

wages, but he does receive monies in his business, you may order a till-tap, a seizure of monies in the "till" conducted by the levying officer in your area.

Bank accounts are too easily transferable. They're good only if you can surprise him and get to them before he has an opportunity to withdraw his funds.

His car would be a good source of funds if he didn't already owe more on it that it's worth or if he didn't own such a klunker, both of which are likely. The other problem with trying to squeeze money out of a car to satisfy a judgment is the complicated nature of the conversion. Have you ever tried to raise some quick cash by selling a vehicle you own? It can be an involved process, one which never yields as much as you thought it would. Selling a car which someone else owns involves more work and requires more upfront money paid to the sheriff or marshal than the previous two assets. It should be a last resort.

Consider the other assets revealed during the examination for what they're worth. If they look attachable, go after them.

Setting Up the Collection

At this point, do not have a change of heart about the tenant's intentions. Do not set up a payment schedule and have the tenant make payments directly to you. He may implore you not to put his livelihood in danger by garnishing his wages. Don't listen to him. You aren't putting his livelihood in danger unless his wages are already being garnished for some other debts. His employer cannot fire him for one garnishment order. Forego garnishing his wages right away only if he promises to pay the entire judgment to you within three days and if he gives you a plausible source for the funds. Otherwise, get thee to the sheriff or marshal's office, fill out the proper forms there, pay the upfront money required, and let them handle the collection. The tenant has to pay the fees for their service anyway.

The fee for garnishing wages is $21; for attaching a bank account, it's $25; for a till-tap, it's $75; and for selling a vehicle, there's an upfront deposit of $600-900 (varies by county).

Remember that tenants may try to hide their assets after the examination. Move quickly before they put their assets out of your reach.

Enlisting the Services of a Collection Agency

Sometimes collecting a judgment yourself is easy; sometimes it's not. After learning what's involved, you may not want to spend your time playing sleuth and trying to collect the judgment yourself. If so, you may get a collection agency to do it for you. Yes, there are people who make their living collecting other people's debts. They are in business to handle collections impersonally and professionally.

For their services, collection agencies charge forty to fifty percent of all they collect, but just remember that half of nothing is nothing. If they don't get any money for you, they get none for themselves. Even for a fat forty or fifty percent of a few hundred dollars, they're not going to turn over every rock looking for your debtor and his assets. You should provide them with some solid information so they will know to look only under iron-pyrite rocks weighing about fifty pounds located within the city limits of Bakersfield. That kind of information is helpful.

To enlist the services of a collection agency, give them the judgment form from your court case, sign an "Assignment of Judgment" (they'll have one handy) authorizing them to collect your debt for you, and wait. You may be pleasantly surprised one day long after you've forgotten the matter when checks start coming in the mail. Don't, of course, be the least bit surprised if they don't, because they probably won't. Be content with the tenant's departure, for with that you have accomplished your primary goal anyway—to minimize your losses and regain the possession of a rental dwelling which you can rent to a paying customer.

Selling the Judgment

Some savvy people make a good living out of buying money judgments for pennies on the dollar and then collecting the full amount of what's owed. You may not even have to contact these people. They may contact you. They scour courthouse records looking for the names of judgment creditors.

If nobody contacts you and you're interested in selling your judgment, ask the court clerk for the name of somebody. She'll know.

Depending upon their assessment of your eagerness to sell and the likelihood of their collecting, they will pay you anywhere from 5 to 40% of the judgment. Consider what they first offer you and bargain with them if you'd rather apply your time to things other than collecting judgments. At least they pay you something, and they pay it to you right away. That's better than nothing.

Filing an Acknowledgment of Satisfaction of Judgment

If the tenant ever does pay the entire amount of the judgment, you must file with the court something called an Acknowledgment of Satisfaction of Judgment. It's a form which becomes part of the county's public records, alerting one and all, especially the credit bureau, that the tenant has paid you everything he owed you as a result of your court case. It's essentially the tenant's "reward" for paying off the debt. While it doesn't eliminate altogether the appearance of the involuntary judgment indebtedness from the tenant's credit report (that remains for seven years), it does serve as a kind of counterbalance and proves that the tenant does pay up, however reluctantly and however late.

File the form only when the tenant has paid you in full, not before. The court clerk will supply you with a copy; use a pen to fill it out. It's a standard Judicial Council form like the half-dozen others used in eviction proceedings, and since you have filled out several such forms already, this one won't be any mystery to you.

Because this particular form is used in many kinds of court cases which result in money judgments, not just evictions, you will see some things on the form which don't apply to you. Don't let them confuse you.

Count yourself lucky if you ever have to file one and be sure you file it promptly. You have no right to delay making public the fact that the tenant has paid up.

- Tap the cosigner to pay the evicted tenant's bill.
- One way to exact revenge is to smirch your evicted tenant's credit rating.
- Another is to give him an IRS 1099-MISC.
- File an abstract of judgment in case the tenant ever buys or sells any real property.
- Go after the tenant most likely to have the bucks; he's responsible for the whole judgment.
- Don't assume that a disappearing tenant is gone forever; he's around somewhere.
- Use any of numerous legal ways to discover where the tenant's assets are.
- Make use of the sheriff or marshal to ensure payment.
- Use a collection agency or sell the judgment if you'd rather not collect it yourself.
- File an Acknowledgement of Satisfaction of Judgment when you finally do get paid.

14
Coping with Other Related Matters

Besides regaining possession of your rental dwelling and collecting the money which is owed to you, the primary concerns of previous chapters, you may have occasion to be concerned with a variety of other related matters. You may need to know, for example, what you ought to do with the belongings your tenant left behind when you evicted him, how to handle an apparent abandonment, how to get rid of a renter who stopped paying you his garage rent, how to evict a lodger from your home, how to oust a discharged manager, what to do about squatters, when to pursue a Writ of Immediate Possession, why the baggage lien law is practically useless to you, what's different about military tenants, how to respond to a landlord who is asking you for a recommendation on the tenant you're evicting, how to handle deposit refunds when the tenant hasn't provided adequate notice that he's vacating, or what to do when you have to evict a Section 8 tenant. Matters such as these appear in this final chapter, which I hope will help you avoid some unnecessary legal entanglements.

Disposing of the Remains

There is always the slim possibility that an evicted tenant will leave you with a crock full of silver dollars and three Nikons; with a dwelling full of greasy pots, black kettles, and thrift-shop furniture; or, more likely, with some piles of tattered clothing, dust balls, and dozens of poopy Pampers. You should know how to dispose of these things legally, exposing yourself to as little liability as possible.

As landlord again in possession of your real property, you must take charge of the tenant's personal property which remains. You have no choice in the matter, for the sheriff or marshal nowadays can assist you only in removing the humanity left on the premises and not in removing anything else. He won't even help you inventory the stuff that's left behind. You're on your own in handling that.

If you can possibly locate your former tenant, try to make arrangements with him to remove his remaining belongings on or before the day set for the eviction, but if you cannot find him anywhere, determine the approximate value of the belongings yourself before doing anything else. If you believe they have a resale value of less than $300, you may dispose of them after fifteen days in any way you choose. You may keep all the pennies you can find, wear the old clothes, toss the Pampers, give away the settee, and sell the pots and kettles. If you have any doubts about your own ability as an appraiser of secondhand goods, you might want to call a thrift shop and ask them for an estimate, giving them everything as a donation in exchange for a receipt stating that the value of all the items is equal to less than $300. If you are the least bit suspicious that your former tenant may be trying to trap you into disposing of his junk, only to claim later that it consisted of nothing but his priceless family heirlooms, take pictures of every room and its contents before you ever touch a thing. Then call the thrift-shop appraiser.

If the belongings are worth $300 or more, you may not dispose of them so easily. You should photograph and inventory everything first and then decide whether to leave things where they are or move them. If you leave them in place, storage charges would be equivalent to the per-diem rent from the date of the eviction.

Since you undoubtedly want the dwelling available again for renting right away, you should move the tenant's goods into "a place of safe-keeping" as soon as possible, and you must return them upon demand, charging only a reasonable sum for the storage itself. Whatever you do, don't hold the tenant's goods until he pays all that he owes you. Be reasonable and you'll

NOTICE
OF BELIEF OF ABANDONMENT
(Real Property)

TO: Delwyn Lewno

Muretta Lewno

Address:

999 Sweet Street
(Street Address)

Littleton   California   91111
(City)   (State)   (Zip)

This notice is given pursuant to Section 1951.3 of the California Civil Code concerning the above-described real property rented by you. The rent on this property has been due and unpaid for fourteen (14) or more consecutive days, and the owner/manager believes that you have abandoned the property.

This real property will be deemed abandoned within the meaning of Section 1951.2 of the Civil Code, and your tenancy shall terminate on ___February 25, XXXX___ which is not less than eighteen (18) days after this notice is deposited in the United States Mail unless before such date the undersigned receives at the address indicated below a written notice from you stating BOTH of the following: (1) Your intent not to abandon the real property, and (2) An address at which you may be served by certified mail in any action for unlawful detainer of the real property.

You are required to pay the rent due and unpaid on this real property as required by your rental agreement. Failure to do so can lead to a court proceeding against you.

Date of mailing this notice: ___February 7, XXXX___

Lester Landlord

Owner/Manager
(signature)

Lester Landlord
123 Neat Street
Littletown, CA 91111

Name & Address of Owner/Manager
(typed or printed)

stay out of trouble.

According to Civil Code §1174, you must keep these goods in storage for at least fifteen days before putting them up for sale, and you must advertise the sale in a local newspaper at least five days before the sale is held. The proceeds must first be applied to the storage costs and to the costs incurred in holding the sale; then they may be applied to your judgment; and after that, whatever is left over must be returned to the tenant. If he is nowhere to be found, the balance must be turned over to the county within thirty days.

Don't be too worried that conducting these sales will interfere with your other leisure-time activities. Tenants simply don't trust their landlords enough to leave valuable belongings behind when they're being evicted. I've never yet had to play the auctioneer in such a situation, but I'm glad that I know what's involved anyway, in case I have to do it someday, just as I'm glad that I can milk a cow, program a computer, fly an airplane, and change a flat tire.

Abandonment

Occasionally a tenant, along with all of his belongings, will skip out entirely without your knowledge, or he may simply disappear and leave all of his personal property behind. Maybe he'll owe you some rent, and maybe he won't. Whereas California law (Civil Code §1951.2 and 1951.3) does have specific procedures to follow in these cases, the procedures do take a minimum of 29 days.

Now, 29 days is a long time to wait if you feel 98% certain that the tenant has already abandoned the place and removed his worldly possessions. You're going to be anxious to get into that empty dwelling, fix it up, and get it rented again. But if you are only 71% certain that he has abandoned the place and you want to avoid all the rigmarole of conducting a full-scale unlawful detainer action to regain possession, 29 days might not seem like such a long time. After all, when you consider that an unlawful detainer filed against a tenant who can't be found and served with any of the required papers in person is going to take a minimum of 28 days, and that's only if all goes extremely well, why, what's 29 days? Not only that, unlike an unlawful detainer, abandonment procedures bypass the court system altogether, so there's little paperwork to prepare and there's

no filing fee to pay.

Think of an abandonment proceeding's 29 days as entirely relative. Don't overlook it as a very useful way to regain possession under certain circumstances.

Whatever the circumstances, you would be wise to try tracking down the missing tenant yourself to learn of his intentions before using this legal procedure. Begin your tracking by looking at the tenant's rental application and telephoning every personal and business reference given there, starting with the "person to contact in an emergency" if there is one listed on the application. Then contact the neighbors for clues to his whereabouts. Finally, when all else fails, contact the police. That should yield some leads. If it doesn't, use the following legal procedure.

As it does in regular unlawful detainer actions, the law requires that you first notify the tenant in writing of your intentions whenever you suspect abandonment. The notice you must use is called a Notice of Belief of Abandonment, but you may not use it at all until fourteen unpaid rent days have passed. Then you may deliver the notice to the tenant in person (yes, that's what the law says), or you may send it by first-class mail (get a "Certificate of Mailing" at the post office for 55¢). You must wait fifteen days after personal service or eighteen days after service by mail before you can legally claim abandonment. If the tenant does answer your notice, he must do so in writing. He must indicate that he does not intend to abandon the premises, and he must provide you with an address where he may be served by certified mail with a complaint for unlawful detainer.

If the tenant fails to answer your abandonment notice within the prescribed fifteen- or eighteen-day waiting period, you may take possession without ever having to set foot inside the courthouse. Just go right into your rental dwelling, and start your usual preparations for new tenants.

Although you do receive possession of your property through this procedure, you do not receive a money judgment. You have to go to court for that. You'll have to decide for yourself how good your chances are of ever collecting. What good's a money judgment if there's nobody available to pay it?

If there is any personal property remaining on the premises when you take possession, you must handle it a little bit differently from the way you

NOTICE OF RIGHT TO RECLAIM ABANDONED PERSONAL PROPERTY

TO: Huddle Rund

Address:

458 Sweet Street
(Street Address)

Littleton   California   91111
(City)   (State)   (Zip)

When vacated, the premises described above contained the following personal property:

One green upholstered chair, one black-and-white television, assorted men's clothes, and various kitchen gadgets

Unless you pay the reasonable cost of storage for all the above-described personal property and take possession of the property which you claim not later than eighteen (18) days after this notice is deposited in the United States Mail, this personal property may be disposed of pursuant to Civil Code Section 1988.

Check the ONE box below which applies:

[X] Because this property is believed to be worth less than $300, it may be kept, sold, or destroyed without further notice if you fail to reclaim it within the time limit indicated **below.**

[ ] Because this property is believed to be worth more than $300, it will be sold if you fail to reclaim it. It will be sold at a public sale after notice has been given by publication. You have the right to bid on the property at this sale. After the property is sold and the costs of storage, advertising, and sale are deducted, the remaining money will be turned over to the county. You may claim the remaining money at any time within one year after the county receives the money.

Date of mailing this notice: ___February 7, XXXX___
Date of expiration of this notice: ___February 25, XXXX___

You may claim this property at: 444 Neat Street, Littletown, CA 91111

Lester Landlord
Owner/Manager
(signature)

Lester Landlord
123 Neat Street
Littletown, CA 91111
Name & Address of Owner/Manager
(typed or printed)

handle the remains left after an eviction. Civil Code §1988 spells out the procedure. You should inventory the property first, store it, and then send the tenant a Notice of Right to Reclaim Abandoned Property, stating that he has eighteen days to reclaim his things. After that period, you may keep, sell, or destroy it if you believe it is worth less than $300. If you believe it is worth more than $300, you must advertise that you are auctioning off his property, and then you may go ahead and auction it off. The proceeds of this sale go first to storage costs and sale expenses, then to delinquent rent and costs; whatever surplus there is beyond that must be turned over to the county.

You may proceed with a nonpayment-of-rent unlawful detainer action at the same time you are pursuing an abandonment if you wish, for a Notice of Belief of Abandonment has no effect on the use of a 3-Day Notice to Pay Rent or Quit. They may be used independently of each other and concurrently as well.

Nosy landlords never have abandonment problems. They know what their tenants are up to all the time. You needn't become nosy to avoid abandonment problems. You can avoid them through good communications and circumspection.

Self-Service Storage Areas and Garages

California has a Self-Service Storage Facility Act (Business & Professional Code §21700) which governs mini-storage units and garages used strictly for storing personal property. Specifically excluded from this act are storage areas or garages rented with a residence, storage areas or garages used as a residence, and warehouses. If you are renting out a garage to somebody and have a separate rental agreement for it, then chances are good that this relationship comes under the SSSFA. Should the renter stop paying you the rent, you'll find that evicting him is relatively easy. The procedure is much like the one used for an abandonment because it calls for similar notice periods and involves no court action in most cases.

Here's what you do when the renter fails to pay his rent. Wait fourteen days following the rent due date. Then send the renter a Preliminary Lien Notice by certified mail to his last known address and to whatever alternative ad-

dress appears on the rental agreement (the agreement must provide a space for an alternative address, whether the renter gives one or not). Here's the notice format:

```
PRELIMINARY LIEN NOTICE
TO [leave a blank for the
renter's name and full address].
    You owe, and have not paid,
rent and/or other charges for the
use of storage [identify the
storage area by space number or
other identifier] at [give the
address of the storage facility].
    These charges total $[amount]
and have been due for more than
14 days. They are itemized as
follows: [give due date, descrip-
tion, and amount].  If this sum
is not paid in full before [give
a date at least 14 days from
mailing], your right to use the
storage space will terminate, you
will be denied access, and an
owner's lien on any stored prop-
erty will be imposed.
    You may pay this sum and may
contact the owner at [give your
name, full address, and your
telephone number].
    [Date it and sign it.]
```

Fourteen days later, having received anything less than the full amount of the rent due, you may lock the renter out, enter the space, and remove the renter's property to a place of safekeeping. You must then send the renter a Notice of Lien Sale just as you did the preliminary notice. Here's the format:

```
NOTICE OF LIEN SALE
TO [leave a blank for the
renter's name and full address].
    Your right to use the storage
space [identify the storage area
by space number or other identi-
fier] at [give the address of the
storage facility] has terminated.
You no longer have access to the
stored property.
    The stored property is subject
to a lien in the amount of [give
```

```
the same amount shown in the PRE-
LIMINARY LIEN NOTICE].  The
stored property will be sold to
satisfy this lien after [specify
a date not less than fourteen
days following the date of mail-
ing] unless the amount of the
lien is paid in full or you com-
plete and return by certified
mail the enclosed DECLARATION IN
OPPOSITION TO LIEN SALE form.
     You may claim any excess sale
proceeds above the lien amount
and the costs of sale at any time
within one year following the
sale, but after one year, the ex-
cess proceeds will be turned over
to the county.
     [Date it and sign it.]
```

Along with the Notice of Lien Sale, you must send a relatively simple Declaration in Opposition to Lien Sale form for the renter to fill out. Here's its format:

```
     DECLARATION IN OPPOSITION
            TO LIEN SALE
     I, [leave a blank for the
renter's name], have received the
notice of lien sale of the prop-
erty stored at [leave a blank for
the location and space number, if
any].
     I oppose the lien sale of the
property. My address is: [leave a
blank for the renter's street ad-
dress, city, state, and zip].
     I understand that the lien-
holder may file an action in
court against me, and if a judg-
ment is given in his or her fa-
vor, I may be liable for the
court costs. I declare under pen-
alty of perjury that the forego-
ing is true and correct, and that
this declaration was signed by me
on [leave a blank for the date]
at [leave a blank for the place].
     [Leave a blank for the renter's
signature.]
```

If you must take the renter to court because he has returned the declaration, follow the procedure in B&P §21710. If you must hold a sale, follow the procedure in B&P §21707 for advertising it, conducting it, and disposing of the proceeds.

Evicting a Lodger

Should you be renting out a room in your own house to a lodger or a roomer, as they're sometimes called, and should you want to evict that person because he has stopped paying you the rent money or because you're not getting along well enough to live under one roof anymore, you're probably pretty miserable about the situation. It's much like being stuck in a bad marriage.

Well, consider yourself lucky in this one respect at least, that you do not have to go to all the trouble of filing an unlawful detainer as outlined in chapter 5 in order to evict your lodger. The eviction procedure for lodgers is much simpler than the standard eviction procedure because the law recognizes that you and a lodger with whom you are having a disagreement are living in close proximity under strained circumstances and that you have to resolve the matter between yourselves reasonably quickly, or there could be some "fire" started by the friction.

Take note, however, that you may use this abbreviated procedure only if you have one lodger, no more, and only where you as the owner have retained the "right of access" to your entire dwelling, including the area occupied by the lodger. If you are renting out a self-sufficient in-law apartment located within your dwelling and you have not retained the right of access to the apartment (having keys to the place does not give you the right of access; apartment owners retain keys to their units, but they do not have the right of access), then you cannot use this procedure. You must follow the standard eviction procedure instead.

So what is this abbreviated procedure for evicting lodgers?

Civil Code §1946.5 explains it in legal terms, and you should take a look at the code before you attempt to evict your lodger (see Appendix B).

In layman's terms, it's the simplest procedure possible, one which puts real teeth into notices and real meaning into the time limits given on those notices. You simply serve the lodger a notice appropriate to the situation, for example, a 3-Day Notice to Pay Rent or Quit in a nonpayment-of-rent situation, the same as you would serve any other tenant (you would be wise to have somebody else serve the notice for you so you'll have someone other than yourself available to testify on your behalf should the tenant later claim in court that nobody served him). If the lodger fails to satisfy the demands of the notice within the time limits allowed, he has violated California Penal Code §602.3 (see Appendix B), and you may make a "citizen's arrest" under Penal Code §837. If the tenant won't leave, you may call the local law enforcement agency and have the lodger formally arrested. An officer removes him from the premises, and he's gone. He's evicted. That's all there is to it. You do not have to go to all the trouble and expense of getting a court judgment and a Writ of Possession.

This truly is a summary eviction. Would that every landlord could use the same procedure for any tenant!

Unfortunately, there's a horsefly in this marvelous ointment. If the tenant won't cooperate by leaving voluntarily and you have to resort to calling in the troops, you might find yourself at a sudden impasse.

Unless your local law enforcement agency already has experience with this procedure or unless you know the people there and they know you, they're going to be reluctant to help. They're going to want a higher authority. Your word is not enough authority for them. They're so accustomed to acting only when they have some court-generated paperwork that they tend to be lost without it. Consequently, you may have to press your case pretty hard to get any action out of them.

Rather than expecting law enforcement people to jump when you call them to have a lodger evicted bodily, prepare yourself for some resistance. Approach them correctly, and you might get the action you want.

Begin by gathering up your paperwork—copies of the rental agreement, the notice you served most recently, and any other relevant papers you may have. Become conversant with the applicable laws. Read them carefully and make copies. Then make an appointment to see somebody at your local law enforcement agency who has the authority to decide whether to take action or not. Argue your case before that person, show him

the paperwork, and see what happens.

In spite of what you see in films and on television, law enforcers in real life tend to ask questions first and shoot afterwards. They want to make sure that they are well within the law before they take any action at all. They don't want to do something which will make them look like fools or cause them grief later, especially now that they're fair game for every loaded video camera pointed in their direction. Don't blame them if they're none too eager to drag your lodger out of your house by the scruff of his neck. They know only too well what the consequences might be for them should they make the wrong move.

Because yours may be the one and only lodger eviction case your local law enforcement agency has ever encountered or ever will encounter, you will probably know more about evicting lodgers than they do. Try convincing them that you know what you're doing, that you have complied with the law, and that you would like them merely to carry out the enforcement. Maybe they will help you, and maybe they won't.

If you can't get any action out of your local law enforcement agency, don't despair. You still have any number of choices for getting rid of that lodger. Here are some—intimidate the lodger into leaving by "moving" somebody else into the same room; show him the law about lodger evictions and give him an ultimatum to be out in one hour, at which time you say that you will cause enough of a disturbance so that your neighbors will call the cops and you will have the lodger arrested for trespassing; deny the lodger access to his lodgings, that is, change the locks when he's gone and lock him out; or follow the same formal eviction procedure which everybody else follows at this stage, just as if the lodger were a tenant in your apartment house.

None of these choices is particularly agreeable, but then, you're stuck in a disagreeable situation anyway, and you'll likely have to do something disagreeable to force the lodger out and restore your life to normalcy.

Every choice except the last one would seem to be an illegal or quasi-legal "self-help" eviction method. It's not. Remember, your situation is not like that of other landlords. Your "tenant" is living with you, so he's more like a house guest than a tenant, and when you and he are not getting along, he's like a house guest who has overstayed his welcome. The law restores possession to you upon expiration of the notice you gave the lodger. Just because you can't convince a law enforcement agency to remove the lodger bodily doesn't mean that you have any less of a right to possession. You have every right to possession. You have every right to put him out on the street yourself. Having him arrested is almost a formality, something which puts the law enforcement establishment's official stamp of approval on the eviction and ensures that nobody gets hurt.

You don't need this stamp of approval, but you do need to ensure that nobody gets hurt, and the best thing you can do to keep the peace is to surround yourself with people. Confront your lodger in the company of others—friends, relatives, or neighbors. You want witnesses. You want moral support. And you want physical support if necessary. If you're too angry with the lodger to talk calmly and you doubt your ability to maintain control over yourself and the situation, you might even want somebody else to do the talking for you.

Whatever you do, be careful. Make absolutely certain that you are in full compliance with the law. Reread the law on the whole lodger eviction procedure. Document and date every step you've taken so far in trying to settle your grievance with the lodger, in giving him proper notice, and in trying to get a law enforcer to remove him. Then take action.

Do nothing to anger the lodger other than put him out. Do not touch him unless he touches you first. Don't even act physically threatening. Return his belongings when he asks for them, return his deposit if you owe him anything, but don't let him back inside the dwelling.

Should he sue you later, you will have what you need to defend yourself in court.

Discharged Manager

Every so often you may be faced with one of the following situations involving a resident manager: You have learned quite by accident that your manager is embezzling funds; you have bought a building which has a manager whom you want to replace; your tenants have begun grumbling to you that the manager is always trying to convert them to his latest religion; you have found your manager drunk on the job; your manager no longer seems interested in exterior maintenance, and the building is beginning to look run-down; over the past three weeks, your manager

has given two tenants black eyes; although told repeatedly that the toilet was leaking and the hot water heater wasn't working in Apartment 6, your manager neglected to do anything about these problems, so the tenant withheld his rent, and you failed to evict him when you tried because he rightly used the warranty-of-habitability defense; or you can't seem to get along with your manager, no matter what.

These are distressing situations, to say the least, and you may want to avoid doing anything about them because you know there will only be unpleasantries involved when you do, but you have a business to run. You simply cannot afford to ignore these situations, nor can you afford to get drawn into the personal dramas certain to occur when you discharge a resident manager. You must think of your business first.

So what do you do? What can you do?

If the matter is urgent enough, such as your having caught a manager embezzling funds, you will have to find someone to manage the place immediately on a temporary basis. Once discovered, the embezzler must not be allowed access to your funds. After you have provided for temporary management, you can deal with the villain himself. Threaten to turn him over to the police if he hasn't moved out completely within twenty-four hours. If he doesn't move out, call the police and at the same time serve him with a summons and complaint. The written employment termination notice you give him is the only notice you need to serve to initiate unlawful detainer proceedings against him.

If the matter is not particularly urgent, such as your incompatibility with the manager or the manager's negligence of responsibilities, you should handle it differently. Determine, first of all, whether you want to let him continue living where he is. If so, give him a written notice stating when his employment is terminated, when his rent is to begin, and how much that rent will be. Then he won't be able to claim in court that his rent was another sum. Give him the amount of notice you have agreed upon in the management agreement, twenty-four hours, seven days, or at most thirty days. Lacking a management agreement, give him thirty days' notice unless his pay period is every week or twice a month. In that case, the notice period should correspond to his pay period.

If you elect to require him to leave upon termination of his employment (wise in most cases; necessary if there are special resident manager's quarters), state in his notice of termination that you want him to move out. Then, if he doesn't move in the time allotted, you may initiate an unlawful detainer against him as soon as his termination becomes effective.

Follow the failure-to-vacate procedure in chapter 8 (you don't need to give him further notice, of course), but you should explain in an attachment to the complaint that the defendant is a licensee, not a tenant, that you and the defendant have had an employer-employee relationship, that you have discharged the defendant from employment, and that you wish to reclaim possession of the dwelling occupied by the defendant as a condition of employment.

Squatters

"Squatters? I've never had any trouble with squatters before. Why would they ever choose my place to squat?"

There are any number of reasons. They might have thought that you didn't care about the property and would be grateful to have someone living there, that you were off on a vacation and wouldn't notice, that you had inherited the property and were waiting for it to clear probate, that you were waiting for a wrecker to tear the place down, that you were a skinflint and should be skinned, that you lived far away and weren't keeping tabs on the place, that you owned so much property you had forgotten about this one, that you were involved in a partnership breakup and couldn't agree what to do with the property, or that you were a government agency with surplus property managed by bureaucrats. Sound crazy? Sure, but there are people in this world who think that you and I owe them a roof over their heads, and given the opportunity, they'll seize that roof. They don't care who owns it.

European landlords know a lot about squatters. They are so overwhelmed with squatters that many of them have had to guard their vacant rental properties like fortresses, using 24-hour guards, electronic alarms, Doberman patrols, and all but impregnable locks, just to keep these pesky people out. England alone is said to have tens of thousands of them. Some are so persistent and so brazen that they will even try to move in by creating a diversion and then sneaking past the guards.

Fortunately the situation has yet to reach those lows here in California because the housing shortage isn't quite so chronic, and our laws aren't quite so archaic. Still, you may occasionally encounter someone who, unbeknownst to you, has set up housekeeping in one of your vacant rentals, and you may wonder what can be done about it.

Consider, first of all, what has happened, that your real property has actually been stolen out from under your nose just as certainly as someone might break in and steal your VCR, your Colt .45, your Radarange, your wedding rings, or your sterling silver. The only difference here is that the squatters can't spirit your property away into hiding. It remains attached to the earth, a particular place with a street address and, of course, a tax assessor's parcel number. You know where the thieves are and you know they aren't going to leave voluntarily, for if they do, they will be relinquishing what they have stolen.

Squatters are committing a criminal act, to be sure, and you have every right to feel wronged. You have been wronged. Consequently, you may tend to cast yourself in the role of a self-appointed vigilante with right on your side. You may want to burst into the place with weapons drawn and boot them out bodily. If you enjoy confrontations and danger and you wouldn't mind risking a few years cooling your heels with society's losers or you have great confidence in your attorney's abilities, strap your six-shooters to your belt, burst into the place, and go after the squatters with all your firepower. Try to resist this approach if you can. It's unreasonable, it's dangerous, it's illegal, and you're likely to widow your wife and orphan your children.

Instead, call the police and talk the situation over with them. Tell them that someone has "stolen your property," that you know where the thieves are, and that you'd like help from the police in reclaiming it. These are terms understood by police anywhere. Telling the police that there are squatters living in a rental dwelling you own will not elicit the same response. Incidentally, you or someone representing you should take an active role in this attempt to reclaim your property. Do not leave it entirely up to the police. Accompany them when they first visit the squatters. Help direct the efforts to clarify the situation for everyone and get the squatters out.

So long as the squatters acknowledge that they

have no legal claim to possession, the police visit should be sufficient to get them out. If they claim that they have a legal right, say an oral agreement with the owner, then the police won't be of much help, and you will have to resort to other means.

If you encounter indifference from the police about your problem, you should get someone else to accompany you on a visit to the premises, in broad daylight if possible. It would be helpful if this person had a football player's neck, a basketball player's height, an iron pumper's chest, and a Sicilian surname, but if such a person is unavailable, any adult will do. Tell the squatters that you have rented the premises to your friend here and he has a valid rental agreement entitling him to move in that very day. They must leave right now, or you will have to call the police in to make them leave. After you've said all that, stay there until they start packing. It might help if you have a U-Haul truck or trailer with you to confirm your statement that your "new tenant" is ready to move in.

You might resort to the primary stratagem used by European landlords who discover squatters on their property, a stratagem similar to what the Feds used when they evicted the Indian squatters from Alcatraz some years back. Keep watch on the place patiently until all or nearly all of the squatters (at least the ringleaders) have left the premises. Then arrive with a large enough entourage and move the squatters' belongings out into the street. If you have waited until the squatters least expected to be evicted, you should encounter little or no resistance. Should there be any resistance at all, stay right there yourself, and send a cohort to call the police immediately. In a ticklish confrontation like the one you've forced, the police must respond, and now it'll be your word against the squatters', and you should prevail, especially if you have some paperwork to prove your case. Be resolute. Don't leave the place without getting your property back. Then, once you are successful in evicting the squatters, secure the place well and have a neighbor look after it for you.

Should these efforts fail, don't do anything really drastic, like burying mines in the yard or setting demolition charges around the periphery of the building and then threatening the squatters' lives if they don't leave. Follow the legal procedure to get them out.

Of course, there is one. It requires serving them with a Notice to Quit first, giving them five days to get out. That's right, I did say five days! Don't ask me why the laws give a squatter more notice time than a deadbeat tenant; they just do.

Use the straightforward Notice to Quit form for starters. Be sure you check the box next to "forceable entry" and put a "5" in the line next to "days."

Try various subterfuges to get the squatters' names if possible (question the neighbors or literally sift through the squatters' garbage looking for names if you have to). On the notice you may list the names as numbered "Does," but you'll need to know their real names by the time you get the judgment because the sheriff or marshal will not be able to carry out the Writ of Possession unless the actual names of the occupants are listed.

After that, you should proceed not with an unlawful detainer, but rather with a forcible detainer according to CCP §1159-60. Consult the latest edition of The Rutter Group's *California Practice Guide: Landlord-Tenant* in your court's law library for more information and the proper forms.

Writ of Immediate Possession

You may still file for a Writ of Immediate Possession just as you may still file a lien against your tenant's personal property using the baggage lien law, but neither one is used that much anymore. In 1970, the writ was emasculated just enough to make it virtually useless except for a narrow range of applications.

Today, according to CCP §1166a, a writ will be issued only if you can prove any one of the following: 1) the defendant resides out of state; 2) he has departed from the state; 3) he cannot, after due diligence, be found in the state; or 4) he has concealed himself to avoid service of summons.

Prior to 1970, one could get a Writ of Immediate Possession in California by proving either that the tenant was bankrupt or that he lacked property sufficient to repay the damages sought by the landlord. As you might imagine, those two grounds, when added to the four above, made this writ quite a bit more useful then as compared to its restricted version now.

But if you feel you can prove that your tenant

falls into any of the four categories above, you might want to secure a Writ of Immediate Possession because it will do exactly what its name says it will do, give you immediate possession, after you make a court appearance.

The procedure starts out like any other unlawful detainer and only changes when the process server who is trying to serve the tenants informs you that they are avoiding service or could be out of state. That's when you file a motion for writ of possession per CCP §1166a (see Appendix B).

This motion must state that the writ of possession you are requesting applies to all tenants, subtenants, if any, named claimants, if any, and any other occupants of the premises. And it should ask for an order shortening the time of notice of the hearing on the motion because the underlying unlawful detainer action is entitled to a summary proceeding.

After you learn from the court when the hearing on your motion will be held, you must serve the tenants with a notice informing them of the date and time of the hearing (served according to CCP §1011). The notice must state that they have the right to file affidavits with the court and to appear and testify at the hearing. It must also state that if the tenants do not appear, the plaintiff/landlord will apply to the court for a writ of possession.

Then comes something different. The judge will require you to "file an undertaking," that is, post a bond, which would be used to compensate the tenants for damages if you later fail to get a judgment for possession or if your unlawful detainer action is later dismissed.

Be aware that some judges are very reluctant to grant an order for immediate possession because they believe that tenants should have their "day in court."

Be aware that some local eviction control ordinances (only rent control areas have eviction controls) may prohibit the use of CCP §1166a in their jurisdictions.

Be aware that you should submit a written declaration (see Declaration for Default Judgment in Lieu of Personal Testimony for format) of facts before the hearing and that your declaration should be specific about where the tenants are and how you discovered their whereabouts. It should give whatever information you have about how the premises are being damaged, if they are

being damaged, and about how the premises are being used for illegal acts, if they are. You should get a declaration from the process server, too, listing all of his previously unsuccessful attempts to serve the tenants.

Be aware that an order for immediate possession is different from a judgment for possession even though they both result in an eviction of the tenants. Once you receive an order for immediate possession, you may still have to seek an official termination of the tenancy from the court, but at least you'd be rid of the tenants in short order.

In spite of these drawbacks, which you should be aware of before using CCP §1166a, you might find certain occasions when this procedure will serve you well.

The Baggage Lien Law

You've heard of the baggage lien law, haven't you? Yes, there truly is such a thing, but, no, it's not of much use to you. You can't just walk right into the dwelling of a tenant who's behind in the rent and seize his belongings any more.

The correct lawful procedure is so involved, and the exemptions are so numerous as to render this law virtually useless to landlords. You must first file a suit and obtain a court order before you may legally remove any of the tenant's nonexempted possessions, and, to be sure, you will find little of what most tenants own is not exempt from seizure. Even if you do get a court order to remove those household and personal items which are not considered basic under the law, you may remove them only during daylight hours. Then you must obtain a court judgment against the tenant and give the tenant another month to redeem his goods. Finally, at long last, you do get to dispose of the seized possessions at a public sale after first giving adequate notice of the sale.

Even though the law as it now reads is virtually useless to you, don't become so disgusted that you try summarily confiscating the tenant's belongings anyway to compensate yourself for rent owed. Tenants become ruffled when that happens, and you can get into more trouble than you can handle.

Some time ago a landlady in Germany seized an American serviceman's stereo set for nonpayment of rent, so he stole a cannon from the armory, wheeled it up in front of his apartment house, and threatened to blow the place up.

There's enough tension in this business without your raising the level higher.

Forget about the baggage lien law. Instead, follow the appropriate eviction proceedings, get the tenant out, and get a money judgment as well. Money is better than baggage any day.

The Military Tenant

You may have noticed that the Request for Entry of Default introduced in chapter 5 includes a Declaration of Non-Military Status that you have to fill out if you want your long-sought default entered as a matter of record. You cannot obtain a default judgment and get the tenant evicted without first signing this request declaring that your tenant is a civilian. Well, then, what happens if you have been blithely pursuing an unlawful detainer action against a military tenant, only to discover at this point that you can't get a default judgment unless you swear to a falsehood? Is all your work thus far for naught?

Maybe it is and maybe it isn't. If you also named the military person's spouse in your suit, proceed against her alone just as you would against any other civilian. When the spouse is evicted, the military tenant will generally accompany her.

Another possibility is to hope that the military tenant will go ahead and make a response to your complaint so you won't have to complete a Declaration of Non-Military Status. The only place one appears, remember, is on the Request for Entry of Default, and you won't have to file a request if the tenant responds to the complaint.

You might want to skip the normal court procedure altogether when you deal with a military person. Because military people are subject to military procedures (you know how Beetle Bailey's sergeant treats him in the comics), you could proceed against a military tenant by calling his commanding officer and asking for help in resolving the payment or tenancy problem, whatever it is. The armed services have the power to order a pay allotment proportional to salary to pay for rent of any premises occupied by a military person, his spouse, child, or other dependents. You'll likely be pleasantly surprised by the speedy response.

By the way, should there be any more major military activity in the future, such as the war in the Persian Gulf, watch the media for possible temporary restrictions on rent collections and evictions as they affect military personnel, and pay heed.

Tenant Recommendations

The tenants you evict are going to find someone else to rent from when they leave your place. They're not going to disappear off the face of the earth, idle a while in purgatory, be jailed for a few years, or wander the streets with other homeless nomads just because you've evicted them. They're going to be out looking for a new place to live in just as soon as you kick them out, and they'll find one, too.

So what do you say, then, when another landlord calls you to ask for a recommendation on someone you're in the process of evicting? Do you tell the whole truth and risk not being able to get rid of the tenants because of a bad recommendation, especially when you're in the early stages of an eviction and you're trying your hardest to get them to leave voluntarily without going to court and losing lots of money and time? Or do you tell none of the truth, just to slough your lousy tenants off on some unsuspecting landlord.

The truth is that you don't have to lie about the tenants you're evicting. Lying will only fill you with regrets later. Nor do you have to tell the whole truth about the tenants either. That'll also fill you with regrets. Instead, don't say anything either positive or negative about them. Say something like this, "I have been advised not to give recommendations on any of my tenants because you might sue me if I give them a good recommendation and they turn out to be bad tenants for you, and they might sue me if I give them a bad recommendation and my judgment is proven wrong." Almost every landlord can understand that explanation, concerned as all of us are about potential lawsuits.

Let the other landlord figure out whether to rent to your old tenants from other information available to him. You, then, can have a clear conscience that you haven't wronged either him, your departing tenants, or yourself.

Deposit Refunds

Frequently, tenants will give an indefinite notice that they plan to move and then give you a definite moving date three days before they actually do move. Naturally they believe that if they leave the place reasonably clean and undamaged, and if they are current in their rent, you owe them their entire deposit plus whatever rent they have paid for those days following the day they are expecting to vacate.

The truth is that if they have a month-to-month tenancy and pay their rent every month, they normally owe you rent for thirty days following the day when they give you a 30-day notice in writing that they intend to move, unless you have agreed with them in advance to a shorter notice period.

Hence, if they have paid you their rent for all of May and they tell you on May 12th that they're leaving May 16th, they owe you rent through June 11th, rather than through May 16th, and you may take the balance out of their security deposit if you choose.

As a practical matter, however, you would be wise to compromise on the rent you charge vacating tenants, especially when you can reasonably expect to find another tenant quickly. You see, you may not legally collect double rent. If you argue with the vacating tenant over how much rent he owes and you succeed in collecting rent from him for twenty days following his move-out date, you're going to have to refund any rent he paid for the period beginning with the first day you receive rent from the new tenant.

There's another practical matter you should keep in mind. You want to make certain that there is enough of a deposit refund available as an incentive for the vacating tenants to leave the place in good condition. The more of a refund they can expect to receive, the better they'll leave the place. When a tenant gives me one week's notice and asks me how much of his deposit he'll get back if he leaves the place clean, I tell him he'll get back all of it except for $50 or $100, which I tell him is to compensate for his giving such short notice. I could hold back more of the deposit because of the short notice, maybe all of it and still be within the law, but that's not going to get me a clean rental.

Evicting the Section 8 Tenant

Section 8 tenants know that the rental assistance they get through HUD's Section 8 Housing Program is a good deal. They get to live in rental housing which isn't located in a "housing project," and they pay only a fraction of the market rent for their dwelling. The government pays the balance.

They know that they had to do a lot to qualify for Section 8 assistance, and they know that Section 8 funds are limited.

Many people who have qualified for assistance aren't receiving any because there's almost always a shortage of funds. They just have to wait until more funds become available or until somebody currently receiving funds is disqualified.

So, if some Section 8 tenants lose their entitlement by increasing their income or doing something foolish like failing to make their rent payments, they lose out on the assistance for a long time to come, perhaps forever. If they can succeed somehow in getting requalified, they must go to the end of the line and wait for funds to become available.

While they're receiving assistance, Section 8 tenants tend to behave. They pay their rent on time, and they abide by whatever rules apply to them as tenants. They don't want to lose out on a good deal.

Of course, there are always some Section 8 tenants who have to be evicted because they stop paying their share of the rent money or they break the rules.

Evicting them does involve a little extra work, I'll grant you, but considering all that you have to do for an ordinary eviction anyway, this extra work doesn't amount to much.

Let's see what's involved should you ever have to evict Section 8 tenants yourself.

First, we'll assume that you have already exhausted every amicable method you know of to resolve whatever it is that is causing you to think about evicting your Section 8 tenants. Having done that, you must serve the tenants with an appropriate notice, and the notice must include a "good cause."

What constitutes a good cause depends upon whether you are proceeding against the tenants during the term of their fixed-term rental agreement (lease) or upon expiration of the agreement. Some good causes, such as failure to pay, disturbing the neighbors, destroying the property, and breaking the law, may be used at any time, whereas other good causes, such as the landlord's wanting to occupy or remodel the premises or end Section 8 involvement, would apply only at the expiration of a fixed-term agreement.

At the same time that you serve the tenants with a notice, you must notify the agency administering your local Section 8 program that you intend to evict the tenants. Sending them a copy of the notice along with a note advising them of your intention to evict the tenants is sufficient. The agency does not get involved in the eviction. It's a matter between you and the tenants.

Now, if the tenants were paying all of the rent themselves and you served them with a notice to pay rent or quit or a notice to terminate tenancy, you must not accept any rent from them to cover the period following the expiration date of the notice. Were you to accept any rent for that period, the tenant could contend that you had negated the notice or that you had entered into a new agreement.

In the case of Section 8 tenants, however, they are the ones paying "rent"; the agency is not. The agency is merely making housing assistance payments to the landlord to make up the shortfall between the market rent and the rent paid by the tenant. Housing assistance payments are not rent. They're an independent subsidy made on behalf of the tenant and on the basis of an agreement between HUD and the landlord. You may continue accepting HUD's payments even during an eviction [*Savett v. Davis* (1994) 29 CA4th Supp. 13, 19-20, 34 CR2d 550, 554].

As for what you should include on a notice to pay rent or quit issued to a Section 8 tenant, you should include just what the tenant is obligated to pay and nothing more. That's the rent. Don't even mention what HUD is paying you.

These few considerations aside, evicting a Section 8 tenant is no different from evicting any other tenant.

- Unload abandoned personal goods legally.
- If you suspect abandonment, try to locate the tenant yourself while you follow the legal procedure to reclaim the premises.
- Use the Self-Service Storage Facility Act procedure for evicting renters from storage areas.
- To evict a lodger from your home, use the uncomplicated and speedy eviction procedure especially designed for such situations.
- Settle rental dwelling questions concurrently with discharging a manager.
- Play a squatter's game to get squatters out.
- Forget about using the baggage lien law.
- Consider using a writ of immediate possession when tenants can't be found or when you know they're avoiding service.
- Be fair in calculating deposit refunds, but don't cheat yourself.
- You can't evict military tenants through municipal court, so use other methods.
- When asked, give neither a positive nor a negative recommendation about a tenant you're evicting.
- Go ahead and evict your Section 8 tenants when you must, but remember to give a "good cause" in your notice and to inform the agency responsible for administering the program.

Forms

Page Numbers

To assist you in finding the blank forms you seek, we put small page numbers in the forms' corners. When you go to copy the forms, either white-out the page numbers, cut them off, or fold the corners of the pages over so the numbers will not show up on your copies.

Number of Copies to Make

The numbers in parentheses following the form names above are the number of copies, in- cluding the original, which you should make if you are dealing with a single defendant; add one copy of each form for each additional defendant.

Make an original plus one copy of your notice first; serve the copy and keep the original. (NOTE: You may serve tenants collectively or individually. If you serve them collectively, you won't need an extra notice for each additional defendant; if you serve them individually, you will need an extra for each additional defendant.) Then, if you have to pursue the eviction as an unlawful detainer later, you will be able to make more copies. If you decide to attach a copy of the notice to the complaint as an exhibit, you will need an additional copy of the notice for each copy of the complaint you prepare. If you do not attach a copy to the complaint, you won't need to make any more copies of the notice, no matter how many co-tenants you're trying to evict. You will, however, need to serve separate notices to sub-tenants (anyone who is subletting) and to cosigners, if there are any.

When using the prejudgment claim procedure, you will need to make three copies of the Prejudgment Claim of Right to Possession form and three additional copies of the summons and complaint. Do not fill out the prejudgment form; it's for the tenant to fill out. You may not even have to supply copies of the form; some process servers supply them for you.

For each defendant who must be served by substituted service or posting, add one copy of the summons, complaint, exhibits, and attachments.

Remember, the numbers given here are minimums. Follow this rule of thumb whenever you're in doubt—*Always make enough copies of every form so you have one for yourself.* Then, if need be, you can make more copies of that form instead of having to make up another "original" or pay the clerk $1 each for each copy she makes on the court's copy machine. The dollar-per-copy charge is supposed to discourage you from using the court as a copy service. Take the hint!

Copy these forms on one side only. Your copies should have one blank side.

Judicial Council Forms

The forms with the capitalized names have been approved or adopted by the Judicial Council of California and are available from most courts. You may copy and use these here if you wish.

Please note that the Judicial Council changes their forms periodically. You will always find the latest versions available for downloading from their Web site. See Resources for the address.

Some of the Judicial Council forms have two printed sides, and some of those have their back sides printed upside down. Copy them exactly that way; your court may refuse to accept them on two separate sheets.

You may copy the seven pages of the Form Interrogatories on seven sheets of paper or on two sides of four sheets. No pages need be copied upside down.

Local Forms

Courts have certain forms of their own for routine tasks, such as the various judgment forms and the Memorandum to Set Case for Trial. Likewise, sheriffs' and marshals' offices have their own forms for routine tasks, such as the Instructions to Levying Officer form.

Sometimes you absolutely must use the forms which they provide to you, and sometimes you may use a similar form designed for the same purpose, such as those provided here.

Ask whether you may use the forms here before you go to the trouble of filling them out.

Unlawful Detainer Summary

Not mentioned anywhere in the text, the optional Unlawful Detainer Summary form shown on page 216 merely summarizes your case. It's a cover sheet of sorts to accompany your paperwork.

Clerks like the form because they prefer to see everything in one place so they don't have to waste time shuffling through a bunch of papers looking for the pertinent facts of each case. Your using the form may actually expedite your case somewhat because the clerk knows she needs little time to process your paperwork. She can look at one form and find everything she needs.

Although you may use this form anytime, the most appropriate time to use it is when you are applying for your judgment.

PAYMENT PLEDGE

Dear Landlord/Landlady:

On or before _____, I promise to pay you
$_____ for rent and other charges now owing on the dwelling
which I rent from you located at the following address:

_____
(Street Address)

_____
(City)   (State)   (Zip)

I expect to be receiving sufficient funds to pay you from the
following sources:

Name	Address	Phone	Amount Expected

Should you wish to, you have my authorization to verify
these sources.

If I fail to honor this pledge, I understand that I will be
evicted and that this pledge will be used against me as evidence
of my bad faith in paying what I owe.

____ I acknowledge receipt of a 3-Day Notice to Pay Rent or
Quit as required by law to begin eviction proceedings. I
understand that the 3-Day Notice may show a balance owed which is
different from that given above because a 3-Day Notice by law can
demand only delinquent rent. I also understand that the
three-day period mentioned in this Notice is being extended to
the date given above, at which time I promise to pay you what I
owe. If I fail to pay on or before that date, you have the right
to continue the legal eviction (unlawful detainer) procedure
against me without having to serve me another 3-Day Notice to Pay
Rent or Quit. I have already been served. I am being given the
extra time to pay only as a courtesy and only this once.

Signed _____

Dated _____

3-DAY NOTICE TO PAY RENT OR QUIT

TO: _____

_____

_____

_____

and all other tenants in possession of the premises described as:

_____
(Street Address)

_____
(City)   (State)   (Zip)

PLEASE TAKE NOTICE that the rent is now due and payable on the above-described premises which you currently hold and occupy.

Your rental account is delinquent in the amount itemized as follows:

Rental period _____ through _____

RENT DUE $_____

less partial payment of $_____

equals TOTAL RENT DUE of $_____

YOU ARE HEREBY REQUIRED to pay said rent in full within three (3) days or to remove from and deliver up possession of the above-described premises, or legal proceedings will be instituted against you to recover possession of said premises, to declare the forfeiture of the Lease or Rental Agreement under which you occupy said premises and to recover rents and damages, together with court costs and attorney's fees, according to the terms of your Lease or Rental Agreement.

Dated: _____   _____
                                                        Owner/Manager

PROOF OF SERVICE

I, the undersigned, being at least 18 years of age, declare under penalty of perjury that I served the above notice, of which this is a true copy, on the following person(s) in possession in the manner(s) indicated below: _____

☐ On _____, I handed the notice to the person(s) in possession personally.

☐ On _____, after attempting personal service, I handed the notice to a person of suitable age and discretion at the residence/business of the person(s) in possession, AND I deposited a true copy in the U.S. Mail, in a sealed envelope with postage fully prepaid, addressed to him/her/them at his/her/their place of residence (date mailed, if different _____).

☐ On _____, after attempting service in both manners indicated above, I posted the notice in a conspicuous place at the residence of the tenant(s), AND I deposited a true copy in the U.S. Mail, in a sealed envelope with postage fully prepaid, addressed to him/her/them at his/her/their place of residence (date mailed, if different _____).

Executed on _____, at _____, California.

Served by _____

NOTICE TO PERFORM COVENANT

TO: _____

_____

_____

_____

and all other tenants in possession of the premises described as:

_____
(Street Address)

_____
(City)   (State)   (Zip)

PLEASE TAKE NOTICE that you have violated the following covenant(s) in your Lease or Rental Agreement:

You are hereby required within _____ days to perform the aforesaid covenant(s) or to deliver up possession of the above-described premises which you currently hold and occupy.

If you fail to do so, legal proceedings will be instituted against you to recover said premises and such damages as the law allows.

This notice is intended to be a _____-day notice to perform the aforesaid covenant(s). It is not intended to terminate or forfeit the Lease or Rental Agreement under which you occupy said premises. If, after legal proceedings, said premises are recovered from you, the owners will try to rent the premises for the best possible rent, giving you credit for sums received and holding you liable for any deficiencies arising during the term of your Lease or Rental Agreement.

Dated: _____   _____
                                                    Owner/Manager

PROOF OF SERVICE

I, the undersigned, being at least 18 years of age, declare under penalty of perjury that I served the above notice, of which this is a true copy, on the following person(s) in possession in the manner(s) indicated below: _____

☐ On _____, I handed the notice to the person(s) in possession personally.

☐ On _____, after attempting personal service, I handed the notice to a person of suitable age and discretion at the residence/business of the person(s) in possession, AND I deposited a true copy in the U.S. Mail, in a sealed envelope with postage fully prepaid, addressed to him/her/them at his/her/their place of residence (date mailed, if different _____).

☐ On _____, after attempting service in both manners indicated above, I posted the notice in a conspicuous place at the residence of the tenant(s), AND I deposited a true copy in the U.S. Mail, in a sealed envelope with postage fully prepaid, addressed to him/her/them at his/her/their place of residence (date mailed, if different _____).

Executed on _____, at _____, California.

Served by _____

174

NOTICE TO TERMINATE TENANCY

TO: _____

_____

_____

_____

and all other tenants in possession of the premises described as:

_____
(Street Address)

_____
(City)   (State)   (Zip)

PLEASE TAKE NOTICE that you are hereby required within _____ days to remove from and deliver up possession of the above-described premises, which you currently hold and occupy.

This notice is intended for the purpose of terminating the Lease or Rental Agreement by which you now hold possession of the above-described premises, and should you fail to comply, legal proceedings will be instituted against you to recover possession, to declare said Lease or Rental Agreement forfeited, and to recover rents and damages for the period of the unlawful detention.

Dated: _____   _____
                                                             Owner/Manager

---

PROOF OF SERVICE

I, the undersigned, being at least 18 years of age, declare under penalty of perjury that I served the above notice, of which this is a true copy, on the following tenant(s) in possession in the manner(s) indicated below: _____

☐ On _____, I handed the notice to the tenant(s) personally.

☐ On _____, after attempting personal service, I handed the notice to a person of suitable age and discretion at the residence/business of the tenant(s), AND I deposited a true copy in the U.S. Mail, in a sealed envelope with postage fully prepaid, addressed to the tenant(s) at his/her/their place of residence (date mailed, if different _____).

☐ On _____, after attempting service in both manners indicated above, I posted the notice in a conspicuous place at the residence of the tenant(s), AND I deposited a true copy in the U.S. Mail, in a sealed envelope with postage fully prepaid, addressed to the tenant(s) at his/her/their place of residence (date mailed, if different _____).

☐ On _____, I sent by certified mail a true copy of the notice addressed to the tenant(s) at his/her/their place of residence.

Executed on _____, at _____, California.

Served by _____

3-DAY NOTICE TO QUIT
FOR WASTE, NUISANCE, OR UNLAWFUL ACTS

TO:_____

_____

_____

_____

and all other tenants in possession of the premises described as:

_____
(Street Address)

_____
(City)   (State)   (Zip)

PLEASE TAKE NOTICE that you are hereby required within three (3) days to deliver up possession of the above-described premises which you currently hold and occupy because you have committed the following waste, nuisance, or unlawful act(s):

As a consequence of your having committed the foregoing acts, your Lease or Rental Agreement is hereby declared canceled under California law (CCP §1161.4).

Should you fail to comply with this notice, legal proceedings will be instituted against you to recover said premises and such damages as the law allows.

Dated: _____   _____
                                                          Owner/Manager

---

PROOF OF SERVICE

I, the undersigned, being at least 18 years of age, declare under penalty of perjury that I served the above notice, of which this is a true copy, on the following person(s) in possession in the manner(s) indicated below: _____

☐ On _____, I handed the notice to the person(s) in possession personally.

☐ On _____, after attempting personal service, I handed the notice to a person of suitable age and discretion at the residence/business of the person(s) in possession, AND I deposited a true copy in the U.S. Mail, in a sealed envelope with postage fully prepaid, addressed to him/her/them at his/her/their place of residence (date mailed, if different _____).

☐ On _____, after attempting service in both manners indicated above, I posted the notice in a conspicuous place at the residence of the tenant(s), AND I deposited a true copy in the U.S. Mail, in a sealed envelope with postage fully prepaid, addressed to him/her/them at his/her/their place of residence (date mailed, if different _____).

Executed on _____, at _____, California.

Served by _____

NOTICE TO QUIT

TO:_____

_____

_____

_____

and all other tenants in possession of the premises described as:

_____
(Street Address)

_____
(City)   (State)   (Zip)

PLEASE TAKE NOTICE that your possession of the above-described premises is without the consent of the owner and is in violation of California law regarding
[ ] forceable entry (CCP §1159 & §1160).
[ ] holdover after foreclosure or execution (CCP §1161a).

You are hereby required to remove from and deliver up possession of said premises within _____ days, or legal proceedings will be instituted against you to recover said premises and such damages as the law allows.

Dated: _____   _____
                                                      Owner/Manager

---

PROOF OF SERVICE

I, the undersigned, being at least 18 years of age, declare under penalty of perjury that I served the above notice, of which this is a true copy, on the following person(s) in possession in the manner(s) indicated below: _____

☐ On _____, I handed the notice to the person(s) in possession personally.

☐ On _____, after attempting personal service, I handed the notice to a person of suitable age and discretion at the residence/business of the person(s) in possession, AND I deposited a true copy in the U.S. Mail, in a sealed envelope with postage fully prepaid, addressed to him/her/them at his/her/their place of residence (date mailed, if different _____).

☐ On _____, after attempting service in both manners indicated above, I posted the notice in a conspicuous place at the residence of the tenant(s), AND I deposited a true copy in the U.S. Mail, in a sealed envelope with postage fully prepaid, addressed to him/her/them at his/her/their place of residence (date mailed, if different _____).

Executed on _____, at _____, California.

Served by _____

72-HOUR NOTICE TO VACATE

(Recreational Vehicles)

TO:_____

_____

_____

_____

and all other occupants in possession of the premises described as:

_____
(Street Address)

_____
(City)   (State)   (Zip)

PLEASE TAKE NOTICE that you have failed to pay for your occupancy or failed to comply with the reasonable written rules and regulations of the park provided to you upon registration. You are hereby required within seventy-two (72) hours to remove from and deliver up possession of the above-described premises which you currently hold and occupy.

Should you fail to comply with this notice, your recreational vehicle will be removed from the park pursuant to the procedure described in that part of the California Civil Code (CCC §799.20 et seq.) commonly known as the Recreational Vehicle Park Occupancy Law.

Dated: _____   _____
                                                    Owner/Manager

---

PROOF OF SERVICE

I, the undersigned, being at least 18 years of age, declare under penalty of perjury that I served the above notice, of which this is a true copy, on the person(s) indicated below and in the manner(s) indicated below:

☐ On _____, I handed the notice to the occupant(s) personally.

☐ On _____, after attempting personal service, I handed the notice to a person of suitable age and discretion at the address above or at the place of business of the occupant(s), AND I posted a true copy in a conspicuous place at the address above, AND I deposited a true copy in the U.S. Mail, in a sealed envelope with postage fully prepaid, addressed to the occupant(s) at the address above. I also deposited a true copy in the U.S. Mail, in a sealed envelope with postage fully prepaid, addressed to the occupant(s) at the following address given on their registration agreement:

_____.

☐ On _____, I [cross out one] (sent by certified mail) (hand-delivered) a true copy of the notice to the police or sheriff's department serving the area where the premises are located.

Executed on _____, at _____, California.

Served by _____

30-DAY NOTICE TO VACATE

(Recreational Vehicles)

TO: _____

_____

_____

_____

and all other tenants in possession of the premises described as:

_____
(Street Address)

_____
(City)   (State)   (Zip)

PLEASE TAKE NOTICE that you are hereby required within thirty (30) days to remove your recreational vehicle from and deliver up possession of the above-described premises which you currently hold and occupy.

This notice is intended, pursuant to California Civil Code §799.66, for the purpose of terminating the right of occupancy by which you now hold possession of the above-described premises.

Should you fail to comply with this notice, legal proceedings will be instituted against you to remove your recreational vehicle from the above-described premises, to recover possession of the above-described premises, to declare forfeited whatever rental agreement you may have, and to recover rents and damages for the period of unlawful detention.

Dated: _____   _____

Owner/Manager

PROOF OF SERVICE

I, the undersigned, being at least 18 years of age, declare under penalty of perjury that I served the above notice, of which this is a true copy, on the following tenant(s) in possession in the manner(s) indicated below: _____

☐ On _____, I handed the notice to the tenant(s) personally.

☐ On _____, after attempting personal service, I handed the notice to a person of suitable age and discretion at the address above or at the place of business of the tenant(s), AND I deposited a true copy in the U.S. Mail, in a sealed envelope with postage fully prepaid, addressed to the tenant(s) at the address above (date mailed, if different _____).

☐ On _____, after attempting service in both manners indicated above, I posted the notice in a conspicuous place at the address above, AND I deposited a true copy in the U.S. Mail, in a sealed envelope with postage fully prepaid, addressed to the tenant(s) at the address above (date mailed, if different _____).

☐ On _____, I sent by certified mail one true copy of the notice addressed to the tenant(s) at the address above and another addressed to the tenant(s) at the following address given on their registration agreement _____.

Executed on _____, at _____, California.

Served by _____

3-DAY NOTICE TO PAY RENT OR QUIT

TO: _____

_____ and all other residents or occupants in possession of the premises described as:

_____

PLEASE TAKE NOTICE that the rent is now due and payable on the above-described premises which you currently hold and occupy. Your rental account is delinquent in the amount itemized as follows:

Rental period_____ through _____   RENT DUE $_____

less partial payment of $_____

equals TOTAL RENT DUE of $_____

YOU ARE HEREBY REQUIRED to pay said rent in full within three (3) days or to deliver up possession of the above-described premises to the park manager, who is authorized to receive same, or legal proceedings will be instituted against you to recover possession of said premises, to declare the forfeiture of the Lease or Rental Agreement under which you occupy said premises and to recover rents and damages, together with court costs and attorney's fees, according to the terms of your Lease or Rental Agreement.

3-DAY NOTICE TO PERFORM COVENANT OR QUIT

PLEASE TAKE NOTICE that you have also failed to perform that covenant in your Lease or Rental Agreement requiring that certain other charges be paid along with your rent. These charges are itemized as follows:

Other charges _____ TOTAL other charges due $_____

You are hereby required to perform this covenant within three (3) days or to deliver up possession of the above-described premises to the park manager. If you fail to do so, legal proceedings will be instituted against you to recover said charges and to recover said premises and such damages as the law allows.

PLEASE NOTE WELL: If you fail to pay the total amount of rent due and owing within three days, your tenancy is terminated. The additional time period allowed in the "60-Day Notice" below is strictly to give you time to locate a place to move your mobilehome. It does not extend the time you have to pay what you owe.

You may advertise your mobilehome for sale and sell or transfer it if you wish, but you may not represent that it may remain where it is when sold or transferred. In fact, it may not remain where it is. It must be moved.

60-DAY NOTICE TO TERMINATE TENANCY

PLEASE TAKE NOTICE that you are hereby required within sixty (60) days to deliver up possession of the above-described premises, which you currently hold and occupy. Compliance with this notice requires removal of your mobilehome so that the space can be re-let.

Rent being delinquent, this notice is being given for good cause, and it is intended, pursuant to California Civil Code §§798-9, commonly known as the "Mobilehome Residency Law," for the purpose of terminating the Lease or Rental Agreement by which you now hold possession of the above-described premises.

SHOULD YOU FAIL TO COMPLY WITH THIS (THESE) NOTICE(S), legal proceedings will be instituted against you to recover possession, to declare said Lease or Rental Agreement forfeited, and to recover rents and damages for the period of unlawful detention. Your mobilehome may be sold at a sheriff's sale to pay for any money judgment entered in favor of the park owner.

Please be advised that your rent, utility bills, and other charges on said premises are due and payable up to and including the date of termination of your tenancy under this notice.

Dated: _____   _____
                                                                              Owner/Manager

PROOF OF SERVICE

I, the undersigned, being at least 18 years of age, declare under penalty of perjury that I served the above notice, of which this is a true copy, on the above-mentioned resident(s) in possession in the manner(s) indicated below:

☐ On _____, I handed the notice to the resident(s) personally.

☐ On _____, after attempting personal service, I handed the notice to a person of suitable age and discretion at the residence/business of the resident(s), AND I deposited a true copy in the U.S. Mail, in a sealed envelope with postage fully prepaid, addressed to the resident(s) at his/her/their place of residence (date mailed, if different _____).

☐ On _____, after attempting service in both manners indicated above, I posted the notice in a conspicuous place at the residence of the resident(s), AND I deposited a true copy in the U.S. Mail, in a sealed envelope with postage fully prepaid, addressed to the resident(s) at his/her/their place of residence (date mailed, if different _____).

☐ On _____, in addition to service on the resident(s) as described above, I deposited a true copy of the notice in the U.S. Mail, in a sealed envelope with postage fully prepaid, addressed to the legal and registered owner(s) (if other than resident(s)) as follows: [legal owner] _____;
[registered owner] _____.

Executed on _____, at _____, California. Served by _____

60-DAY NOTICE TO TERMINATE TENANCY

TO: _____

_____

_____

_____

and all other residents or occupants in possession of the premises described as:

_____
(Street Address)

_____
(City)   (State)   (Zip)

PLEASE TAKE NOTICE that you are hereby required within sixty (60) days to deliver up possession of the above-described premises, which you currently hold and occupy. Compliance with this notice requires removal of your mobilehome so that the space can be re-let.

This notice is intended, pursuant to California Civil Code §§798-9, commonly known as the "Mobilehome Residency Law," for the purpose of terminating the Lease or Rental Agreement by which you now hold possession of the above-described premises.

SHOULD YOU FAIL TO COMPLY WITH THIS NOTICE, legal proceedings will be instituted against you to recover possession, to declare said Lease or Rental Agreement forfeited, and to recover rents and damages for the period of unlawful detention. Your mobilehome may be sold at a sheriff's sale to pay for any money judgment entered in favor of the park owner.

This notice is being given for good cause as follows:

Please be advised that your rent, utility bills, and other charges on said premises are due and payable up to and including the date of termination of your tenancy under this notice.

Dated: _____ _____
                                                    Owner/Manager

PROOF OF SERVICE

I, the undersigned, being at least 18 years of age, declare under penalty of perjury that I served the above notice, of which this is a true copy, on the following resident(s) in possession in the manner(s) indicated below: _____

☐ On _____, I handed the notice to the resident(s) personally.

☐ On _____, after attempting personal service, I handed the notice to a person of suitable age and discretion at the residence/business of the resident(s), AND I deposited a true copy in the U.S. Mail, in a sealed envelope with postage fully prepaid, addressed to the resident(s) at his/her/their place of residence (date mailed, if different _____).

☐ On _____, after attempting service in both manners indicated above, I posted the notice in a conspicuous place at the residence of the resident(s), AND I deposited a true copy in the U.S. Mail, in a sealed envelope with postage fully prepaid, addressed to the resident(s) at his/her/their place of residence (date mailed, if different _____).

☐ On _____, in addition to service on the resident(s) as described above, I deposited a true copy of the notice in the U.S. Mail, in a sealed envelope with postage fully prepaid, addressed to the legal and registered owner(s) (if other than resident(s)) as follows:

LEGAL OWNER _____

REGISTERED OWNER _____

Executed on _____, at _____, California.

Served by _____

NOTICE
OF BELIEF OF ABANDONMENT
(Real Property)

TO: _____

_____

_____

_____

Address:

_____
(Street Address)

_____
(City)   (State)   (Zip)

This notice is given pursuant to Section 1951.3 of the California Civil Code concerning the above-described real property rented by you. The rent on this property has been due and unpaid for fourteen (14) or more consecutive days, and the owner/manager believes that you have abandoned the property.

This real property will be deemed abandoned within the meaning of Section 1951.2 of the Civil Code, and your tenancy shall terminate on _____ which is not less than eighteen (18) days after this notice is deposited in the United States Mail unless before such date the undersigned receives at the address indicated below a written notice from you stating BOTH of the following: (1) Your intent not to abandon the real property, and (2) An address at which you may be served by certified mail in any action for unlawful detainer of the real property.

You are required to pay the rent due and unpaid on this real property as required by your rental agreement. Failure to do so can lead to a court proceeding against you.

Date of mailing this notice: _____

_____
Owner/Manager
(signature)

_____

_____

Name & Address of Owner/Manager
(typed or printed)

NOTICE OF RIGHT TO RECLAIM ABANDONED PERSONAL PROPERTY

TO:_____

_____

_____

_____

Address:

_____
(Street Address)

_____
(City)   (State)   (Zip)

When vacated, the premises described above contained the following personal **property:**

Unless you pay the reasonable cost of storage for all the above-described personal property and take possession of the property which you claim not later than eighteen (18) days after this notice is deposited in the United States Mail, this personal property may be disposed of pursuant to Civil Code Section 1988.

Check the ONE box below which applies:

☐ Because this property is believed to be worth less than $300, it may be kept, sold, or destroyed without further notice if you fail to reclaim it within the time limit indicated **below.**

☐ Because this property is believed to be worth more than $300, it will be sold if you fail to reclaim it. It will be sold at a public sale after notice has been given by publication. You have the right to bid on the property at this sale. After the property is sold and the costs of storage, advertising, and sale are deducted, the remaining money will be turned over to the county. You may claim the remaining money at any time within one year after the county receives the money.

Date of mailing this notice:_____

Date of expiration of this notice: _____

You may claim this property at:

_____
Owner/Manager
(signature)

_____

_____

_____
Name & Address of Owner/Manager
(typed or printed)

1

2

3

4

5

6

7

8

9

10

11

12

13

14

15

16

17

18

19

20

21

22

23

24

25

26

27

28

29

ATTORNEY OR PARTY WITHOUT ATTORNEY *(Name and Address)*:	TELEPHONE NO.:	*FOR COURT USE ONLY*

ATTORNEY FOR *(Name)*:

INSERT NAME OF COURT, JUDICIAL DISTRICT, AND BRANCH COURT, IF ANY:

CASE NAME:

CIVIL CASE COVER SHEET (Case Cover Sheets)	CASE NUMBER:

1. ☐ Case category *(Insert code from list below for the ONE case type that best describes the case)*:

01 Abuse of Process
02 Administrative Agency Review
03 Antitrust/Unfair Business Practices
04 Asbestos
05 Asset Forfeiture
06 Breach of Contract/Warranty
07 Business Tort
08 Civil Rights *(Discrimination, False Arrest)*
09 Collections *(Money Owed, Open Book Accounts)*
10 Construction Defect
11 Contractual Arbitration
12 Declaratory Relief
13 Defamation *(Slander, Libel)*
14 Eminent Domain/Inverse Condemnation
15 Employment *(Labor Commissioner Appeals, EDD Actions, Wrongful Termination)*
16 Fraud
17 Injunctive Relief

18 Insurance Coverage/Subrogation
19 Intellectual Property
20 Enforcement of Judgment *(Sister State, Foreign, Out-of-Country Abstracts)*
21 Partnership and Corporate Governance
22 PI/PD/WD—Auto *(Personal Injury/Property Damage/ Wrongful Death)*
23 PI/PD/WD—Nonauto
24 Product Liability
25 Professional Negligence *(Medical or Legal Malpractice, etc.)*
26 Real Property *(Quiet Title)*
27 RICO
28 Securities Litigation
29 Tax Judgment
30 Toxic Tort/Environmental
31 Unlawful Detainer—Commercial
32 Unlawful Detainer—Residential
33 Wrongful Eviction
34 Other: _____

2. Type of remedies sought *(check all that apply)*: a. ☐ Monetary b. ☐ Nonmonetary c. ☐ Punitive
3. Number of causes of action:
4. Is this a class action suit? ☐ Yes ☐ No

Date:

....
(TYPE OR PRINT NAME)

▶

_____
(SIGNATURE OF PARTY OR ATTORNEY FOR PARTY)

NOTE TO PLAINTIFF

- This cover sheet shall accompany each civil action or proceeding, except those filed in small claims court or filed under the Probate Code, Family Law Code, or Welfare and Institutions Code.
- File this cover sheet in addition to any cover sheet required by local court rule.
- Do not serve this cover sheet with the complaint.
- This cover sheet shall be used for statistical purposes only and shall have no effect on the assignment of the case.

Form Adopted by Rule 982.2
Judicial Council of California
982.2(b)(1) [New July 1, 1996]

CIVIL CASE COVER SHEET
(Case Cover Sheets)

SUMMONS
(CITACION JUDICIAL)

UNLAWFUL DETAINER—EVICTION
(PROCESO DE DESAHUCIO—EVICCION)

NOTICE TO DEFENDANT: *(Aviso a acusado)*

FOR COURT USE ONLY
(SOLO PARA USO DE LA CORTE)

YOU ARE BEING SUED BY PLAINTIFF:
(A Ud. le está demandando)

You have *5 DAYS* after this summons is served on you to file a typewritten response at this court. (To calculate the five days, count Saturday and Sunday, but do not count other court holidays.)

A letter or phone call will not protect you. Your typewritten response must be in proper legal form if you want the court to hear your case.

If you do not file your response on time, you may lose the case, you may be evicted, and your wages, money, and property may be taken without further warning from the court.

There are other legal requirements. You may want to call an attorney right away. If you do not know an attorney, you may call an attorney referral service or a legal aid office *(listed in the phone book)*.

Después de que le entreguen esta citación judicial usted tiene un plazo de **5 DIAS** para presentar una respuesta escrita a máquina en esta corte. (Para calcular los cinco días, cuente el sábado y el domingo, pero no cuente ningún otro día feriado observado por la corte.)

Una carta o una llamada telefónica no le ofrecerá protección; su respuesta escrita a máquina tiene que cumplir con las formalidades legales apropiadas si usted quiere que la corte escuche su caso.

Si usted no presenta su respuesta a tiempo, puede perder el caso, le pueden obligar a desalojar su casa, y le pueden quitar su salario, su dinero y otras cosas de su propiedad sin aviso adicional por parte de la corte.

Existen otros requisitos legales. Puede que usted quiera llamar a un abogado inmediatamente. Si no conoce a un abogado, puede llamar a un servicio de referencia de abogados o a una oficina de ayuda legal (vea el directorio telefónico).

The name and address of the court is: *(El nombre y dirección de la corte es)*

CASE NUMBER *(Número del caso)*

The name, address, and telephone number of plaintiff's attorney, or plaintiff without an attorney, is:
(El nombre, la dirección y el número de teléfono del abogado del demandante, o del demandante que no tiene abogado, es)

(Must be answered in all cases) An **unlawful detainer assistant (B&P 6400-6415)** ☐ did **not** ☐ did for compensation give advice or assistance with this form. *(If plaintiff has received any help or advice for pay from an unlawful detainer assistant, state)*:

a. Assistant's name: b. Telephone No.:

c. Street address, city, and ZIP:

d. County of registration: e. Registration No.:   f. Expires on *(date)*:

Date:
(Fecha)   Clerk, by _____ , Deputy
                                            (Actuario)   *(Delegado)*

[SEAL]

NOTICE TO THE PERSON SERVED: You are served

1. ☐ as an individual defendant.
2. ☐ as the person sued under the fictitious name of *(specify)*:

3. ☐ on behalf of *(specify)*:

    under: ☐ CCP 416.10 (corporation)   ☐ CCP 416.60 (minor)
           ☐ CCP 416.20 (defunct corporation)   ☐ CCP 416.70 (conservatee)
           ☐ CCP 416.40 (association or partnership) ☐ CCP 416.90 (individual)
           ☐ other:

4. ☐ by personal delivery on *(date)*:
       (See reverse for Proof of Service)

PLAINTIFF:	CASE NUMBER
DEFENDANT:	

PROOF OF SERVICE

1. **At the time of service I was at least 18 years of age and not a party to this action, and I served copies** of the (specify documents):

2. a. **Party served** (specify name of party as shown on the documents served):

   b. **Person served:** □ party in item 2a □ other (specify name and title or relationship to the party named in item 2a):

   c. **Address:**

3. **I served the party named in item 2**
   a. □ **by personally delivering the copies** (1) on (date): (2) at (time):
   b. □ **by leaving the copies** with or in the presence of (name and title or relationship to person indicated in item 2b):
      (1) □ **(business)** a person at least 18 years of age apparently in charge at the office or usual place of business of the person served. I informed him or her of the general nature of the papers.
      (2) □ **(home)** a competent member of the household (at least 18 years of age) at the dwelling house or usual place of abode of the person served. I informed him or her of the general nature of the papers.
      (3) on (date): (4) at (time):
      (5) □ A **declaration of diligence** is attached. (Substituted service on natural person, minor, conservatee, or candidate.)
   c. □ **by mailing** the copies to the person served, addressed as shown in item 2c, by first-class mail, postage prepaid.
      (1) on (date): (2) from (city):
      (3) □ with two copies of the Notice and Acknowledgment of Receipt and a postage-paid return envelope addressed to me
      (4) □ to an address outside California with return receipt requested. (Attach completed form.) →
   d. □ **by causing copies to be mailed.** A declaration of mailing is attached.
   e. □ **other** (specify other manner of service and authorizing code section):

4. The "**Notice to the Person Served**" (on the summons) was completed as follows:
   a. □ as an individual defendant.
   b. □ as the person sued under the fictitious name of (specify):
   c. □ on behalf of (specify):
      under: □ CCP 416.10 (corporation) □ CCP 416.60 (minor) □ other:
      □ CCP 416.20 (defunct corporation) □ CCP 416.70 (conservatee)
      □ CCP 416.40 (association or partnership) □ CCP 416.90 (individual)

5. **Person serving** (name, address, and telephone number):
   a. **Fee for service:** $
   b. □ Not a registered California process server
   c. □ Exempt from registration under B&P § 22350(b)
   d. □ Registered California process server
      (1) □ Employee or independent contractor
      (2) Registration No.:
      (3) County:
      (4) Expiration (date):

6. □ **I declare** under penalty of perjury under the laws of the State of California that the foregoing is true and correct.

7. □ **I am a California sheriff, marshal, or constable and I certify that the foregoing is true and correct.**

Date: _____

▶ _____
(SIGNATURE)

ATTORNEY OR PARTY WITHOUT ATTORNEY *(Name and Address)*:	TELEPHONE NO.:	FOR COURT USE ONLY

ATTORNEY FOR *(Name)*:

NAME OF COURT:
STREET ADDRESS:
MAILING ADDRESS:
CITY AND ZIP CODE:
BRANCH NAME:

PLAINTIFF:

DEFENDANT:

[ ] DOES 1 TO _____

COMPLAINT—Unlawful Detainer*

CASE NUMBER:

1. a. Plaintiff is (1) [ ] an individual over the age of 18 years (4) [ ] a partnership
      (2) [ ] a public agency (5) [ ] a corporation
      (3) [ ] other *(specify)*:
   b. [ ] Plaintiff has complied with the fictitious business name laws and is doing business under the fictitious name of *(specify)*:

2. Defendants named above are in possession of the premises located at *(street address, apt. No., city, and county)*:

3. Plaintiff's interest in the premises is [ ] as owner [ ] other *(specify)*:

4. The true names and capacities of defendants sued as Does are unknown to plaintiff.

5. a. On or about *(date)*: defendants *(names)*:

      (1) agreed to rent the premises for a [ ] month-to-month tenancy [ ] other tenancy *(specify)*:
      (2) agreed to pay rent of $ payable [ ] monthly [ ] other *(specify frequency)*:
      The rent is due on the [ ] first of the month [ ] other day *(specify)*:
   b. This [ ] written [ ] oral agreement was made with
      (1) [ ] plaintiff (3) [ ] plaintiff's predecessor in interest
      (2) [ ] plaintiff's agent (4) [ ] other *(specify)*:
   c. [ ] The defendants not named in item 5a are
      (1) [ ] subtenants (2) [ ] assignees (3) [ ] other *(specify)*:
   d. [ ] The agreement was later changed as follows *(specify)*:

   e. [ ] A copy of the written agreement is attached and labeled Exhibit 1.

6. [ ] a. Defendants *(names)*:
      were served the following notice on the same date and in the same manner:
      (1) [ ] 3-day notice to pay rent or quit (4) [ ] 3-day notice to quit
      (2) [ ] 3-day notice to perform covenants or quit (5) [ ] 30-day notice to quit
      (3) [ ] other *(specify)*:
   b. (1) On *(date)*: , the period stated in the notice expired at the end of the day.
      (2) Defendants failed to comply with the requirements of the notice by that date.
   c. All facts stated in the notice are true.
   d. [ ] The notice included an election of forfeiture.
   e. [ ] A copy of the notice is attached and labeled Exhibit 2.
   f. [ ] One or more defendants was served (1) with a different notice, or (2) on a different date, or (3) in a different manner, as stated in attachment 6f. *(Check item 7c and attach a statement providing the information required by items 6a–e and 7 for each defendant.)*

*NOTE: Do not use this form for evictions after sale (Code Civ. Proc., § 1161a).

(Continued on reverse)

Form Approved by the
Judicial Council of California
982.1(90) [Rev. July 1, 1996]

COMPLAINT—Unlawful Detainer

Civil Code, § 1940 et seq.;
Code of Civil Procedure, § 425.12

PLAINTIFF (Name):	CASE NUMBER:
DEFENDANT (Name):	

7. a. ☐ The notice in item 6a was served on the defendants named in item 6a as follows:

    (1) ☐ by personally handing a copy to defendant on (date):

    (2) ☐ by leaving a copy with (name or description):   , a person

        of suitable age and discretion, on (date):   at defendant's ☐ residence ☐ business

        AND mailing a copy to defendant at defendant's place of residence on (date):

        because defendant cannot be found at defendant's residence or usual place of business.

    (3) ☐ by posting a copy on the premises on (date):   (☐ and giving a copy to a person found

        residing at the premises) AND mailing a copy to defendant at the premises on (date):

        (a) ☐ because defendant's residence and usual place of business cannot be ascertained OR

        (b) ☐ because no person of suitable age or discretion can be found there.

    (4) ☐ (not for 3-day notice; see Civil Code section 1946 before using) by sending a copy by certified or registered

        mail addressed to defendant on (date):

    (5) ☐ (not for residential tenancies; see Civil Code section 1953 before using) in the manner specified in a written

        commercial lease between the parties.

  b. ☐ (Name):   was served on behalf of all defendants who signed a joint written rental agreement.

  c. ☐ Information about service of notice on the defendants named in item 6f is stated in attachment 7c.

8. ☐ Plaintiff demands possession from each defendant because of expiration of a fixed-term lease.

9. ☐ At the time the 3-day notice to pay rent or quit was served, the amount of **rent due** was $

10. ☐ The fair rental value of the premises is $ per day.

11. ☐ Defendants' continued possession is malicious, and plaintiff is entitled to statutory damages under Code of Civil Procedure section 1174(b). (State specific facts supporting a claim up to $600 in attachment 11.)

12. ☐ A written agreement between the parties provides for attorney fees.

13. ☐ Defendants' tenancy is subject to the local rent control or eviction control ordinance of (city or county, title of ordinance, and date of passage):

    Plaintiff has met all applicable requirements of the ordinances.

14. ☐ Other allegations are stated in attachment 14.

15. Plaintiff remits to the jurisdictional limit, if any, of the court.

16. PLAINTIFF REQUESTS

  a. possession of the premises.

  b. costs incurred in this proceeding.

  c. ☐ past due rent of $

  d. ☐ reasonable attorney fees.

  e. ☐ forfeiture of the agreement.

  f. ☐ damages at the rate stated in item 10 from (date):   for each day defendants remain in possession through entry of judgment.

  g. ☐ statutory damages up to $600 for the conduct alleged in item 11.

  h. ☐ other (specify):

17. ☐ Number of pages attached (specify):

    UNLAWFUL DETAINER ASSISTANT (Business and Professions Code sections 6400–6415)

18. (must be answered in all cases) An unlawful detainer assistant ☐ did **not** ☐ did for compensation give advice or assistance with this form. (If plaintiff has received **any** help or advice for pay from an unlawful detainer assistant, state):

  a. Assistant's name: b. Telephone No.:

  c. Street address, city, and ZIP:

  d. County of registration: e. Registration No.:   f. Expires on (date):

    ▶

. . . .   _____

(TYPE OR PRINT NAME)   (SIGNATURE OF PLAINTIFF OR ATTORNEY)

VERIFICATION

(Use a different verification form if the verification is by an attorney or for a corporation or partnership.)

I am the plaintiff in this proceeding and have read this complaint. I declare under penalty of perjury under the laws of the State of California that the foregoing is true and correct.

Date:

    ▶

. . . .   _____

(TYPE OR PRINT NAME)   (SIGNATURE OF PLAINTIFF)

NOTICE: EVERYONE WHO LIVES IN THIS RENTAL UNIT MAY BE EVICTED BY COURT ORDER. READ THIS FORM IF YOU LIVE HERE AND IF YOUR NAME IS NOT ON THE ATTACHED SUMMONS AND COMPLAINT.

1. If you live here and you do not complete and submit this form within 10 days of the date of service shown on this form, you will be evicted without further hearing by the court along with the persons named in the Summons and Complaint.
2. If you file this form, your claim will be determined in the eviction action against the persons named in the Complaint.
3. If you do not file this form, you will be evicted without further hearing.

CLAIMANT OR CLAIMANT'S ATTORNEY *(Name and Address)*:

TELEPHONE NO.:

FOR COURT USE ONLY

ATTORNEY FOR *(Name)*:

NAME OF COURT:

STREET ADDRESS:

MAILING ADDRESS:

CITY AND ZIP CODE:

BRANCH NAME:

PLAINTIFF:

DEFENDANT:

PREJUDGMENT CLAIM OF RIGHT TO POSSESSION

CASE NUMBER:

(To be completed by the process server)
DATE OF SERVICE:

(Date that this form is served or delivered, and posted, and mailed by the officer or process server)

Complete this form only if ALL of these statements are true:
1. You are NOT named in the accompanying Summons and Complaint.
2. You occupied the premises on or before the date the unlawful detainer (eviction) Complaint was filed.
3. You still occupy the premises.

I DECLARE THE FOLLOWING UNDER PENALTY OF PERJURY:

1. My name is *(specify)*:

2. I reside at *(street address, unit No., city and ZIP code)*:

3. The address of "the premises" subject to this claim is *(address)*:

4. On *(insert date)*: [   ], the landlord or the landlord's authorized agent filed a complaint to recover possession of the premises. *(This date is the court filing date on the accompanying Summons and Complaint.)*

5. I occupied the premises on the date the complaint was filed *(the date in item 4)*. I have continued to occupy the premises ever since.

6. I was at least 18 years of age on the date the complaint was filed *(the date in item 4)*.

7. I claim a right to possession of the premises because I occupied the premises on the date the complaint was filed *(the date in item 4)*.

8. I was not named in the Summons and Complaint.

9. I understand that if I make this claim of right to possession, I will be added as a defendant to the unlawful detainer (eviction) action.

10. *(Filing fee)* I understand that I must go to the court and pay a filing fee of $ or file with the court the form "Application for Waiver of Court Fees and Costs." I understand that if I don't pay the filing fee or file with the court the form for waiver of court fees within 10 days from the date of service on this form (excluding court holidays), I will not be entitled to make a claim of right to possession.

(Continued on reverse)

CP10.5 [New January 1, 1991]

PREJUDGMENT CLAIM OF RIGHT TO POSSESSION

Code of Civil Procedure, §§ 415.46, 715.010, 715.020, 1174.25

> **NOTICE: If you fail to file this claim, you will be evicted without further hearing.**

11. *(Response required within five days after you file this form)* I understand that I will have *five days* (excluding court holidays) to file a response to the Summons and Complaint after I file this Prejudgment Claim of Right to Possession form.

12. **Rental agreement.** I have *(check all that apply to you)*:
   a. ☐ an oral rental agreement with the landlord.
   b. ☐ a written rental agreement with the landlord.
   c. ☐ an oral rental agreement with a person other than the landlord.
   d. ☐ a written rental agreement with a person other than the landlord.
   e. ☐ other *(explain)*:

I declare under penalty of perjury under the laws of the State of California that the foregoing is true and correct.

> WARNING: Perjury is a felony punishable by imprisonment in the state prison.

Date:

. . . . ▶ _____
(TYPE OR PRINT NAME)   (SIGNATURE OF CLAIMANT)

> **NOTICE:** If you file this claim of right to possession, the unlawful detainer (eviction) action against you will be determined at trial. At trial, you may be found liable for rent, costs, and, in some cases, treble damages.

—NOTICE TO OCCUPANTS—

YOU MUST ACT AT ONCE if all the following are true:
1. **You are NOT named in the accompanying Summons and Complaint.**
2. **You occupied the premises on or before the date the unlawful detainer (eviction) complaint was filed.** *(The date is the court filing date on the accompanying Summons and Complaint.)*
3. **You still occupy the premises.**

(Where to file this form) You can complete and SUBMIT THIS CLAIM FORM WITHIN 10 DAYS from the date of service (on the reverse of this form) at the court where the unlawful detainer (eviction) complaint was filed.

(What will happen if you do not file this form) If you do not complete and submit this form (and pay a filing fee or file the form for proceeding in forma pauperis if you cannot pay the fee), YOU WILL BE EVICTED.

After this form is properly filed, you will be added as a defendant in the unlawful detainer (eviction) action and your right to occupy the premises will be decided by the court. *If you do not file this claim, you will be evicted without a hearing.*

1

2

3

4

5

6

7

IN THE MUNICIPAL COURT OF _____ JUDICIAL DISTRICT,

COUNTY OF _____, STATE OF CALIFORNIA

_____,)
               Plaintiff,)   NO.
    vs.   )
)   DECLARATION FOR
_____,)   DEFAULT JUDGMENT
           Defendant.)   IN LIEU OF PERSONAL
_____)   TESTIMONY (CCP 585.4)

I, _____, declare

that if sworn as a witness, I would testify competently within my

personal knowledge to the following facts:

1. That I am the plaintiff herein and the owner of the premises

located at _____, in the City of

_____, County of _____,

State of California.

2. That on _____, prior to filing this

action, the defendant rented said premises from me by _____

agreement and agreed to pay the sum of $_____ per month rental,

payable in advance on the _____ day of each and every calendar month

thereafter, current per month rental value being the sum of $_____

or $_____ per day.

3. That by virtue of said agreement, defendant went into

possession of said premises and still continues to hold and occupy same.

4. That on _____, I caused the defendant to be served with a written notice stating the amount of rent due and requiring payment thereof or possession of the premises within three days after service of the notice.

5. That when at least three days had elapsed after service of said notice on defendant and no part of said rent had been paid, I caused the defendant to be served with a Summons and Complaint on

_____.

6. Said defendant has failed to answer the Summons and Complaint within five days following service.

WHEREFORE, I pray that this Court render a judgment by default against the defendant for restitution of said premises, for costs of $_____, for past due rent of $_____, for damages at the rate of $_____ per day, and for forfeiture of the agreement.

I declare under penalty of perjury that the foregoing is true and correct.

Executed on _____, at City of _____, County of _____, State of California.

_____
Plaintiff

ATTORNEY OR PARTY WITHOUT ATTORNEY *(Name and Address)*:	TELEPHONE NO.:	FOR COURT USE ONLY

ATTORNEY FOR *(Name)*:

Insert name of court and name of judicial district and branch court, if any:

PLAINTIFF:

DEFENDANT:

REQUEST FOR (Application)	☐ ENTRY OF DEFAULT ☐ CLERK'S JUDGMENT ☐ COURT JUDGMENT	CASE NUMBER:

1. TO THE CLERK: On the complaint or cross-complaint filed
   a. On *(date)*:
   b. By *(name)*:
   c. ☐ Enter default of defendant *(names)*:

   d. ☐ I request a court judgment under CCP 585(b), (c), 989, etc. *(Testimony required. Apply to the clerk for a hearing date, unless the court will enter a judgment on an affidavit under CCP 585(d).)*
   e. ☐ Enter clerk's judgment
      (1) ☐ For restitution of the premises only and issue a writ of execution on the judgment. CCP 1174(c) does not apply. (CCP 1169) ☐ Include in the judgment all tenants, subtenants, named claimants, and other occupants of the premises. The Prejudgment Claim of Right to Possession was served in compliance with CCP 415.46.
      (2) ☐ Under CCP 585(a). *(Complete the declaration under CCP 585.5 on the reverse (item 4).)*
      (3) ☐ For default previously entered on *(date)*:

2. **Judgment to be entered**

	Amount	Credits Acknowledged	Balance
a. Demand of complaint	$	$	$
b. Statement of damages (CCP 425.11) *(superior court only)*†			
(1) Special	$	$	$
(2) General	$	$	$
c. Interest	$	$	$
d. Costs *(see reverse)*	$	$	$
e. Attorney fees	$	$	$
f. **TOTALS**	$	$	$

   g. **Daily damages** were demanded in complaint at the rate of: $ per day beginning *(date)*:

3. ☐ *(check if filed in an unlawful detainer case)* **UNLAWFUL DETAINER ASSISTANT** information is on the reverse *(complete item 3)*.

Date:

▶

. . . .
(TYPE OR PRINT NAME)   (SIGNATURE OF PLAINTIFF OR ATTORNEY FOR PLAINTIFF)

† *Personal injury or wrongful death actions only.*

FOR COURT USE ONLY	(1) ☐ Default entered as requested on *(date)*: (2) ☐ Default NOT entered as requested *(state reason)*:

Clerk, by: _____

(Continued on reverse)

Form Adopted by the
Judicial Council of California
982(a)(6) [Rev. July 1, 1996*]

REQUEST FOR ENTRY OF DEFAULT
(Application to Enter Default)

Code of Civil Procedure, §§ 585-587, 1169

*See note on reverse.

3. **UNLAWFUL DETAINER ASSISTANT** *(Business and Professions Code sections 6400–6415)* An **unlawful detainer assistant**
☐ did **not** ☐ did for compensation give advice or assistance with this form. *(If declarant has received **any** help or advice for pay from an unlawful detainer assistant, state)*:
   a. Assistant's name: b. Telephone No.:
   c. Street address, city, and ZIP:

   d. County of registration: e. Registration No.:   f. Expires on *(date)*

4. ☐ **DECLARATION UNDER CCP 585.5** *(Required for clerk's judgment under CCP 585(a))* This action
   a. ☐ is ☐ is not on a contract or installment sale for goods or services subject to CC 1801, etc. (Unruh Act).
   b. ☐ is ☐ is not on a conditional sales contract subject to CC 2981, etc. (Rees-Levering Motor Vehicle Sales and Finance Act).
   c. ☐ is ☐ is not on an obligation for goods, services, loans, or extensions of credit subject to CCP 395(b).

5. **DECLARATION OF MAILING (CCP 587)** A copy of this Request for Entry of Default was
   a. ☐ **not mailed** to the following defendants whose addresses are **unknown** to plaintiff or plaintiff's attorney *(names)*:

   b. ☐ **mailed** first-class, postage prepaid, in a sealed envelope addressed to each defendant's attorney of record or, if none, to each defendant's last known address as follows:
      (1) Mailed on *(date)*:   (2) To *(specify names and addresses shown on the envelopes)*:

I declare under penalty of perjury under the laws of the State of California that the foregoing items 3, 4, and 5 are true and correct.
Date:

.... ▶ _____
(TYPE OR PRINT NAME)   (SIGNATURE OF DECLARANT)

6. **MEMORANDUM OF COSTS** *(Required if judgment requested)* **Costs and Disbursements** are as follows (CCP 1033.5):
   a. Clerk's filing fees . . . . $
   b. Process server's fees . . . . $
   c. Other *(specify)*: . . . . $
   d. . . . . $
   e. **TOTAL** . . . . $ _____
   f. ☐ Costs and disbursements are waived.

I am the attorney, agent, or party who claims these costs. To the best of my knowledge and belief this memorandum of costs is correct and these costs were necessarily incurred in this case.

I declare under penalty of perjury under the laws of the State of California that the foregoing is true and correct.
Date:

.... ▶ _____
(TYPE OR PRINT NAME)   (SIGNATURE OF DECLARANT)

7. ☐ **DECLARATION OF NONMILITARY STATUS** *(Required for a judgment)* No defendant named in item 1c of the application is in the military service so as to be entitled to the benefits of the Soldiers' and Sailors' Civil Relief Act of 1940 (50 U.S.C. appen. § 501 et seq.).

I declare under penalty of perjury under the laws of the State of California that the foregoing is true and correct.
Date:

.... ▶ _____
(TYPE OR PRINT NAME)   (SIGNATURE OF DECLARANT)

NOTE: Continued use of form 982(a)(6) (Rev. Sept. 30, 1991) is authorized until June 30, 1997, *except* in unlawful detainer proceedings.

ATTORNEY OR PARTY WITHOUT ATTORNEY (Name and Address) : TELEPHONE NO.:	FOR COURT USE ONLY
ATTORNEY FOR (Name) :	
NAME OF COURT AND ADDRESS:	
PLAINTIFF: DEFENDANT:	CASE NUMBER:

UNLAWFUL DETAINER
DEFAULT JUDGMENT
BY CLERK
FOR POSSESSION OF REAL
PROPERTY ONLY

The Defendant(s) hereinafter named, having been regularly served with summons and copy of complaint, having failed to appear and answer plaintiff's complaint within the time allowed by law, and the default of said defendant(s) having been duly entered; upon application of plaintiff to the Clerk for Judgment for Restitution and pursuant to the provisions of 1169 of the Code of Civil **Procedure,**

IT IS ADJUDGED that Plaintiff(s)

have and recover from Defendant(s)

the restitution and possession of those certain premises situated, lying and being in the County of _____, State of California, and more particularly described as follows, to-wit:

This judgment ☐ does ☐ does not include all tenants, subtenants, named claimants, and other occupants of the premises.

I hereby certify this to be a true copy of the Judgment in the above action.

Judgment entered on _____ _____ , Clerk

Judgment Book_____ Page_____ By _____ , Deputy Clerk

UNLAWFUL DETAINER DEFAULT JUDGMENT BY CLERK
(For Possession of Real Property Only)

ATTORNEY OR PARTY WITHOUT ATTORNEY (Name and Address) : TELEPHONE NO.:	FOR COURT USE ONLY
ATTORNEY FOR (Name) :	
NAME OF COURT AND ADDRESS:	
PLAINTIFF:	
DEFENDANT:	CASE NUMBER:

**AMENDED
UNLAWFUL DETAINER
DEFAULT JUDGMENT**

The Defendant(s) hereinafter named, having been regularly served with summons and copy of complaint, having failed to appear and answer plaintiff's complaint within the time allowed by law, and the default of said defendant(s) having been duly entered, and after having heard the testimony and considered the evidence, or pursuant to affidavit on file herein, the Court ordered the following JUDGMENT:

IT IS ORDERED AND ADJUDGED that Plaintiff(s)

have and recover from Defendant(s)

the restitution and possession of those certain premises situated, lying and being in the County of _____, State of California, and more particularly described as follows, to-wit:

possession of premises restored to plaintiff on   through judgment pursuant to CCP §1169 dated.

It is further Ordered, Adjudged, and Decreed that said plaintiff(s) have and recover from said defendant(s)

Rents and Damages	
Interest	
Costs	
Attorney Fees	
TOTAL	

And that the lease or agreement under which said defendant(s) hold(s) said premises be, and the same is hereby declared, forfeited, void, and of no effect.

Dated: . . . .
                                                                    Judge of the Municipal Court

I hereby certify this to be a true copy of the Judgment in the above action.

Judgment entered on _____   _____ , Clerk

Judgment Book_____ Page_____ By _____ , Deputy Clerk

CCP 585, 664, 668, 1033 1/2, 1169, 1174

AMENDED UNLAWFUL DETAINER DEFAULT JUDGMENT

ATTORNEY OR PARTY WITHOUT ATTORNEY (Name and Address) : TELEPHONE NO.:	FOR COURT USE ONLY
ATTORNEY FOR (Name) :	
NAME OF COURT AND ADDRESS:	
PLAINTIFF: DEFENDANT:	CASE NUMBER:

**UNLAWFUL DETAINER
DEFAULT JUDGMENT**

The Defendant(s) hereinafter named, having been regularly served with summons and copy of complaint, having failed to appear and answer plaintiff's complaint within the time allowed by law, and the default of said defendant(s) having been duly entered, and after having heard the testimony and considered the evidence, or pursuant to affidavit on file herein, the Court ordered the following JUDGMENT:

IT IS ORDERED AND ADJUDGED that Plaintiff(s)

have and recover from Defendant(s)

the restitution and possession of those certain premises situated, lying and being in the County of _____, State of California, and more particularly described as follows, to-wit:

It is further Ordered, Adjudged, and Decreed that said plaintiff(s) have and recover from said defendant(s)　　　　Rents and Damages

Interest

Costs

Attorney Fees _____

TOTAL

And that the lease or agreement under which said defendant(s) hold(s) said premises be, and the same is hereby declared, forfeited, void, and of no effect.

.... days stay of execution.

Dated: ....

....
Judge of the Municipal Court

I hereby certify this to be a true copy of the Judgment in the above action.

Judgment entered on _____   _____ , Clerk

Judgment Book_____ Page_____ By_____ , Deputy Clerk

UNLAWFUL DETAINER DEFAULT JUDGMENT

198

Name, Address, and Telephone No. of Attorney(s)

Space Below for Use of Court Clerk Only

Attorney(s) for

MUNICIPAL COURT OF CALIFORNIA, COUNTY OF _____
_____ **JUDICIAL DISTRICT**

Plaintiff(s)

VS.

Defendant(s)

Case Number

MEMORANDUM TO SET CASE FOR TRIAL

I hereby represent to the court that this case is at issue, and request that it be set for trial.

Nature of the case: <u>Unlawful Detainer</u> _____

Jury trial _____ demanded. Time necessary for trial: _____
       (is or is not)   (Estimate carefully)

This case _____ entitled to legal preference in setting <u>C.C.P. 1179a</u>
       (is or is not)   (If so, state reasons)

_____ . Reporter _____ requested.
                                                                        (is or is not)

The following dates are NOT acceptable to me: _____
_____

Names, addresses and telephone numbers of attorneys for other parties, or of parties appearing in person:

Dated: _____   _____
                                                    (Note: Must be signed by attorney or party requesting setting)

PROOF OF SERVICE BY MAIL — CCP 1013a, 2015.5

I declare that: I am a (resident of / employed in) the county of _____, California.
                                                            (County where mailing occurred)

I am over the age of eighteen years and not a party to the within entitled cause; my (business / residence) address is:
_____

On _____, I served the attached MEMORANDUM TO SET CASE FOR TRIAL on the
                  (Date)
_____ <u>defendant(s)</u> _____ in said cause, by placing a true copy thereof enclosed in a sealed envelope

with postage thereon fully prepaid, in the United States mail at _____ addressed as follows:

I declare under penalty of perjury that the foregoing is true and correct, and that this declaration was executed on
_____, at _____, California.
            (Date)   (Place)

_____   _____
          (Type or Print Name)   (Signature)

MUNICIPAL COURT OF CALIFORNIA, COUNTY OF _____
_____ **JUDICIAL DISTRICT**

Plaintiff(s)	Case Number
VS	**JUDGMENT**
Defendant(s)	

Department   Judge   Reporter

This cause came on for trial on _____, a jury trial having been waived, Plaintiff(s) appearing by attorney(s):

Defendant(s) appearing by attorney(s):

The Court, having considered the evidence, and no [if requested, cross out 'no'] statement of decision having been requested, ordered the following judgment:
It is adjudged that

recover from

the restitution and possession of those premises situated in the County of _____, State of California, and more particularly described as

and the sum of $_____ principal, $_____ attorney fee, $_____ interest, $_____ costs.
TOTAL JUDGMENT $_____

Approved: _____
                                  Judge of the Municipal Court

Minutes of
This Judgment was entered on
in the Register of Actions.   , Clerk

By _____
                         Deputy Clerk

Clerk's Certificate of Service by Mail (CCP 1013a[3])
I, Clerk of the above-named court, do certify that I am not a party to the above-entitled cause; that on the date shown below I served the foregoing document by depositing a true copy thereof, enclosed in a separate, sealed envelope, with the postage thereon fully prepaid, in the United States mail at _____, California, each of which envelopes was addressed respectively to the persons and addresses shown above said document.

_____, California   , Clerk

Dated _____

By _____
                         Deputy Clerk

Judgment (Trial - Unlawful Detainer)

	COURT USE ONLY
COURT ADDRESS: **PLAINTIFF:** **DEFENDANT:**	

APPLICATION FOR ISSUANCE OF WRIT OF : ☐ **POSSESSION** ☐ **SALE** ☐ **OTHER**_____	**CASE NUMBER**

I, the undersigned, say : I am the ☐ Judgment Creditor

☐ attorney for the Judgment Creditor

☐ assignee of record of the Judgment Creditor

in the above-entitled action and that the following judgment was: (check if applicable)

☐ entered on _____ .

☐ entered on _____ .

In favor of the Judgment Creditor as follows (name and address) :

against the Judgment Debtor(s) as follows (name and address) :

for the amount of :

$ _____ Principal

$ _____ Accrued Costs

$ _____ Attorney Fees

$ _____ Interest

$ _____ TOTAL

and the possession of the premises located at :

The daily rental value of the property as of the date the complaint was filed is :

$ _____

It is prayed that a writ as checked above be issued to the

The writ will be directed to _____
(Law Enforcement Agency and Location)

I declare under the penalty of perjury under the Laws of the State of California that the foregoing is true and correct.

Executed on _____ at _____ , California

_____
Signature

APPLICATION FOR WRIT OF POSSESSION / SALE

ATTORNEY OR PARTY WITHOUT ATTORNEY (Name and Address): TELEPHONE NO.:	FOR RECORDER'S USE ONLY

☐ Recording requested by and return to:

☐ ATTORNEY FOR   ☐ JUDGMENT CREDITOR   ☐ ASSIGNEE OF RECORD

NAME OF COURT:
STREET ADDRESS:
MAILING ADDRESS:
CITY AND ZIP CODE:
BRANCH NAME:

PLAINTIFF:

DEFENDANT:

WRIT OF ☐ EXECUTION (Money Judgment) ☐ POSSESSION OF ☐ Personal Property ☐ Real Property ☐ SALE	CASE NUMBER:

1. **To the Sheriff or any Marshal or Constable of the County of:**

   You are directed to enforce the judgment described below with daily interest and your costs as provided by law.

2. **To any registered process server:** You are authorized to serve this writ only in accord with CCP 699.080 or CCP 715.040.

3. *(Name)*:

   is the ☐ judgment creditor ☐ assignee of record
   whose address is shown on this form above the court's name.

4. **Judgment debtor** *(name and last known address)*:

9. ☐ See reverse for information on real or personal property to be delivered under a writ of possession or sold under a writ of sale.

10. ☐ This writ is issued on a sister-state judgment.

11. Total judgment . . . . $

12. Costs after judgment (per filed order or memo CCP 685.090) . . . . $

13. Subtotal *(add 11 and 12)* . . . . $ _____

14. Credits . . . . $

15. Subtotal *(subtract 14 from 13)* . . . . . . $ _____

16. Interest after judgment (per filed affidavit CCP 685.050) . . . . $

17. Fee for issuance of writ . . . . $

18. **Total** *(add 15, 16, and 17)* . . . . $ _____

☐ additional judgment debtors on reverse

5. **Judgment entered** on *(date)*:

6. ☐ **Judgment renewed** on *(dates)*:

7. **Notice of sale** under this writ
   a. ☐ has not been requested.
   b. ☐ has been requested *(see reverse)*.

8. ☐ Joint debtor information on reverse.

[SEAL]

19. Levying officer:
   (a) Add daily interest from date of writ (at the legal rate on 15) of . . . . $
   (b) Pay directly to court costs included in 11 and 17 (GC 6103.5, 68511.3, CCP 699.520(i)) . . . . $

20. ☐ The amounts called for in items 11-19 are different for each debtor. These amounts are stated for each debtor on Attachment 20.

Issued on *(date)*:   Clerk, by _____, Deputy

— NOTICE TO PERSON SERVED: SEE REVERSE FOR IMPORTANT INFORMATION. —

(Continued on reverse)

Form Approved by the Judicial Council of California
EJ-130 [Rev. January 1, 1997*]

WRIT OF EXECUTION

Code of Civil Procedure, §§ 699.520, 712.010, 715.010
*See note on reverse.

— Items continued from the first page —

4. ☐ **Additional judgment debtor** (name and last known address):

7. ☐ **Notice of sale** has been requested by (name and address):

8. ☐ **Joint debtor** was declared bound by the judgment (CCP 989-994)
   a. on (date):   a. on (date):
   b. name and address of joint debtor: b. name and address of joint debtor:

   c. ☐ additional costs against certain joint debtors (itemize):

9. ☐ (Writ of Possession or Writ of Sale) **Judgment** was entered for the following:
   a. ☐ Possession of real property: The complaint was filed on (date):   **(Check (1) or (2)):**
      (1) ☐ The Prejudgment Claim of Right to Possession was served in compliance with CCP 415.46.
             The judgment includes all tenants, subtenants, named claimants, and other occupants of the premises.
      (2) ☐ The Prejudgment Claim of Right to Possession was NOT served in compliance with CCP 415.46.
             (a) $ was the daily rental value on the date the complaint was filed.
             (b) The court will hear objections to enforcement of the judgment under CCP 1174.3 on the following
                 dates (specify):
   b. ☐ Possession of personal property
        ☐ If delivery cannot be had, then for the value (itemize in 9e) specified in the judgment or supplemental order.
   c. ☐ Sale of personal property
   d. ☐ Sale of real property
   e. Description of property:

— NOTICE TO PERSON SERVED —

WRIT OF EXECUTION OR SALE. Your rights and duties are indicated on the accompanying Notice of Levy.
WRIT OF POSSESSION OF PERSONAL PROPERTY. If the levying officer is not able to take custody of the property, the levying
officer will make a demand upon you for the property. If custody is not obtained following demand, the judgment may be enforced
as a money judgment for the value of the property specified in the judgment or in a supplemental order.
WRIT OF POSSESSION OF REAL PROPERTY. If the premises are not vacated within five days after the date of service on the
occupant or, if service is by posting, within five days after service on you, the levying officer will remove the occupants from the real
property and place the judgment creditor in possession of the property. Except for a mobile home, personal property remaining on
the premises will be sold or otherwise disposed of in accordance with CCP 1174 unless you or the owner of the property pays the
judgment creditor the reasonable cost of storage and takes possession of the personal property not later than 15 days after the
time the judgment creditor takes possession of the premises.
► A Claim of Right to Possession form accompanies this writ (unless the Summons was served in compliance with CCP 415.46).

EJ-130 [Rev. January 1, 1997*]   **WRIT OF EXECUTION**   Page two

ATTORNEY OR PARTY WITHOUT ATTORNEY *(Name and Address)*

TELEPHONE NO

FOR COURT USE ONLY

ATTORNEY FOR *(Name)*

Insert name of court and name of judicial district and branch court, if any:

PLAINTIFF/PETITIONER:

DEFENDANT/RESPONDENT:

REQUEST FOR DISMISSAL

☐ **Personal Injury, Property Damage, or Wrongful Death**
   ☐ **Motor Vehicle**   ☐ **Other**
☐ **Family Law**
☐ **Eminent Domain**
☐ **Other** *(specify)*:

CASE NUMBER:

— **A conformed copy will not be returned by the clerk unless a method of return is provided with the document.** —

1. **TO THE CLERK:** Please **dismiss** this action as follows:

  a. (1) ☐ With prejudice   (2) ☐ Without prejudice

  b. (1) ☐ Complaint   (2) ☐ Petition
     (3) ☐ Cross-complaint filed by *(name)*:   on *(date)*:
     (4) ☐ Cross-complaint filed by *(name)*:   on *(date)*:
     (5) ☐ Entire action of all parties and all causes of action
     (6) ☐ Other *(specify)*:*

Date:

▶

(SIGNATURE)

(TYPE OR PRINT NAME OF ☐ ATTORNEY ☐ PARTY WITHOUT ATTORNEY)

* If dismissal requested is of specified parties only, of specified causes of action only, or of specified cross-complaints only, so state and identify the parties, causes of action, or cross-complaints to be dismissed.

Attorney or party without attorney for:

☐ Plaintiff/Petitioner   ☐ Defendant/Respondent
☐ Cross-complainant

2. **TO THE CLERK:** Consent to the above dismissal is hereby given.**

Date:

▶

(SIGNATURE)

(TYPE OR PRINT NAME OF ☐ ATTORNEY ☐ PARTY WITHOUT ATTORNEY)

** If a cross-complaint—or Response (Family Law) seeking affirmative relief—is on file, the attorney for cross-complainant (respondent) must sign this consent if required by Code of Civil Procedure section 581(i) or (j).

Attorney or party without attorney for:

☐ Plaintiff/Petitioner   ☐ Defendant/Respondent
☐ Cross-complainant

(To be completed by clerk)

3. ☐ Dismissal entered as requested on *(date)*:
4. ☐ Dismissal entered on *(date)*:   as to only *(name)*:
5. ☐ Dismissal **not entered** as requested for the following reasons *(specify)*:

6. ☐ a. Attorney or party without attorney notified on *(date)*:
     b. Attorney or party without attorney not notified. Filing party failed to provide
       ☐ a copy to conform   ☐ means to return conformed copy

Date: Clerk, by _____, Deputy

Form Adopted by the
Judicial Council of California
982(a)(5) [Rev. January 1, 1997]

REQUEST FOR DISMISSAL

Code of Civil Procedure, § 581 et seq.
Cal. Rules of Court, rules 383, 1233

```
 1

 2

 3

 4

 5

 6

 7

 8        IN THE MUNICIPAL COURT OF _____ JUDICIAL DISTRICT,

 9        COUNTY OF _____, STATE OF CALIFORNIA

10

11        _____,)
                         Plaintiff,)          NO.
12              vs.                  )
                                     )         STIPULATION FOR ENTRY
13        _____,)     OF JUDGMENT
                         Defendant.)
14        _____)

15            Plaintiff(s) and Defendant(s) named above hereby agree to settle

16       the above-entitled action, which is for unlawful detainer of premises

17       located at

18       in the city of

19       in the above-named county, state of California.

20            The settlement terms and conditions are as follows (applicable

21       paragraphs are checked):

22            [ ] Plaintiff shall have immediate judgment for restitution of

23       premises. Execution on this judgment shall [cross out one] (not be

24       stayed)  (be stayed until                                ).

25            [ ] Defendant(s) agree to vacate the premises on or before

26

27            [ ] Defendant(s) agree to pay Plaintiff(s) the sum of $            ,

28       of which $            is payment in full of the rent owing for the

29       period from                            through                        ,
```

1 and of which $ is for the following:

2

3 Defendant(s) agree to pay this sum [cross out one] (immediately) (on or

4 before   ). If Defendant(s) fail to pay as

5 agreed, Plaintiff(s) shall make an ex parte application to the court

6 for a judgment or amended judgment for the portion of this sum owing

7 and for immediate restitution of the premises.

8   [ ] The deposits of $ being held for security on the

9 premises shall be applied as follows:

10

11   [ ] Plaintiff(s) and Defendant(s) agree to drop any and all other

12 claims they may have made against one another as landlord(s) and as

13 tenant(s).

14   [ ] Plaintiff(s) and Defendant(s) agree that this stipulation

15 makes no conclusion as to which side has prevailed in this legal

16 action.

17

18 Dated:

19
                        _____
20   Plaintiff(s)

21 Dated:

22
                        _____
23   Defendant(s)

24

25

26

27

28

29

MUNICIPAL COURT OF CALIFORNIA, COUNTY OF _____

_____ **JUDICIAL DISTRICT**

Plaintiff(s)

VS

Defendant(s)

Case Number

**JUDGMENT
PURSUANT TO STIPULATION**

COURT JUDGE   Reporter

The parties having stipulated that judgment may be entered in favor of plaintiff(s) and against defendant(s), and stipulation having been made in court, the court ordered the following judgment pursuant to said stipulation:

It is adjudged that plaintiff(s)

have and recover from defendant(s)

$_____ principal, $_____ attorney fee, $_____ interest, $_____ costs.

TOTAL JUDGMENT $_____

It is further ordered:

Minutes of
Judgment entered on
in the Register of Actions.

Clerk of the Court

By . . . .
                                                            Deputy Clerk

JUDGMENT PURSUANT TO STIPULATION

ATTORNEY OR PARTY WITHOUT ATTORNEY *(Name and Address)*:

TEL. NO.:

ATTORNEY FOR *(Name)*:

NAME OF COURT AND JUDICIAL DISTRICT AND BRANCH COURT, IF ANY:

SHORT TITLE OF CASE:

UNLAWFUL DETAINER ASSISTANT
(Check one box): An unlawful detainer assistant ☐ did ☐ did not for compensation give advice or assistance with this form. *(If one did, state the following)*:

ASSISTANT'S NAME:

ADDRESS:

TEL. NO.:

COUNTY OF REGISTRATION:

REGISTRATION NO.:

EXPIRES *(DATE)*:

FORM INTERROGATORIES — UNLAWFUL DETAINER
Asking Party:

Answering Party:

Set No.:

CASE NUMBER:

Sec. 1. Instructions to All Parties

(a) These are general instructions. *For time limitations, requirements for service on other parties, and other details, see Code of Civil Procedure section 2030 and the cases construing it.*

(b) These interrogatories do not change existing law relating to interrogatories nor do they affect an answering party's right to assert any privilege or objection.

Sec. 2. Instructions to the Asking Party

(a) These interrogatories are designed for optional use in unlawful detainer proceedings.

(b) There are restrictions that generally limit the number of interrogatories that may be asked and the form and use of the interrogatories. For details, read Code of Civil Procedure section 2030(c).

(c) In determining whether to use these or any interrogatories, you should be aware that abuse can be punished by sanctions, including fines and attorney fees. See Code of Civil Procedure sections 128.5 and 128.7.

(d) Check the box next to each interrogatory that you want the answering party to answer. Use care in choosing those interrogatories that are applicable to the case.

(e) Additional interrogatories may be attached.

Sec. 3. Instructions to the Answering Party

(a) An answer or other appropriate response must be given to each interrogatory checked by the asking party. Failure to respond to these interrogatories properly can be punished by sanctions, including contempt preceedings, fine, attorneys fees, and the loss of your case. See Code of Civil Procedure sections 128.5, 128.7, and 2030.

(b) As a general rule, within five days after you are served with these interrogatories, you must serve your responses on the asking party and serve copies of your responses on all other parties to the action who have appeared. See Code of Civil Procedure section 2030 for details.

(c) Each answer must be as complete and straightforward as the information reasonably available to you permits. If an interrogatory cannot be answered completely, answer it to the extent possible.

(d) If you do not have enough personal knowledge to fully answer an interrogatory, say so, but make a reasonable and good faith effort to get the information by asking other persons or organizations, unless the information is equally available to the asking party.

(e) Whenever an interrogatory may be answered by referring to a document, the document may be attached as an exhibit to the response and referred to in the response. If the document has more than one page, refer to the page and section where the answer to the interrogatory can be found.

(f) Whenever an address and telephone number for the same person are requested in more than one interrogatory, you are required to furnish them in answering only the first interrogatory asking for that information.

(g) Your answers to these interrogatories must be verified, dated, and signed. You may wish to use the following form *at the end of your answers:*

''I declare under penalty of perjury under the laws of the State of California that the foregoing answers are true and correct.

_____   _____   ''
(DATE)   (SIGNATURE)

Sec. 4. Definitions

Words in **BOLDFACE CAPITALS** in these interrogatories are defined as follows:

(a) **PERSON** includes a natural person, firm, association, organization, partnership, business, trust, corporation, or public entity.

(b) **PLAINTIFF** includes any **PERSON** who seeks recovery of the **RENTAL UNIT** whether acting as an individual or on someone else's behalf and includes all such **PERSONS** if more than one.

(Continued)

Page 1 of 7

Form Approved by the
Judicial Council of California
FI-128 [Rev. July 1, 1987]
[Page 1 revised July 1, 1996]

**FORM INTERROGATORIES
UNLAWFUL DETAINER**

CCP 2030, 2033.5

(c) **LANDLORD** includes any **PERSON** who offered the **RENTAL UNIT** for rent and any **PERSON** on whose behalf the **RENTAL UNIT** was offered for rent and their successors in interest. **LANDLORD** includes all **PERSONS** who managed the **PROPERTY** while defendant was in possession.

(d) **RENTAL UNIT** is the premises **PLAINTIFF** seeks to recover.

(e) **PROPERTY** is the building or parcel (including common areas) of which the **RENTAL UNIT** is a part. (For example, if **PLAINTIFF** is seeking to recover possession of apartment number 12 of a 20-unit building, the building is the **PROPERTY** and apartment 12 is the **RENTAL UNIT**. If **PLAINTIFF** seeks possession of cottage number 3 in a five-cottage court or complex, the court or complex is the **PROPERTY** and cottage 3 is the **RENTAL UNIT**.)

(f) **DOCUMENT** means a writing, as defined in Evidence Code section 250, and includes the original or a copy of handwriting, typewriting, printing, photostating, photographing, and every other means of recording upon any tangible thing and form of communicating or representation, including letters, words, pictures, sounds, or symbols, or combinations of them.

(g) **NOTICE TO QUIT** includes the original or copy of any notice mentioned in Code of Civil Procedure section 1161 or Civil Code section 1946, including a 3-day notice to pay rent and quit the **RENTAL UNIT**, a 3-day notice to perform conditions or covenants or quit, a 3-day notice to quit, and a 30-day notice of termination.

(h) **ADDRESS** means the street address, including the city, state, and zip code.

Sec. 5. Interrogatories

The following interrogatories have been approved by the Judicial Council under section 2033.5 of the Code of Civil Procedure for use in unlawful detainer proceedings:

CONTENTS

70.0 General

[Either party may ask any applicable question in this section.]

☐ 70.1 State the name, **ADDRESS**, telephone number, and relationship to you of each **PERSON** who prepared or assisted in the preparation of the responses to these interrogatories. (Do not identify anyone who simply typed or reproduced the responses.)

☐ 70.2 Is **PLAINTIFF** an owner of the **RENTAL UNIT**? If so, state:
(a) the nature and percentage of ownership interest;
(b) the date **PLAINTIFF** first acquired this ownership interest.

☐ 70.3 Does **PLAINTIFF** share ownership or lack ownership? If so, state the name, the **ADDRESS**, and the nature and percentage of ownership interest of each owner.

☐ 70.4 Does **PLAINTIFF** claim the right to possession other than as an owner of the **RENTAL UNIT**? If so, state the basis of the claim.

☐ 70.5 Has **PLAINTIFF'S** interest in the **RENTAL UNIT** changed since acquisition? If so, state the nature and dates of each change.

☐ 70.6 Are there other rental units on the **PROPERTY**? If so, state how many.

☐ 70.7 During the 12 months before this proceeding was filed, did **PLAINTIFF** possess a permit or certificate of occupancy for the **RENTAL UNIT**? If so, for each state:

(a) the name and **ADDRESS** of each **PERSON** named on the permit or certificate;
(b) the dates of issuance and expiration;
(c) the permit or certificate number.

☐ 70.8 Has a last month's rent, security deposit, cleaning fee, rental agency fee, credit check fee, key deposit, or any other deposit been paid on the **RENTAL UNIT**? If so, for each item state:

(a) the purpose of the payment;
(b) the date paid;
(c) the amount;
(d) the form of payment;
(e) the name of the **PERSON** paying;
(f) the name of the **PERSON** to whom it was paid;
(g) any **DOCUMENT** which evidences payment and the name, **ADDRESS**, and telephone number of each **PERSON** who has the **DOCUMENT**;
(h) any adjustments or deductions including facts.

☐ 70.9 State the date defendant first took possession of the **RENTAL UNIT**.

☐ 70.10 State the date and all the terms of any rental agreement between defendant and the **PERSON** who rented to defendant.

☐ 70.11 For each agreement alleged in the pleadings:

(a) identify all **DOCUMENTS** that are part of the agreement and for each state the name, **ADDRESS**, and telephone number of each **PERSON** who has the **DOCUMENT**;
(b) state each part of the agreement not in writing, the name, **ADDRESS**, and telephone number of each **PERSON** agreeing to that provision, and the date that part of the agreement was made;
(c) identify all **DOCUMENTS** that evidence each part of the agreement not in writing and for each state the name, **ADDRESS**, and telephone number of each **PERSON** who has the **DOCUMENT**;
(d) identify all **DOCUMENTS** that are part of each modification to the agreement, and for each state

the name, **ADDRESS**, and telephone number of each **PERSON** who has the **DOCUMENT** (see also § 71.5);

(e) state each modification not in writing, the date, and the name, **ADDRESS**, and telephone number of the **PERSON** agreeing to the modification, and the date the modification was made (see also § 71.5);

(f) identify all **DOCUMENTS** that evidence each modification of the agreement not in writing and for each state the name, **ADDRESS**, and telephone number of each **PERSON** who has the **DOCUMENT** (see also § 71.5).

☐ 70.12 Has any **PERSON** acting on the **PLAINTIFF'S** behalf been responsible for any aspect of managing or maintaining the **RENTAL UNIT** or **PROPERTY**? If so, for each **PERSON** state:

(a) the name, **ADDRESS**, and telephone number;
(b) the dates the **PERSON** managed or maintained the **RENTAL UNIT** or **PROPERTY**;
(c) the **PERSON'S** responsibilities.

☐ 70.13 For each **PERSON** who occupies any part of the **RENTAL UNIT** (except occupants named in the complaint and occupants' children under 17) state:

(a) the name, **ADDRESS**, telephone number, and birthdate;
(b) the inclusive dates of occupancy;
(c) a description of the portion of the **RENTAL UNIT** occupied;
(d) the amount paid, the term for which it was paid, and the person to whom it was paid;
(e) the nature of the use of the **RENTAL UNIT**;
(f) the name, **ADDRESS**, and telephone number of the person who authorized occupancy;
(g) how occupancy was authorized, including failure of the **LANDLORD** or **PLAINTIFF** to protest after discovering the occupancy.

☐ 70.14 Have you or anyone acting on your behalf obtained any **DOCUMENT** concerning the tenancy between any occupant of the **RENTAL UNIT** and any **PERSON** with an ownership interest or managerial responsibility for the **RENTAL UNIT**? If so, for each **DOCUMENT** state:

(a) the name, **ADDRESS**, and telephone number of each individual from whom the **DOCUMENT** was obtained;
(b) the name, **ADDRESS**, and telephone number of each individual who obtained the **DOCUMENT**;
(c) the date the **DOCUMENT** was obtained;
(d) the name, **ADDRESS**, and telephone number of each **PERSON** who has the **DOCUMENT** (original or copy).

71.0 Notice

[If a defense is based on allegations that the 3-day notice or 30-day **NOTICE TO QUIT** *is* **defective in form or content**, *then either party may ask any applicable question in this section.]*

☐ 71.1 Was the **NOTICE TO QUIT** on which **PLAINTIFF** bases this proceeding attached to the complaint? If not, state the contents of this notice.

☐ 71.2 State all reasons that the **NOTICE TO QUIT** was served and for each reason:

(a) state all facts supporting **PLAINTIFF'S** decision to terminate defendant's tenancy;

(b) state the names, **ADDRESSES**, and telephone numbers of all **PERSONS** who have knowledge of the facts;
(c) identify all **DOCUMENTS** that support the facts and state the name, **ADDRESS**, and telephone number of each **PERSON** who has each **DOCUMENT**.

☐ 71.3 List all rent payments and rent credits made or claimed by or on behalf of defendant beginning 12 months before the **NOTICE TO QUIT** was served. For each payment or credit state:

(a) the amount;
(b) the date received;
(c) the form in which any payment was made;
(d) the services performed or other basis for which a credit is claimed;
(e) the period covered;
(f) the name of each **PERSON** making the payment or earning the credit;
(g) the identity of all **DOCUMENTS** evidencing the payment or credit and for each state the name, **ADDRESS**, and telephone number of each **PERSON** who has the **DOCUMENT**.

☐ 71.4 Did defendant ever fail to pay the rent on time? If so, for each late payment state:

(a) the date;
(b) the amount of any late charge;
(c) the identity of all **DOCUMENTS** recording the payment and for each state the name, **ADDRESS**, and telephone number of each **PERSON** who has the **DOCUMENT**.

☐ 71.5 Since the beginning of defendant's tenancy, has **PLAINTIFF** ever raised the rent? If so, for each rent increase state:

(a) the date the increase became effective;
(b) the amount;
(c) the reasons for the rent increase;
(d) how and when defendant was notified of the increase;
(e) the identity of all **DOCUMENTS** evidencing the increase and for each state the name, **ADDRESS**, and telephone number of each **PERSON** who has the **DOCUMENT**.

[See also section 70.11(d) — (f).]

☐ 71.6 During the 12 months before the **NOTICE TO QUIT** was served was there a period during which there was no permit or certificate of occupancy for the **RENTAL UNIT**? If so, for each period state:

(a) the inclusive dates;
(b) the reasons.

☐ 71.7 Has any **PERSON** ever reported any nuisance or disturbance at or destruction of the **RENTAL UNIT** or **PROPERTY** caused by defendant or other occupant of the **RENTAL UNIT** or their guests? If so, for each report state:

(a) a description of the disturbance or destruction;
(b) the date of the report;
(c) the name of the **PERSON** who reported;
(d) the name of the **PERSON** to whom the report was made;
(e) what action was taken as a result of the report;
(f) the identity of all **DOCUMENTS** evidencing the report and for each state the name, **ADDRESS**, and telephone number of each **PERSON** who has each **DOCUMENT**.

71.8 Does the complaint allege violation of a term of a rental agreement or lease (other than nonpayment of rent)? If so, for each covenant:
(a) identify the covenant breached;
(b) state the facts supporting the allegation of a breach;
(c) state the names, **ADDRESSES**, and telephone numbers of all **PERSONS** who have knowledge of the facts;
(d) identify all **DOCUMENTS** that support the facts and state the name, **ADDRESS**, and telephone number of each **PERSON** who has each **DOCUMENT**.

71.9 Does the complaint allege that the defendant has been using the **RENTAL UNIT** for an illegal purpose? If so, for each purpose:
(a) identify the illegal purpose;
(b) state the facts supporting the allegations of illegal use;
(c) state the names, **ADDRESSES**, and telephone numbers of all **PERSONS** who have knowledge of the facts;
(d) identify all **DOCUMENTS** that support the facts and state the name, **ADDRESS**, and telephone number of each **PERSON** who has each **DOCUMENT**.

[Additional interrogatories on this subject may be found in sections 75.0, 78.0, 79.0, and 80.0.]

72.0 Service

*[If a defense is based on allegations that the **NOTICE TO QUIT** was **defectively served**, then either party may ask any applicable question in this section.]*

72.1 Does defendant contend (or base a defense or make any allegations) that the **NOTICE TO QUIT** was defectively served? If the answer is "no," do not answer interrogatories 72.2 through 72.3.

72.2 Does **PLAINTIFF** contend that the **NOTICE TO QUIT** referred to in the complaint was served? If so, state:
(a) the kind of notice;
(b) the date and time of service;
(c) the manner of service;
(d) the name and **ADDRESS** of the person who served it:
(e) a description of any **DOCUMENT** or conversation between defendant and the person who served the notice.

72.3 Did any person receive the **NOTICE TO QUIT** referred to in the complaint? If so, for each copy of each notice state:
(a) the name of the person who received it;
(b) the kind of notice;
(c) how it was delivered;
(d) the date received;
(e) where it was delivered;
(f) the identity of all **DOCUMENTS** evidencing the notice and for each state the name, **ADDRESS**, and telephone number of each **PERSON** who has the **DOCUMENT**.

73.0 Malicious Holding Over

[If a defendant denies allegations that defendant's continued possession is malicious, then either party may ask any applicable question in this section. Additional questions in section 75.0 may also be applicable.]

73.1 If any rent called for by the rental agreement is unpaid, state the reasons and the facts upon which the reasons are based.

73.2 Has defendant made any attempts to secure other premises since the service of the **NOTICE TO QUIT** or since the service of the summons and complaint? If so, for each attempt:
(a) state all facts indicating the attempt to secure other premises;
(b) state the names, **ADDRESSES**, and telephone numbers of all **PERSONS** who have knowledge of the facts;
(c) identify all **DOCUMENTS** that support the facts and state the name, **ADDRESS**, and telephone number of each **PERSON** who has each **DOCUMENT**.

73.3 State the facts upon which **PLAINTIFF** bases the allegation of malice.

74.0 Rent Control and Eviction Control

74.1 Is there an ordinance or other local law in this jurisdiction which limits the right to evict tenants? If your answer is no, you need not answer sections 74.2 through 74.6.

74.2 For the ordinance or other local law limiting the right to evict tenants, state:
(a) the title or number of the law;
(b) the locality.

74.3 Do you contend that the **RENTAL UNIT** is exempt from the eviction provisions of the ordinance or other local law identified in section 74.2? If so, state the facts upon which you base your contention.

74.4 Is this proceeding based on allegations of a need to recover the **RENTAL UNIT** for use of the **LANDLORD** or the landlord's relative? If so, for each intended occupant state:
(a) the name;
(b) the residence **ADDRESSES** from three years ago to the present;
(c) the relationship to the **LANDLORD**;
(d) all the intended occupant's reasons for occupancy;
(e) all rental units on the **PROPERTY** that were vacated within 60 days before and after the date the **NOTICE TO QUIT** was served.

74.5 Is the proceeding based on an allegation that the **LANDLORD** wishes to remove the **RENTAL UNIT** from residential use temporarily or permanently (for example, to rehabilitate, demolish, renovate, or convert)? If so, state:
(a) each reason for removing the **RENTAL UNIT** from residential use;
(b) what physical changes and renovation will be made to the **RENTAL UNIT**;
(c) the date the work is to begin and end;
(d) the number, date, and type of each permit for the change or work;

(e) the identity of each **DOCUMENT** evidencing the intended activity (for example, blueprints, plans, applications for financing, construction contracts) and the name, **ADDRESS**, and telephone number of each **PERSON** who has each **DOCUMENT**.

☐ **74.6** Is the proceeding based on any ground other than those stated in sections 74.4 and 74.5? If so, for each:
(a) state each fact supporting or opposing the ground;
(b) state the names, **ADDRESSES**, and telephone numbers of all **PERSONS** who have knowledge of the facts;
(c) identify all **DOCUMENTS** evidencing the facts and state the name, **ADDRESS**, and telephone number of each **PERSON** who has each **DOCUMENT**.

75.0 Breach of Warranty to Provide Habitable Premises

[If plaintiff alleges nonpayment of rent and defendant bases his defense on allegations of implied or express breach of warranty to provide habitable residential premises, then either party may ask any applicable question in this section.]

☐ **75.1** Do you know of any conditions in violation of state or local building codes, housing codes, or health codes, conditions of dilapidation, or other conditions in need of repair in the **RENTAL UNIT** or on the **PROPERTY** that affected the **RENTAL UNIT** at any time defendant has been in possession? If so, state:
(a) the type of condition;
(b) the kind if corrections or repairs needed;
(c) how and when you learned of these conditions;
(d) how these conditions were caused;
(e) the name, **ADDRESS**, and telephone number of each **PERSON** who has caused these conditions.

☐ **75.2** Have any corrections, repairs, or improvements been made to the **RENTAL UNIT** since the **RENTAL UNIT** was rented to defendant? If so, for each correction, repair, or improvement state:
(a) a description giving the nature and location;
(b) the date;
(c) the name, **ADDRESS**, and telephone number of each **PERSON** who made the repairs or improvements;
(d) the cost;
(e) the identity of any **DOCUMENT** evidencing the repairs or improvements;
(f) if a building permit was issued, state the issuing agencies and the permit number of your copy.

☐ **75.3** Did defendant or any other **PERSON** during 36 months before the **NOTICE TO QUIT** was served or during defendant's possession of the **RENTAL UNIT** notify the **LANDLORD** or his agent or employee about the condition of the **RENTAL UNIT** or **PROPERTY**? If so, for each written or oral notice state:
(a) the substance;
(b) who made it;
(c) when and how it was made;
(d) the name and **ADDRESS** of each **PERSON** to whom it was made;
(e) the name and **ADDRESS** of each person who knows about it;
(f) the identity of each **DOCUMENT** evidencing the notice and the name, **ADDRESS**, and telephone number of each **PERSON** who has it;

(g) the response made to the notice;
(h) the efforts made to correct the conditions;
(i) whether the **PERSON** who gave notice was an occupant of the **PROPERTY** at the time of the complaint.

☐ **75.4** During the period beginning 36 months before the **NOTICE TO QUIT** was served to the present, was the **RENTAL UNIT** or **PROPERTY** (including other rental units) inspected for dilapidations or defective conditions by a representative of any governmental agency? If so, for each inspection state:
(a) the date;
(b) the reason;
(c) the name of the governmental agency;
(d) the name, **ADDRESS**, and telephone number of each inspector;
(e) the identity of each **DOCUMENT** evidencing each inspection and the name, **ADDRESS**, and telephone number of each **PERSON** who has it.

☐ **75.5** During the period beginning 36 months before the **NOTICE TO QUIT** was served to the present, did **PLAINTIFF** or **LANDLORD** receive a notice or other communication regarding the condition of the **RENTAL UNIT** or **PROPERTY** (including other rental units) from a governmental agency? If so, for each notice or communication state:
(a) the date received;
(b) the identity of all parties;
(c) the substance of the notice or communication;
(d) the identity of each **DOCUMENT** evidencing the notice or communication and the name, **ADDRESS**, and telephone number of each **PERSON** who has it.

☐ **75.6** Was there any corrective action taken in response to the inspection or notice or communication identified in sections 75.4 and 75.5? If so, for each:
(a) identify the notice or communication;
(b) identify the condition;
(c) describe the corrective action;
(d) identify of each **DOCUMENT** evidencing the corrective action and the name, **ADDRESS**, and telephone number of each **PERSON** who has it.

☐ **75.7** Has the **PROPERTY** been appraised for sale or loan during the period beginning 36 months before the **NOTICE TO QUIT** was served to the present? If so, for each appraisal state:
(a) the date;
(b) the name, **ADDRESS**, and telephone number of the appraiser;
(c) the purpose of the appraisal;
(d) the identity of each **DOCUMENT** evidencing the appraisal and the name, **ADDRESS**, and telephone number of each **PERSON** who has it.

☐ **75.8** Was any condition requiring repair or correction at the **PROPERTY** or **RENTAL UNIT** caused by defendant or other occupant of the **RENTAL UNIT** or their guests? If so, state:
(a) the type and location of condition;
(b) the kind of corrections or repairs needed;
(c) how and when you learned of these conditions;
(d) how and when these conditions were caused;
(e) the name, **ADDRESS**, and telephone number of each **PERSON** who caused these conditions;

(f) the identity of each **DOCUMENT** evidencing the repair (or correction) and the name, **ADDRESS**, and telephone number of each **PERSON** who has it.

[See also section 71.0 for additional questions.]

76.0 Waiver, Change, Withdrawal, or Cancellation of Notice to Quit

[If a defense is based on waiver, change, withdrawal, or cancellation of the NOTICE TO QUIT, then either party may ask any applicable question in this section.]

☐ 76.1 Did the **PLAINTIFF** or **LANDLORD** or anyone acting on his or her behalf do anything which is alleged to have been a waiver, change, withdrawal, or cancellation of the **NOTICE TO QUIT**? If so:
(a) state the facts supporting this allegation;
(b) state the names, **ADDRESSES**, and telephone numbers of all **PERSONS** who have knowledge of these facts;
(c) identify each **DOCUMENT** that supports the facts and state the name, **ADDRESS**, and telephone number of each **PERSON** who has it.

☐ 76.2 Did the **PLAINTIFF** or **LANDLORD** accept rent which covered a period after the date for vacating the **RENTAL UNIT** as specified in the **NOTICE TO QUIT**? If so:
(a) state the facts;
(b) state the names, **ADDRESSES**, and telephone numbers of all **PERSONS** who have knowledge of the facts;
(c) identify each **DOCUMENT** that supports the facts and state the name, **ADDRESS**, and telephone number of each **PERSON** who has it.

77.0 Retaliation and Arbitrary Discrimination

[If a defense is based on retaliation or arbitrary discrimination, then either party may ask any applicable question in this section.]

☐ 77.1 State all reasons that the **NOTICE TO QUIT** was served or that defendant's tenancy was not renewed and for each reason:
(a) state all facts supporting **PLAINTIFF'S** decision to terminate or not renew defendant's tenancy;
(b) state the names, **ADDRESSES**, and telephone numbers of all **PERSONS** who have knowledge of the facts;
(c) identify all **DOCUMENTS** that support the facts and state the name, **ADDRESS**, and telephone number of each **PERSON** who has it.

78.0 Nonperformance of the Rental Agreement by Landlord

[If a defense is based on nonperformance of the rental agreement by the LANDLORD or someone acting on the LANDLORD'S behalf, then either party may ask any applicable question in this section.]

☐ 78.1 Did the **LANDLORD** or anyone acting on the **LANDLORD'S** behalf agree to make repairs, alterations, or improvements at any time or provide services to the **PROPERTY** or **RENTAL UNIT**? If so, for each agreement state:
(a) the substance of the agreement;

(b) when it was made;
(c) whether it was written or oral;
(d) by whom and to whom;
(e) the name and **ADDRESS** of each person who knows about it;
(f) whether all promised repairs, alterations, or improvements were completed or services provided;
(g) the reasons for any failure to perform;
(h) the identity of each **DOCUMENT** evidencing the agreement or promise and the name, **ADDRESS**, and telephone number of each **PERSON** who has it.

☐ 78.2 Has **PLAINTIFF** or **LANDLORD** or any resident of the **PROPERTY** ever committed disturbances or interfered with the quiet enjoyment of the **RENTAL UNIT** (including, for example, noise, acts which threaten the loss of title to the property or loss of financing, etc.)? If so, for each disturbance or interference, state:
(a) a description of each act;
(b) the date of each act;
(c) the name, **ADDRESS**, and telephone number of each **PERSON** who acted;
(d) the name, **ADDRESS**, and telephone number of each **PERSON** who witnessed each act and any **DOCUMENTS** evidencing the person's knowledge;
(e) what action was taken by the **PLAINTIFF** or **LANDLORD** to end or lessen the disturbance or interference.

79.0 Offer of Rent by Defendant

[If a defense is based on an offer of rent by a defendant which was refused, then either party may ask any applicable question in this section.]

☐ 79.1 Has defendant or anyone acting on the defendant's behalf offered any payments to **PLAINTIFF** which **PLAINTIFF** refused to accept? If so, for each offer state:
(a) the amount;
(b) the date;
(c) purpose of offer;
(d) the manner of the offer;
(e) the identity of the person making the offer;
(f) the identity of the person refusing the offer;
(g) the date of the refusal;
(h) the reasons for the refusal.

80.0 Deduction from Rent for Necessary Repairs

[If a defense to payment of rent or damages is based on claim of retaliatory eviction, then either party may ask any applicable question in this section. Additional questions in section 75.0 may also be applicable.]

☐ 80.1 Does defendant claim to have deducted from rent any amount which was withheld to make repairs after communication to the **LANDLORD** of the need for the repairs? If the answer is "no," do not answer interrogatories 80.2 through 80.6.

☐ 80.2 For each condition in need of repair for which a deduction was made, state:
(a) the nature of the condition;
(b) the location;
(c) the date the condition was discovered by defendant;
(d) the date the condition was first known by **LANDLORD** or **PLAINTIFF**;

(e) the dates and methods of each notice to the **LANDLORD** or **PLAINTIFF** of the condition;

(f) the response or action taken by the **LANDLORD** or **PLAINTIFF** to each notification;

(g) the cost to remedy the condition and how the cost was determined;

(h) the identity of any bids obtained for the repairs and any **DOCUMENTS** evidencing the bids.

☐ 80.3 Did **LANDLORD** or **PLAINTIFF** fail to respond within a reasonable time after receiving a communication of a need for repair? If so, for each communication state:

(a) the date it was made;

(b) how it was made;

(c) the response and date;

(d) why the delay was unreasonable.

☐ 80.4 Was there an insufficient period specified or actually allowed between the time of notification and the time repairs were begun by defendant to allow **LANDLORD** or **PLAINTIFF** to make the repairs? If so, state all facts on which the claim of insufficiency is based.

☐ 80.5 Does **PLAINTIFF** contend that any of the items for which rent deductions were taken were not allowable under law? If so, for each item state all reasons and facts on which you base your contention.

☐ 80.6 Has defendant vacated or does defendant anticipate vacating the **RENTAL UNIT** because repairs were requested and not made within a reasonable time? If so, state all facts on which defendant justifies having vacated the **RENTAL UNIT** or anticipates vacating the rental unit.

81.0 Fair Market Rental Value

*[If defendant denies **PLAINTIFF** allegation on the fair market rental value of the **RENTAL UNIT**, then either party may ask any applicale question in this section. If defendant claims that the fair market rental value is less because of a breach of warranty to provide habitable premises, then either party may also ask any applicable question in section 75.0]*

☐ 81.1 Do you have an opinion on the fair market rental value of the **RENTAL UNIT**? If so, state:

(a) the substance of your opinion;

(b) the factors upon which the fair market rental value is based;

(c) the method used to calculate the fair market rental value.

☐ 81.2 Has any other **PERSON** ever expressed to you an opinion on the fair market rental value of the **RENTAL UNIT**? If so, for each **PERSON**:

(a) state the name, **ADDRESS**, and telephone number;

(b) state the substance of the **PERSON's** opinion;

(c) describe the conversation or identify all **DOCUMENTS** in which the **PERSON** expressed an opinion and state the name, **ADDRESS**, and telephone number of each **PERSON** who has each **DOCUMENT**.

☐ 81.3 Do you know of any current violations of state or local building codes, housing codes, or health codes, conditions of dilapidation or other conditions in need of repair in the **RENTAL UNIT** or common areas that have affected the **RENTAL UNIT** at any time defendant has been in possession? If so, state:

(a) the conditions in need of repair;

(b) the kind of repairs needed;

(c) the name, **ADDRESS**, and telephone number of each **PERSON** who caused these conditions.

Name, Address, and Telephone No. of Attorney(s)

Space Below for Use of Court Clerk Only

Attorney(s) for

| **AMENDMENT TO COMPLAINT** | **COURT OF** | **CASE NUMBER:** |

vs.

Plaintiff(s)

Defendant(s)

FICTITIOUS NAME (NO ORDER REQUIRED)

Upon filing the complaint herein, plaintiff(s) being ignorant of the true name of a defendant, and having designated said defendant in the complaint by the fictitious name of

_____

and having discovered the true name of said defendant to be

_____

hereby amends the complaint by inserting such true name in place and stead of such fictitious name wherever it appears in said complaint.

_____
Plaintiff(s)/Attorney(s) for Plaintiff(s)

INCORRECT NAME/ADDRESS (ORDER REQUIRED)

Plaintiff(s) having designated a defendant in the complaint by the incorrect name/address of

_____

and having discovered the true name/address of said defendant to be

_____

hereby amends the complaint by inserting such true name/address in place and stead of such incorrect name/address wherever it appears in said complaint.

_____
Plaintiff(s)/Attorney(s) for Plaintiff(s)

ORDER

Proper cause appearing, the above amendment to the complaint is allowed.

Dated: _____   _____
Presiding Judge

AMENDMENT TO COMPLAINT
CCP §§473-474

INSTRUCTIONS TO LEVYING OFFICER SERVING WRIT
(POSSESSION OF REAL PROPERTY)

_____

Plaintiff

-vs-

_____

Defendant

_____

Date

_____

Court (Case) Number

To:

By virtue of the accompanying Writ in the above entitled action, you are hereby instructed to RETURN POSSESSION OF THE PROPERTY DESCRIBED BELOW TO THE CREDITOR:

_____

Street Address (include apt. no.)

_____

City/Zip Code

WHEN YOU ARE READY TO DELIVER POSSESSION OF THE PROPERTY, CONTACT:

_____

Name

_____

Address

_____

City/Zip Code

_____

Phone (8 AM - 11 AM)

_____

Signature (Creditor or Creditor's Attorney)

_____

Print/Type Name

_____

Address

_____

City/State/Zip Code

_____

Phone (8 AM - 5 PM)

Court Date: _____ Time: _____ Dept: _____ Judge: _____

UNLAWFUL DETAINER CASE SUMMARY

CASE
Title:
Number:
Defendant(s):

Property Address:

TENANCY
Date Tenancy Began:
Initial Rent:
Current Rent:
Security Deposit:

NOTICE
Notice Served:
Date of Notice:
Date Notice Expired:

SUMMONS/COMPLAINT
Date Summons/Complaint Filed:
Date Summons/Complaint Served:

REQUEST
1) Forfeiture of the Agreement
2) Past Due Rent . . . .
3) DAMAGES
Date Damages Begin:
Date Damages End:
Damages Per Day:
TOTAL DAMAGES:
4) Costs . . . .
5) Restitution of the Premises

JUDGMENT
Immediate Possession OR Stay of _____ Days (circle one)

Past Due Rent $_____

Damages $_____

Costs $_____

Judge (name) _____ Dept./Time_____

ATTORNEY OR PARTY WITHOUT ATTORNEY *(Name and Address)*: TELEPHONE NO.: *FOR COURT USE ONLY*

ATTORNEY FOR *(Name)*:

NAME OF COURT:
STREET ADDRESS:
MAILING ADDRESS:
CITY AND ZIP CODE:
BRANCH NAME:

PLAINTIFF:

DEFENDANT:

CASE NUMBER:

APPLICATION AND ORDER FOR APPEARANCE AND EXAMINATION

☐ **ENFORCEMENT OF JUDGMENT**   ☐ **ATTACHMENT (Third Person)**
☐ Judgment Debtor ☐ Third Person

ORDER TO APPEAR FOR EXAMINATION

1. TO *(name)*:
2. YOU ARE ORDERED TO APPEAR personally before this court, or before a referee appointed by the court, to
   a. ☐ furnish information to aid in enforcement of a money judgment against you.
   b. ☐ answer concerning property of the judgment debtor in your possession or control or concerning a debt you owe the judgment debtor.
   c. ☐ answer concerning property of the defendant in your possession or control or concerning a debt you owe the defendant that is subject to attachment.

Date: Time: Dept. or Div.:   Rm.:
Address of court ☐ shown above ☐ is:

3. This order may be served by a sheriff, marshal, constable, registered process server, **or** the following specially appointed person *(name)*:

Date: ▶ _____
(SIGNATURE OF JUDGE OR REFEREE)

This order must be served not less than 10 days before the date set for the examination.
IMPORTANT NOTICES ON REVERSE

APPLICATION FOR ORDER TO APPEAR FOR EXAMINATION

1. ☐ Judgment creditor ☐ Assignee of record ☐ Plaintiff who has a right to attach order
   applies for an order requiring *(name)*:   to appear and furnish information
   to aid in enforcement of the money judgment or to answer concerning property or debt.
2. The person to be examined is
   ☐ the judgment debtor
   ☐ a third person (1) who has possession or control of property belonging to the judgment debtor or the defendant or (2) who owes the judgment debtor or the defendant more than $250. An affidavit supporting this application under CCP §491.110 or §708.120 is attached.
3. The person to be examined resides or has a place of business in this county or within 150 miles of the place of examination.
4. ☐ This court is **not** the court in which the money judgment is entered or *(attachment only)* the court that issued the writ of attachment. An affidavit supporting an application under CCP §491.150 or §708.160 is attached.
5. ☐ The judgment debtor has been examined within the past 120 days. An affidavit showing good cause for another examination is attached.

I declare under penalty of perjury under the laws of the State of California that the foregoing is true and correct.
Date:

▶

.... *(TYPE OR PRINT NAME)* ....   _____
(SIGNATURE OF DECLARANT)

Form Approved by the
Judicial Council of California
AT-138, EJ-125 [New July 1, 1984]

**APPLICATION AND ORDER
FOR APPEARANCE AND EXAMINATION
(Attachment—Enforcement of Judgment)**

CCP 491.110, 708.110, 708.120

218

AT-138, EJ-125
[New July 1, 1984]

APPLICATION AND ORDER FOR APPEARANCE AND EXAMINATION
(Attachment—Enforcement of Judgment)

Page two

APPEARANCE OF JUDGMENT DEBTOR (ENFORCEMENT OF JUDGMENT)

NOTICE TO JUDGMENT DEBTOR If you fail to appear at the time and place specified in this order, you may be subject to arrest and punishment for contempt of court, and the court may make an order requiring you to pay the reasonable attorney fees incurred by the judgment creditor in this proceeding.

APPEARANCE OF A THIRD PERSON (ENFORCEMENT OF JUDGMENT)

(1) **NOTICE TO PERSON SERVED** If you fail to appear at the time and place specified in this order, you may be subject to arrest and punishment for contempt of court, and the court may make an order requiring you to pay the reasonable attorney fees incurred by the judgment creditor in this proceeding.

(2) **NOTICE TO JUDGMENT DEBTOR** The person in whose favor the judgment was entered in this action claims that the person to be examined pursuant to this order has possession or control of property which is yours or owes you a debt. This property or debt is as follows (Describe the property or debt using typewritten capital letters):

If you claim that all or any portion of this property or debt is exempt from enforcement of the money judgment, you must file your exemption claim in writing with the court and have a copy personally served on the judgment creditor not later than three days before the date set for the examination. You must appear at the time and place set for the examination to establish your claim of exemption or your exemption may be waived.

APPEARANCE OF A THIRD PERSON (ATTACHMENT)

NOTICE TO PERSON SERVED If you fail to appear at the time and place specified in this order, you may be subject to arrest and punishment for contempt of court, and the court may make an order requiring you to pay the reasonable attorney fees incurred by the plaintiff in this proceeding.

APPEARANCE OF A CORPORATION, PARTNERSHIP, ASSOCIATION, TRUST, OR OTHER ORGANIZATION

It is your duty to designate one or more of the following to appear and be examined: officers, directors, managing agents, or other persons who are familiar with your property and debts.

1

2

3

4

5

6

7

8   IN THE MUNICIPAL COURT OF _____ JUDICIAL DISTRICT,

9   COUNTY OF _____, STATE OF CALIFORNIA

10

11   _____,)
                          Plaintiff,)   No.
12   vs.   )
)   APPLICATION AND
13   _____,)   DECLARATION FOR
                          Defendant.)   ORDER OF POSTING
14   _____)   OF SUMMONS

15   Application is hereby made for an order directing service of

16   summons in the above-entitled matter on above-named Defendant by

17   posting of said summons on the premises located at

18

19

20   The complaint in this action, which is for unlawful detainer, was

21   filed on   , and the summons was duly issued on

22

23   Said Defendant is a necessary party to this action. Said

24   Defendant cannot, with reasonable diligence, be served in any other

25   manner specified by Section 415.47 of the Code of Civil Procedure.

26   Defendant's place of employment is unknown to the Plaintiff, and a

27   reasonable search of public records does not disclose any address for

28   said Defendant; hence, said Defendant's whereabouts are unknown.

29   Reasonable diligence in attempting service is set forth in the

1 Declaration of   on file herein and attached hereto.

2   WHEREFORE, Plaintiff prays that the Court issue its order

3 directing service of the summons against the Defendant by posting of

4 the summons at

5 pursuant to provisions of Section 415.45 of the Code of Civil

6 Procedure.

7   I declare under penalty of perjury that the foregoing is true and

8 correct.

9   Executed on   , at City of   ,

10 County of   , State of California.

11

12

13   _____

14   Plaintiff

15

16

17

18

19

20

21

22

23

24

25

26

27

28

29

IN THE MUNICIPAL COURT OF _____ JUDICIAL DISTRICT,

COUNTY OF _____, STATE OF CALIFORNIA

_____,)
                Plaintiff,)
      vs.   )   NO.
)
_____,)   ORDER FOR
              Defendant.)   POSTING OF SUMMONS
_____)   (CCP 415.45)

Upon reading and filing the Plaintiff's Application and Declaration for Order of Posting of Summons, the Court appears satisfied therefrom that a cause of action for unlawful detainer exists against Defendant in the above-mentioned action and that summons on the complaint has been duly issued out of the above-entitled court in this action and that said Defendant cannot with reasonable diligence be served in any manner specified by Section 415.10 and 415.50 of the Code of Civil Procedure for the reasons that the whereabouts of said Defendant are unknown, and that reasonable diligence has been expended in attempting to serve the summons as set forth in the declaration on file herein.

IT IS HEREBY ORDERED that the service of said summons in this action be made on Defendant by posting of the summons for a period of not less

1 than ten (10) days on the premises located at

2

3

4 THE COURT ALSO ORDERS that a copy of the summons and complaint

5 shall be mailed forthwith by certified mail to Defendant at his

6 last known address, to wit:

7

8 Dated:

9 _____

JUDGE OF THE MUNICIPAL COURT

10

11

12

13

14

15

16

17

18

19

20

21

22

23

24

25

26

27

28

29

IN THE MUNICIPAL COURT OF _____ JUDICIAL DISTRICT,

COUNTY OF _____, STATE OF CALIFORNIA

_____,)
        Plaintiff,)
    vs.   )   NO.
)
_____,)   COMPLAINT FOR
        Defendant.)   UNLAWFUL DETAINER
_____)   (CCP §1161a)

Plaintiff alleges as follows:

  1. At all times mentioned herein, plaintiff was and now is a competent adult residing in the City of _____, County of _____, State of California.

  2. Plaintiff is the owner of the premises located at _____ in the City of _____, County of _____, State of California.

  3. Plaintiff believes that defendants are competent adults residing in the City of _____, County of _____, State of California.

  4. The true names and capacities of defendants sued as Does are unknown to plaintiff. Plaintiff will seek leave of court to amend this complaint when said true names and capacities have been determined.

  5. At all times mentioned herein, each of the defendants,

1   including the defendants served as Does herein, was the agent and/or

2   employee of each of the remaining defendants and in doing what is

3   mentioned herein was acting within the scope of such agency and/or

4   employment. Plaintiff is further informed and believes and thereupon

5   alleges that each of the defendants, including the defendants served as

6   Does herein, claims some type of possessory interest in the premises.

7   6. Defendants entered into possession of the Premises as owners

8   of record. Defendants are no longer owners of record, nor are they

9   tenants of the current owner of record.

10   7. Plaintiff has acquired ownership interest in the premises and

11 consequent right to possession. Plaintiff is now the owner of record,

12 holding legal entitlement to the premises as [select one]:

13 [ ] purchaser from the defendants through a voluntary sale.

14 [ ] purchaser upon foreclosure against the defaulting defendants.

15 [ ] purchaser under writ of execution against the defendants.

16 [ ] purchaser under a power of sale provision contained in a deed of

17 trust executed by the defendants.

18 [ ] purchaser under the default provisions of a conditional sale

19 contract or security agreement.

20   8. Plaintiff has complied with all legal requirements for

21 perfecting the title as evidenced by Exhibit A.

22   9. Plaintiff caused the defendants to be served with a written

23 notice to quit. Said notice required defendants to deliver possession

24 of the premises within three days following service of the notice. A

25 copy of this notice is attached hereto as Exhibit B and incorporated

26 herein by this reference.

27   10. The notice to quit was served on the defendants pursuant to

28 CCP Section 1162 in the manner shown on the Proof of Service, which is

29 a part of Exhibit B.

11. The period stated in the notice to quit expired on

_____, and defendants failed to comply with the notice by that date, that is, they failed to quit the premises and deliver up possession to plaintiff.

12. Defendants continue in possession of the premises without plaintiff's permission or consent.

14. Plaintiff is entitled to immediate possession of the premises.

13. Plaintiff is informed and believes and thereupon alleges that the reasonable rental value of the premises is the sum of $_____ per day, and damages to plaintiff caused by defendants' unlawful detention thereof have accrued at said rate since _____ [date after notice to quit expired] and will continue to accrue at said rate so long as defendants remain in possession of the premises.

WHEREFORE, plaintiff prays judgment against defendants, and each of them, as follows:

1. For immediate possession of the premises;

2. For damages at the rate of $_____, according to proof at trial, for each day defendants continue in possession of the premises, commencing _____.

3. For costs of suit incurred herein; and

4. For such other and further relief as the court may deem just and proper.

DATED: _____ SIGNED: _____

[Verification attached]

VERIFICATION

I, the undersigned, certify and declare that I have read the foregoing complaint and know its contents. The statement following the box checked is applicable.

[ ] I am a party to this action. The matters stated in the document described above are true of my own knowledge and belief except as to those matters stated on information and belief, and as to those matters I believe them to be true.

[ ] I am [ ] an officer [ ] a partner [ ] a _____ of _____, a party to this action, and am authorized to make this verification on its behalf. I am informed and believe and on that ground allege that the matters stated in the document described above are true.

[ ] I am the attorney, or one of the attorneys for _____, a party to this action. Such party is absent from the county where I or such attorneys have their offices and is unable to verify the document described above. For that reason, I am making this verification for and on behalf of that party. I am informed and believe and on that ground allege that the matters stated in said document are true.

Executed on _____, at _____.

I declare under penalty of perjury under the laws of the State of California that the foregoing is true and correct.

SIGNED: _____

Appendix A

Posting

Posting, one of the options available to you for serving especially elusive tenants a Summons and Complaint, involves several steps [see CCP §415.45(b); see also Green v. Lindsey (U.S. Sup.Ct. 1982) 102 S.Ct. 1874, 72 L.Ed.2d 249]:

1. Instruct the process server to make three attempts to serve the papers and then return them to you with enough information so you can proceed to get an order for posting.

2. Check the information regarding the process server's three attempts and make sure that they were made on three different days, each at a different time of the day. Two might be made in the morning and one in the evening, for example.

3. Prepare an Application and Declaration for Order of Posting of Summons and an Order for Posting of Summons in this appendix.

4. Take to the court clerk the process server's signed statement that the defendant could not be found, as well as the two forms just mentioned for securing the order of posting. Ask her to submit them to a judge for a signature. Depending on how busy everybody is, you may be able to wait for them then or you may have to return and pick them up later.

5. Take your papers back to the sheriff or marshal and have him post the Summons and Complaint on the tenant's main entry and also send a copy of each by certified mail to the defendant at his last known address. The posting must take place before the mailing.

6. Wait fifteen days for a response [CCP §415.45(c)].

Does

Whenever you discover that the fictitious "DOES 1 to 10," whom you referred to in your Summons and Complaint, are real people with real names, you'll have to amend the Complaint or you won't be able to evict them.

Once you find out who they are, which is sometimes the most difficult part of all and may involve your having to "sift through the garbage" (attorneys' expression not necessarily meant to be literal) looking for their real names, you may file an Amendment to Complaint form and then have them served with a copy of the Summons, Complaint, and the Amendment.

In the absence of a Judicial Council form for this purpose, the form provided here should suffice to substitute a real person's name for a Doe. This is a dual-purpose form which works both for changing fictitious names to real names and for changing incorrect names to real names. "Does" are fictitious names and changing them does not require that you secure a judge's signature. You need use only the top two-thirds of the form for changing fictitious names. If you want to, you may use the same form for changing more than one fictitious name at a time.

These are the steps you should take to change "Does" to real names:

1. Make sure that your original Summons and Complaint always include "DOES 1 to 10" (10 is usually enough to include everybody who wasn't specifically named, but there's nothing to prevent you from using a larger number) as defendants.

2. Find out the real names of any adults living on the premises whom you didn't know before.

3. Complete the upper two-thirds of the Amendment to Complaint form.

4. File the Amendment to Complaint form with the court clerk.

5. Serve each of your newly discovered Does individually with a copy of the Summons, Complaint, and the Amendment to Complaint.

6. Wait five days following service for these defendants to respond.

7. Continue the eviction as usual.

```
1   Lester Landlord & Leslie Landlord
    123 Neat Street
2   Littletown, California 91111
    415-123-4567
3   Plaintiff in Propria Persona

4

5

6

7

8       IN THE MUNICIPAL COURT OF __LITTLETOWN__ JUDICIAL DISTRICT,

9       COUNTY OF _____SADDLEBACK_____, STATE OF CALIFORNIA

10
    LESTER LANDLORD
11  LESLIE LANDLORD                  ,)
                         Plaintiff,)    No. 1234567890
12          vs.                   )
    RICHARD ROTTER                )      APPLICATION AND
13  HAZEL ROTTER                 ,)      DECLARATION FOR
                         Defendant.)    ORDER OF POSTING
14  _____ )       OF SUMMONS
```

15   Application is hereby made for an order directing service of

16 summons in the above-entitled matter on above-named Defendant by

17 posting of said summons on the premises located at

18   456 Sweet Street

19   Littletown, California 91111

20   The complaint in this action, which is for unlawful detainer, was

21 filed on July 2, XXXX   , and the summons was duly issued on

22 July 2, XXXX.

23   Said Defendant is a necessary party to this action. Said

24 Defendant cannot, with reasonable diligence, be served in any other

25 manner specified by Section 415.47 of the Code of Civil Procedure.

26 Defendant's place of employment is unknown to the Plaintiff, and a

27 reasonable search of public records does not disclose any address for

28 said Defendant; hence, said Defendant's whereabouts are unknown.

29   Reasonable diligence in attempting service is set forth in the

You will find a blank copy of this form in the FORMS section of this book and in Eviction Forms Creator.

1   Declaration of   Sheriff   on file herein and attached hereto.

2   WHEREFORE, Plaintiff prays that the Court issue its order

3   directing service of the summons against the Defendant by posting of

4   the summons at 456 Sweet Street, Littletown, California

5   pursuant to provisions of Section 415.45 of the Code of Civil

6   Procedure.

7   I declare under penalty of perjury that the foregoing is true and

8   correct.

9   Executed on July 7, XXXX   , at City of Littletown   ,

10   County of Saddleback   , State of California.

11

12

13   *Lester Landlord*
                                    Plaintiff

14

15

16

17

18

19

20

21

22

23

24

25

26

27

28

29

You will find a blank copy of this form in the FORMS section of this book and in Eviction Forms Creator.

```
 1   Lester Landlord & Leslie Landlord
     123 Neat Street
 2   Littletown, California 91111
     415-123-4567
 3   Plaintiff in Propria Persona

 4

 5

 6

 7

 8        IN THE MUNICIPAL COURT OF _____LITTLETOWN_____ JUDICIAL DISTRICT,

 9        COUNTY OF _____SADDLEBACK_____, STATE OF CALIFORNIA

10   LESTER LANDLORD
     LESLIE LANDLORD
11   _____,)
                    Plaintiff,)
12          vs.              )        NO. 1234567890
     RICHARD ROTTER          )
13   HAZEL ROTTER            )
     _____,)          ORDER FOR
                 Defendant.)          POSTING OF SUMMONS
14   _____)        (CCP 415.45)

15        Upon reading and filing the Plaintiff's Application and

16   Declaration for Order of Posting of Summons, the Court appears

17   satisfied therefrom that a cause of action for unlawful detainer exists

18   against Defendant in the above-mentioned action and that summons on the

19   complaint has been duly issued out of the above-entitled court in this

20   action and that said Defendant cannot with reasonable diligence be

21   served in any manner specified by Section 415.10 and 415.50 of the Code

22   of Civil Procedure for the reasons that the whereabouts of said

23   Defendant are unknown, and that reasonable diligence has been expended

24   in attempting to serve the summons as set forth in the declaration on

25   file herein.

26

27   IT IS HEREBY ORDERED that the service of said summons in this action be

28   made on Defendant by posting of the summons for a period of not less

29
```

You will find a blank copy of this form in the FORMS section of this book and in Eviction Forms Creator.

1 than ten (10) days on the premises located at

2

3   456 Sweet Street, Littletown, California 91111

4 THE COURT ALSO ORDERS that a copy of the summons and complaint

5 shall be mailed forthwith by certified mail to Defendant at his

6 last known address, to wit:

7   456 Sweet Street, Littletown, California 91111

8 Dated: July 7, XXXX

9   *Denise Berger*

          ─────────────────────────
          JUDGE OF THE MUNICIPAL COURT

You will find a blank copy of this form in the FORMS section of this book and in Eviction Forms Creator.

Name, Address, and Telephone No. of Attorney(s)

Lester Landlord & Leslie Landlord
123 Neat Street
Littletown, California 91111

415-123-4567

Attorney(s) for Plaintiff in Propria Persona

Space Below for Use of Court Clerk Only

AMENDMENT TO COMPLAINT

MUNICIPAL COURT OF CALIFORNIA
COUNTY OF SADDLEBACK
LITTLETOWN JUDICIAL DISTRICT

CASE NUMBER:
1234567890

Lester Landlord
Leslie Landlord

Otto Rowe

vs.

Plaintiff(s)

Defendant(s)

FICTITIOUS NAME (NO ORDER REQUIRED)
Upon filing the complaint herein, plaintiff(s) being ignorant of the true name of a defendant, and having designated said defendant in the complaint by the fictitious name of

Doe 1 and Doe 2

and having discovered the true name of said defendant to be

Jennifer Rowe and Max Rowe

hereby amends the complaint by inserting such true name in place and stead of such fictitious name wherever it appears in said complaint.

Lester Landlord
Plaintiff(s)/Attorney(s) for Plaintiff(s)

INCORRECT NAME/ADDRESS (ORDER REQUIRED)
Plaintiff(s) having designated a defendant in the complaint by the incorrect name/address of

and having discovered the true name/address of said defendant to be

hereby amends the complaint by inserting such true name/address in place and stead of such incorrect name/address wherever it appears in said complaint.

Plaintiff(s)/Attorney(s) for Plaintiff(s)

ORDER
Proper cause appearing, the above amendment to the complaint is allowed.

Dated: _____

_____
Presiding Judge

AMENDMENT TO COMPLAINT
CCP §§473-474

efc

You will find a blank copy of this form in the FORMS section of this book and in Eviction Forms Creator.

Appendix B

Codes Relevant to Unlawful Detainers

Code of Civil Procedure §1166a

(a) Upon filing the complaint, the plaintiff may, upon motion, have immediate possession of the premises by a writ of possession of a manufactured home, mobilehome, or real property issued by the court and directed to the sheriff of the county, or constable or marshal, for execution, where it appears to the satisfaction of the court, after a hearing on the motion, from the verified complaint and from any affidavits filed or oral testimony given by or on behalf of the parties, that the defendant resides out of state, has departed from the state, cannot, after due diligence, be found within the state, or has concealed himself or herself to avoid the service of summons. The motion shall indicate that the writ applies to all tenants, subtenants, if any, named claimants, if any, and any other occupants of the premises.

(b) Written notice of the hearing on the motion shall be served on the defendant by the plaintiff in accordance with the provisions of Section 1011, and shall inform the defendant as follows: "You may file affidavits on your own behalf with the court and may appear and present testimony on your own behalf. However, if you fail to appear, the plaintiff will apply to the court for a writ of possession of a manufactured home, mobilehome, or real property."

(c) The plaintiff shall file an undertaking in such sum as shall be fixed and determined by the judge, to the effect that, if the plaintiff fails to recover judgment against the defendant for the possession of the premises or if the suit is dismissed, the plaintiff will pay to the defendant such damages, not to exceed the amount fixed in the undertaking, as may be sustained by the defendant by reason of such dispossession under the writ of possession of a manufactured home, mobilehome, or real property.

(d) If, at the hearing on the motion, the findings of the court are in favor of the plaintiff and against the defendant, an order shall be entered for the immediate possession of the premises.

(e) The order for the immediate possession of the premises may be enforced as provided in Division 3 (commencing with Section 712.010) of Title 9 of Part 2.

(f) For the purposes of this section, references in Division 3 (commencing with Section 712.010) of Title 9 of Part 2 and in subdivisions (e) to (m), inclusive, of Section 1174, to the "judgment debtor" shall be deemed references to the defendant, to the "judgment creditor" shall be deemed references to the plaintiff, and to the "judgment of possession or sale of property" shall be deemed references to an order for the immediate possession of the premises.

Code of Civil Procedure §1169

If at the time appointed any defendant served with a summons does not appear and defend, the clerk, or the judge if there is no clerk, upon written application of the plaintiff and proof of the service of summons and complaint, shall enter the default of any defendant so served, and, if requested by the plaintiff, immediately shall enter judgment for restitution of the premises and shall issue a writ of execution thereon. Thereafter, the plaintiff may apply to the court for any other relief demanded in the complaint, including the costs, against the defendant, or defendants, or against one or more of the defendants. [NOTE: Attorneys generally advise landlords to wait until the tenant has been evicted before going back into court for a money judgment. They fear that the two judgments, the earlier of which might be superseded by the latter, could result in confusion and delay.]

Code of Civil Procedure §715.050

Except with respect to enforcement of a judgment for money, a writ of possession issued pursuant to a judgment for possession in an unlawful detainer action shall be enforced pursuant to this chapter without delay, notwithstanding receipt of notice of the filing by the defendant of a bankruptcy proceeding.

This section does not apply to a writ of possession issued for possession of a mobilehome or manufactured home, as those terms are defined in subdivision (a) of Section 1161a, and does not apply to a writ of possession issued for possession of real property in a mobilehome park subject to the Mobilehome Residency Law (Chapter 2.5 (commencing with Section 798) of Title 2 of Part 2 of Division 2 of the Civil Code), or to a manufactured housing community, as defined in Section 18801 of the Health and Safety Code.

Civil Code §1946.5

(a)   The hiring of a room by a lodger on a periodic basis within a dwelling unit occupied by the owner may be terminated by either party giving written notice to the other of his or her intention to terminate the hiring, at least as long before the expiration of the term of the hiring as specified in Section 1946. The notice shall be given in a manner prescribed in Section 1162 of the Code of Civil Procedure or by certified or registered mail, restricted delivery, to the other party, with a return receipt requested.

(b)   Upon expiration of the notice period provided in the notice of termination given pursuant to subdivision (a), any right of the lodger to remain in the dwelling unit or any part thereof is terminated by operation of law. The lodger's removal from the premises may thereafter be effected pursuant to the provisions of Section 602.3 of the Penal Code or other applicable provisions of law.

(c)   As used in this section, "lodger" means a person contracting with the owner of a dwelling unit for a room or room and board within the dwelling unit personally occupied by the owner, where the owner retains a right of access to all areas of the dwelling unit occupied by the lodger and has overall control of the dwelling unit.

(d)   This section applies only to owner-occupied dwellings where a single lodger resides. Nothing in this section shall be construed to determine or affect in any way the rights of persons residing as lodgers in an owner-occupied dwelling where more than one lodger resides.

Penal Code §602.3

(a)   A lodger who is subject to Section 1946.5 of the Civil Code and who remains on the premises of an owner-occupied dwelling unit after receipt of a notice terminating the hiring, and expiration of the notice period, provided in Section 1946.5 of the Civil Code is guilty of an infraction and may, pursuant to Section 837, be arrested by the owner for the offense. Notwithstanding Section 853.5, the requirement of that section for release upon a written promise to appear shall not preclude an assisting peace officer from removing the person from the owner-occupied dwelling unit.

(b)   The removal of a lodger from a dwelling unit by the owner pursuant to subdivision (a) is not a forcible entry under the provisions of Section 1159 of the Code of Civil Procedure and shall not be a basis for civil liability under that section.

(c)   Chapter 5 (commencing with Section 1980) of Title 5 of Part 4 of Division 3 of the Civil Code applies to any personal property of the lodger which remains on the premises following the lodger's removal from the premises pursuant to this section.

(d)   Nothing in this section shall be construed to limit the owner's right to have a lodger removed under other provisions of law.

(e)   Except as provided in subdivision (b), nothing in this section shall be construed to limit or affect in any way any cause of action an owner or lodger may have for damages for any breach of the contract of the parties respecting the lodging.

(f)   This section applies only to owner-occupied dwellings where a single lodger resides. Nothing in this section shall be construed to determine or affect in any way the rights of persons residing as lodgers in an owner-occupied dwelling where more than one lodger resides.

Appendix C
Important Ruling Relevant to Unlawful Detainers and Bankruptcies
In re Smith, 105 B.R. 50 (Bkrtcy. C.D.Cal. 1989)
Vincent P. Zurzolo, Bankruptcy Judge, August 30, 1989

I. INTRODUCTION

Mike Marquand, dba San Marcos Apartments, ("Movant") filed and served a motion (the "Motion") pursuant to 11 U.S.C. §362(d) for relief from the automatic stay provided by 11 U.S.C. §362(a) (the "Stay"). In the Motion, Movant seeks an order relieving him of the Stay so he may enforce a "Judgment for Unlawful Detainer" (the "Judgment") obtained by Movant in the Municipal Court of the State of California, County of Los Angeles ("the State Court"). Movant obtained the Judgment in the State Court to regain possession of residential real property commonly known as 15238 Orange Avenue, No. 111, Paramount, California (the "Apartment"), from Sanya Smith ("Debtor"), the debtor in this Chapter 7 bankruptcy case.

The Motion is not unique or rare; I have heard over one hundred such motions in each month since April, 1988, when I assumed the bench. With few and insignificant variations, these hundreds of motions involve facts identical to those I find below.

II. FACTS

On June 30, 1988, Debtor entered into an Apartment Rental Agreement (the "Rental Agreement") with Movant. Under the terms of the Rental Agreement, Debtor agreed to pay Movant $695.00 per month beginning on July 1, 1988. On or about June 1, 1989, Debtor failed to pay the agreed-upon monthly rent to Movant. Thereafter, on June 10, 1989, Movant served a Notice to Pay Rent or Surrender Possession of Premises pursuant to Cal. Code of Civ. Proc. §1161. Debtor did not pay the overdue rent. Movant then filed a complaint for unlawful detainer in the State Court (the "Complaint") on June 30, 1989. Debtor did not appear or otherwise respond to the Complaint.

On July 17, 1989, the Judgment was awarded to Movant. Before Movant could enforce the Judgment to regain possession of the Apartment, Debtor filed her Voluntary Petition Under Chapter 7 of the United States Bankruptcy Code in the United States Bankruptcy Court, Central District of California on July 28, 1989. Movant was the only creditor listed on Debtor's Bankruptcy Schedules.

On August 1, 1989, Movant filed the Motion. On August 3, 1989, Movant served notice of the Motion and the Motion on Debtor by United States Mail. The Motion was heard on August 30, 1989. Debtor did not appear at the hearing or file any type of opposition to the Motion.

III. THE PROLIFERATION OF "UNLAWFUL DETAINER" CASE FILINGS

More than 39,000 Chapter 7 bankruptcy cases are filed in the Central District of California annually.[1] A significant portion of these cases are apparently filed solely for the purpose of staying a residential landlord from dispossessing a debtor/tenant from a rented apartment or house. There is no exact count of these "unlawful detainer cases pending in this district, but over the past several months, eighty percent of the motions for relief from Stay filed in Chapter 7 cases that I have heard involve residential unlawful detainer actions.

That these cases are filed solely for the purpose of staying enforcement of unlawful detainer judgments can be inferred from several facts: the commencement of the case by the filing of a "bare bones" petition without any schedules or statement of affairs ever being filed; the listing of no, few, or false creditors, if schedules are indeed filed; the failure of the debtor to appear at the mandatory section 341(a) meeting of creditors; and the refusal of debtors in these cases to comply with the requirements of the Bankruptcy Code, the Bankruptcy Rules, or this court's Local Rules and thereby failing to obtain a discharge.

The debtor/tenant almost never appears at the hearing on the landlord/movant's motion for relief from the Stay. When a debtor/tenant does appear, I always inquire as to the purpose of the bankruptcy case filing. Invariably the debtor tells me that he or she filed in order to stay his or her eviction from residential real property.

IV. THE ROLE OF THE "BANKRUPTCY MILLS"

A principal, and perhaps the primary, reason for the proliferation of these unlawful detainer bankruptcy cases is the advice given to these debtor/tenants by some lawyers and many paralegals who are in business to advise low-income and legally unsophisticated individuals regarding the filing of bankruptcy cases.

Some of these lawyers and paralegals provide valuable services for reasonable compensation to those who are in financial distress and who seek the "fresh start" a Chapter 7 or Chapter 13 discharge provides. Unfortunately there are many others who mislead debtor/tenants into believing that filing a bankruptcy case will stay unlawful detainer evictions for an extended period of time and that no detrimental consequences will occur. These "bankruptcy mills" often take several hundreds of dollars in fees from debtor/tenants who cannot afford to pay rent in the first place.

Often these debtor/tenants are not advised that the filing of a bankruptcy case will have a deleterious effect on their credit records. In fact, many debtor/tenants who have appeared in my court have told me that these "bankruptcy mills" do not even disclose to these debtor/tenants that they were filing bankruptcy—rather, they are led to believe they are obtaining some appropriate form of legal relief in our legal system, which is all too often complex and intimidating to the lay-person.

Of course, not all of these debtor/tenants are innocent victims. Many have learned to manipulate the bankruptcy court system on their own, without the help of any of the "bankruptcy mills." These pro se debtor/tenants will often file not one, but two or more bankruptcies in order to delay improperly the enforcement of an unlawful detainer judgment. Landlords who have sought relief from the Stay before me have testified that some of these manipulative debtor/tenants have boasted that they can use (or misuse) the bankruptcy court system to delay the landlord's efforts to evict them for several months while paying no rent.

V. THE EFFECT ON BANKRUPTCY COURTS

As discussed in section III above, the bankruptcy courts in the Central District of California are flooded with Chapter 7 and Chapter 13 cases filed solely for the purpose of delaying unlawful detainer evictions. Inevitably and swiftly following the filing of these cases is the filing of motions for relief of the Stay by landlords who are temporarily thwarted by this abuse of the bankruptcy court system. Nearly every bankruptcy judge in the Central District of California allows residential landlords to seek relief from the Stay in these unlawful detainer bankruptcy cases on shortened notice.[2] Thus, contrary to the false representations made by the "bankruptcy mills," the debtor/tenants generally obtain only a brief respite from the consummation of the unlawful detainer evictions, after having paid hundreds of dollars to these mills.

The United States Trustee for the Central District of California has joined forces with the United States Attorney in an attempt to put these "bankruptcy mills" out of business.[3] These laudable efforts have met with little success. This is due to the ease with which operators of these bankruptcy mills can shuck one business identity, assume another, change location, and continue to defraud an unending supply of debtor/tenants and abuse the protection afforded by the Stay.

The Bankruptcy Court for the Central District of California is the busiest bankruptcy court in the nation, with over 50,000 bankruptcy case filings a year.[4] The mountain of paperwork that accompanies the thousands of abusive "unlawful detainer" case filings places an unnecessary burden on our already over-worked and undercompensated clerk's office. Of course, this mountain of paperwork flows from our Clerk's Office to the chambers of our judges when landlords file their relief from Stay motions. Because of the increased workload caused by these blatantly abusive unlawful detainer case filings, our court has had to establish special procedures dismissing these cases as quickly as possible so that the court's dockets and the clerk's files will not become more choked with paperwork than they already are.

These relief from Stay motions are rarely contested and are never lost, as long as the moving party provides adequate notice of the motion and competent evidence to establish a prima facie case. Thus, bankruptcy courts in our district hear dozens of these Stay motions weekly, none of which involves any justiciable controversies of fact or law.

VI. THE SCOPE OF THE STAY
A. Property of the Estate

Section 362(a) provides in pertinent part: [A] petition filed under Section 301, 302, or 303 of this title... operates as a stay, applicable to all entities of...

(1) The commencement or continuation, including the issuance or employment of process, of a judicial, administrative, or other action or proceeding against the debtor that was or could have been commenced before the commencement of the case under this title, or to recover a claim against the debtor that arose before the commencement of the case under this title;

(2) The enforcement, against the debtor or against property of the estate, of a judgment obtained before the commencement of a case under this title;

(3) any act to obtain possession of property of the estate, or property from the estate, or property from the estate, or to exercise control over property of the estate....(Emphasis added.)

The term "property of the estate," as used in section 362(a), is defined in section 541(a)(1) to include:

[A]ll legal or equitable interests of the debtor in property as of the commencement of the case.

[1] A bankruptcy court must look to state law to determine what "legal or equitable interests" the debtor had at the commencement of the case. See Butner v. United States, 440 U.S. 48, 99 S.Ct. 914, 59 L.Ed.2d 136 (1979); In re Farmers Markets, Inc., 792 F.2d 1400 (9th Cir. 1986); and In re Schewe, 94 B.R. 938 (Bankr. W.D. Mich. 1989).

[2] The United States Court of Appeals for the Ninth Circuit has interpreted California law as to whether a tenant retains any property interest once a lease has been terminated. In the case of In re Windmill Farms, Inc., 841 F.2d 1467 (1988), the Ninth Circuit held that a lease of real property is terminated under California law when the lessor affirms his elec-

tion to terminate the lease as expressed in a notice to pay rent or quit which the lessor has previously served upon the lessee. Id. at 1469-71. This affirmation of the termination of the lease by the lessor is usually accomplished by the filing of a complaint for unlawful detainer. Thus, if the lessor properly notifies the lessee of the lessor's intention to terminate the lease, the unpaid rent is not paid within the appropriate period of notice, and the lessor affirms his intention to terminate the lease by, at least, filing a complaint for unlawful detainer, the lease is terminated and the lessee retains no property interest with regards to the leased real property, except, perhaps, for one—the right to obtain relief from forfeiture of the lease under California Code of Civil Procedure §1179.[5]

[3] In this case, Debtor failed to pay her rent, Movant gave appropriate notice to Debtor of his intention to terminate Debtor's tenancy if she did not pay her overdue rent, Debtor failed to pay her overdue rent, and Movant affirmed his intention to terminate the tenancy by filing a Complaint. Further, Movant obtained the Judgment which declared his termination of Debtor's tenancy of the Apartment. Therefore it follows from the analysis present in Windmill Farms that the bankruptcy estate of Debtor has absolutely no property interest in the Rental Agreement, or the tenancy it created, which was terminated prior to the commencement of this bankruptcy case. Debtor's retention of physical possession of the Apartment is not a property interest recognized by law.[6]

It is arguable that Debtor's bankruptcy estate does retain a property interest in the right to seek relief from forfeiture under Cal. Code of Civ. Proc. §1179. No Chapter 7 debtor or trustee has ever sought to exercise this right in any of the residential unlawful detainer cases that I have heard. This is due to the fact that such tenancies have absolutely no value to the bankruptcy estate and its creditors and that these unlawful detainer bankruptcy cases rarely, if ever, have any assets that would enable the bankruptcy trustee to fulfill the condition in Cal. Code Civ. Proc. §1179 for relief from forfeiture—"full payment of rent due." That relief from forfeiture rights have no meaning in residential unlawful detainer cases is recognized in our Local Bankruptcy Rule 112(1)(a) which provides that the Chapter 7 trustee in such cases neither need be named as a responding party in, nor served with, motions for relief, from Stay to enforce unlawful detainer judgments against residential real property.[7]

Based upon the foregoing authorities, I conclude that neither Debtor nor the bankruptcy estate herein has any legal or equitable property interest in the Debtor's Rental Agreement or the Apartment due to the termination of Debtor's tenancy prior to the commencement of this bankruptcy case. Therefore, the Stay does not enjoin the Movant from taking any action to regain possession of the Apartment. As a result, it is not necessary for the Movant to obtain relief from the Stay in order to regain possession of the Apartment.[8]

B. The Debtor

[4] It appears from the language of section 362(a)(2), quoted in section VI above, that the Stay enjoins Movant from enforcing an unlawful detainer judgment against Debtor, even though the Stay does not prohibit Movant from regaining possession of the Apartment. I believe, however, that the only practical construction of 362(a)(1), (2) and (3) would be that these subsections operate to enjoin an entity from continuing an action or enforcing a judgment against a debtor that would either interfere with the administration of the bankruptcy estate or violate the discharge of debt which gives debtors a "fresh start," a goal sought by debtors who file bankruptcy in good faith.[9] For example, if a landlord, or any other creditor, attempted to enforce a judgment for money damages against the Debtor or the bankruptcy estate, 11 U.S.C. §362(a)(2) would clearly enjoin such conduct.

As discussed above, those individuals who file bankruptcy cases to stay unlawful detainers usually do not seek a "fresh start" discharge of debt. They are only seeking to delay improperly the landlord from obtaining possession of his property. This delay provides no benefit to the bankruptcy estate or creditors of the estate.

The purpose of the Stay is to give the bankruptcy estate and its fiduciary, either the trustee or the debtor-in-possession, an opportunity to gather together the assets of the estate, determine their value, and liquidate or reorganize them. This goal of the Stay is not achieved by applying it to a landlord's attempt to regain possession of residential real property wrongfully being held by a debtor/tenant.

Instead, if the Stay is allowed to enjoin a landlord from completing a residential eviction, a completely different end is achieved—that of allowing unscrupulous manipulators, the "bankruptcy mills," to prey upon the desperate and ignorant tenants who come to them for help and are defrauded out of money which could better be used to pay rent to their current landlords or to obtain new living quarters.

Another consequence of holding that the Stay applies to residential unlawful detainer evictions is that the cost of doing business as a residential landlord rises with the additional expense of hiring lawyers not only to pursue an eviction in the state court but also to obtain relief from the Stay in Bankruptcy Court. This added cost necessarily increases the rent that must be paid by low-income tenants in the Los Angeles area, which is one of the most expensive urban rental markets in the country.[10] The ever increasing rents for low-income housing, of course, only makes it harder for tenants to pay their rent and therefore leads to more abusive bankruptcy filings.[11] Thus, this vicious cycle repeats and repeats.

[5] Based upon the foregoing, I conclude that the Stay does not enjoin a landlord from regaining possession of residential premises from a wrongfully holding-over bankruptcy debtor/tenant, as long as the landlord seeks only to repossess the property and not to enforce any other portion of his unlawful detainer judgment against the debtor and the bankruptcy estate, such as collecting money damages.

VII. Conclusion

This opinion may be viewed by some as judicial legislation. I observe that this abuse of the bankruptcy court system has been communicated to Congress.[12] Congress has failed to address the problem, perhaps because landlords of residential real property do not have as loud a lobbying voice as commercial landlords who have been able to effect large and significant revisions in the Bankruptcy Code in order to protect their interests. See 11 U.S.C. §365(b)(3) and §365(c)(3) as amended by the Bankruptcy Amendments and Federal Judgeship Act of 1984.

I further observe that this opinion will have absolutely no effect on this problem unless residential landlords, and the attorneys who represent them, call it to the attention of the state courts that issue unlawful detainer judgments and convince those state courts to order the proper state law enforcement officials to evict debtor/tenants without first requiring residential landlords to obtain relief from the Stay. If this chain of events results, there is a chance that this wide-spread and daily abuse of the Bankruptcy Court system and the shameless defrauding of thousands of tenant victims will cease.

Based upon my conclusion that the Stay does not enjoin Movant to enforce the Judgment with no further delay, I hereby authorize Movant, to the extent that such authority is required, to enforce the Judgment to regain possession of the Apartment from Debtor.

Nevertheless, in the interests of justice, and to allow Movant to enforce the Judgment with no further delay, I hereby authorize Movant, to the extent that such authority is required, to enforce the Judgment to regain possession of the Apartment from Debtor.

---

1. See "The Federal Judicial Workload Statistics," Dec. 1988 edition, Administrative Office of the United States Courts, Statistical Analysis and Reports Division.

2. See Local Bankruptcy Practice Manual for the Central District of California, (Professional Education Systems, Inc., 1989) pp. 366-367

3. See Los Angeles Times, "Petition Mills Dupe Many Into False Bankruptcies," May 8, 1989, Sec. I, pp. 1, 23-24.

4. See "The Federal Judicial Workload Statistics," Dec. 1988 edition, Administrative Office of the United States Courts, Statistical Analysis and Reports Division.

5. In re Windmill Farms, supra at 1469, the Ninth Circuit held that if a trustee was able to obtain relief from forfeiture of the lease pursuant to CCP §1179, then the lease would be "resurrected" and the bankruptcy estate would regain its property interest in the lease and the subject real property.

6. Many courts have held that actual, physical possession of premises subject to a month-to-month tenancy or lease does not constitute a legal or equitable interest in property within the meaning of section 541. In re Kennedy, 39 B.R. 995, 997 (C.D. Cal. 1984); In re Youngs, 7 B.R. 69, 71 (Bankr.D.Mass.1980); In re Depoy, 29n B.R. 466, 470 (Bankr.N.D.Ind.1983)

7. Even if a trustee or debtor wished to obtain relief from forfeiture for a terminated residential lease, nothing in this opinion precludes either party from seeking such relief in the appropriate forum.

8. In some ways, the above analysis is analogous to the Bankruptcy Code's treatment of property that technically is property of the estate but which is of inconsequential value or benefit to the estate. Section 542(a) provides as follows:

   An entity, other than a custodian, in possession, custody, or control, during the case, of properties that the trustee may use, sell, or lease under Section 363 of this title, or that the debtor may exempt under section 542 of this title, shall deliver to the trustee, and account for, such property or the value of such property, unless such property is of inconsequential value or benefit to the estate. (Emphasis added.)

   If an entity has possession of property of the estate that is of inconsequential value or benefit to the estate, section 542 excuses that entity from turning it over to the trustee. Similarly, if a landlord seeks possession of residential real property that is no longer property of the estate, it does not follow that the Stay should enjoin the landlord from doing so.

9. H.R.Rep. No 95-595, 95th Cong. 1st Sess. 340-342 (1977), U.S. Code Cong. & Admin. News 1978 pp. 5787, 6296-6299 reprinted in King, Klee, and Levin, Collier on Bankruptcy (15th Ed. 1988) Appendix 2.

10. See recent study done by Roulac Real Estate Consulting Group; Deloitte, Haskins & Sells and Institute of Real Estate Management, August, 1989.

11. See Los Angeles Times, "Crowded Courtrooms Serve as Battleground for L.A.'s Eviction Wars," June 11, 1989, Part II, p. 1.

12. Letter of the Honorable Alan M. Ahart dated March 17, 1989, a copy of which is on file with this court.

References

Books & Booklets

(Your county has a law library which is usually located in or near the courthouse and is open to everyone, not just attorneys. You'll find most of these books and booklets available there; those which aren't, you'll likely find at your public library. Because most of them are expensive and tend to become dated rather quickly, take a close look at them before you decide to add them to your own library.)

Brown, David; Ralph Warner. *The Landlord's Law Book, Volume 1: Rights and Responsibilities.* Nolo Press, 950 Parker St., Berkeley, CA 94710, (510) 549-1976.

Two attorneys wrote this book specifically to demystify the law for California landlords and landladies. By and large, they succeed.

Brown, David. *The Landlord's Law Book, Volume 2: Evictions.* Nolo Press, 950 Parker St., Berkeley, CA 94710, (510) 549-1976.

Should you want a second opinion on eviction matters, take a look at this book. It covers pretty much the same ground as *The Eviction Book for California*, and it's pretty expensive, but it bears the distinction of having been written by an attorney, for whatever that's worth to you.

California Apartment Association. *California Rental Housing Reference Book.* California Apartment Association, 1414 K St., Suite 610, Sacramento, CA 95814, (916) 447-7881.

This book contains the laws, case citings, and forms which are relevant to the landlording business in California today. Having your own copy handy will save you many trips to the library to look up this law or that case. It has dozens of forms which have been reviewed by the CAA and its attorneys and also by the State Attorney General's office, so you can expect them to incorporate whatever's pertinent in the latest laws and legal interpretations. It even includes a rental application and a rental agreement in Spanish.

California Apartment Law Information Foundation. *Unlawful Detainer Study.* California Apartment Law Information Foundation (CALIF), 621 S. Westmoreland Ave., Suite 101, Los Angeles, CA 90005, (213) 251-9665.

This 44-page booklet reports and analyzes unlawful detainer (UD) statistical data like nobody's business and concludes that the $337,181,139 which long-suffering landlords lose every year in untaxed rental value while they're pursuing UDs is everybody's business. The report is full of startling statistics and conclusions about UDs. CALIF is a non-profit organization dedicated to opening the eyes of the public to the plight of the landlord. Give it your support. I do.

California Department of Consumer Affairs Legal Office. *California Tenants, Your Rights and Responsibilities.* Department of Consumer Affairs, P.O. Box 310, Sacramento, CA 95802.

Although this fifty-page booklet covers landlord-tenant matters from a tenant's point of view, landlords find it helpful, too. Not only does it provide a succinct overview of the eviction procedure, it examines the rental process from the git-go, when tenants first start looking for a place to live, and it serves as a good introduction to the many laws which apply to residential tenancies. For a free copy, write to the address above. Enclose a stamped (postage sufficient for four ounces), self-addressed envelope (at least 7" x 10") for delivery, and while you're at it, ask for a list of other Consumer Affairs' publications.

California Department of Consumer Affairs Legal Office. *Small Claims Court Handbook.* Department of Consumer Affairs, P.O. Box 310, Sacramento, CA 95802.

If you wish to pursue your case in small claims court or if your tenant is suing you there, you should read this booklet to learn how to prepare and present your side of the case most effectively. Like the booklet above, this one is free.

DeLaive, Janet, ed. *Legal Secretary's Handbook (California).* The Rutter Group, 15760 Ventura Blvd., Suite 630, Encino, CA 91436, (818) 990-3260.

This informational cornucopia is a two-volume "law library" for legal secretaries, the real workhorses in law offices. It includes only one chapter on unlawful detainers specifically, but it has much information on other related matters, such as motions, appeals, writs, demurrers, pleadings, attachments, general procedures, court filing fees, and the like. In addition, there are samples galore.

Eriksen, Ronald. *How to Find Missing Persons.* Loompanics Unlimited, P.O. Box 1197, Port Townsend, WA 98368, (206) 385-5087.

Though most of what is in this book is scrupulous stuff, some of it is not, but then you just may have to check your scruples at the door before you go out hunting for an unscrupulous tenant who's disappeared owing you a bunch of money.

Fisher, Roger; William Ury. *Getting to Yes: Negotiating Agreement Without Giving In.* Penguin Books, 40 West 23rd St., New York, NY 10010.

Written by two professors who have spent years studying how people can best resolve their conflicts without giving in to the opposition and without resorting to physical force or the legal system, this very practical manual offers scores of ideas which you might try when you're having tenant problems. Because some of the book's examples are drawn from landlord-tenant situations, you can see how the ideas apply directly to you as a landlord.

Friedman, Terry; David Garcia; and Mark Hagarty. *California Practice Guide: Landlord-Tenant.* The Rutter Group, 15760 Ventura Blvd., Suite 630, Encino, CA 91436, (818) 990-3260.

Three attorneys with vastly different perspectives on landlord-tenant matters collaborated to write this guide. One usually represents landlords; one usually represents tenants; and the third is a judge who has heard more than his share of landlord-tenant litigation. They have examined the subject backwards, forwards, rightside-up, upside-down, and inside-out. Though written for attorneys, it has a practical side as well and can prove useful to the landlord who handles his own evictions. Unfortunately, it's the most expensive of all the books listed here.

HALT. *Using the Law Library, A Nonlawyer's Guide.* HALT, 1319 F Street, NW, Suite 300, Washington, DC 20004, (202) 347-9600.

Part of HALT's Citizens Legal Manuals series, this particular volume prepares the nonlawyer to use the resources of a law library as knowledgeably as any bona fide member of the bar, maybe even as knowledgeably as any jailhouse lawyer. HALT, by the way, is an acronym for "Help Abolish Legal Tyranny," a national public interest organization "dedicated to the principle that all

people in the United States should be able to dispose of their legal affairs in a simple, affordable and equitable manner." That's just what you're trying to do in handling an eviction yourself, isn't it? HALT is worthy of your support, and with support, it makes copies of the Citizens Legal Manuals series available as premiums.

Moskovitz, Myron; Peter Honigsberg; and David Finkelstein. *California Eviction Defense Manual.* California Continuing Education of the Bar, 2300 Shattuck Ave., Berkeley, CA 94704, (800) 924-3924.

This law book, written for tenants' attorneys, offers some valuable insights into the defenses concocted by those who consider most landlords unscrupulous. Such people must certainly lie awake nights thinking up new legal stratagems to thwart all of us filthy-rich landlords and landladies. A supplement, the latest of which is included in the price of the manual itself, is published every June.

Moskovitz, Myron; Ralph Warner; and Charles Sherman. *California Tenants' Handbook.* Nolo Press, 950 Parker St., Berkeley, CA 94710, (510) 549-1976.

Tenants who are having trouble with their landlord seek out this book and scour it for remedies. Some landlords and landladies think of it as the enemy's battle plan and consider it offensive. Some of it is. But it's primarily defensive, and it gives you a chance to consider the tenant's point of view for a change.

National Housing Law Project. *HUD Housing Programs: Tenants' Rights.* National Housing Law Project, 614 Grand Avenue, Oakland, CA 94610, (510) 251-9400.

You think you got problems! Take a look at this enormous bo5ok sometime. It'll remove the blinders from your eyeballs. It cites case after case which legal-aid attorneys have brought against public housing projects; that's right, public housing projects! You might conclude from a cursory examination that public housing administrators are bumbling fools, that poor people are more litigious than a lawyer's daughter, that legal-aid attorneys are relentless, and that whoever is paying the bills must be as blind as justice herself, and you wouldn't be far wrong. As Pogo was wont to say, "I has met the enemy, and he is us."

Computer Software

Eviction Forms Creator™ (California). (IBM-PC running Windows and Macintosh) ExPress, P.O. Box 1639, El Cerrito, CA 94530-4639, (510) 236-5496.

Sooner or later, somebody had to write a computer program which could fill out eviction forms. Because nobody else did it, I wrote it myself. Whether you're doing one eviction or hundreds, this program will save you both time and frustration. You enter information only once, and that same information is used wherever it's needed to fill out virtually all the eviction forms, including the Judicial Council forms. The program is simple to understand and easy to use. To see the program's main menu, go to page 253.

Periodicals

Apartment and Property Owners Association Magazine. Your Association, (see association listings for the one nearest you). 6, 10, or 12 issues a year, advertising; included with membership.

Most California apartment and property owners associations publish their own magazines or newsletters which, among other things, help to keep their members up-to-date on legal matters.

The Robert Bruss California Real Estate Law Newsletter. Robert Bruss, 251 Park Road, Suite 200, Burlingame, CA 94010, (800) 736-1736. 12 issues a year, no advertising.

In this fascinating eight-page newsletter, Robert Bruss, the nationally syndicated real estate writer, reviews current California court decisions involving real estate. As you might imagine, a fair number of these decisions affect landlord-tenant matters in general and evictions specifically. Mr. Bruss uses his skills as an attorney, real estate entrepreneur, and real estate writer to detail each case, analyze the resulting decision, and explain why this particular case is important, all in layman's terms. Anyone with an interest in California real estate can understand and profit from this information.

Services

Tele-Lawyer. Tele-Lawyer, P.O. Box 12927, Las Vegas, NV 89112, (800) 835-3529, Monday through Friday, 9 a.m. to 5 p.m.

What won't "they" think of next? Now you can dial an 800 number, give the operator your MasterCard or Visa number, request to speak to a lawyer specializing in landlord-tenant matters, ask your specific legal questions, and get an expert's legal opinion without having to wait for an appointment, without even having to leave your home or office. The expert who will be answering your queries will have years of experience in this field and should know the answers straightaway. If not, he will research the matter and call you back. Tele-Lawyer charges $3 per minute and claims that most calls require ten to fifteen minutes. That works out to $30-45 for the average call.

The Tele-Lawyer law firm neither makes referrals nor accepts cases. It generates revenue strictly by selling "legal expertise by the minute" over the telephone. Consequently, when you call Tele-Lawyer, you won't encounter anybody who is trying to sell you the services of a particular lawyer in order to get a referral fee, nor will you encounter anybody who wants to take your case. A Tele-Lawyer lawyer simply wants to give you the best possible answers to your questions while you're on the telephone.

Don't call Tele-Lawyer if you feel completely overwhelmed by an eviction you're pursuing. In that situation, call a local lawyer who specializes in landlord-tenant law and turn over your case to him.

Call Tele-Lawyer if you feel that the answers to a few unsettling questions will help you pursue your case on your own.

Web Sites

(Where the Internet (World Wide Web) will take us in the future is anybody's guess, but it has already changed the way we gather information, and it can save you a lot of time when you're pursuing an eviction.)

http://www.courtinfo.ca.gov/judicialcouncil/—Here's where you'll find a complete list of all the Judicial Council forms. If you've heard that a certain form has changed, but you want to verify that it has and also obtain a copy in Adobe Acrobat format, go to this site.

http://www.courtinfo.ca.gov/otherwebsites/—Here's where you will find a list of the county courts which have their own Web sites. If your county court is on the list, there will be a link to its site, and you should find information about the locations of the courts in your county, their hours, and their fees.

http://www.landlording.com—This is my own Web site where you will find current information about my books and software. You will also find a page called "What's New?" where I comment on subjects of current interest to landlords.

http://www.leginfo.ca.gov/calaw.html—Maintained by the State of California, this site makes available all of the state's current codes (laws), including those found in the Code of Civil Procedure and the Civil Code, which are the codes most relevant to evictions. Because the state itself maintains this site, you know that the codes are current.

http://tenant.net—Maintained by tenant advocates, this site has nothing good to say about landlords and landladies. Indeed, it likens us to vermin, but it has some links which may prove useful if you want to find the particulars about the rent control board in your area.

Glossary

Abandonment—giving up possession without notifying the landlord.

Abstract of Judgment—a lien recorded in a county where a judgment debtor (someone named in a judgment) has assets.

Accrue—accumulating or adding up over a period of time; rent "accrues" every day the tenant remains in possession of the landlord's real property.

Affidavit—a sworn, written statement.

Affirmative Defense—a defense based more on new evidence than on a denial of the charges.

Alternative—a choice given to the tenant in a notice such as a 3-Day Notice to Pay Rent or Quit; the tenant may either pay up or vacate.

Answer—legal paper filed soon after summons which states the defendant's defense in response to the plaintiff's complaint; it assures the defendant of a trial.

Automatic Stay (Bankruptcy Court)—halt of a case's legal proceedings as a result of a bankruptcy filing by either plaintiff or defendant; legal "monkey wrench" used by tenants who want to delay their evictions.

Baggage Lien Law—unless you're running a hotel or motel, forget it.

Breach of Contract—breaking something agreed upon in a lease or rental agreement.

Case Number—a number assigned by the court clerk when the legal papers are first filed; thereafter, the case is known by that number.

Civil Code—state laws relating to noncriminal matters; includes laws such as those covering discrimination, tenants' rights, and security deposits; abbreviated as CC.

Code of Civil Procedure—state laws governing how civil matters are to be conducted legally; abbreviated as CCP.

Complaint—a statement of the plaintiff's case.

Constructive Eviction—either an actual disturbance by the landlord of the tenant's possession of the premises or any substantial interference with the tenant's quiet enjoyment of the premises; examples are removing the front door or cutting down the stairway to a second-floor entrance.

Constructive Service—serving a notice without giving it to the defendant personally; leaving it with someone of "suitable age and discretion" and mailing a copy or posting it in a conspicuous place at the residence and mailing a copy.

Court of Jurisdiction—court which has the responsibility for deciding matters concerning property in its general area.

Covenant—an expressed or implied promise appearing in a lease or rental agreement; here's a sample of a covenant: "Tenants agree to keep from making loud noises and disturbances and to play music and broadcast programs at all times so as not to disturb other people's peace and quiet."

Covenant of Quiet Enjoyment—landlord's implied promise that he will not disturb the tenant's possession of the premises.

Damages—amount of money awarded by the court to compensate for loss or injury; in nonpayment cases, damages equal unpaid rent following the final rental period mentioned in the 3-day notice.

Declaration for Default Judgment in Lieu of Personal Testimony per CCP 585.4—sworn, written statement by the plaintiff, restating what was included in the complaint and asking the court to enter a judgment in the plaintiff's favor because the defendant failed to answer the summons; it takes the place of a personal appearance at a prove-up trial; availability of this declaratory procedure is up to the discretion of each judicial district.

Declaration of Service—a statement signed by one who served certain papers and attesting to how and when they were served.

Default—failure to respond to a court summons within a given time limit.

Defendant—one against whom a case is brought; one who is being sued; opposite of plaintiff.

Demurrer—legal paper responding to plaintiff's complaint and asserting that there is no cause of action at all; in a demurrer the defendant is saying, in effect, that even if what the plaintiff states in his complaint is true, the plaintiff still doesn't have a case; the defendant's response is essentially, "So what?"

Entry of Default—recording in public records the lack of a response to the filing of a lawsuit.

Estoppel Defense—legal defense alleging that the plaintiff may not depart from precedents already set in order to win a judgment; in an unlawful detainer for nonpayment, a 3-Day Notice to Pay Rent or Quit would be considered premature if served before the date when the landlord was accustomed to collecting rent and not considering it late.

Eviction—the actual removal of tenants from real property through a legal process; loosely used to refer to the process itself as well as to the removal of tenants even though there has been no legal process.

Execution—carrying out of the judgment; in an unlawful detainer action, an execution no longer results in the hanging or other permanent dispatch of the tenant; execution results only in the tenant's expulsion from the property and in an effort to collect monies owed.

Ex Parte—Latin for "on behalf of a single party"; an "ex parte" action is the legal equivalent of a surprise attack because it gives the other party, the adversary, no notice nor any opportunity to respond; "ex parte" actions are subject to a speedy review upon application by the adversary.

Filing—entering your legal papers into the records of the court; accomplished after you have prepared the summons and complaint.

Forcible Entry—taking possession without a legal right to the property; a landlord using a passkey to dispossess a tenant who has a legal right to live where he is and a squatter who takes over a vacant residence are both guilty of forcible entry.

Forfeiture—loss of the right to possess a property for failure to comply with the rental agreement.

Injunction—a court order restraining someone from a certain activity; it is supposed to prevent future injuries, not compensate for past injuries.

In Forma Pauperis—this Latin expression means literally "in the manner of a pauper"; someone who claims to be too poor to pay normal court costs may file a paper to this effect and not have to pay them.

In Re—another Latin expression, it means "in the matter of," as in *In Re Smith*; captions of legal citations regarding nonadversarial judicial proceedings, such as bankruptcies and probates, use the *in re* surname format; adversarial judicial proceedings are commonly referred to in the *plaintiff v. defendant* format.

Judicial Council of California—state agency charged by the legislature with the responsibility for providing both the form and the content of various forms used in courts throughout California.

Judgment—outcome of the court hearing or trial.

Judgment by Default—ruling made by a judge in the landlord's favor after the tenant has been given a certain period of time to respond to the summons and complaint and has failed to do so; landlord must apply for the judgment by default; it is not granted automatically.

Lien Sale—procedure necessary for recouping monies owed by self-service storage renters who stop paying their rent or abandon their property.

Memorandum to Set Case for Trial—form used to secure a trial in a contested case.

Motion to Quash Service—legal paper responding to the plaintiff's complaint; may assert that the summons itself or its service is somehow defective or that the cause of action is not really for unlawful detainer and hence fails to qualify for summary proceedings.

Motion to Strike—legal paper responding to the plaintiff's complaint and asserting that there are irrelevancies or redundancies in the complaint or that it contains some other defect, such as the absence of a verification or an improper request for damages.

Movant—a party, not named in an action, who brings a motion into court.

Nail and Mail—expression used to characterize service which involves posting a copy of the paper to be served and mailing a copy to the defendant at his last known address.

Notice to Pay Rent or Quit—a notice advising the delinquent tenant that he must either pay the rent owing within a certain period, generally three days, or move out; this notice must precede any unlawful detainer for nonpayment of rent.

Notice to Perform Covenant—a notice advising the tenant that he is breaking his lease or rental agreement; this notice must precede any unlawful detainer for breach of contract.

Notice to Vacate—the sheriff or marshal's final five-day warning before actual removal of the tenants.

Nuisance—anything harmful to the health, offensive to the senses, or otherwise adversely affecting the enjoyment of life or property.

Order for Posting—see "posting."

Penal Code—state laws governing criminal matters; includes information about performing a citizen's arrest in the eviction of a lodger; abbreviated as PC; don't confuse this abbreviation with "personal computer" or "politically correct."

Performance of Covenants—fulfilling the obligations agreed upon in a contract.

Personal Service—serving legal documents by handing them to someone directly.

Place Plaintiff in Quiet Possession—court instruction to the sheriff or marshal to evict a tenant and give possession to the plaintiff who won an eviction action.

Plaintiff—the one bringing a case to court; the one suing.

Plaintiff in Propria Persona—"in propria persona" is a Latin expression meaning literally that the plaintiff is "in his own person" or is representing himself before the court; usually the expression is shortened to "Plaintiff in Pro Per" or even to "In Pro Per"; in a legal context, it means the same as "Pro Se."

Pleading Paper—paper with line numbers down the left side; in the context of this book, pleading paper is used for attachments to the unlawful detainer complaint, for a Declaration for Default Judgment in Lieu of Personal Testimony, and for a few other documents.

Posting—alternative method of service; requires court order and adds ten days to time allowed for answer but requires no one to be present to receive the papers; papers are taped, stapled, or otherwise attached to a conspicuous place on the property.

Pray—ask or plead.

Prejudgment Claim of Right to Possession—form served along with the summons and complaint; anyone filing this claim becomes a defendant; all others give up their right to claim later that they had a right of possession.

Prima Facie—a Latin phrase which means "at first sight"; "prima facie evidence" is evidence which would seem to support a fact, although it might be refuted.

Process—legal papers bringing a matter before a court of law.

Process Server—someone who serves legal papers; cannot be party to the suit.

Proof of Service—see "declaration of service."

Pro Se—another Latin phrase meaning "for oneself"; anyone acting as his own attorney is acting "Pro Se"; in a legal context, it means the same as "In Pro Per."

Prove-up Trial—plaintiff's personal appearance in court to prove the allegations made in the complaint and ask for a default judgment.

Pursuant to—according to or following.

Quit—take your belongings and leave the property.

Relief from Automatic Stay—permission from a bankruptcy court enabling a landlord to proceed with eviction proceedings against a tenant who has filed for bankruptcy.

Request for Entry of Default—a request for the clerk to record that the defendant failed to respond to the summons.

Restitution—return; ordinarily the plaintiff in an unlawful detainer asks for the "restitution" or return of the premises among other things.

Retaliatory Eviction—unlawful detainer defense used when the landlord is alleged to be getting revenge against his tenants for exercising their legal rights.

Self-Help Eviction—use of any methods, legal or illegal, which do not involve court proceedings and result ultimately in the tenant's vacating the premises; bribery and cutting off utilities are both self-help methods; bribery is legal; cutting off utilities is not.

Service—the serving of legal papers on someone affected by them.

Small Claims Court—a civil court where people argue their own cases without attorneys; unlawful detainers are no longer heard in small claims court.

Stay—a postponement or delay, as in a "stay of

execution"; generally, a stay is a win for a tenant and a loss for a landlord because it means that the tenant gets more time to occupy the premises without having to pay rent.

Stipulation—agreement between plaintiff and defendant as to how a judge is to decide an issue.

Substituted Service—serving legal papers on a substitute rather than handing them directly to the defendant; extends the waiting period by ten days.

Summons—a notice requiring that one appear in court or before a court official.

Summary Proceeding—a prompt and simple hearing which is abbreviated by law; unlawful detainers are summary proceedings.

Superior Court—court used for unlawful detainers when either the rent or the total judgment exceeds the limits of a municipal court.

Thirty-Day Notice to Terminate Tenancy—a notice used in situations where you want tenants to leave for reasons of your own; this notice must precede any eviction for failure to vacate; in certain California cities, notably those with rent control, this notice may be used only for "just cause," e.g., demolition, occupancy by a close relative, etc.

Three-Day Notice—any of several different kinds of 3-day notices, the two most common being for nonpayment of rent and for breach of contract.

Unlawful Detainer—wrongfully keeping real property that belongs to someone else; see "unlawful detainer proceeding."

Unlawful Detainer Proceeding—the legal proceeding necessary for eviction; frequently abbreviated as "unlawful detainer."

Verification—a statement required at the end of every complaint to acknowledge that the facts are as stated.

Warehouseman's Lien—in the case of a mobilehome park eviction, the park owner's right to sell the mobilehome to satisfy the amount owed by the mobilehome's legal owner.

Warranty of Habitability—landlord's implied obligation to provide a dwelling which is fit for human occupancy; this right of the tenant cannot be signed away.

Waste—destruction of property.

Writ—written authority from a court for the sheriff or marshal to carry out a judgment.

Writ of Execution—court authorization for the sheriff or marshal to seize a defendant's property or money in order to satisfy a judgment.

Writ of Immediate Possession—the result of a procedure used when tenants are hiding to avoid service or are known to be out of state.

Writ of Possession—court authorization for the sheriff or marshal to remove a tenant from a property and return possession to the plaintiff who successfully sued for eviction.

California Apartment and Property Owners Associations

ALAMEDA COUNTY
(NORTHERN)
Rental Housing Association
2201 Broadway, Suite 311
Oakland, CA 94612
(510) 893-9873

ALAMEDA COUNTY
(SOUTHERN)
Rental Housing Owners
Association of Southern
Alameda County
1264 "A" St.
Hayward, CA 94541
(510) 537-0340

BERKELEY
Berkeley Property Owners
Association
2005 Hopkins
Berkeley, CA 94707
(510) 525-3666

CENTRAL COAST
Central Coast Rental Housing
Association
P.O. Box 101
Santa Maria, CA 93456
(805) 928-3988

CHICO
North Valley Property Owners
Association
813 East Fifth Ave.
Chico, CA 95926-2702
(916) 345-1321

CONTRA COSTA/NAPA/
SOLANO COUNTIES
Rental Housing Association
1070 Concord Ave., Suite 120
Concord, CA 94520
(510) 686-3234

FOOTHILL (PASADENA)
Foothill Apartment Association
424 N. Lake Ave., Suite 104
Pasadena, CA 91101-1202
(818) 793-5873
(213) 681-5106

FRESNO
CAA/Greater Fresno Division
980 Ninth St., Suite 2150
Sacramento, CA 95814
(209) 252-5125

KERN COUNTY
CAA/Kern County Division
980 Ninth St., Suite 2150
Sacramento, CA 95814
(805) 322-3288

LONG BEACH/
SOUTHERN CITIES
Apartment Association
California Southern Cities
4120 Atlantic Ave.
Long Beach, CA 90807
(310) 426-8341

Apt. Owners Association
3550 Long Beach Blvd.,
Suite D-4
Long Beach, CA 90807
(562) 595-6700

CAA/Southern Los Angeles
County Chapter
P.O. Box 3278
Long Beach, CA 90803-0278
(800) 305-7522

LOS ANGELES
Apartment Association of
Greater Los Angeles
621 S. Westmoreland Ave.
Los Angeles, CA 90005
(213) 384-4131

Apartment Owners Association
5455 Wilshire Blvd., #1009
Los Angeles, CA 90036
(213) 937-8811

MARIN
Marin Income Prop. Assn.
P.O. Box 150315
San Rafael, CA 94915
(415) 491-4461

MERCED COUNTY
Rental Prop. Association of
Merced County
P.O. Box 2455
Merced, CA 95344
(209) 723-4797

MODESTO
Rental Property Association of
Central California
400 12th St., Suite 14
Modesto, CA 95354
(209) 529-3055

MONTEREY COUNTY
Apt. Assn of Monterey County
975 Cass St.
Monterey, CA 93940
(408) 649-4704

NAPA COUNTY
(See Contra Costa/Napa/
Solano Counties)

NORTH COAST
North Coast Rental Housing
Association
P.O. Box 12172
Santa Rosa, CA 95406
(707) 526-9526

ORANGE COUNTY
Apt. Assn. of Orange County
12822 Garden Grove Blvd.,
Suite D
Garden Grove, CA 92643
(714) 638-5550

Apartment Owners Association
11752 Garden Grove Blvd.
Garden Grove, CA 92643
(714) 539-6000

PASADENA
(See Foothill)

POMONA VALLEY
(See San Bernardino County/
Pomona Valley)

SACRAMENTO
Sacramento Valley
Apartment Association
221 Lathrop Way, Suite M
Sacramento, CA 95815
(916) 920-1120

SAN BERNARDINO
COUNTY/
POMONA VALLEY
Apartment Association of
Greater Inland Empire
400 N. Mountain Ave.,
Suite 311
Upland, CA 91786
(909) 949-0711

SAN DIEGO
San Diego County
Apartment Association
2727 Camino Del Rio So.,
Suite 327
San Diego, CA 92108
(619) 297-1000

Apartment Owners Association
1660 Hotel Circle North,
Suite 640
San Diego, CA 92108
(619) 294-7900

SAN FERNANDO
VALLEY/VENTURA
COUNTY
Apartment Owners Association
15025 Oxnard St., Ste. 200
Van Nuys, CA 91411
(818) 988-9200

SAN FRANCISCO
San Francisco
Apartment Association
333 Hayes St., Suite 100
San Francisco, CA 94102
(415) 255-2288

SAN JOAQUIN COUNTY
San Joaquin
Rental Property Association
840 N. El Dorado St.
Stockton, CA 95202
(209) 944-9266

SANTA BARBARA
Santa Barbara
Rental Property Association
3887 State St., Suite 7
Santa Barbara, CA 93105
(805) 687-7007

SANTA MONICA
Action Apartment Association
2812 Santa Monica Blvd.,
Suite 203
Santa Monica, CA 90404
(310) 828-7628

SOLANO COUNTY
(See Contra Costa/Napa/
Solano Counties)

SOUTH BAY/
SOUTHERN CITIES
(See Long Beach/Southern
Cities)

TRI-COUNTY
Tri-County
Apartment Association
792 Meridian Way, Suite A
San Jose, CA 95126-3899
(408) 297-0483

VENTURA COUNTY
(See San Fernando Valley/
Ventura County)

❦ ❦ ❦

CALIFORNIA
(State Association)
California
Apartment Association
980 Ninth St., Suite 2150
Sacramento, CA 95814
(916) 447-7881

Index

Eviction Forms Creator™

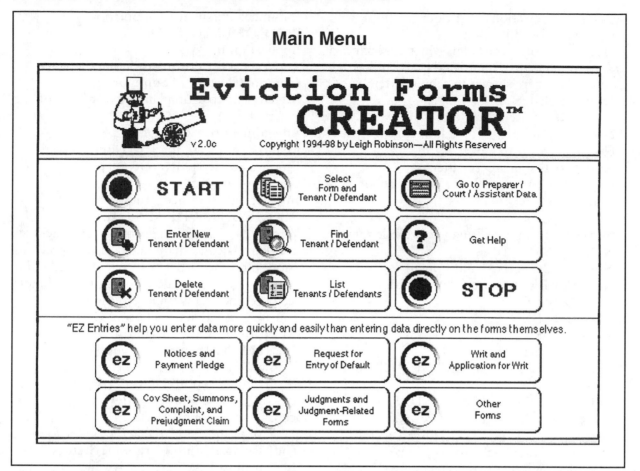

Eviction Forms Creator creates the various forms you need to evict a tenant legally through the California court system. It creates them the modern way, on a computer, rather than the old fashioned way, on a typewriter.

Using Eviction Forms Creator, even the worst of typists, those who have to eyeball the key caps and strike the right keys with conscious effort, can create perfect eviction forms which are sure to please the people who count whenever there's an eviction in the legal works, that is, the court clerk and the judge.

Eviction Forms Creator is designed to be so easy to use that it doesn't require a thick user's manual and hours of study time. In fact, once you understand a little bit about what makes the program "tick," what you need to do to load it onto your computer, what you need to do to navigate through it easily, and what you need to do to get it to print the forms correctly, you'll be ready to crank out great-looking eviction forms from sunup to sundown.

When using Eviction Forms Creator, you save time because you enter information only once, and that same information is used wherever it's needed to fill out all the forms. Once you enter information about yourself as the preparer of the forms, for example, you never have to enter that information again. The same goes for the court(s) you use and for each of the tenants you are evicting.

The forms you can create with Eviction Forms Creator begin with the various legal notices designed to alert tenants to the owner's intent to evict, and they end with the Writ of Execution, which gives the sheriff or marshal the authority to turn the tenants out and return possession of the property to the rightful owner.

These forms include both those which have specific legal wording requirements and those which have specific legal wording and formatting requirements, that is, the Judicial Council forms. (The Judicial Council is charged by the state legislature with the responsibility of providing uniformity in the forms used in state courts.)

The program works just as well for those who

do their own evictions as it does for those who do evictions for others.

Here is a list of all the forms which are included in Eviction Forms Creator (the seven Judicial Council forms are shown in capital letters):

Payment Pledge
Notice to Pay Rent or Quit
Notice to Pay, etc. (Mobilehomes)
Notice to Perform Covenant
Notice to Terminate Tenancy
Notice to Quit for Waste, Nuisance, or Unlawful Acts
Notice to Quit
Notice to Terminate Tenancy (Mobilehomes)
Notice to Vacate (RVs)
Notice of Belief of Abandonment
Notice of Right to Reclaim Abandoned Personal Property
COVER SHEET
SUMMONS
COMPLAINT
PREJUDGMENT CLAIM OF RIGHT TO POSSESSION
REQUEST FOR ENTRY OF DEFAULT
Clerk's Default Judgment (five versions)
Court's Default Judgment (three versions)
Judgment After Trial (two versions)
Amended Judgment (three versions)
Declaration for Default Judgment in Lieu of Personal Testimony
Judgment Pursuant to Stipulation
WRIT OF EXECUTION
Application for Writ
Application for Posting of Summons
Order for Posting of Summons
Attachment to Complaint (two copies of the same form)
Amendment to Complaint
Memo to Set Case for Trial (four versions)
Proof of Service [Memo to Set]
Case Summary
Instructions to Officer (three versions)
REQUEST FOR DISMISSAL

Version 2.0 of Eviction Forms Creator includes more than twice as many forms as the previous version, fifty-one rather than twenty-five, and it has the added advantage of being fully editable directly on the forms themselves.

You may use Eviction Forms Creator on an IBM-PC or an Apple Macintosh.

The IBM-PC must be running Windows 3.1, Windows 95, or Windows NT. It must have a hard drive, Microsoft Universal Printer Driver 3.1.4 or later, a pointing device (mouse or trackball), and a dot matrix, laser, or ink-jet printer capable of printing in Arial and Courier fonts.

The Macintosh must be running System 7.0 or higher. It must have a hard drive and a dot-matrix, laser, or ink-jet printer, capable of printing in Helvetica and Courier fonts.

Order Forms

ExPRESS, P.O. BOX 1639, EL CERRITO, CA 94530-4639

Dear ExPress:

I'm a scrupulous property owner, and I'd like copies of your materials for my very own. Hurry up with my order. I need all the help I can get right now.

Please send me:

_____ copies of *Landlording*	@ $24.95	$_____
_____ copies of *The Eviction Book for California*	@ $23.95	$_____
_____ copies of *Landlording*® (*The Forms Diskette*)	@ $39.95	$_____
_____ copies of *Eviction Forms Creator*™	@ $59.95	$_____
_____ copies of *Pushbutton Landlording*®	@ $129.95	$_____
> > > > SALES TAX FOR CALIFORNIA RESIDENTS > > > >		$_____
	Shipping and handling	$ 2.00
	TOTAL	$_____

My computer uses DOS___, Windows___ (Version___), Macintosh OS___

PLEASE SEND TO

_____

_____

_____

ExPRESS, P.O. BOX 1639, EL CERRITO, CA 94530-4639

Dear ExPress:

I'm an unscrupulous property owner who's merciless, lowdown, and greedy, and I'll pay double the usual price for your stuff just to lay my hands on all that great information. It may even reform me. Who knows?

Please send me:

_____ copies of *Landlording*	@ $49.90	$_____
_____ copies of *The Eviction Book for California*	@ $47.90	$_____
_____ copies of *Landlording*® (*The Forms Diskette*)	@ $79.90	$_____
_____ copies of *Eviction Forms Creator*™	@ $119.90	$_____
_____ copies of *Pushbutton Landlording*®	@ $259.90	$_____
> > > > SALES TAX FOR CALIFORNIA RESIDENTS > > > >		$_____
	Shipping and handling	$ 4.00
	TOTAL	$_____

My computer uses DOS___, Windows___ (Version___), Macintosh OS___

PLEASE SEND TO

_____

_____

_____

ExPRESS, P.O. BOX 1639, EL CERRITO, CA 94530-4639

Dear ExPress:

I'm not a property owner yet, but I think I'd like to be one some day, and I'd certainly like to know what I'm doing. Show me.

Please send me:

_____ copies of *Landlording*	@ $24.95	$_____
_____ copies of *The Eviction Book for California*	@ $23.95	$_____
_____ copies of *Landlording*® (*The Forms Diskette*)	@ $39.95	$_____
_____ copies of *Eviction Forms Creator*™	@ $59.95	$_____
_____ copies of *Pushbutton Landlording*®	@ $129.95	$_____
> > > > SALES TAX FOR CALIFORNIA RESIDENTS > > > >		$_____
	Shipping and handling	$ 2.00
	TOTAL	$_____

My computer uses DOS___, Windows___ (Version___), Macintosh OS___

PLEASE SEND TO

_____

_____

_____

Use one of these forms and mail it with your check or money order, OR call ExPRESS at (510) 236-5496 and charge to your MasterCard or Visa. Visit our Web site at http://www.landlording.com